T0183501

Lecture Notes in Computer Science　　　8593

Commenced Publication in 1973
Founding and Former Series Editors:
Gerhard Goos, Juris Hartmanis, and Jan van Leeuwen

Guevara Noubir · Michel Raynal (Eds.)

Networked Systems

Second International Conference, NETYS 2014
Marrakech, Morocco, May 15–17, 2014
Revised Selected Papers

 Springer

Editors
Guevara Noubir
Northeastern University
Boston, MA
USA

Michel Raynal
Université de Rennes 1
Rennes Cedex
France

ISSN 0302-9743   ISSN 1611-3349   (electronic)
ISBN 978-3-319-09580-6   ISBN 978-3-319-09581-3   (eBook)
DOI 10.1007/978-3-319-09581-3

Library of Congress Control Number: 2014946230

LNCS Sublibrary: SL5 – Computer Communication Networks and Telecommunications

Springer Cham Heidelberg New York Dordrecht London

Printed on acid-free paper

Springer is part of Springer Science+Business Media (www.springer.com)

Message from the General Chairs

The recent development of the Internet as well as mobile networks, together with the progress of cloud computing technology, has changed the way people perceive computers, communicate, and do business. Today's Internet carries huge volumes of personal, business, and financial data, much of which are accessed wirelessly through mobile devices. In addition, cloud computing technology is providing a shared pool of configurable computing resources (hardware and software: e.g., networks, servers, storage, applications, and services) that are delivered as services over a diversity of networks technologies. Advances in Web technologies, social networking, and middleware platforms have provided new opportunities for the implementation of novel applications and the provision of high-quality services over connected devices. This allows participatory information sharing, interoperability, and collaboration on the World Wide Web. All these technologies can be gathered under the umbrella of networked systems.

After the great success of the First International Conference on Networked Systems, NETYS 2013, NETYS 2014 took place during May 15–17, 2014, in Marrakech, Morocco. It provided a forum for presenting best practices and novel algorithms, results, and techniques on networked systems. The conference gathered researchers and experts from all over the world to address the challenging issues related to networked systems such as multi-core architectures, concurrent and distributed algorithms, middleware environments, storage clusters, social networks, peer-to-peer networks, sensor networks, wireless and mobile networks, as well as privacy and security measures to protect such networked systems and data from attack and abuse.

We would like to express our cordial thanks to our partners and sponsors for their trust and support. A special thanks goes to Springer-Verlag, which has ensured that the proceedings, since the first edition of NETYS, have reached a wide readership throughout the world. We are grateful to the Program Committee co-chairs, the session chairs and the Program Committee members for their excellent work and we wish to take this opportunity to congratulate all the authors for the high quality displayed in their papers and to thank all the participants for their support and interest. Finally, no conference can be a success without the precious contribution of the Organizing Committee, which we thank for their dedication and hard work to make this conference a success.

July 2014

Mohammed Erradi
Rachid Guerraoui

Message from the Program Committee Chairs

The International Conference on Networked Systems (NETYS) is establishing itself as a high-quality forum bringing together researchers and engineers from both the theory and practice of networked systems.

NETYS 2014 was fortunate to attract a high interest among the community, and received 80 submissions from 15 countries and four continents. These figures indicate that NETYS has gained worldwide visibility. This fairly high number of submissions provided an excellent opportunity for a high-quality program, but also called for a demanding and laborious paper evaluation process. The 31 members of the Technical Program Committee worked efficiently and responsibly under tight time constraints to produce a total of 183 reviews that provided the basis for the final paper selection. As a result of this process, 20 regular papers, and six short papers, were finally selected for presentation at the main conference. The program was further enriched by two keynote presentations offered by world-renowned researchers in the field: Professor Mohamed G. Gouda (UT Texas), who gave a talk on "Communication Without Repudiation," and Professor Seif Haridi (KTH Royal Institute of Technology, Stockolm), who gave a talk on "Big Data and Cloud Computing." A special thank you to both of them.

We are grateful to all authors who trusted us with their work; without them there would be no conference. The final result would not have been possible without the dedication and hard work of many colleagues. Special thanks are due to members of the Program Committee, and to all external referees for the quality and depth of the reviews, and their sense of responsibility and responsiveness under very tight deadlines. Last but not least, a warm thanks to the conference chairs, Mohammed Erradi (ENSIAS, Rabat) and Rachid Guerraoui (EPFL), for their continuous help and friendship.

Guevara Noubir
Michel Raynal

Organization

Program Committee

Sergio Arevalo	Polytechnic University, Madrid, Spain
Gildas Avoine	UCL, UK
Najib Badache	Cerist, Algeria
Karim Baina	ENSIAS, Rabat, Morocco
Roberto Baldoni	Rome University, Italy
Carole Delporte	LIAFA, University of Paris V, France
Amr El Abbadi	University of Santa Barbara, CA, USA
Mohamed Erradi	ENSIAS, Rabat, Morocco
Hugues Fauconnier	LIAFA, University of Paris V, France
Mounia Fredj	ENSIAS, Rabat, Morocco
Bernd Freisleben	Marburg University, Germany
Benoit Garbinato	UNIL, Switzerland
Vijay Garg	UT Austin, USA
Mohamed G. Gouda	UT Austin, USA
Vincent Gramoli	Sydney University, Australia
Maurce Herlihy	Brown University, USA
Zahi Jarir	Cadi Ayyad University, Morocco
Mohamed Jmaiel	Université de Sfax, Tunisia
Anne-Marie Kermarrec	Inria, Rennes, France
Darek Kowalski	University of Liverpool, UK
Loukas Lazos	University of Arizona, USA
Ibrahim Matta	Boston University, USA
Hassan Mountassir	Université de Franche-Comté, France
Guevara Noubir	Northeastern University, USA
Panos Papadimitratos	KTH, Sweden
Vivien Quéma	INPG, Grenoble, France
Michel Raynal	IRISA, France
Luis Rodrigues	Technical University, Lisbon, Portugal
Gregor von Bochmann	University of Ottawa, Canada

Additional Reviewers

Ataee, Shabnam	Chaari, Tarak
Bagaa, Miloud	Chakir, Boutaina
Bendjoudi, Ahcene	Chang, Yen-Jung
Bostanipour, Behnaz	Chapuis, Bertil
Bridgman, John	Chauhan, Himanshu

Cheikhrouhou, Saoussen
Del Pozzo, Antonella
Di Luna, Giuseppe Antonio
Diegues, Nuno
Doudou, Messaoud
Doumi, Karim
Du, Xiaofei
Georgiou, Theodore
Hung, Wei-Lun
Jamaa, Maissa B.

Lasla, Noureddine
Leitão, João
Loulou, Monia
Mdhaffar, Afef
Moro, Arielle
Nawab, Faisal
Ouadjaout, Abdelraouf
Petroni, Fabio
Sahin, Cetin
Zellou, Ahmed

Keynote Talks

Communication Without Repudiation: The Unanswered Question

Mohamed G. Gouda

University of Texas at Austin, Austin, TX 78712, USA
gouda@cs.utexas.edu

Abstract. A non-repudiation protocol is to be executed by two parties, say S and R, in order to (1) enable S to send some text to R then receive some non-repudiated evidence that R has indeed received the text, and (2) enable R to receive both the sent text from S and some non-repudiated evidence that this text was indeed sent from S to R. Since 1995, tens of non-repudiation protocols have been proposed, but every one of these protocols seems to suffer from one or more well-known problems. For example, most protocols assume the existence of a third party that is trusted by both S and R. This observation reminds us that the following core question has never been answered. Can there be a non-repudiation protocol that does not suffer from any of these problems?

Research Challenges in Data-Intensive Cloud Computing

Seif Haridi

KTH Royal Institute of Technology, Sweden
haridi@kth.se

Abstract. I will focus in this talk on what is next in the area of cloud computing and data-intensive computational frameworks. In particular as cloud computing in data centers is becoming today's technology, research efforts are shifting to the challenges in multi data-centers cloud environments, especially in distributed services across multiple data centers. Also for big data applications, the tools are changing from simple Map-Reduce frameworks into full fledged data analytic stacks for processing and querying large data sets in various forms. These new tools make it much easier for application developers to create value out of data. We will present the current state of research in these areas and outline the related research challenges.

Contents

Keynote Talk: Communication Without Repudiation: The Unanswered Question

Mohamed G. Gouda[✉]

University of Texas at Austin, Austin, TX 78712, USA
gouda@cs.utexas.edu

Abstract. A non-repudiation protocol is to be executed by two parties, say S and R, in order to (1) enable S to send some text to R then receive some non-repudiated evidence that R has indeed received the text, and (2) enable R to receive both the sent text from S and some non-repudiated evidence that this text was indeed sent from S to R. Since 1995, tens of non-repudiation protocols have been proposed, but every one of these protocols seems to suffer from one or more well-known problems. For example, most protocols assume the existence of a third party that is trusted by both S and R. This observation reminds us that the following core question has never been answered. Can there be a non-repudiation protocol that does not suffer from any of these problems?

1 Introduction

The Internet supports many security services that are well-established and well-utilized. These services can be invoked by different parties, as these parties communicate over the Internet, in order to ensure that the communications between the parties remain secure. An example list of these services is as follows:

- Availability services (to defend against denial of service attacks)
- Authentication services (to defend against one party impersonating a second party while it communicates with a third party)
- Confidentiality services (to defend against eavesdropping attacks)
- Integrity services (to defend against the corruption of a message after the message is constructed and sent by its original source and before it is received by its ultimate destination)
- Freshness services (to defend against message replay attacks)
- Access control services (to defend against intrusion attacks)
- Anonymity services (to defend against identifying which party is communicating with which other party)

Famously absent from such a list is a "non-repudiation service", which defends against repudiation attacks where one party sends a message then repudiates that it has sent the message or where a second party receives the message then repudiates that it has ever received the message. The absence of a well-established non-repudiation service over the Internet is troubling, especially since such a service has been proposed and promoted since 1995. See for example [1,2].

© Springer International Publishing Switzerland 2014
G. Noubir and M. Raynal (Eds.): NETYS 2014, LNCS 8593, pp. 1–8, 2014.
DOI: 10.1007/978-3-319-09581-3_1

One possible reason that no non-repudiation service has ever been well-established over the Internet is that every "non-repudiation protocol" that has been proposed to implement such a service has suffered from one or more of the following three problems:

(a) **Trusted Third Party:**
Most non-repudiation protocols assume the existence of a third party that can be trusted by all parties that invokes the non-repudiation service. Even worse, some non-repudiation protocols assume the existence of a very invasive trusted third party, one that participates in transmitting (i.e. sending or receiving) every message that is transmitted during every execution of these protocols.

(b) **No Tolerance of Message Loss or Corruption:**
Some non-repudiation protocols assume that some specified messages that are transmitted during the execution of the protocol can neither be lost nor corrupted.

(c) **Synchronized Clocks:**
Some non-repudiation protocols assume that their parties have tightly synchronized clocks.

For example, the well-cited non-repudiation protocols of Zhou and Gollmann [3,4] suffer from problems (a) and (c), whereas the protocol of Markowitch and Roggeman [5] suffers from problem (b). More recently, the protocol of Hernandez-Ardieta, Gonzalez-Tablas, and Alvarez [6] suffers from problems (a) and (c). In fact, every non-repudiation protocol that has been proposed in the past seems to suffer from one or more of these three problems; see for example [7].

These observations remind us that the following core question concerning non-repudiation protocols have never been answered. Can there be a non-repudiation protocol that does not suffer from any of the three problems (a), (b), and (c) stated above?

From past experience, the effort needed to show that the answer to such a question is "Yes" is much less than the effort needed to show that the answer is "No". Therefore, naturally, one should first attempt to show that the answer to this question is "Yes". Only when all these attempts fail should one consider showing that the answer to this question is "No".

To show that the answer to this core question is "Yes", one merely needs to exhibit a non-repudiation protocol that satisfies the following three conditions.

1. The exhibited protocol does not involve a trusted third party.
2. The exhibited protocol tolerates the loss and corruption of sent messages.
3. The exhibited protocol does not require the participating parties to have tightly synchronized clocks.

But before we venture into exhibiting a non-repudiation protocol, we need first to present our specification of non-repudiation protocols.

2   Specification of Non-repudiation Protocols

In this section, we present our specification of non-repudiation protocols. Any correct design of a non-repudiation protocol is required to satisfy this specification.

A non-repudiation protocol is to be executed by two parties, say S and R. This protocol is required to satisfy the following five conditions.

(a) **Guaranteed Termination:**
Every execution of the protocol, by both S and R, is guaranteed to terminate in a finite time.

(b) **Termination of S:**
Party S terminates only after S sends some text to R and only after S receives some non-repudiated evidence that R has indeed received the sent text.

(c) **Termination of R:**
Party R terminates only after R receives both the sent text from S and some non-repudiated evidence that this text was indeed sent from S to R.

(d) **Opportunism of S:**
If during the protocol execution, party S reaches a state st after it has received the non-repudiated evidence that R has indeed received the sent text, then S can neither send nor receive any message at state st.

(e) **Opportunism of R:**
If during the protocol execution, party R reaches a state st after it has received the non-repudiated evidence that the text was indeed sent from S to R, then R can neither send nor receive any message at state st.

3   Preliminary Design of a Non-repudiation Protocol

In this section, we outline our first attempt to showing that the answer to the core question stated in Sect. 1 is "Yes". In this first attempt, we exhibit a non-repudiation protocol that, we hoped, satisfies the three properties (1) through (3) stated in Sect. 1.

Unfortunately, it turns out that this initial protocol, called the NR-1 protocol, suffers from two problems. First, the NR-1 protocol does not satisfy our specification of non-repudiation protocols stated in Sect. 2. (In other words, the NR-1 protocol is an erroneous non-repudiation protocol that needs to be corrected.)

Second, although the NR-1 protocol satisfies the two properties (1) and (3) stated in Sect. 1, it does not satisfy property (2).

Therefore, the first task of our future research agenda is to modify the NR-1 protocol so that it no longer suffers from these two problems while maintaining the fact that it satisfies the two properties (1) and (3) stated in Sect. 1.

Our design of the NR-1 protocol is based on three simple ideas: message alternation, message acceptance, and collected evidence. Next, we describe each one of these ideas in some detail.

(a) **Message Alternation:**
Party S sends its text to party R in a sequence of n txt messages.
When R receives the next expected txt message from S, R sends back an ack message to S acknowledging the reception of the txt message.
When S receives an ack message from R acknowledging the reception of the latest txt message, S executes exactly one of the following two actions. First, if the latest txt message is not (yet) the n-th txt message to R, then S sends the next txt message to R. Second, if the latest txt message is the n-th txt message to R, then S terminates.
The flow of messages in the NR-1 protocol can be outlined as follows:

$$S \longrightarrow R : txt1$$
$$S \longleftarrow R : ack1$$
$$S \longrightarrow R : txt2$$
$$S \longleftarrow R : ack2$$
$$...$$
$$S \longrightarrow R : txtn$$
$$S \longleftarrow R : ackn$$

Each txt message is of the form:

$$txt(S, R, ss, sq, < text >, < sign.by\ S >)$$

− txt is the message type
− S is the identity of message sender R is the identity of message receiver
− ss is an identifier of the current protocol session between S and R
− sq is the sequence number of the message in the sequence of n txt messages
− $< text >$ is the sent text in the message.
− $< sign.by S >$ is the message signature using the private key of the message sender S

Each ack message is of the form:

$$ack(R, S, ss, sq, < text >, < sign.by\ R >)$$

− ack is the message type
− R is the identity of message sender
− S is the identity of message receiver
− ss is an identifier of the current protocol session between S and R
− sq is the sequence number of the txt message being acknowledged by this ack message
− $< text >$ is the text in the txt message being acknowledged by this ack message
− $< sign.by R >$ is the message signature using the private key of the message sender R

(b) **Message Acceptance:**
During each execution of the NR-1 protocol, S keeps track of the latest sent txt message from S to R and R keeps track of the latest sent ack message from R to S.

Initially, S constructs the first txt message whose sequence number is 1, sends this message to R, and makes this message the latest sent txt message from S to R. Also initially, R constructs an ack message whose sequence number is 0 and whose text is empty and makes this message the latest sent ack message from R to S (even though this message was never sent from R to S).

When S receives an ack message from R, S compares the latest sent txt message with the received ack message and determines, based on this comparison, whether or not to accept the received ack message.

Let the latest sent txt message and the received ack message be as follows:

$$txt(S, R, ss, sq, < text >, < sign.by\ S >)$$

$$ack(R, S, ss', sq', < text' >, < sign.by\ R >)$$

Then S accepts the received ack message iff the following four conditions hold:

- $ss = ss'$
- $sq = sq'$
- $< text >=< text' >$
- $< sign.by\,R >$ is the correct signature of the ack message using the private key of R

If S accepts the received ack message, then S executes one of the following two actions. First, if the sequence number of the latest sent txt message is n, then S terminates. Second, if the sequence number of the latest sent txt message is less than n, then S constructs the next txt message and sends it to R. (Now, this txt message becomes the latest sent txt message from S to R.)

If S does not accept the received ack message, then S discards this message and sends the latest txt message to R.

Similarly, when R receives a txt message from S, R compares the latest sent ack message with the received txt message and determines, based on this comparison, whether or not to accept the received txt message.

Let the latest sent ack message and the received txt message be as follows

$$ack(R, S, ss, sq, < text >, < sign.by\ R >)$$

$$txt(S, R, ss', sq', < text' >, < sign.by\ S >)$$

Then R accepts the received txt message iff the following three conditions hold:

- $ss = ss'$
- $sq + 1 = sq'$

- $< sign.by\,S >$ is the correct signature of the txt message using the private key of S

If R accepts the received $txt(S, R, ss', sq', < text' >, < sign.by\,S >)$ message, then R constructs the message $ack(R, S, ss', sq', < text' >, < sign.by\,R >)$ and sends it to S. (Now, this ack message is the latest sent ack message.)

If R does not accept the received txt message, then R discards this message.

(c) **Collected Evidence:**

During the execution of the NR-1 protocol, S needs to collect non-repudiated evidence that R has indeed received the text that is sent from S to R. This collected evidence consists simply of the sequence of n ack messages that were sent by R and received and accepted by S. Note that R cannot repudiate this evidence because these messages contain the correct session identifier and correct sequence numbers and are signed by the private key of R, which only R knows.

Also during the execution of the NR-1 protocol, R needs to collect non-repudiated evidence that S is the one that had sent the text to R. This collected evidence simply consists of the sequence of n txt messages that were sent by S and received and accepted by R. Note that S cannot repudiate this evidence because these messages contain the correct session identifier and correct sequence numbers and are signed by the private key of S, which only S knows.

As mentioned earlier, the NR-1 protocol suffers from two problems. First, it does not satisfy our specification of non-repudiation protocols stated in Sect. 2. Second, this protocol does not tolerate message loss and corruption. Therefore, as mentioned earlier, the first task in our research agenda is to modify the NR-1 protocol so that it no longer suffers from these two problems and to verify the correctness of the modified protocol.

(Verifying the correctness of a non-repudiation protocol is not a trivial task. In fact, as discussed in [8,9], several non-repudiation protocols were shown to be incorrect after these protocols were published in the literature.)

4   A General Non-repudiation Protocol

As specified in Sect. 2 above, a non-repudiation protocol involves two parties, named S and R. Recall that the goal of this protocol is to achieve non-repudiation when party S sends some text to party R.

Clearly, one can envision a more general non-repudiation protocol that involves $(k + 1)$ parties, named $S, R.1, \ldots,$ and $R.k$. The goal of this more general protocol is to achieve non-repudiation when party S sends the same text to each of the parties $R.1$ through $R.k$.

Two well-known general non-repudiation protocols are presented in [10,11]. Unfortunately both of these protocols assume the existence of a trusted third party.

Therefore, the second task in our research agenda is to exhibit a general non-repudiation protocol that satisfies the three properties (1) through (3) stated in

Sect. 1. In other words, the exhibited protocol (1) will not involve a trusted third party, (2) will tolerate the loss and corruption of sent messages, and (3) will not require the participating parties to have tightly synchronized clocks.

Our design of this general non-repudiation protocol can use as a "module" our design of the 2-party non-repudiation protocol in the first task in our research agenda.

5 A Certified Email Service Without a Trusted Party

Non-repudiation protocols can be used in implementing certified email services [12,13]. Recently several certified mail services have been deployed over the Internet [14,15]. Examples of these services are as follows:

1. The Austrian Document Delivery System (or DDS for short) was deployed in 2004
2. The Italian Posta Elettronica Certificata (or PEC for short) service was deployed in 2005
3. The German De-Mail service was deployed in 2010
4. The Slovenian Moja.Posta.Si service is deployed and currently being operated by the Slovenian Post
5. Several companies, e.g. "CertifiedMail", "ReturnReceipt", "ZixMail", and "PrivaSphere", have offered certified email services in 2007.

Unfortunately, each one of these services is based on a 2-party non-repudiation protocol that involves a very invasive trusted third party, one that participates in transmitting (i.e. sending or receiving) every message that is transmitted during any execution of the protocol.

Therefore, the third task in our research agenda is to plan a certified mail service that does not rely on the existence of a trusted third party or relies on a least invasive trusted party. In fact, this planned certified mail service can be based on the 2-party non-repudiation protocol which we will design in the first task in our research agenda.

6 Concluding Remarks

Despite many published papers on non-repudiation protocols, the following core question concerning these protocols has remained unanswered. Can there be a non-repudiation protocol that does not suffer from three well-known problems (namely the need for a trusted third party, the intolerance of message loss and corruption, and the need for tightly synchronized clocks)? We believe (at least till now) that the answer to this question is "Yes". And in this presentation, we have described our early efforts that we hope will lead to answering this question.

Acknowledgement. The presentation in this paper has originated from extensive discussions with my two Ph.D. students Mr. Muqeet Ali and Ms. Rezwana Reaz. I am grateful for all their help.

References

1. Herda, S.: Non-repudiation: constituting evidence and proof in digital cooperation. Comput. Stand. Interf. **17**(1), 69–79 (1995)
2. Cox, B., Tygar, D., Sirbu, M.: NetBill security and transaction protocol. In: Proceedings of USENIX Workshop on Electronic Commerce, pp. 77–88, July 1995
3. Zhou, J., Gollmann, D.: A fair non-repudiation protocol. In: Proceedings of the IEEE Symposium on Security and Privacy, pp. 55–61, May 1996
4. Zhou, J., Gollmann, D.: An efficient non-repudiation protocol. In: Proceedings of the IEEE Computer Security Foundations Workshop, pp. 126–132, June 1997
5. Markowitch, O., Roggeman, Y.: Probabilistic non-repudiation without trusted third party. In: Proceedings of the Conference on Security in Communication Networks, September 1999
6. Hernandez-Ardieta, J., Gonzalez-Tablas, A., Alvarez, B.: An optimistic fair exchange protocol based on signature policies. Comput. Secur. **27**(7–8), 309–322 (2008)
7. Kremer, S., Markowitch, O., Zhou, J.: An intensive survey of fair non-repudiation protocols. Comput. Commun. **25**(17), 1606–1621 (2002)
8. Muntean, C., Dojen, R., Coffey, T.: Establishing and preventing a new replay attack on a non-repudiation protocol. In: Proceedings of the 5-th IEEE International Conference on Intelligent Computer Communication and Processing (ICCP), pp. 283–290, August 2009
9. Chen, M., Wu, K., Xu, J., He, P.: A new method for formalizing optimistic fair exchange protocols. In: Soriano, M., Qing, S., López, J. (eds.) ICICS 2010. LNCS, vol. 6476, pp. 251–265. Springer, Heidelberg (2010)
10. Kremer, S., Markowitch, O.: A multi-party non-repudiation protocol. In: Qing, S., Eloff, J.H.P. (eds.) Information Security for Global Information Infrastructures. IFIP, vol. 47, pp. 271–280. Springer, Heidelberg (2000)
11. Markowitch, O., Kremer, S.: A multi-party optimistic non-repudiation protocol. In: Won, D. (ed.) ICISC 2000. LNCS, vol. 2015, pp. 109–122. Springer, Heidelberg (2001)
12. Zhou, J., Onieva, J., Lopez, J.: Optimized multi-party certified email protocols. Inf. Manag. Comput. Secur. **13**(5), 350–366 (2005)
13. Ferrer-Gomilla, J., Onieva, J., Payeras, M., Lopez, J.: Certified electronic mail: properties revisited. Comput. Secur. **29**(2), 167–179 (2010)
14. Oppliger, R.: Providing certified mail services on the Internet. IEEE Secur. Priv. **5**(1), 16–22 (2007)
15. Tauber, A.: A survey of certified mail systems provided on the Internet. Comput. Secur. **30**(6–7), 464–485 (2011)

Leader Election in Rings with Homonyms

Carole Delporte-Gallet[(⊠)], Hugues Fauconnier, and Hung Tran-The

LIAFA- Université Paris-Diderot, Paris, France
{cd,hf,Hung.Tran-The}@liafa.univ-paris-diderot.fr

Abstract. Considering the case of homonyms processes (some processes may share the same identifier) on a ring, we give here a necessary and sufficient condition on the number of identifiers to enable leader election. We prove that if l is the number of identifiers then message-terminating election is possible if and only if l is greater than the greatest proper divisor of the ring size even if the processes do not know the ring size. If the ring size is known, we propose a process-terminating algorithm exchanging $O(n \log(n))$ messages that is optimal.

1 Introduction

The goal of the model of homonym processes [10] is to be an extension of the classical model in which every process has its own unique identity and the model in which the processes are fully anonymous. With homonyms, processes have an identifier coming from a set of identifiers $\mathcal{L}$ and as we always assume that each identifier is the identifier of at least one process, if $|\mathcal{L}|$ is equal to the number of processes n each process has its own identity and $|\mathcal{L}|$ is 1, the processes are fully anonymous. But the cases where $0 < |\mathcal{L}| < n$ are rather natural and useful. For example in communication signatures [9], signatures are identifiers and process groups share the same signature to maintain some kind of privacy (it could be impossible to distinguish between processes with the same identifier). Moreover it is generally very costly to assign unique identities to processes and some mechanisms for this (e.g. name servers, hash function) do not avoid to have sites with the same identifier.

Until now homonyms have been mainly studied in the context of process failures (Byzantine, omission, crash) for the Consensus problem [4, 10–12] and it has been proved that in many cases unique identifiers are not needed.

A classical and fundamental problem in distributed algorithms is the leader election problem. The main purpose of our paper is to study the leader election problem in the framework of homonyms processes and determine in which way identifiers are needed. In this paper we restrict ourselves to ring topologies (of known or unknown size). We give necessary and sufficient conditions on $|\mathcal{L}|$ the number of identifiers enabling to solve the leader election problem.

From years, many results have been proved concerning the leader election problem depending on the network topology (e.g. [2,5,7,22,23]). Clearly some

This work is supported by the ANR DISPLEXITY.

© Springer International Publishing Switzerland 2014
G. Noubir and M. Raynal (Eds.): NETYS 2014, LNCS 8593, pp. 9–24, 2014.
DOI: 10.1007/978-3-319-09581-3_2

of our results, in particular impossibility results, in the framework of homonyms may be deduced from those results. Nevertheless the results and algorithms given in this paper are rather simple and neat. Moreover they depend only on the number of identifiers and not on their layout.

More than thirty years ago it has been proved that with anonymous processes there is, in general, no deterministic solution for the leader election problem [2].

To avoid impossibility results, randomization is a well known technique to break symmetry and randomized election algorithms have been considered on a variety of network topology (e.g. ring, tree, complete graph) in, for example, [1,17,21], but in this paper we do consider only deterministic algorithms.

The main purpose of our work is to study how to break symmetry with homonymous and not the properties of communication graphs. Hence we restrict ourselves to leader election in (bidirectional) rings with homonyms.

Concerning anonymous processes in rings, Dijkstra [13] observed that, with a particular communication model called central demon, a deterministic leader election algorithm cannot exist if the ring size is a composite number. Several papers [6,16] present leader election algorithms for anonymous rings of prime size with some kinds of demons. In this paper we consider asynchronous message passing and with this model of communication it is easy to verify that no deterministic election algorithm is possible with anonymous processes. On the other hand, if each process has its own identity the election on a ring is easy. Between these extremes, weakening anonymous condition with homonyms processes, it is interesting to determine how many identifiers are sufficient and necessary to have a deterministic election algorithm.

More precisely we directly prove that there are deterministic solutions for election on a ring if and only if the number of identifiers is strictly greater than the greatest proper divisor of the ring size and we explicitly give a solution. For example, if the ring size is a prime number, then there is a deterministic election algorithm if and only there are at least two identifiers.

An interesting point is the fact that this necessary and sufficient condition on the number of identifiers holds even if the ring size is not known by processes when we consider deterministic message terminating algorithms (i.e. processes do not terminate but only a finite number of messages are exchanged). Moreover in the last section when the number of identifiers is known, we propose a deterministic process terminating election algorithm exchanging $0(n \log(n))$ messages. This message complexity is clearly optimal [19].

2 Model and Definition

We consider a distributed message-passing system of n processes ($n \geq 2$). There are neither process failures nor link failures. In the following, we establish some results assuming that process knows n and some results without this knowledge. Each process gets an identifier from a set of identifiers $\mathcal{L} = \{1, 2, \ldots, l\}$. We assume that each identifier is assigned to at least one process, that knows it, but some processes may share the same identifier. Processes with the same identifier have the same deterministic algorithm. In our paper, we sometimes refer to individual processes using names like p, but these names cannot be used by the processes themselves in their algorithm. The identifier of a process p is denoted $Id(p)$.

Message-passing communication between processes is asynchronous. Processes are organized in a bidirectional ring, so that a process can send messages to its two neighbors. The communication channels are reliable and Fifo. The distance from p to q, say $d(p,q)$, is 1 plus the number of processes between p and q in the clockwise ring. Note that if $p_0, ..., p_{k-1}$ are any k different processes in the ring $\sum_{i=0}^{i=k-1} d(p_i, p_{i+1 \mod k}) = n$

A sequence of n identifiers represents a ring of size n. For example $< 1, 2, 3, 3, 1, 2, 3, 3 >$ is the ring of Fig. 1. All rotations or reflections of this sequence represent the same ring (i.e. $< 2, 3, 3, 1, 2, 3, 3, 1 >$ denotes also the ring of Fig. 1).

We consider the *leader election* problem. Each process has a boolean variable *Leader* and a process is *elected* if its variable *Leader* is equal to true.

Definition 1. *A process p is a leader if eventually it is elected forever: there is a time τ after which the variable Leader of p is forever equal to true.*

An algorithm solves the leader election problem if there is a unique leader. We consider two variants of this problem *process-terminating* and *message-terminating*. In the case of process-terminating, eventually all processes terminate, in a case of message-terminating, eventually there is no message exchanged.

Definition 2. *An algorithm solves process-terminating leader election problem for n processes if for any ring of size n: (1)(leader) there is a unique leader, and (2)(process-terminating) eventually all processes terminate.*

Note that process-terminating leader election problem is equivalent to the problem where each process takes an irrevocable decision to be leader or not.

Definition 3. *An algorithm solves message-terminating leader election problem for n processes if for any ring of size n : (1)(leader) there is a unique leader, and (2)(message-terminating) eventually there is no exchanged message.*

Definition 4. *If x is an integer, the greatest proper divisor of x, $gpd(x)$, is the greatest divisor of x excluding x itself.*

Note that if x is prime, $gpd(x) = 1$. From this definition we get:

Proposition 1. *If $x \geq 2$, then $x/gpd(x) \geq 2$.*

3   Impossibility Results

To strengthen our results, we prove them when the communication is synchronous. So we can assume that we have a round model in which in each round a process (1) may send a message to its two neighbors, (2) waits δ (during this time it receives the messages sent by its neighbors if any), and (3) computes its new state according to its current state and the received messages.

3.1   Size n Known by Processes

The following result can be deduced from [5, 8, 22], but in our case it is easier to show it directly.

Theorem 1. *Assuming that n is known by all processes and $|\mathcal{L}| \leq gpd(n)$, process-terminating leader election for n processes is unsolvable.*

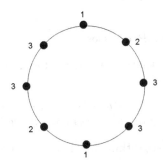

Fig. 1. An example: $n = 8$, $|\mathcal{L}| = 3$.

Proof. We show this theorem by contradiction. Assume that there exists an algorithm $\mathcal{Alg}$ that solves process-terminating leader election problem for n processes. We construct a ring of size n in which process terminating leader election problem is unsolvable. If $|\mathcal{L}| = 1$, all processes have the same identifier and we are in an anonymous system. From the classical result [2], process terminating leader election is unsolvable in an anonymous ring and in synchronous case. Thus the proposition holds. Now, consider that $|\mathcal{L}| \geq 2$.

Let k be $gpd(n)$. We call a k-segment a sequence of k processes positioned in the clockwise direction as follows: the process with identifier 1 is positioned at the first position of the segment, the process with identifier 2 at the second position of the segment,..., process having identifier $(|\mathcal{L}| - 1)$ at the $(|\mathcal{L}| - 1)$th position of the segment. $k - |\mathcal{L}| + 1$ remaining processes having identifier $|\mathcal{L}|$ are positioned from the $|\mathcal{L}|$th to the kth position. We can construct a ring of size n by n/k continuous segments. They are symmetrically distributed in the ring. For example, $n = 8, |\mathcal{L}| = 3$ (see Fig. 1).

It is straightforward to verify, by induction on the number of rounds, that in every round, the n/k processes with the identical positions on the segments are in identical states. (All processes with identical positions on the segments have the same identifier, they start in the same state and execute the same code).

Consider the round τ, at which all processes have terminated, they end up in the same state.

If one process in some segment is leader then every process with the identical position of another segment is also leader. Then n/k processes are leader. By Proposition 1, n/k is greater than 2, contradicting the fact that $\mathcal{Alg}$ solves the leader election problem and we must have a unique leader.

Theorem 2. *Assuming that n is known by all processes and $|\mathcal{L}| \leq gpd(n)$, message-terminating leader election for n processes is unsolvable.*

Proof. We show this theorem by contradiction. Assume that there exists an algorithm that solves message terminating leader election problem for n processes. The proof is the same that the proof of Theorem 1 but instead of considering the round τ, at which all processes have terminated, we consider the round τ after which no message are exchanged.

3.2   Size n Unknown by Processes

If n is unknown, that means that the algorithm for a process with some identifier is the same for any values of n.

Theorem 3. *Even if $|\mathcal{L}| > gpd(n)$, there exists no algorithm for process-terminating leader election if the processes don't know the ring size.*

Proof. Assume there is an algorithm $\mathcal{Alg}$ that solves process-terminating leader election for n processes.

Let $S = <i_1, i_2, ..., i_n>$ be a ring of size n, consider an execution e of $\mathcal{Alg}$ on this ring. By hypothesis, there exists r such that after r rounds all processes have terminated and exactly one process in S is *leader*.

We consider the ring $S' = <j_1, ..., j_m>$ of size $2n$ that is composed by $<i_1, i_2, ..., i_n>$ 2 times. s_1, s_2 denotes these 2 segments. Consider now an execution of $\mathcal{Alg}$ on S'. After r rounds, the kth process of segment s_1 and the kth process of segment s_2 is at each end of round in the same state that the kth process of S in the execution e. Then after r rounds, all processes in s_1 and s_2 terminate. As in execution e there is exactly one leader, in the execution of $\mathcal{Alg}$ on S' there are at least 2 leaders contradicting the fact that $\mathcal{Alg}$ solves the leader election problem.

4   Deterministic Leader Election with Homonyms

4.1   The Simple Protocol

The model we consider in this subsection is essentially a model of population protocol [3], the only difference is that here the state of an agent is an integer and hence an agent is not a finite state automaton. We present a very simple election protocol in this model.

In the *simple protocol* we consider a set, $\mathcal{A}$, of fully anonymous agents, each agent a is described by an automaton. The state of an agent is an integer initialized at some value $v_a > 0$ for agent a. As in population protocol, two agents may meet together, in this case if agent a meets agent b then they both change their states following the rule R (s_x denote the state of agent x before the meeting and s'_x the state for agent x after the meeting):

$$\text{if } s_a > s_b \text{ then } s'_a = s_b + s_a \text{ and } s'_b = 0$$

If $s_a = s_b$ the states of the agents are not modified.

A global state, S of the system is the states of each agent: for global state S and agent a, $S(a)$ is the value of s_a in this state.

Let $V = \Sigma_{a \in \mathcal{A}} v_a$. An easy induction proves that the sum of the states of each agent is invariant, hence for each global state S of the system, we have $\Sigma_{a \in \mathcal{A}} S(a) = V$.

On the other hand, assuming that each agent meets infinitely often all the other agents, it is easy to verify that eventually a global state will be reached such that all agent states are either equal to 0 or to some common value M. Moreover after such a global state T, any meeting between agents will not change T. Hence, the protocol converges to a global state T such that there is a M for all $a \in \mathcal{A}$ we have $T(a) = M$ or $T(a) = 0$.

Remark that $M \geq \max\{v_a | a \in \mathcal{A}\}$. If $Lead$ is the set of agents with state equal to M in global state T, then from the invariant ($\Sigma_{a \in \mathcal{A}} S(a) = V$) we deduce $M \times |Lead| = V$ and hence M and $|Lead|$ divide V.

To summarize:

Lemma 1. *The simple protocol converges to a global state T such that there is an integer M and a set $Lead$ of agents such that for all $a \in Lead$ we have $T(a) = M$ and for all $a \in \mathcal{A} \setminus Lead$ we have $T(a) = 0$.*

The set $Lead$ may be considered as the set of the leaders and:

Lemma 2. *The simple protocol is a leader election if and only if $\max\{v_a \in \mathcal{A}\} > gpd(V)$. Moreover the state of the leader is equal to V.*

In particular, if V is prime and there are at least two agents a and b such that $v_a \neq v_b$, then $Lead$ is a singleton and hence the simple protocol is a leader election.

4.2   Message-Terminating Leader Election in a Ring with Homonyms

Assuming that the number of identifiers is strictly larger than the greatest proper divisor of the ring size, we propose a message-terminating leader election in a ring of unknown size with homonyms. The algorithm is described in Fig. 2.

Consider a ring of n processes with homonymous processes and let $\mathcal{L}$ be the set of identifiers. Assuming that the ring is oriented, in the following, next (resp. previous) will denote the next process (resp. previous process) for the clockwise direction.

We first give some intuitions about the algorithm. Roughly speaking, the algorithm realizes in parallel leader elections for each set of processes having the same identifier. These elections are based on the same principles as in the simple protocol and when the election converges the chosen processes have an estimate est of the ring size. For each identifier i, at least one process (but perhaps several) is eventually elected, and eventually each leader for identifier l has the same estimate est of the ring size. Moreover, these estimates of the ring

var: $Id, state = active, est = 0, Leader = false, \forall i \in \mathcal{L}\ L[i] = 0;$
1 **procedure** $Compute()$
2 **begin**
3   /* compute distance to the next active process with identifier Id */
4   **send**$(right, Id)$ to next
5   **receive**$(ALeft, Id, v)$ from next
6     $est = v$
7   /* compute distance to the previous active process with identifier Id */
8   **send**$(left, Id)$ to previous
9   **receive**$(Aright, Id, v)$ from previous
10    $leftest := v$
11   **if** $est < leftest$ **then**
12       $state = passive$
13   **send**$(restart)$ to next
14   **send**$(restart)$ to previous
15   **else if** $est = leftest$ **then send**$(publish, Id, est)$ to next
16 **end of procedure**

initially
17 $Compute()$

messages
18   **on receive**$(left, i)$ from previous
19   **if** $state = active \wedge i = Id$ **then send**$(ARight, i, 1)$ to previous
20   **else send** $(left, i)$ to next
21   **on receive**$(right, i)$ from next
22   **if** $state = active \wedge i = Id$ **then send**$(ALeft, i, 1)$ to next
23   **else send** $(right, i, v)$ to next
24   **on receive**$(Aright, i, v)$ from previous $\wedge (state = passive \vee i \neq Id)$
25   **send**$(ARight, i, v + 1)$ to next
26   **on receive**$(Aleft, i, v)$ from next $\wedge (state = passive \vee i \neq Id)$
27   **send**$(Aleft, i, v + 1)$ to previous
28   **on receive**$(restart)$
29       $Compute()$
30   **on receive**$(publish, i, v)$
31   **if** $L[i] < v$ **then**
32       $L[i] = v$
33   **send**$(publish, i, v)$ to next
34       $(*, j) = \max\{(L[j], j) | j \in \mathcal{L}\}$
35   **if** $(j = Id) \wedge state = active$
36   **then** $Leader = true$
37   **else** $Leader = false$

Fig. 2. Message-terminating leader election algorithm for identifier Id.

size are strictly lower than n if more than one leader is elected, and is equal to n when there is only one leader for identifier i.

We now describe more precisely the leader election for processes with the same identifier i. A process is initially *active* and may become definitely *passive*.

Only an active process may be a leader. Each active process having i as identifier computes the distance to the next (Lines 3–6) and the previous (Lines 8–10) active process with the same identifier. This computation is easy: a process p with identifier i sends a message $right$ and a message $left$ to respectively its successor and its predecessor on the ring. These messages are retransmitted (in the same direction) by all passive processes or processes with identifier different from i. When the first active process with identifier i receives one of these messages it sends back a message ($Aleft$, respectively $Aright$) with a counter to the initiator of the message. The counter is incremented in each node that retransmits the message until the message reaches p. When received by p, the counter associated with a message $Aleft$ gives the distance between p and the next active process with identifier i. This distance is recorded by p in its variable est. In the same way, p will get the distance to its previous active process and stores it in variable $leftest$.

If the estimate est is strictly lower than $leftest$ then p becomes passive (Line 11) and sends message $restart$ to next and previous active processes with identifier i (Lines 13 and 14) these messages lead to a computation of the distances for these processes (Lines 28–29).

The point is here that the behaviour of the nodes emulates the simple protocol. For this, considering the ring with the processes having the same identifier i, and let the state s_p of p for the simple protocol be the value of est for p. We obtain an emulation of the simple protocol. Indeed, as est is the distance to the next process with identifier i, the sum of all the s_p is equal to n. When a process becomes passive we may consider that it sets s_p to 0 and that the previous active process q updates s_q to $s_q + s_p$. Hence the moves of the algorithm emulate the rule R of the simple algorithm.

From Lemma 1 the election for identifier i stabilizes to a set $Lead$ of processes that we call leaders for identifier i, of agents having the same estimate est. Moreover, if the cardinality of $\mathcal{L}$ is greater than the greatest proper divisor of n, for at least one identifier, say l, from Lemma 2 the leader election for identifier i eventually gives only one leader for i. It remains to choose one identifier among the identifiers leading to one leader. This is done by choosing the identifier whose the estimate is the biggest (using order of identifiers if more than one identifier is the biggest). Then a process leader with this identifier considers itself as the global leader (variable $Leader$ Lines 30–37).

An active process with identifier i may be a leader for this identifier only if the values est and $leftest$ are the same (else the election is not "stabilized" for this identifier). To collect information about leaders for each identifier, when est equals to $leftest$, an active process with identifier i sends a message $publish$ with its estimation of the ring size (Line 15) that will circulate on the ring (in such a way that at most n messages are generated). All active processes in the ring maintain an array L containing for each identifier the best estimation of the ring size. Then each active process chooses (s, i) as the max among all the $(T[j], j)$ (ordered by $(a, b) < (a', b')$ if and only if $a < a'$ or $a = a'$ and $b < b'$) and considers itself as the (global leader) if its identifier is i.

Proposition 2. *If $|\mathcal{L}| > gpd(n)$, algorithm of Fig. 2 is a message-terminating election algorithm with homonyms.*

Proof. We only give the main steps of the proof.

Adapting the proof of Lemma 1 we get the main Lemma:

Lemma 3. *For each identifier i, there is a non empty set L_i of processes with identifier i and there is $v > 0$ such that (1) there is a time after which L_i is the set of active processes with identifier i, (2) v is greater or equal the maximum of distance on the ring between processes with identifier i, and (3) $n = v \times |L_i|$.*

Under the condition of this previous lemma, we say that the election on identifier i converges to L_i with estimate v for the size of the ring.

Lemma 4. *If the election for identifier i converges to estimate e then for any estimate est of processes with identifier i, $e \leq est$.*

If the election for identifier i converges to set L_i and $p \in L_i$, p eventually sends a *publish* message. As *publish* messages reach all processes with Lemma 4 we get:

Lemma 5. *If the election for identifier i converges to estimate e then eventually at each process $L[i] = e$.*

We say that process p chooses identifier i as leader if after Line 30 for some x $(e, j) = (x, i)$. Call a process with variable *Leader* equal to true a winner, and a process with variable *Leader* equal to false a looser.

Lemma 6. *Eventually all processes choose the same identifier i as leader. Then eventually all processes with identifiers different from i are forever looser and only active processes with identifiers equal to i are forever winner.*

Lemma 7. *If $|\mathcal{L}| > gpd(n)$, then for at least one identifier i, there are p and q with identifier i such that the distance from p to q is greater than $gpd(n)$.*

Proof. Indeed let $G(i)$ be the set of processes with identifier i and $d_i(p)$ be the distance on the ring to the next process with identifier i (if the next such process is p itself $d_i(p) = n$) clearly $\sum_{p \in G(i)} d_i(p) = n$.

Let $M = \{i \in \mathcal{L} | \max\{d_i(p)|p \in G(i)\} > gpd(n)\}$. By contradiction assume that $M = \emptyset$, then for all $i \in \mathcal{L}$: $\sum_{p \in G(i)} d_i(p) = n \leq gpd(n) \cdot |G(i)|$. Thus

$$gpd(n) \cdot n = gpd(n) \cdot \left(\sum_{i \in \mathcal{L}} |G(i)|\right) = \sum_{i \in \mathcal{L}} gpd(n) \cdot |G(i)| \geq |\mathcal{L}|n$$

Hence $gpd(n) \geq |\mathcal{L}|$ a contradiction.

Then from Lemma 3:

Lemma 8. *If $|\mathcal{L}| > gpd(n)$ then for at least one $i \in \mathcal{L}$ the election converges to a singleton with estimate n.*

From Lemmas 8 and 6, we deduce that eventually only one process is winner and all other processes are looser. A simple verification enables to proves that only a finite number of messages are exchanged, finishing the proof of the proposition.

If n, the ring size, is known algorithm of Fig. 2 may easily be changed to get a process-terminating leader election algorithm. Essentially for each identifier active processes verifies that there is only one leader for the identifier by sending a message *Probe*. Details are given in Fig. 3.

```
/* replace Line 15 of Algorithm of Figure 2 */
  if (est = leftest) then
    if est = n then send(publish, Id, n)
    else send(Probe, Id, est, true, 1) to next

/* replace Line 30 to 37 of Algorithm of Figure 2 */
  on receive(publish, i, v)
    L[i] = v
    if ∀k ∈ L L[k] ≠ 0 then
      if (Id = max{j ∈ L|L[j] = n}) ∧ (state = active) then
        Leader = true
        send(Terminate)
        terminate
      send(publish, i, v) to next

/* code for messages Terminate */
  on receive(Terminate)
    Leader = False
    send(Terminate)
    terminate

/* code for messages Probe */
  on receive(Probe, i, v, b, c)
    if (c = n) ∧ (b = true) then send(publish, i, v)
    else if (c < n) then
      if ((Id ≠ i) ∨ (state = passive)) then send(Probe, i, v, b, c + 1) to next
      else
        if est = v then send (Probe, l, v, b, c + 1)
        else send (Probe, i, v, false, c + 1)
```

Fig. 3. From message-terminating to process-terminating.

Proposition 3. *If $|\mathcal{L}| > gpd(n)$ and n is known by processes, algorithm of Fig. 3 is a process-terminating election algorithm with homonyms.*

Remarks. It is only for simplify the code that we refer in the algorithm to $\mathcal{L}$. $\mathcal{L}$ is used only in algorithm Fig. 2 for array L indexed by identifiers in Lines 30–34. Instead of array L it is possible to deal with an ordered list without a priori knowledge of the set of identifiers. Hence we get a deterministic message-terminating election algorithm with neither the knowledge of the ring size neither the knowledge of the number of identifiers.

In the same way, if $|\mathcal{L}| > gpd(n)$, if n is not a prime number, n is lower or equal to $|\mathcal{L}|^2$. With the knowledge of $|\mathcal{L}|$ we get a bound on n, it is easy to adapt the algorithm of Fig. 3 in such a way we obtain process-terminating election algorithm with only the knowledge of $|\mathcal{L}|$.

5   A Process Terminating Leader Election Algorithm with $O(n \times \log(n))$ Messages

5.1   Definitions

We encode in a multi-sequence, a number of processes and a set of identifiers. A *multi-sequence* is a sequence $((a_1, i_1), (a_2, i_2), ..., (a_u, i_u))$, where for each $1 \leq h \leq u$, i_h is an identifier, a_h is the multiplicity of i_h, and $i_1 < i_2 < ... < i_u$. For a multi-sequence $\mathcal{I} = ((a_1, i_1), (a_2, i_2), ..., (a_u, i_u))$, $Id(\mathcal{I}) = \{i_1, i_2, ..., i_u\}$ and $nb(\mathcal{I}) = a_1 + a_2 + ... + a_u$. We define a total order on such multi-sequences. Given two sequences $\mathcal{I} = ((a_1, i_1), (a_2, i_2), ..., (a_u, i_u))$ and $\mathcal{J} = ((b_1, j_1), (b_2, j_2), ..., (b_v, j_v))$, we say that $\mathcal{I} < \mathcal{J}$ if

- it exists $k \leq min\{u, v\}$ such that
  - for every $0 \leq h < k$: $i_{u-h} = j_{v-h}$ and $a_{u-h} = b_{v-h}$
  - $i_{u-k} < j_{v-k}$ or $(i_{u-k} = j_{v-k}$ and $a_{u-k} < b_{v-k})$
  or
- $u < v$ and for every $0 \leq h < u$: $i_{u-h} = j_{v-h}$ and $a_{u-h} = b_{v-h}$

It can be easily verified that we have defined a total order between multi-sequence. In the following $<>$ denotes the empty multi-sequence and $\oplus$ is the operator adding an element to a multi-sequence.

5.2   Algorithm

Our leader election algorithm uses a similar approach to the ones in [15,20], where processes have distinct identifiers. Recall that in their algorithms, each process is initially active. Processes that are passive, simply forward the message they receive. At each step, an active process sends a message with its identifier to its both neighbors and receives messages from its both nearest active neighbors.

If one of the received messages contains an identifier greater than its own identifier then it becomes passive. Otherwise, it starts a new step. If a process receives its own message (i.e. a message with its own identifier) then the process becomes leader. The algorithm terminates after $O(\log(n))$ steps, and each step requires $2n$ messages.

In our algorithm, we keep the idea that each process is initially active and, at each step, each remaining active process p will exchange messages with its two nearest active neighbors and it will determine if it becomes passive (as for the previous algorithm).

But to determine if a process p becomes passive we use not only the identifiers of its two nearest active neighbors q and s but also the distances $d(p, q)$ and $d(p, s)$ and the identifiers of the processes between p and q and p and s.

We encode these two last information in multi-sequence and we use the total order on these multi-sequences.

The algorithm ensures that p and q are active and neighbors then the information they get each other are the same: if p receives from its left $(Id(q), \mathcal{D_L})$ then q receives from its right $(Id(p), \mathcal{D_R})$ with $\mathcal{D_R} = \mathcal{D_L}$.

After the exchange of messages, p compares $(Id(q), \mathcal{D_L})$ and $(Id(s), \mathcal{D_R})$ that it received from its two nearest active neighbors. If the number of processes between itself and its neighbors is the size of the ring, this process is the only active process. Then it is the leader. It sends a message STOP in order that all passive processes terminate and it terminates. If the number of processes between itself and its neighbors is different from the ring size, the process becomes passive if (1) $Id(p) < Id(q)$ or $Id(p) < Id(r)$ or (2) if $Id(p) = Id(q) = Id(s)$ and ($\mathcal{D_R} < \mathcal{D_L}$ or $\mathcal{D_R} = \mathcal{D_L}$) (condition (2) is an adaptation for homonyms). Otherwise, it remains active and starts a new step.

If we consider three consecutive active processes by the previous rules at least one of them become passive. In each step, at least a third of active processes are hence eliminated. By repetitive application of these rules eventually it remains only at most one active process (the ring structure ensures that if two processes are active at least one will be eliminated). Thus after $O(\log(n))$ steps, it remains at most one process.

But we have to avoid that all processes become passive. The fact that $|\mathcal{L}|$ is greater than the greatest proper divisor of n ensures that it is impossible that there is a subset of processes with the same identifier such that the distance between them is the same and the set of identifiers of processes between them are the same (see Lemma 10).

Thus, the algorithm will finish with only one active process. The algorithm is described in more details in Fig. 4.

We give below the main steps of the proof of this theorem and we sketch their proofs. By abuse of language we say that a process is active (resp. passive) if its *status* variable is *active* (resp. *passive*). As channels are FIFO, a computation of an active process can be decomposed in (asynchronous) rounds. As long as a process is active and has not terminate, it executes a round: it waits to receive messages from the left and the right and computes its new state after receiving them. We name s_p^r the state of p after r rounds. Let s_p^0 denotes the initial state. If a process is terminated or passive in s_p^r then for all r' greater than $s_p^{r'} = s_p^r$.

Directly from the algorithm we have:

Lemma 9. *If process q is active at s_q^r and p is its the nearest active right neighbor (i.e. the nearest right neighbor p such that p is active in s_p^r) then if q receives $\mathcal{D}_R^q$ from its right and p receives $\mathcal{D}_L^p$ from its left then $\mathcal{D}_R^q = \mathcal{D}_L^p$.*

Lemma 10. *Let G be a subset of processes with the same identifier, there do not exist a set of identifiers $\mathcal{I}$ and an integer x such that for any two processes p and q of G, there are x processes between p and q and the set of identifiers of processes between p and q is $\mathcal{I}$.*

Code for a process with identifier i

```
 1  status = "active"
 2  Leader = false
 3  send(i, <>, 1) in both directions

 4  for ever
 5     if status = "passive" then
 6        wait until received a message:
 7           On receiving (j, 𝒟):
 8              send(j, 𝒟 ⊕ < i >) in the same direction

 9           On receiving (STOP):
10              send(STOP) in the same direction; halt

11     if status = "active" then
12        wait until received a message from the left and the right:
13        assume that (j_R, 𝒟_R) came from right and (j_L, 𝒟_L) came from left
14        if nb(𝒟_R) = n then Leader = true; send(STOP) to left; halt
15        else if (i < j_R or i < j_L) or (i = j_R = j_L and (𝒟_R < 𝒟_L or 𝒟_R = 𝒟_L ) )
16           then status = "passive"
17           else send(i, <>, 1) in both directions
```

Fig. 4. $O(n \log(n))$ algorithm for process terminating leader election

Proof. Assume that there exists a subset G of processes with the same identifier, a set of identifier $\mathcal{I}$ and an integer x such that for any two processes p and q of G, there are x processes between p and q and the set of identifiers of processes between p and q is $\mathcal{I}$. Note that $x \geq |\mathcal{I}|$. We have $n = |G| * x$, then (1) x is a divisor of n. As for each identifier, the ring contains at least one process with this identifier, we get $\mathcal{I} = \mathcal{L}$.

Then $x \geq gpd(n)$, with (1) this implies that G contains only one process.

Lemma 11. *For all r, there is at least one process p active in s_p^r.*

Proof. We show this property by induction, it holds trivially for $r = 0$. Assume it is true until $r - 1$. Assume for contradiction that all processes become passive in r. Let G be the set of processes that changes its state from active to passive in round r.

If G contains at least two processes with a different identifier, we consider the subset H of G that contain the processes with the greatest identifier. As there is a process in G with another identifier, there is at least one process in H that has from right active neighbor a process in $H \setminus G$. From condition line 15, this process remains active.

If all processes in G have the same identifier, by Lemma 10, for at least one process we have $\mathcal{D}_L > \mathcal{D}_R$. From condition Line 15, this process remains active.

Lemma 12. *For $r > 0$, let $x = |\{p|p$ is active in $s_p^{r-1}\}|$, we have $|\{p|p$ is active in $s_p^r\}| \le (2/3) * x + x \mod 3$.*

Proof. Consider the set $\{p|p$ is active in $s_p^{r-1}\}$) and $x = |\{p|p$ is active in $s_p^{r-1}\}|$. We split this set in sets of three processes that are neighbors in the ring (it remains $x \mod 3$ processes). Consider some sets of three processes $\{p, q, v\}$ and assume that p is the left neighbor of q and x its right neighbor.

If p and q or q and v have not the same identifier then the process with the smallest identifiers become passive. Let $\mathcal{D}_R^q$ and $\mathcal{D}_L^q$ the values that it receives from its nearest active neighbors. If they have the same identifier, q remains active only if $\mathcal{D}_R^q > \mathcal{D}_L^q$ but in this case by Lemma 9, p becomes passif.

Lemma 13. *For $r > 0$, let $|\{p|p$ is active in $s_p^{r-1}\}| = 2$, we have $|\{p|p$ is active in $s_p^r\}| = 1$.*

Proof. It remains two active processes, let p and q be these processes.

If p and q have not the same identifier then the process with the smallest identifiers become passive. Let $\mathcal{D}_R^q$ and $\mathcal{D}_L^q$ the values that it receives from its nearest active neighbors. If p and q have the same identifier, q remains active only if $\mathcal{D}_R^q > \mathcal{D}_L^q$ but in this case by Lemma 9, p becomes passive.

From Lemmas 11, 12 and 13, we deduce that eventually it remains only one active process. Directly from the algorithm this process becomes leader and propagates the termination by sending a STOP messages.

Theorem 4. *If n is known by processes and $|\mathcal{L}| > gpd(n)$ then there exists an algorithm that solves process terminating leader election with $O(n \log(n))$ messages.*

6   Concluding Remarks

Given a ring of size n, $gpd(n)$ identifiers are needed to have a deterministic election algorithm. If n is a prime number then two identifiers are sufficient, but in the worst case when n is even $n/2$ (hence $O(n)$) identifiers are needed. Moreover, if there is a deterministic solution for leader election, then we do not have any penalty: there is an election with the same order of number of exchanged messages as when all processes have their own identity. Then limiting the number of identifiers without avoiding the existence of deterministic election algorithm is mainly interesting if some properties of the size ring are known (e.g. this size is a prime number).

The leader election problem has been studied in framework similar to homonyms: [5,7,8,22,23] consider "partially anonymous", [14] "nonunique label" and [18] "partially eponymous". Some of the results in these papers are similar to the ones we present here but we present our results, restricted to the ring topology, in term of number of process identifiers rather than properties of the general communication graph. Even if [14] concerns rings with asynchronous communication, our algorithm, with our conditions on $|\mathcal{L}|$ gets the optimality in term of messages that is not achieved in a more general framework by [14].

References

1. Abrahamson, K., Adler, A., Gelbart, R., Higham, L., Kirkpatrick, D.: The bit complexity of randomized leader election on a ring. SIAM J. Comput. **18**(1), 12–29 (1989)
2. Angluin, D.: Local and global properties in networks of processors (extended abstract). In: Proceedings of the Twelfth Annual ACM Symposium on Theory of Computing, STOC '80, pp. 82–93. ACM, New York (1980)
3. Angluin, D., Aspnes, J., Diamadi, Z., Fischer, M.J., Peralta, R.: Computation in networks of passively mobile finite-state sensors. Distrib. Comput. **18**(4), 235–253 (2006)
4. Arévalo, S., Anta, A.F., Imbs, D., Jiménez, E., Raynal, M.: Failure detectors in homonymous distributed systems (with an application to consensus). In: ICDCS, pp. 275–284 (2012)
5. Boldi, P., Shammah, S., Vigna, S., Codenotti, B., Gemmell, P., Simon, J.: Symmetry breaking in anonymous networks: characterizations. In: ISTCS, pp. 16–26 (1996)
6. Burns, J.E., Pachl, J.K.: Uniform self-stabilizing rings. ACM Trans. Program. Lang. Syst. **11**(2), 330–344 (1989)
7. Chalopin, J., Godard, E., Métivier, Y.: Election in partially anonymous networks with arbitrary knowledge in message passing systems. Distrib. Comput. **25**(4), 297–311 (2012)
8. Chalopin, J., Métivier, Y., Morsellino, T.: Enumeration and leader election in partially anonymous and multi-hop broadcast networks. Fundam. Inform. **120**(1), 1–27 (2012)
9. Chaum, D., van Heyst, E.: Group signatures. In: Davies, D.W. (ed.) EUROCRYPT 1991. LNCS, vol. 547, pp. 257–265. Springer, Heidelberg (1991)
10. Delporte-Gallet, C., Fauconnier, H., Guerraoui, R., Kermarrec, A.-M., Ruppert, E., Tran-The, H.: Byzantine agreement with homonyms. In: PODC, pp. 21–30. ACM (2011)
11. Delporte-Gallet, C., Fauconnier, H., Tran-The, H.: Byzantine agreement with homonyms in synchronous systems. In: Bononi, L., Datta, A.K., Devismes, S., Misra, A. (eds.) ICDCN 2012. LNCS, vol. 7129, pp. 76–90. Springer, Heidelberg (2012)
12. Delporte-Gallet, C., Fauconnier, H., Tran-The, H.: Homonyms with forgeable identifiers. In: Even, G., Halldórsson, M.M. (eds.) SIROCCO 2012. LNCS, vol. 7355, pp. 171–182. Springer, Heidelberg (2012)
13. Dijkstra, E.W.: Self-stabilizing systems in spite of distributed control. Commun. ACM **17**(11), 643–644 (1974)
14. Dobrev, S., Pelc, A.: Leader election in rings with nonunique labels. Fundam. Inform. **59**(4), 333–347 (2004)
15. Franklin, R.: On an improved algorithm for decentralized extrema finding in circular configurations of processors. Commun. ACM **25**(5), 336–337 (1982)
16. Huang, S.-T.: Leader election in uniform rings. ACM Trans. Program. Lang. Syst. **15**(3), 563–573 (1993)
17. Kutten, S., Pandurangan, G., Peleg, D., Robinson, P., Trehan, A.: Sublinear bounds for randomized leader election. In: Frey, D., Raynal, M., Sarkar, S., Shyamasundar, R.K., Sinha, P. (eds.) ICDCN 2013. LNCS, vol. 7730, pp. 348–362. Springer, Heidelberg (2013)

18. Mavronicolas, M., Michael, L., Spirakis, P.G.: Computing on a partially eponymous ring. Theor. Comput. Sci. **410**(6–7), 595–613 (2009)
19. Pachl, J.K., Korach, E., Rotem, D.: Lower bounds for distributed maximum-finding algorithms. J. ACM **31**(4), 905–918 (1984)
20. Peterson, G.L.: An o(nlog n) unidirectional algorithm for the circular extrema problem. ACM Trans. Program. Lang. Syst. **4**(4), 758–762 (1982)
21. Xu, Z., Srimani, P.K.: Self-stabilizing anonymous leader election in a tree. In: IPDPS. IEEE Computer Society (2005)
22. Yamashita, M., Kameda, T.: Leader election problem on networks in which processor identity numbers are not distinct. IEEE Trans. Parallel Distrib. Syst. **10**(9), 878–887 (1999)
23. Yamashita, M., Kameda, T.: Modeling k-coteries by well-covered graphs. Networks **34**(3), 221–228 (1999)

Abort Free SemanticTM by Dependency Aware Scheduling of Transactional Instructions

Hillel Avni[1], Shlomi Dolev[2(✉)], Panagiota Fatourou[3], and Eleftherios Kosmas[3]

[1] Tel-Aviv University, Tel Aviv, Israel
hillel.avni@gmail.com
[2] Ben-Gurion University of the Negev, Beersheba, Israel
dolev@cs.bgu.ac.il
[3] FORTH-ICS, University of Crete, Rethymno, Greece
{faturu,ekosmas}@csd.uoc.gr

Abstract. We present a TM system that executes transactions without ever causing any aborts. The system uses a set of *t-var lists*, one for each transactional variable. The instructions of each transaction are placed in the appropriate t-var lists based on which t-variable each of them accesses. A set of worker threads are responsible to execute these instructions. Because of the way instructions are inserted in and removed from the lists, by the way the worker threads work, and by the fact that all the instructions of a transaction are placed in the appropriate t-var lists before doing so for the instructions of any subsequent transaction, it follows that no conflict will ever occur. Parallelism is fine-grained since it is achieved at the level of transactional instructions instead of transactions themselves (i.e., the instructions of a transaction may be executed concurrently).

1 Introduction

In *asynchronous shared memory systems,* *where* threads execute in arbitrary speeds and communication among them occurs by accessing basic shared *primitives* (usually provided by the hardware), having threads executing pieces of code in parallel is not an easy task due to synchronization conflicts that may occur among threads that need to concurrently access non-disjoint sets of shared data. A promising parallel programming paradigm is Transactional Memory (TM) where pieces of code that may access data that become shared in a concurrent environment (such pieces of data are called *transactional variables* or *t-variables*) are indicated as *transactions*. A TM system ensures that the execution of a transaction T will either *succeed*, in which case T *commits* and all its updates become visible, or it will be *unsuccessful*, so T *aborts* and its updates are discarded. Each committed transaction appears as if it has been executed "instantaneously" in some point of its execution interval.

When a conflict between two transactions occurs, TM systems usually abort one of the transactions to ensure consistency; two transactions *conflict* if they

© Springer International Publishing Switzerland 2014
G. Noubir and M. Raynal (Eds.): NETYS 2014, LNCS 8593, pp. 25–40, 2014.
DOI: 10.1007/978-3-319-09581-3_3

both access the same t-variable and at least one of these accesses writes a t-variable. To guarantee *progress*, all transactions should eventually commit. This property, albeit highly desirable, is scarcely ensured by the currently available TM systems; most of these systems do not even ensure that transactions abort only when they violate the considered consistency condition (this property is known as *permissiveness* [13]). The work performed by a transaction that aborts is discarded and it is later re-executed as a new transaction; this incurs a performance penalty. So, the nature of TM is optimistic; if transactions never abort then no work is ever discarded. In terms of achieving good performance, the system should additionally guarantee that parallelism is achieved. So, transactions should not be executed sequentially and global contention points should be avoided. The design of TM algorithms that never abort transactions is highly desirable since they additionally support irrevocable transactions; i.e. transactions that perform irrevocable operations, e.g. I/O operations.

In this paper, we present SemanticTM, an opaque [16] TM algorithm which ensures (1) that transactions complete and never abort (i.e., the strongest progress guarantee), and (2) fine-grain parallelism at the transactional instruction level: in addition to instructions of different transactions, instructions of the same transaction that do not depend on each other can be executed concurrently. So, since SemanticTM ensures wait-freedom, it naturally supports irrevocable operations.

SemanticTM employs a list for each t-variable. The instructions of each transaction are placed in the appropriate lists in FIFO order; specifically, each instruction is executed on a single t-variable, so it is placed in the list of the t-variable that it accesses. A set of worker threads execute instructions from the lists, in order. The algorithm is highly fault-tolerant. Even if some worker threads fail by crashing, all transactions whose instructions have been placed in the lists will be executed. In this paper we focus on relatively simple transactions that access a known set of t-variables, and their codes contain **read** and **write** instructions on them, conditionals (i.e. **if**, **else if**, and **else**), loops (i.e. **for**, **while**, etc.), and function calls. For such transactions, the work of placing the instructions of the transaction in lists can be done at compile time (so there is no need to employ a scheduling component for doing so). Despite this fact, for simplicity, we refer bellow to a scheduling thread (sometimes called scheduler) which undertakes this task. We briefly discuss, in Sect. 4, how to extend SemanticTM to cope with more complicated transactional codes.

We remark that several dependencies may exist among the instructions of a single transaction; specifically, a single instruction may have several dependencies. SemanticTM works well when these dependencies can be predicted statically. By using compiler support, these dependencies become known before the beginning of the execution of the transactions. SemanticTM stores information about them together with the corresponding instruction in the appropriate list. In Sect. 2, we describe the dependencies expected by SemanticTM in order to guarantee the correct execution of the corresponding transactions.

It is worth mentioning that in this work, we do not focus on how these dependencies are extracted. SemanticTM can make use of any existing or future work on dataflow analysis. After its placement in the appropriate list, each transactional instruction is executed as soon as its data are available. Thus, SemanticTM can be thought of as a dataflow algorithm in the sense that it mimics, in software, a dataflow architecture.

In Sect. 3, we present some experimental results where a simplified version of SemanticTM executes simple static transactions testing different conflict patterns among them. In the experiments, SemanticTM exhibits good performance; specifically, in all these experiments, SemanticTM performs better than GccSTM [23] which is an industry software transactional memory standard [23].

The current version of SemanticTM does not support dynamic transactions. A discussion on how this limitation could be overcome is provided in Sect. 4. Since SemanticTM ensures that all transactions will commit, it does not provide any support for explicitly aborting transactions.

Related Work. TM algorithms that never abort transactions has been recently presented in [1, 18]. They use ideas from [25] where a TM system is presented which supports the execution of irrevocable transactions. In the algorithms of [1, 18], read-only transactions are *wait-free*, i.e. each of them is completed successfully within a finite number of steps; a *read-only* transaction never writes a t-variable in contrast to an *update* transaction that performs write operations on such variables. However, these algorithms restrict parallelism by executing all update transactions sequentially using a global lock. SemanticTM guarantees that no transaction aborts while exploiting parallelism between both writers and readers. SemanticTM does not also use any locks and therefore update transactions are also executed in a wait-free way. TM systems that support wait-free read-only transactions are presented in [4, 21]. Update transactions in them may abort and they require locks to execute some of the transactional instructions.

To enhance progress, a lot of research has been performed on designing efficient contention managers and transactional schedulers. A contention manager [15, 24] is a TM component aiming at ensuring progress by providing efficient conflict resolution policies. When two transactions conflict, the contention manager is employed to decide whether simple techniques, like back-off, would be sufficient, or which of the transactions should abort or be paused to allow the other transaction to complete. SemanticTM prevents conflicts from occurring thus making the use of a contention manager unnecessary.

Somewhat closer to the work here, a *transactional scheduler* [2, 3, 5, 6, 11, 19, 27] is a more elaborated TM component which places transactions in a set of queues, usually one for each thread; a set of working threads then execute transactions from these queues. In addition to deciding which transaction to delay or abort when a conflict occurs, and when to restart a delayed or aborted transaction, a scheduler also decides in which scheduling queue the transaction will be placed once its execution will be resumed or restarted. Some of the schedulers always abort one of the two transactions and place it in an appropriate queue to guarantee that the transaction will be restarted only after the conflicting transaction has finished its execution, i.e. they serialize the execution of the two transactions. CarSTM [11], Adaptive Transaction Scheduling [27], and Steal-on-Abort [2] work in this way. In [5], a scheduler was presented which alternates between reading epochs (where priority is given to the execution of read-only transactions) and writing epochs (where the opposite occurs). This technique behaves better for read-dominated [17] and bimodal [5] workloads, for which schedulers like those presented in [2,11,27] may serialize more than necessary. However, the working threads in the algorithm of [5] use locks; additionally, aborts are not avoided. To evaluate a transactional scheduler, competitive analysis is often employed [3,5,14,15] where the total time needed to complete a set of transactions (known as *makespan*) is compared to the makespan of a clairvoyant scheduler [19].

In [12], scheduling is done based on future prediction of the transactions' data sets on the basis of a short history of past transactions and the accesses that they performed. If a transaction is predicted to conflict with an active transaction, it is serialized. To avoid serializing more than necessary in cases of low contention, a heuristic is used where prediction and serialization occur only if the completion rate of transactions falls below a certain threshold.

In [22], a lock-based dependence-aware TM system is presented which dynamically detects and resolves conflicts. Its implementation extends ideas from TL II [10] with support of dependence detection and data forwarding. The algorithm serializes transactions that conflict; in case of aborts, cascading aborts may occur. The current version of SemanticTM copes only with transactions that their data sets are known. However, SemanticTM ensures that all transactions will always commit within a bounded number of steps.

In [20], a database transaction processing system similar to SemanticTM is proposed; database transactions can be thought of as transactions whose data sets are known, in TM concept. Similarly to SemanticTM, consecutive transactional instructions of a transaction are separated into groups, called *actions*, according to the dataset they access, each worker thread is responsible to execute instructions for a disjoint set of datasets, and each action is scheduled to the appropriate thread. Data dependencies between actions are maintained using extra metadata. Specifically, a shared object (additional to database's tables), called *rendezvous point*, is maintained for the dependencies of each action of some transaction; a single action may have several data dependencies and each of those dependencies will be resolved by the corresponding thread. Using these rendezvous points the execution of a transaction is separated into phases, with each phase containing independent actions. A thread initiating the execution of a transaction, schedules the independent actions (of the first phase) to the appropriate worker threads. When a worker thread resolves the last dependency of some rendezvous point, it initiates the next phase of transaction's execution by scheduling the next independent actions of this transaction. However, due to its execution scheme a transaction executed in this system may have to abort, whereas in SemanticTM transactions never abort.

With goals similar to TM, Thread Level Speculation (TLS) [8,9,26] uses compiler support to split a program into several tasks which are speculatively executed and each of them finishes by trying to commit. Whenever a consistency violation is detected the conflicting tasks are appropriately aborted, like in TM. In [7], an algorithm that incorporates TLS support on a TM algorithm has been proposed, where each transaction of the TM program is split into several tasks. In this case, consistency violations may arise as a result of either an intra-transaction conflict (i.e., a conflict between the instruction of the same transaction) or an inter-transaction conflict (i.e., a conflict between instruction of different transactions). In both cases, an appropriate tasks' abort policy ensures that no consistency violation occurs. However, in SemanticTM instead of executing tasks, threads execute sets of instructions, each performed on a specific t-variable (this set may contain instructions of several transactions). So, no conflict ever occurs.

2   SemanticTM

Main Ideas. SemanticTM uses a set of lists, called *t-var lists*, one for each t-variable. A scheduler places the instructions of each transaction in the appropriate t-var lists based on which t-variables each of them accesses. All the instructions of each transaction are placed in the t-var lists before the instructions of any subsequent transaction. The scheduler also records any dependencies that may exist between the instructions of the same transaction. Each of the workers repeatedly chooses, *uniformly at random*, a t-var list and executes the instructions of this list, starting from the first one. Processing transactions in this way ensures that conflicts never occur; so, transactions never abort. Recall that compiler support is employed to know, for each instruction, any dependency that leads to or originates from it. Figure 1 shows the main structure of SemanticTM.

For example, consider transactions T_1 and T_2 of Fig. 2. Without loss of generality, assume that the instructions of T_1 are placed in the t-var lists first. Then, the instructions of lines 1 and 2 of T_1 will be placed in the t-var list for x before the write to x on line 6 of T_2. Similarly, the write to y of line 3 of T_1 will be placed in the t-var list for y before the write to y of line 5 of T_2. Since the worker threads respect the order in which instructions have been inserted in the lists when they execute them, the instructions of T_1 on each t-variable will be executed before the instructions of T_2 on this t-variable, and thus no conflict between them will ever occur.

The set of t-variables accessed by a transaction is its *data set*. We call *control flow statements* the conditionals and loops, and we use the instruction cond to refer to such a statement. The *instructions* of a transaction are read, write, and cond instructions. We call *block* the set of its instructions in the body of a control flow statement; so each cond instruction is associated with a block.

Dependencies. If the execution of an instruction e_1 requires the result of the execution of another instruction e_2, then there is a *dependency* between e_1 and e_2. This dependency is an *input* dependency for e_1 and an *output* dependency for e_2. A dependency between a read and a write is called *data* dependency.1

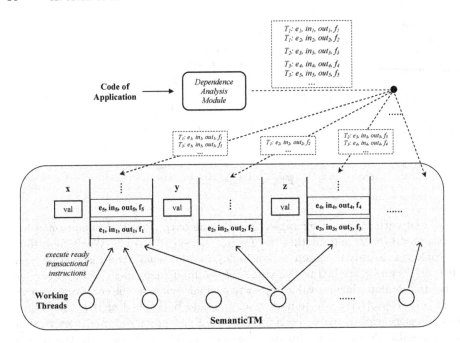

Fig. 1. Main components of SemanticTM. Extraction of transactional instructions and their placement into t-var lists.

We remark that SemanticTM will place five instructions for T_1 (Fig. 2) in the t-var lists: e_1 which is a write to x (line 1), a read e_2 and a write e_3 to x (line 2), a read e_4 on x and a write e_5 to y for line 3. There is an output dependency from e_i to e_{i+1}, $1 \leq i < 5$. Notice that in order to execute line 3, where the assignment on y depends on the value of x, SemanticTM places a read instruction (e_4) on x before the corresponding write instruction (e_5) on y. By doing this, SemanticTM avoids to maintain data dependencies between write instructions (e.g., between e_3 and e_5).

Moreover, SemanticTM does not maintain input dependencies for any read instruction e on a t-variable x, since all writes to x on which e depends have been placed in the t-var list of x before e and thus the read can get the value from the metadata of x (by the way the algorithm works, this value will be consistent). Thus, SemanticTM records input data dependencies only for write and cond instructions (that originate from read instructions). For each such dependency, additional metadata are maintained, including the value of the t-variable, read by the corresponding read instruction, which is also called *value of the dependency*. We remark that each read (write or cond) instruction may have several output (input) data dependencies.

A dependency that either leads to or originates from a cond instruction is called *control* dependency. For each cond instruction, SemanticTM maintains an output control dependency from cond to each instruction e of the block

```
1  x := 3
2  x++
3  y := x
   T1
```

```
4  z := 2
5  y := z
6  x := y
   T2
```

```
7  x := 1
8  if (...) then
9     x := 2
10 else
11    x := 4
12 y := x
   T3
```

```
13 i := 1
14 while (i ≤ 3)          cnt ∈ {0, 1, 2, 3}
15    j := 1              cnt ∈ {0, 1, ..., 15}
16    while (j ≤ 5)       startinneriter ∈ {⊥, 0, 5, 10}
17       j := j + 1       forouteriter ∈ {0, 1, 2, 3}
18    i := i + 1
   T4
```

Fig. 2. Transactions.

associated with it. As an example, there is one output control dependency for instruction 8 (to 9) and another one for instruction 10 (to 11). We assume that for each `write` instruction on a t-variable x, or for each `cond` instruction e, a function f can be applied to the values of the input dependencies of e in order either to calculate the new value of x or to evaluate whether the condition is `true` or `false`, respectively. We remark that f should be applied after all the input data dependencies of e have been resolved[1]. Table 1 provides a brief description of all possible dependencies for each instruction. The state of an instruction is *waiting*, if at least one of its input dependencies has not been resolved, otherwise, it is *ready*; an instruction is *active* if it is either waiting or ready.

Recall that by using compiler support, the dependencies between the instructions of a transaction are known before the beginning of its execution. Each instruction, together with its dependencies (and function), is placed in the appropriate t-var list, as a single *entry*.

Conditionals. Each part of a conditional (`if`, `else if`, `else`) is associated with a `cond` instruction and a block. Therefore, for an `if` ... `then` ... `else` statement, the two `cond`s (for the `if` and the `else` part) and their blocks' transactional instructions will be placed in the appropriate t-var lists. Then, at runtime, one of the two `cond` instructions will be evaluated as `false` so its block's instructions will be invalidated by the working thread that executes this `cond`. A `cond` instruction can be inserted in the t-var list of any t-variable; in the current version of SemanticTM it is placed in the t-var list of the first instruction of its block.

Notice that a transactional instruction of some block, may have *outside-block* dependencies which come from or lead to instructions that does not belong to the block. For instance, there may be outside-block dependencies from the instruction of line 7 to the `cond`s of the `if`...`then` ...`else` or to the instructions of the `cond`s' blocks. Notice that in SemanticTM output outside block dependencies are resolved directly because of the way that the transactional instructions are placed in the t-var lists. For example, to execute line 12, SemanticTM places

[1] Computation on local variables can be included in the code of function f. For this reason, such a function may also be maintained for `read` instructions.

Table 1. Data dependencies between transactional instructions.

Transactional instruction	Dependencies			
	Input		Output	
	Data dep	Control dep	Data dep	Control dep
$e = \mathtt{read}(x)$	In SemanticTM, e has no input data dependencies	if e participates in some block, it has an input control dependency originating from the block's cond	e forwards the value it reads to write and cond instructions that depend on it	if e participates in some loop's block, an output control dependency originates from e to its block's cond
$e = \mathtt{write}(x)$	e may have input data dependencies originating from reads	if e participates in some block, it has an input control dependency originating from the block's cond	In SemanticTM, e has no output data dependencies	if e participates in some loop's block, an output control dependency originates from e to its block's cond
$e = \mathtt{cond}$	e may have input data dependencies originating from reads	if e is a cond of a loop cond, it has input control dependency originating from each of its block's instructions cond		e has output control dependencies to each of its block's instructions

a read instruction e and a write instruction e' in the t-var lists of x and y, respectively. Recall that e as a read instruction does not have an input dependency. However, a dependency exists from e to e'. Moreover, in SemanticTM input outside block dependencies do not exist. As an example, consider that line 12 participates in some block's code; for the same reason (as above), e and e' do not have input outside block dependencies.

Loops. Let e be a transactional instruction that is included in a loop block; let c be the associated cond. SemanticTM places c and each instruction of the block in the appropriate t-var lists only once independently of the number of times that the loop will be executed since this number may be known only at run time. We remark that the execution of e (and c) in some iteration may depend on the execution of some transactional instructions of the previous iteration; we call such a dependency *across-iteration*.

In order to perform c multiple times, an *iteration counter* cnt_c is associated with c. This counter stores the current iteration number of the loop's execution. Moreover, the input control dependency of e is implemented with a counter cnt_e; the same counter is also used to implement the input control dependency of c from e. If $cnt_e = cnt_c + 1$, then the input control dependency of e is resolved, otherwise not; if $cnt_e = cnt_c$, then e has been executed and the input control dependency of c from e is resolved, for the (cnt_c)th iteration. Notice that cnt_e can be either equal to or smaller by one from cnt_c. This is so, since c can initiate a new iteration only after its input control dependencies originating from its block instructions have been resolved, i.e., after all these instructions have been executed for the current iteration; similarly, these instructions can be executed only if their input control dependencies (from c) have been resolved.

To ensure correctness, an *iteration number* is associated with each of the input data dependencies of e (or c); this number is stored together with the corresponding input dependency into a CAS object. When the iteration number of an input data dependency $inDep$ of e (or c) is smaller than cnt_c, it follows that $inDep$ is unresolved for the current iteration; if all input data dependencies of e have their iteration number fields equal to cnt_c, then all data dependencies of e have been resolved and e can be executed. Once e is executed, it resolves the control dependency to c by writing there an iteration number equal to cnt_c; recall that the same action marks e as performed for the current iteration. When all dependencies of c have been resolved c can be executed. If it decides to initiate the next iteration (i.e., its condition is evaluated as true) it increments cnt_c by one to resolve its output control dependencies for the next iteration.

Notice that although (in SemanticTM) e does not have data dependencies with instructions outside the block of c, c may have input data dependencies from instructions outside its block and inside its block; we call them *outer* and *inner* data dependencies, respectively. SemanticTM differentiates them, so that inner dependencies are not taken into consideration when c decides the initiation of the first loop iteration. Also, if the input control dependencies of c are resolved for some iteration, then its inner data dependencies are also resolved for the same iteration; so, c uses them to decide the initiation of the next loop iteration.

Consider a t-var list that contains two instructions e_1 and e_2, in this order, which are included in the same loop block. Assume that there is an across iteration data dependency from e_2 to e_1. We remark that the input across-iteration data dependency of e_1 originating from e_2 should be initialized as resolved in order for e_1 to appropriately become ready for the first iteration of the loop. Also, notice that the execution of e_1 during the second iteration should occur only after the execution of the first-iteration instance of e_2. Since e_1 precedes e_2 in the list, the working threads may have to search which element of the corresponding t-var list is ready (instead of just checking whether the first element of the list is ready). Specifically, t-var list should be searched until an instruction is found that does not participate in the same loop, or until the end of the list if such an instruction does not exist. In this way, the loop instructions are executed as if the loop was unfolded and all its instructions were executed in FIFO order. We remark that the loop in which an instruction participates can be determined using its input control dependency.

Nesting of conds. Let c_2 be a cond that participates in the block of another cond c_1 (so the block of c_2 is *nested* in that of c_1). In SemanticTM, the output control dependencies of c_1 include only c_2 and not any instruction in the block of c_2; respectively, each instruction of the block of c_2 has an output control dependency with c_1.

We consider first the case where c_1 and c_2 are conditionals. During the execution of c_1 by some thread p, p will resolve c_1's output control dependency to c_2. If c_2 is not invalidated, then c_2 and the instruction of its block are executed; otherwise, c_2 and the instructions of its block are invalidated.

We consider now the case where c_1 and c_2 are loops. Each time c_1 initiates a new iteration, c_2 is executed. During its execution, c_2 may execute several iterations of its block code. When its execution completes for some iteration of c_1, c_2 resolves its output control dependency to c_1; from this point on and until the input control dependency of c_2 from c_1 is resolved once more, we say that c_2 is *inactive*.

Recall that c_2 has both inner and outer data dependencies. We remark that, in each iteration of c_1, c_2's outer data dependencies should be resolved before c_2 is executed for the first time for the current iteration of c_1. Notice that, a cond that does not participate in some loop is executed for the first time when its iteration counter equals 0. This is true for c_2, for the first iteration of c_1, but probably in next iterations of c_1 may have a value greater than 0.

To figure out the first time that c_2 is executed for the current iteration of c_1, a *start inner iteration number* $startinneriter_{c_2}$ is associated with c_2. Before the input control dependency of c_2 is resolved, $startinneriter_{c_2}$ is updated (by some working thread executing c_1) so that $startinneriter_{c_2} = cnt_{c_2}$. For example, consider T_4 (Fig. 2), with c_1 and c_2 be the cond instructions of lines 14 and 16, respectively. Notice that $startinneriter_{c_2}$ takes values $\{\perp, 0, 5, 10\}$ (in this order) where $\perp$ is its initial value and the rest are the values of cnt_{c_2} before c_2's loop starts in each iteration of c_1's loop, i.e. $(i-1) * 5$, $1 \leq i \leq 3$, for the ith iteration of c_1's loop.

The case where c_2 is a conditional's cond and c_1 is a loop's cond is similar with the previous one, with the difference that c_2 is executed only once each time c_1 initiates another (outer) loop iteration. Finally, the case where c_2 is a loop's cond and c_1 is a conditional's cond is again similar with the above one (where c_1 and c_2 are both loops), with the difference that c_2's input control dependency is resolved at most once; specifically, if c_1 is evaluated as true.

Worker Threads. Since working threads choose the t-var list to work on uniformly at random, it may happen that several working threads may (concurrently) execute the same instruction. To synchronize workers that execute the same instructions, the following synchronization techniques are employed. For each transactional instruction e, a *status* field (with initial value ACTIVE) is maintained in its entry, indicating that e has not yet been performed. As soon as a working thread completes the execution of e, it changes e's *status* to DONE.

For each t-variable x, SemanticTM maintains a single CAS object which stores the value of x together with a *version number*. This is done in order to atomically update x. Recall that several instances of a write instruction e to some t-variable x which is contained in a loop block are executed (one for each iteration). The working threads executing the same instance of e should use the same old value for x, so that x is updated consistently; also, they should calculate the same new value for x for the current iteration. To ensure this, SemanticTM maintains a CAS object in the record of e which stores the old value of the t-variable to be updated by e and an iteration number; moreover, the new value of x, is calculated by all working threads using the values provided in input data dependencies of e for the current iteration.

We consider now the case where a cond c_2 is nested under a cond c_1 and at least one of them is a loop's cond. In order the working threads executing c_1 to correctly update the $startinneriter_{c_2}$ field of c_2, a CAS object $forouteriter_{c_2}$ is associated with c_2 that maintains the iteration of c_1's loop for which c_2 has started executing. The first step during the execution of c_2 for the first time for some iteration $j > 0$ of c_1 by the corresponding working thread is to update $forouteriter_{c_2}$ so that it is equal to j; recall that before the input control dependency of c_2 from c_1 is resolved for the jth iteration of c_1, $startinneriter_{c_2}$ has been updated with value j. By doing this, thereafter the working threads executing c_1 for iteration j are not able to update $forouteriter_{c_2}$ with a value different than j. Therefore, at each point in time $forouteriter_{c_2}$ is either smaller than one or equal with cnt_{c_1}.

Considering again the example of Fig. 2, with c_1 be the cond of line 14 and c_2 be the cond of line 16, $forouteriter_{c_2}$ takes values $\{0, 1, 2, 3\}$ (in this order) where 0 is its initial value and the rest are the values of cnt_{c_1} in each iteration of c_1's loop; i.e., i, $1 \leq i \leq 3$, for its ith iteration.

3   Experimental Evaluation

In this section, we present some experimental results on the performance of SemanticTM.

The system. We use a Core i7-4770 3.4 GHz Haswell processor, running Linux 3.9.1-64-net1 x86_64. This processor has 4 cores, each with 2 hyperthreads, and hyperthreads enabled. Each core has a private 32 KB 8-way associative level-1 data cache and a 256 KB 8-way level-2 data cache. The chip further includes a shared 8MB level-3 cache. The cache lines are each 64-bytes.

The benchmarks' code was written in C and compiled with GCC-4.8.1. We compare SemanticTM to GccSTM, the gcc's STM support which was introduced in GCC-4.7 [23]. GccSTM is considered as the industry STM standard.

Tested Workload. We study four benchmarks that execute simple static transactions, testing different conflict patterns among them. In each of our benchmarks, we execute 10^5 transactions and have N worker threads $W_1, \ldots, W_N$ work on N tvar-lists $V_1, \ldots, V_N$. For our experiments, we consider a simplified version of SemanticTM which works as follows. Before the beginning of each experiment, a single thread places the instructions of each transaction in each tvar-list. Then, N workers are initiated and worker W_k, $1 \leq k \leq N$, processes all transactional instructions contained in t-var list V_k, for different values on N. This static assignment of workers to lists trades wait-freedom for performance.

The GccSTM code works on N variables as well, and initiates exactly N threads, each executing the same type and number of transactions as in SemanticTM. In both GccSTM and SemanticTM, in each benchmark, each worker thread executes transactions of the same type. We denote by T_i, $1 \leq i \leq 4$, the transactions' type executed in our ith benchmark. The code of T_i executed by W_k is shown in Fig. 3; also, the SemanticTM version of code of T_1 is presented.

1   $V_{(k+1)\%N} \leftarrow V_{(k-2)\%N} + 1$
2   await
3   $V_{(k+2)\%N} \leftarrow V_{(k-1)\%N} + 1$

T_1

4   add **read** to $V_{(k-2)\%N}$
5   add **write** to $V_{(k+1)\%N}$ dep on $V_{(k-2)\%N}$
    followed by **await**
6   add **read** to $V_{(k-1)\%N}$
7   add **write** to $V_{(k+2)\%N}$ dep on $V_{(k-1)\%N}$

T_1 - SemanticTM

8    $V_k \leftarrow V_k + 1$
9   await
10   $V_k \leftarrow V_k + 1$

T_2

11   $V_1 \leftarrow V_1 + 1$
12   await
13   $V_1 \leftarrow V_1 + 1$

T_3

14   $V_1 \leftarrow 10000$
15   **while** $(V_1 \neq 0)$ **do**
16   **if** $(V_1 > 0)$ **then**
17       $V_1 \leftarrow V_1 + 1$
18   **await**
19     $V_k \leftarrow V_k$

T_4

Fig. 3. Code of T_i, $1 \leq i \leq 4$.

We measure the throughput, i.e. the number of transactions that are executed successfully per second. The interesting thing about the workload of the 1st benchmark is that GccSTM, as well as any other optimistic TM algorithm, will abort all transactions while executing line 2. The reason is that while W_k waits by calling await, W_{k-3} writes a t-variable (V_{k-2}) which is contained in W_k's read-set. However, W_k realizes that it has to abort only at commit time. Thus, the longer each transaction waits, the higher is the penalty (in terms of the number of aborted transactions) that an optimistic TM pays. We remark that the use of await is realistic since it simulates the execution of local work which might be necessary.

In the 2nd benchmark, no transaction ever aborts, since each of them accesses a disjoint set of t-variables (W_k accesses only V_k). Using this benchmark, the overhead added by the SemanticTM's implementation is compared against the overhead added by GccSTM. In the 3rd benchmark each transaction increments by one the same shared counter (V_1). Finally, the 4th benchmark studies SemanticTM's performance for transactions with conditionals and loops.

Results. The graphs of Fig. 4 show the performance advantage of SemanticTM in comparison to GccSTM. As expected, this advantage is significant in the 1st experiment, since the abort ratio of GccSTM is very high (for eight threads, it is 8 times faster than GccSTM when wait time is short and 20 times faster when wait time is long). In the 3rd experiment, GccSTM causes a smaller number of aborts, since at the first write, V_1 is locked due to its encounter-time-locking algorithm [23]. Still its performance degrades. However, since the t-var list of V_1

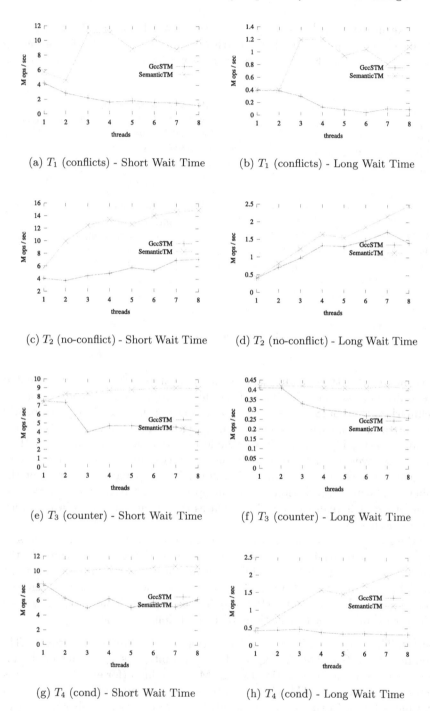

(a) T_1 (conflicts) - Short Wait Time

(b) T_1 (conflicts) - Long Wait Time

(c) T_2 (no-conflict) - Short Wait Time

(d) T_2 (no-conflict) - Long Wait Time

(e) T_3 (counter) - Short Wait Time

(f) T_3 (counter) - Long Wait Time

(g) T_4 (cond) - Short Wait Time

(h) T_4 (cond) - Long Wait Time

Fig. 4. Transactions with long and short wait time, to demonstrate the impact of different amounts of local work.

becomes a bottleneck, SemanticTM is only 2.5 times faster than GccSTM when wait time is short, and 2 times faster when wait time is long.

Finally, the 2nd experiment where no conflicts occur, show that the overhead added by SemanticTM is less than the overhead added by GccSTM, since SemanticTM is almost 2 times faster than GccSTM in this experiment. For a small number of threads, the gap in performance is small for long wait time, since the overhead added by the GccSTM is amortized.

4 Discussion

The current version of SemanticTM assumes that each transaction accesses a known set of t-variables. This can be overcome by using wildcards; a *wildcard* is an instruction which accesses a t-variable known only at runtime. As an example, consider a transaction that accesses an element of an array; however, the exact element becomes known only at runtime. To cope with this (or similar cases), SemanticTM can maintain a t-var list L for the entire array, as well as one list L_i, $1 \leq i \leq m$, for each of its elements, where m is the array size. The scheduler places each instruction e that accesses a (possibly unknown) element of the array in L. When later (at runtime), the specific element i to be accessed by e becomes known, e is moved in list L_i. A similar strategy may work for supporting dynamic memory allocation, if we consider the memory heap as an array.

Recall that in SemanticTM there are output dependencies from all instructions of a block to its cond and vice versa. However, the scheduler may choose to add such dependencies from the block's cond instruction only to those instructions that do not depend on other block instructions, since the rest have dependencies originating from them and therefore they will be executed after them. Moreover, no output control dependencies to a block's cond from those block instructions that do not contribute to the evaluation of the cond are needed. Such optimizations may have positive impact on the performance of SemanticTM.

SemanticTM is currently achieving fine-grain parallelism at the level of transactional instructions by maintaining a t-var list for each t-variable. Its space overhead can be decreased by maintaining a single t-var list for a set of more than one t-variables. So, there is a tradeoff between the space overhead and the granularity of parallelism achieved by it.

Designing a lock-based version of SemanticTM will be simpler than its lock-free version discussed here since it will not have to cope with several threads executing the same instruction.

Acknowledgements. This work has been supported by the project "IRAKLITOS II - University of Crete" of the Operational Programme for Education and Lifelong Learning 2007–2013 (E.P.E.D.V.M.) of the NSRF (2007–2013), co-funded by the European Union (European Social Fund) and National Resources. It has also been supported by the European Commission under the 7th Framework Program through the TransForm (FP7-MC-ITN-238639) project and by the ARISTEIA Action of the Operational Programme Education and Lifelong Learning which is co-funded by the European Social Fund (ESF) and National Resources through the GreenVM project.

The research has also been partially supported by the Rita Altura Trust Chair in Computer Sciences, Lynne and William Frankel Center for Computer Sciences, and Israel Science Foundation (grant number 428/11).

References

1. Afek, Y., Matveev, A., Shavit, N.: Pessimistic software lock-elision. In: Aguilera, M.K. (ed.) DISC 2012. LNCS, vol. 7611, pp. 297–311. Springer, Heidelberg (2012)
2. Ansari, M., Luján, M., Kotselidis, C., Jarvis, K., Kirkham, C., Watson, I.: Steal-on-abort: improving transactional memory performance through dynamic transaction reordering. In: Seznec, A., Emer, J., O'Boyle, M., Martonosi, M., Ungerer, T. (eds.) HiPEAC 2009. LNCS, vol. 5409, pp. 4–18. Springer, Heidelberg (2009)
3. Attiya, H., Epstein, L., Shachnai, H., Tamir, T.: Transactional contention management as a non-clairvoyant scheduling problem. In: Proceedings of the 25th Annual ACM Symposium on Principles of Distributed Computing, PODC '06, ACM, New York, pp. 308–315 (2006)
4. Attiya, H., Hillel, E.: Single-version STMs can be multi-version permissive (extended abstract). In: Aguilera, M.K., Yu, H., Vaidya, N.H., Srinivasan, V., Choudhury, R.R. (eds.) ICDCN 2011. LNCS, vol. 6522, pp. 83–94. Springer, Heidelberg (2011)
5. Attiya, H., Milani, A.: Brief announcement: transactional scheduling for read-dominated workloads. In: Keidar, I. (ed.) DISC 2009. LNCS, vol. 5805, pp. 108–110. Springer, Heidelberg (2009)
6. Attiya, H., Sainz, D.: Relstm: a proactive transactional memory scheduler. In: Proceedings of the 8th ACM SIGPLAN Workshop on Transactional Computing, TRANSACT '13 (2013)
7. Barreto, J., Dragojevic, A., Ferreira, P., Filipe, R., Guerraoui, R.: Unifying thread-level speculation and transactional memory. In: Narasimhan, P., Triantafillou, P. (eds.) Middleware 2012. LNCS, vol. 7662, pp. 187–207. Springer, Heidelberg (2012)
8. Cintra, M., Llanos, D.R.: Design space exploration of a software speculative parallelization scheme. IEEE Trans. Parallel Distrib. Syst. **16**(6), 562–576 (2005)
9. Cintra, M., Martínez, J.F., Torrellas, J.: Architectural support for scalable speculative parallelization in shared-memory multiprocessors. SIGARCH Comput. Archit. News **28**(2), 13–24 (2000)
10. Dice, D., Shalev, O., Shavit, N.N.: Transactional locking II. In: Dolev, S. (ed.) DISC 2006. LNCS, vol. 4167, pp. 194–208. Springer, Heidelberg (2006)
11. Dolev, S., Hendler, D., Suissa, A.: Car-stm: scheduling-based collision avoidance and resolution for software transactional memory. In: Proceedings of the 27th ACM Symposium on Principles of Distributed Computing, PODC '08, pp. 125–134. ACM, New York (2008)
12. Dragojević, A., Guerraoui, R., Singh, A.V., Singh, V.: Preventing versus curing: avoiding conflicts in transactional memories. In: Proceedings of the 28th ACM Symposium on Principles of Distributed Computing, PODC '09, pp. 7–16. ACM, New York (2009)
13. Guerraoui, R., Henzinger, T.A., Singh, V.: Permissiveness in transactional memories. In: Taubenfeld, G. (ed.) DISC 2008. LNCS, vol. 5218, pp. 305–319. Springer, Heidelberg (2008)
14. Guerraoui, R., Herlihy, M., Kapalka, M., Pochon, B.: Robust contention management in software transactional memory. In: OOPSLA '05 Workshop on Synchronization and Concurrency in Object-Oriented Languages (SCOOL '05) (2005)

15. Guerraoui, R., Herlihy, M., Pochon, B.: Toward a theory of transactional contention managers. In: Proceedings of the 24th Annual ACM Symposium on Principles of Distributed Computing, PODC '05, pp. 258–264. ACM, New York (2005)
16. Guerraoui, R., Kapalka, M.: On the correctness of transactional memory. In: Proceedings of the 13th ACM SIGPLAN Symposium on Principles and Practice of Parallel Programming, PPoPP '08, pp. 175–184. ACM, New York (2008)
17. Guerraoui, R., Kapalka, M., Vitek, J.: Stmbench7: a benchmark for software transactional memory. In: Proceedings of the 2nd ACM SIGOPS/EuroSys European Conference on Computer Systems 2007, EuroSys '07, pp. 315–324. ACM, New York (2007)
18. Matveev, A., Shavit, N.: Towards a fully pessimistic stm model. In: 7th ACM SIGPLAN Workshop on Transactional Computing, TRANSACT'12 (2012)
19. Motwani, R., Phillips, S., Torng, E.: Non-clairvoyant scheduling. Theor. Comput. Sci. **130**(1), 17–47 (1994)
20. Pandis, I., Johnson, R., Hardavellas, N., Ailamaki, A.: Data-oriented transaction execution. Proc. VLDB Endow. **3**(1–2), 928–939 (2010)
21. Perelman, D., Fan, R., Keidar, I.: On maintaining multiple versions in stm. In: Proceedings of the 29th ACM SIGACT-SIGOPS Symposium on Principles of Distributed Computing, PODC '10, pp. 16–25. ACM, New York (2010)
22. Ramadan, H.E., Roy, I., Herlihy, M., Witchel, E.: Committing conflicting transactions in an stm. In: Proceedings of the 14th ACM SIGPLAN Symposium on Principles and Practice of Parallel Programming, PPoPP '09, pp. 163–172. ACM, New York (2009)
23. Riegel, T.: Software transactional memory building blocks. Ph.D. thesis, Technische Universität Dresden, Dresden, 01062 Dresden, Germany (2013)
24. Scherer III, W.N., Scott, M.L.: Advanced contention management for dynamic software transactional memory. In: Proceedings of the 24th Annual ACM Symposium on Principles of Distributed Computing, PODC '05, pp. 240–248. ACM, New York (2005)
25. Welc, A., Saha, B., Adl-Tabatabai, A.-R.: Irrevocable transactions and their applications. In: Proceedings of the 20th Annual Symposium on Parallelism in Algorithms and Architectures, SPAA '08, pp. 285–296. ACM, New York (2008)
26. Yiapanis, P., Rosas-Ham, D., Brown, G., Luján, M.: Optimizing software runtime systems for speculative parallelization. ACM Trans. Archit. Code Optim. **9**(4), 391–3927 (2013)
27. Yoo, R.M., Lee, H.-H.S.: Adaptive transaction scheduling for transactional memory systems. In: Proceedings of the 20th Annual Symposium on Parallelism in Algorithms and Architectures, SPAA '08, pp. 169–178. ACM, New York (2008)

Disjoint-Access Parallelism
Does Not Entail Scalability

Rachid Guerraoui and Mihai Letia[✉]

EPFL, Lausanne, Switzerland
{rachid.guerraoui,mihai.letia}@epfl.ch

Abstract. Disjoint Access Parallelism (DAP) stipulates that operations involving disjoint sets of memory words must be able to progress independently, without interfering with each other. In this work we argue towards revising the two decade old wisdom saying that DAP is a binary condition that splits concurrent programs into scalable and non-scalable. We first present situations where DAP algorithms scale poorly, thus showing that not even algorithms that achieve this property provide scalability under all circumstances. Next, we show that algorithms which violate DAP can sometimes achieve the same scalability and performance as their DAP counterparts. We continue to show how by violating DAP and without sacrificing scalability we are able to circumvent three theoretical results showing that DAP is incompatible with other desirable properties of concurrent programs. Finally we introduce a new property called generalized disjoint-access parallelism (GDAP) which estimates how much of an algorithm is DAP. Algorithms having a large DAP part scale similar to DAP algorithms while not being subject to the same impossibility results.

1 Introduction

As multicores have become the norm, writing concurrent programs that are correct and efficient has become more important than ever. In this context, efficiency is no longer just a matter of making a program fast on a specific number of processors, but also ensuring that when the number of processors is increased, the performance of the program also increases proportionally.

In order to simplify the task of algorithm designers, several attempts to characterize scalable programs have been made. Ideally, these properties would be used in the design phase, when directly measuring scalability is impossible, and still guarantee scalable programs.

One such property is Disjoint Access Parallelism (DAP) [15]. Introduced by Israeli and Rappoport, it has been acclaimed to be both necessary and sufficient for ensuring the scalability of concurrent algorithms. In a nutshell, this property stipulates that operations accessing disjoint sets of memory words must be able to progress independently, without interfering with each other.

Unfortunately, it has been shown to be impossible to achieve DAP along with other desirable properties of concurrent algorithms. Ellen et al. [7] showed

© Springer International Publishing Switzerland 2014
G. Noubir and M. Raynal (Eds.): NETYS 2014, LNCS 8593, pp. 41–56, 2014.
DOI: 10.1007/978-3-319-09581-3_4

for instance that it is impossible to build a disjoint-access parallel universal construction that is wait-free, even when considering a very weak definition of disjoint-access parallelism. To illustrate further, Attiya et al. [4] proved that it is impossible to build a disjoint-access parallel transactional memory having read-only transactions that are invisible and always terminate successfully, while Guerraoui and Kapalka [9] showed that it is impossible to design a transactional memory that is both disjoint-access parallel and obstruction-free.

Conventional wisdom seems to consider that DAP programs scale under any circumstances while violating this property is catastrophic for scalability. In this work we contradict the two decade old assumption that DAP is necessary and sufficient for obtaining scalable concurrent programs. We first show situations where disjoint-access parallel programs scale poorly, mainly due to the high synchronization cost of specific hardware. We then show how by modifying DAP algorithms in order to violate this property we still obtain good scalability. Surprisingly perhaps, in some cases we find the non-DAP algorithm to outperform a similar DAP one. Although unintuitive, the fact that an algorithm that is not DAP and performs slightly more work can scale better is most likely due to decreasing contention on shared data in a manner similar to flat combining [11].

We use two data structures to evaluate the impact of violating DAP, one lock-based and one lock-free. The lock-based data structure is a closed addressing hashtable that uses lock striping to prevent concurrent threads from accessing the same bucket of the hashtable. The lock-free one is the multi-word compare-and-swap implementation of Harris et al. [10]. In order to observe the effects of losing DAP under several scenarios, we conduct our measurements on two distinct hardware platforms, one being a multi-socket Opteron while the other is a single-socket Niagara.

Using our new findings we revisit three theoretical proofs showing that disjoint-access parallelism is incompatible with other desirable properties of concurrent programs, such as stronger liveness. Then, by circumventing the proofs we show that violating DAP does not hamper scalability or performance, thus making it possible to achieve the other desirable properties without sacrificing scalability.

So far, disjoint-access parallelism has been thought of as a binary property, and although in some cases violating it has little to no effect, this is by no means a general principle. To quantify how close the scalability of a non-DAP algorithm is to that of a DAP one, we introduce a new notion called Generalized Disjoint-Access Parallelism (GDAP). In short, GDAP quantifies how much of an operation is DAP.

We experiment with violating the DAP property in two distinct ways. First, by adding a global shared counter we allow restricted communication among processes, for instance allowing one process to observe the presence of another. Then, we allow processes to communicate using a shared queue that permits processes to exchange any type of message. As counter increments feature a lower latency compared to queue operations, the non-DAP part is higher in the latter case, having a more pronounced impact on scalability. Similarly, the latency of hashtable operations is lower than that of the multi-word compare-and-swap, leading to a smaller non-DAP part for the latter. When most of the operation is DAP, even though not all of it, i.e. there is a small non-DAP part, the difference in scalability compared to operations that are fully DAP is negligible and in some cases the GDAP algorithm even achieves better performance and scalability. When a large part of the operation is not DAP, scalability is indeed severely hampered.

The rest of the paper is organized as follows. Section 2 reviews disjoint-access parallelism in a standard model of shared memory. Section 3 describes the benchmarks we use to show that DAP is neither sufficient (Sect. 4) nor necessary (Sect. 5) for ensuring scalability. In Sect. 6 we review three previous impossibility results relying on DAP and we show that violating this property, under similar scenarios to those in the proofs, has little impact on scalability. We introduce our new notion of generalized disjoint-access parallelism in Sect. 7 and review related work in Sect. 8.

2   Disjoint Access Parallelism

We consider a standard model of a shared memory system [5]. Under this model, we first recall the notion of disjoint-access parallelism of Israeli and Rappoport [15].

A finite set of *asynchronous processes* $p_1, \ldots, p_n$ are assumed to apply *primitives* to a set of *base objects* $\mathcal{O}$, located in the shared memory. A primitive that does not change the state of a base object is called a *trivial* primitive. As we wish to reason about the practical performance of disjoint-access parallel programs, we consider base objects to be memory locations supporting operations such as read, write, compare-and-swap, and fetch-and-increment.

A *concurrent object* is a data structure, shared among several processes, implemented using algorithms that apply a set of primitives to underlying base objects, and providing to its user a set of higher-level operations. An *implementation* of concurrent object A from a set of base objects $I \subset \mathcal{O}$ is a set of algorithms, one for each operation of object A. The clients of object A cannot distinguish between A and its implementation.

Two operations affecting distinct concurrent objects are said to be *disjoint-access*. A *transaction* is then defined as a special type of operation that invokes operations of more than one concurrent object. Two transactions are said to be disjoint-access if they access disjoint sets of concurrent objects.

Disjoint-Access Parallelism is a condition on concurrent algorithms stating that any two operations or transactions that access disjoint sets of concurrent objects must not apply primitives to the same base object, but must be able to proceed independently, without interfering with each other. This technique ensures that no hot-spots are created by the implementation and is claimed to ensure scalability by reducing the number of cache misses.

To illustrate, consider a Software Transactional Memory that uses the underlying primitives of the shared memory (read, write, C&S, etc.) to provide the user with read/write registers that can then be accessed through atomic transactions. The registers provided by the STM are then the concurrent objects. In this context, if p_i and p'_i are two processes that execute concurrent transactions T_j and T'_j, DAP requires that if transactions T_j and T'_j access disjoint sets of registers, then they must not access the same base object, i.e. the same underlying memory location. This implies that the time required to execute each of the two transactions would be the same, had they been executing in isolation.

An alternative definition of disjoint-access parallelism allows operations or transactions accessing disjoint sets of concurrent objects to apply trivial primitives to the same base object. Disjoint-access parallelism is only violated if at least one of the primitives is non-trivial. We believe this definition to be more useful in practice as hardware can typically execute read operations in parallel, while writes are commonly ordered among themselves and with respect to the reads. When arguing that DAP is not a good measure for scalability in practice, we use the latter definition.

3 Benchmarks

We use two different hardware platforms and two separate applications in order to obtain an ample image of the difference DAP makes in the scalability of concurrent programs.

The first platform is a 48-core AMD Opteron equipped with four AMD Opteron 6172 multi-chip modules that contain two 6-core dies each. We further refer to it as the *Opteron*. The L1 contains a 64 KiB instruction cache as well as a 64 KiB data cache, while the size of the L2 cache is 512 KiB. The L3 cache is shared per die and has a total size of 12 MiB. The cores are running at 2.1 GHz and have access to 128 GiB of main memory.

Our other test platform is a Sun Niagara 2, equipped with a single-die SUN UltraSPARC T2 processor. We further refer to it as the *Niagara*. Based on the chip multi-threading architecture, this processor contains 8 cores, each able to run a total of 8 hardware threads, totaling 64 threads. The L1 cache is shared among the 8 threads of every core and has a 16 KiB instruction cache and 8 KiB data cache. The last level cache (LLC) is shared among all the cores and has a size of 4 MiB. The cores are running at 1.2 GHz and have access to 32 GiB of main memory.

Each data point in our graphs was obtained by averaging three separate runs. For each run we warm up the JVM for 5 s before measuring the throughput for 10 s, obtaining a variation small enough to be negligible. We continue to describe the two applications we use to assess the degree at which disjoint-access parallelism influences scalability in practice.

3.1 Lock-Based Hashtable

Our lock-based implementation is based on the striped hashtable of Herlihy and Shavit [13], which in turn is based on the sequential closed-addressing hashtable.

Hash conflicts are resolved by assigning elements that map to the same hash value into buckets. Each bucket is protected by a distinct lock and can hold any number of elements by storing them in a linked list.

Although a set implemented using a hashtable cannot be regarded as being DAP due to hash collisions, when considering the hashtable data structure, operations involving the same bucket are no longer logically independent. This allows operations affecting the same bucket to synchronize using the same lock while still satisfying DAP. Operations affecting elements that map to different buckets need to acquire different locks and can proceed independently. The hashtable is the data structure of choice for illustrating DAP in the reference book of Herlihy and Shavit [13].

We made two independent modifications to this data structure in order to violate disjoint-access parallelism. We first added a global shared counter that keeps track of the total number of elements in the hashtable. This counter is incremented by every insert and decremented by every remove operation of the hashtable using fetch-and-increment and respectively fetch-and-decrement. The hashtable size operation is present in most frameworks for sequential programming, such as that of the JDK. Although approximating the current size of the hashtable can be done by using weak counters, a strong counter is needed in order to provide a linearizable size operation. We thus explore the compromise of losing disjoint-access parallelism in order to obtain an atomic size operation.

The second modification consisted in adding a concurrent queue, shared among all the processes, and making each update to the hashtable also push or pop an element from this queue. While the global counter consists of the minimum violation of DAP, the higher latency of the queue allows us to observe the effects of having a larger part of the operations violate DAP.

3.2   Multi-word Compare-and-Swap

The multi-word compare-and-swap represents a Java implementation of the algorithm presented by Harris et al. [10]. The algorithm first builds a double-compare single-swap (DCSS) operation out of the compare-and-swap available in hardware and then builds an n-word compare-and-swap operation (NCAS) on top of that. Both the DCSS and NCAS algorithms are based on *descriptors*, making their design non-blocking. Using this mechanism, an operation makes its parameters available so that other processes can provide help in case the initial operation is delayed.

This algorithm is disjoint-access parallel since NCAS operations that affect disjoint sets of memory locations are not required to synchronize among themselves and can proceed in parallel. We again made two independent modifications in order to violate DAP. We first added a global shared counter for keeping track of the number of NCAS operations executed. Although finding this number could have been done by using local counters, we chose this solution in order to obtain a slight violation of disjoint-access parallelism whose impact on scalability we can measure. This solution also allows finding the precise number of NCAS operations executed before the current point in time. The second modification was

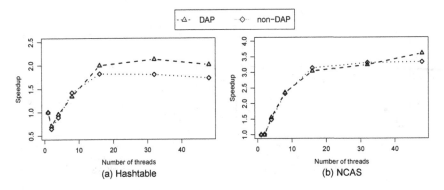

Fig. 1. Speedup obtained when executing 20 % update operations on a hashtable with 1024 elements and buckets of length 4 (a) and NCAS operations of length 8 in a system with 1000 locations (b) on the Opteron.

to make every NCAS operation also perform a push or pop from a concurrent queue, shared among all the processes. Due to the higher latencies incurred by the queue, this modification allows us to test scenarios where operations violate DAP in a larger degree.

4   DAP Does Not Imply Scalability

In this section we contradict the common misconception that disjoint-access parallel algorithms necessarily scale. To this aim, we run both the lock-based hashtable and the NCAS algorithms on the Opteron. On this machine the disjoint-access parallel implementations of both algorithms scale poorly. For the sake of comparison, we also plot on the same graphs the versions of these algorithms where DAP is violated by adding a global shared counter.

In Fig. 1a we show the scalability of the original (DAP) version of our lock-based hashtable. To put it into perspective, we compare to a version where we break disjoint-access parallelism by having a global counter that stores the size of the data structure. Our experiments use buckets of length 4 and 20 % update operations. The DAP version of the hashtable achieves a speedup of only 2.2X on 48 cores compared to the single core performance. The resulting scalability is far from ideal and cannot justify aiming for disjoint-access parallelism when designing a new concurrent algorithm.

In Fig. 1b we plot the speedup obtained when running our implementation of the multi-word compare-and-swap on the Opteron. In this experiment each of the NCAS operations attempts to change the value of 8 memory locations, while the system contains 1000 locations in total. In the case of this algorithm, the DAP version achieves a speedup of only 3.5X on 48 cores. To put it into perspective, we also plot the non-DAP version of the NCAS where each operation increments a global shared counter. In this experiment the two algorithms perform almost identically and for some thread counts the non-DAP version performs

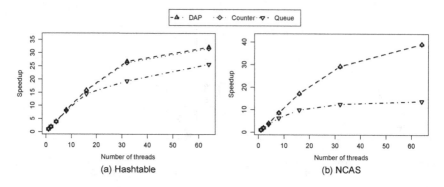

Fig. 2. Speedup obtained when executing 20 % update operations on a hashtable with 1024 elements and buckets of length 4 (a) and NCAS operations of length 8 in a system with 1000 locations (b) on the Niagara.

slightly better. This effect, of having an algorithm that performs strictly more work perform better, is probably caused by decreasing contention on the NCAS locations by using the extra delay provided by the counter. In effect, violating disjoint-access parallelism under this scenario does not bring any performance penalty.

5   Scalability Does Not Imply DAP

In this section we contradict the common misconception that disjoint-access parallelism is a requirement for obtaining scalable concurrent programs. We present experiments using both the lock-based hashtable and the multiword compare-and-swap showing that, for both applications, the non-DAP versions of these algorithms are able to scale. There experiments were conducted on the Niagara machine.

In Fig. 2a we plot the speedup obtained when running the hashtable benchmark with 20 % update operations on a table with 1024 elements and buckets of length 4. Both the DAP and non-DAP version using a counter scale very well, measuring a speedup of 32X on 64 hardware threads. Both versions scale identically to the point that it is hard to distinguish between the two. The non-DAP version using an additional queue scales less but is still able to reach a 25X speedup on 64 hardware threads. Therefore the small violation of DAP obtained when using an additional counter does not hamper scalability at all, while the larger non-DAP part represented by the queue operations, still allows the algorithm to achieve a 25X speedup.

Figure 2b shows the speedup obtained when executing NCAS operations on our Niagara machine. In these tests, each thread picks 8 locations at random, reads their values using the read operation of the algorithm, and attempts to swap them to a random set of new values. We use a total of 1000 locations for this experiment.

Both the DAP and the non-DAP version using a counter obtain a 40X speedup and, as in the case of the hashtable, their performance is indistinguishable, both versions scaling equally well. The non-DAP version using a queue scales significantly less but is still able to reach a 10X speedup on 64 hardware threads. Compared to the hashtable augmented with the queue, this version of the NCAS scales less due to the fact that all the operations use the queue, whereas in the case of the hashtable, only the updates (20 %) were using the queue. Therefore when running our benchmarks on the Niagara machine, disjoint-access-parallelism does not bring any advantage compared to a version of the same algorithm that slightly violates this property by introducing a shared counter. When operations have a larger non-DAP part, such as in the case of adding a shared queue, both the hashtable and the NCAS are able to scale, although not as much as their DAP counterparts.

6 Revisiting Impossibilities

In this section we dissect three published theoretical results that we believe are misleading [4,7,9]. They seem to indicate that we need to sacrifice liveness in order to have scalability: in fact, we must only sacrifice liveness when aiming for disjoint-access parallelism. We put these results to the test by evaluating solutions that circumvent these impossibilities and we show that by weakening DAP, scalability is not affected.

6.1 DAP Vs Obstruction-Freedom

The first result [9] proves that it is impossible to design a transactional memory providing transactions that are at the same time disjoint-access parallel and obstruction-free. The latter condition requires that from any point in the execution of the system, if a transaction executes alone for a long enough period of time, it eventually commits. This allows a transaction having a higher priority to be able to preempt or abort lower priority ones at any time and then be sure to commit.

The authors claim that disjoint-access parallelism prevents artificial "hot spots" that may provoke "useless" cache invalidations, thus decreasing performance. We provide experimental measurements showing that even in the case of programs that violate disjoint-access parallelism and feature such artificial "hot spots", the number of cache invalidations does not increase significantly: performance does not suffer.

Circumventing the critical scenario. The authors present the following scenario for showcasing their impossibility result in a system consisting of four transactional variables, x, y, w and z. Transaction T_1 starts executing, reads value 0 for both w and z and then attempts to write value 1 into both x and y. Then T_1 is delayed just before it commits, and T_2 starts executing, reads value 0 from x, writes 1 to w and commits. We observe that T_1 and T_2 cannot both commit since

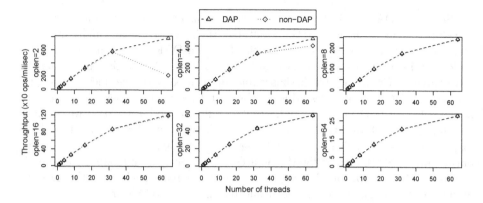

Fig. 3. Throughput obtained when executing NCAS operations of different lengths in a system with 10000 locations on the Niagara.

this would violate serializability. Therefore the latter must write a base object to abort the former, which must then be read by a new transaction T_3 that reads y and updates z. Thus, even if T_2 and T_3 access disjoint sets of transactional objects, the latter must read a base object showing that T_1 has been aborted, and that object must in turn have been written by T_2.

One possible way to circumvent the impossibility is to add a counter C_T to every transaction T in the system. In the example above, consider the counter C_{T1} associated with transaction T_1. The counter initially has the value 0 and transaction T_2, before committing, aborts T_1 by incrementing its counter to 1. When T_3 executes, it reads y and also counter C_{T1}, finding that T_1 was aborted.

We estimate a loose upper bound of the performance impact of such a modification by adding a global shared counter to our NCAS system instead of one for each operation. Furthermore, all our NCAS operations increment this global counter instead of only those participating in scenarios similar to those described by the authors. Note that incrementing is at least as expensive as reading the counter value. These two differences have the effect of increasing contention at least as much, if not more than required to contradict the proof.

Performance. In Fig. 3 we show the throughput of running our NCAS implementation on a system with 10000 locations. The difference between the DAP and the non-DAP version is that the latter increments a global shared counter on every operation. We vary the length of the NCAS operation between 2 and 64. The results show that when using operations of length at least 8, the two versions of the algorithm perform identically. As we observe shorter lengths of the operations, the difference is small for a length of 4 and significant for length 2 but only when running 64 threads. The decrease in performance for the latter case is due to the high contention on the counter caused by the low time required for executing the NCAS. When the NCAS operation needs to write 4 or more locations, contention on the counter decreases and it is no longer a performance bottleneck.

6.2   DAP Vs Invisible Reads and Eventual Commit

Attiya et al. [4] showed that it is impossible to build a transactional memory that is disjoint-access parallel and has read-only transactions that are invisible and always eventually commit. They again built on the assumption that disjoint-access parallelism is necessary for achieving scalability. We show however that violating disjoint-access parallelism in a manner that would circumvent their proof has little or no effect on the scalability of the system.

A transactional memory is said to have invisible read-only transactions if such transactions do not apply any updates to base objects; otherwise read-only transactions are said to be visible. Invisible read-only transactions are desirable since this reduces the number of updates to base objects in read-dominated workloads, thus decreasing the number of cache invalidations.

Circumventing the critical scenario. The authors start by defining a flippable execution, consisting of a single long read-only transaction with a complete update transaction interleaved between every two steps of the read-only trans-action, such that flipping the order of two consecutive updates is indistinguish-able from the initial execution to all the processes. Then they show that in such a flippable execution, the read-only transaction cannot commit. Finally, the authors prove that every disjoint-access parallel transactional memory with invisible read-only transactions has such a flippable execution and the conclu-sion follows. The crux of the proof is building an execution where the read-only transaction misses one of two update transactions. Having all transactions incre-ment a shared counter upon committing would enable the read-only transaction to find both update transactions and a flippable execution would no longer be possible.

Performance. In Fig. 4 we show both the throughput and the cache miss rate obtained when running the NCAS operations on the Opteron. We use again operations of length 8 and we vary the size of system. The size of the L1 data cache is 64 KB, hence systems of 1000 locations fit into the L1. The L2 cache is 512 KB, being able to accommodate a system containing 10000 locations. The L3 cache has a total of 12 MB and is insufficient to accommodate the largest system size.

One of the main arguments in favor of disjoint-access parallelism is that it increases performance by reducing the number of cache misses in the system. Due to this we perform more in-depth measurements of the cache behavior of the two versions of the NCAS algorithm. We measure the LLC cache miss rate due to its high penalties and because on the Opteron it proves to be a good measure of inter-core communication. We use the perf tool [1], which we attach to our benchmark after performing a 5 s warm-up. To prevent the virtual machine from garbage collecting during our measurements, we use a large initial heap size that is not expected to fill.

For small system sizes we see that both versions of the algorithm do not scale. Due to high contention, operations have a high chance of conflicting, causing

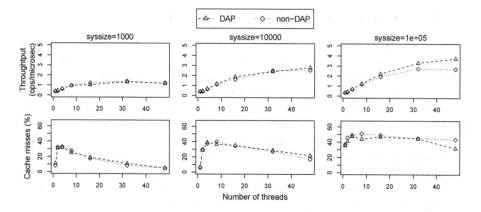

Fig. 4. Throughput and percentage of cache misses obtained when executing NCAS operations of length 8 in a system of different sizes on the Opteron.

them to help each other. As the system size is increased, both algorithms increase in performance but continue to scale poorly. The amount of cache misses is largely the same, with the biggest difference being at 10^5 elements, where a more significant difference in terms of the throughput is observed when reaching 48 cores.

6.3   DAP Vs Wait-Freedom

A universal construction [12] is a concurrent algorithm that takes as input a sequential algorithm and then atomically applies it to a data structure. The main difference between a transactional memory and a universal construction is that the former can complete an operation by returning ABORT, while the latter does not return until it has successfully applied the operation. The universal construction is then equivalent to a transactional memory that reattempts to execute aborted transactions until it succeeds in committing them.

Ellen et al. [7] showed that a universal construction cannot be both disjoint-access parallel and wait-free. Their proof relies on building an unordered linked list with operations append and search. The former adds an element to the end of the list by modifying its tail pointer, while the latter tries to find a specific element by starting from the beginning of the list.

Circumventing the critical scenario. The proof proceeds by having one search operation execute while other processes are continuously executing appends. If the search is not close to the end of the list, it remains disjoint-access with respect to concurrent append operations. However, if the rate at which new elements are appended to the list is faster than the progress of the search operation, the latter will never finish unless the element being searched for is found. It is then sufficient for this element to be different than all the elements being added to the list, and the conclusion follows.

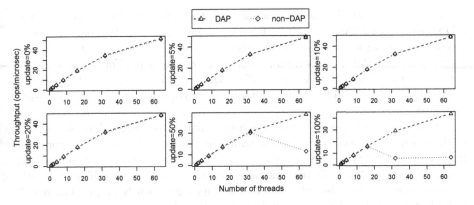

Fig. 5. Throughput obtained when executing different percentages of update operations on a hashtable with 1024 elements and buckets of length 1 on the Niagara.

One simple way of circumventing the assumptions in their proof is to allow processes executing a search to read a base object that was written by a process executing append, even though they access disjoint data items. This object could then inform the search that a specific append has a higher timestamp and can be safely be serialized after it.

Performance. In order to evaluate the effect of violating DAP in such a manner, we modified our non-DAP version of the hashtable such that the search operations read the shared counter incremented by the insert and delete. In Fig. 5 we compare this new non-DAP version of the hashtable to the original DAP version on the Niagara, while varying the update rate between 0 and 100 %. The experiments show that for update rates of up to 20 %, the counter does not affect performance at all. Then, when using 50 % updates, the effect is visible for thread counts larger than 32, while with 100 % updates, the effect becomes visible at 16 threads. As update rates of more than 20 % are less common in practice, we conclude that for most workloads adding the extra counter does not affect throughput and scalability.

7   DAP as a Non-binary Property

So far disjoint-access parallelism has been thought of as a binary property: DAP programs scale, non-DAP programs do not scale. However, in this work we have shown that disjoint-access parallelism is neither necessary (Sect. 5) nor sufficient (Sect. 4) for obtaining scalable concurrent programs. To this end we have shown that violating DAP by itself does not make an impact on scalability. Programs that are "almost DAP" scale as well as their fully DAP counterparts.

In order to quantify how close an algorithm is to being disjoint-access parallel, we extend the notion of DAP to define a property called generalized disjoint-access parallelism (GDAP). This property encompasses the classical notion of disjoint-access parallelism but also algorithms that violate it to a certain degree. GDAP is useful for characterizing situations where algorithm designers choose to give up DAP in order to obtain some other desirable properties by capturing how far the resulting algorithm is from its fully DAP counterpart. For instance, many Software Transactional Memories (STMs) use a shared counter [6,17] in order to achieve faster revalidation or contention management, this way increasing performance.

Intuitively, if an operation OP applies primitives to L base objects, and $1/k$ of these objects are part of a hotspot while the rest is DAP, the only theoretical bound for scalability is when k instances of OP are being executed concurrently. Hence the larger the k factor, the smaller the impact on scalability. In fact, our experiments show that algorithms featuring a sufficiently large k factor still provide the same scalability as fully DAP algorithms and in some cases can outperform them.

Definition 1 (GDAP of order k). *Let $\mathcal{I}$ be the set of implementations of concurrent objects $\mathcal{A}$. If for any two operations OP_i and OP_j such that:*

- *I_i is an implementation of object $A_i \in \mathcal{A}$ and I_j is an implementation of object $A_j \in \mathcal{A}$,*
- *$A_i \neq A_j$,*
- *OP_i is an operation of implementation $I_i \in \mathcal{I}$ and OP_j is an operation of implementation $I_j \in \mathcal{I}$,*
- *I_i applies primitives to base objects O_i and I_j applies primitives to base objects O_j,*
- *$\exists O_i' \subset O_i$ with $(O_i \setminus O_i') \cap O_j = \emptyset$ and $|O_i'| \times k \leq |O_i|$*

then $\mathcal{I}$ said to be GDAP of order k.

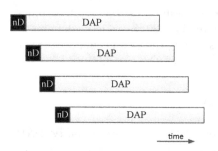

Fig. 6. Execution showing Generalized Disjoint-Access Parallel operations.

Figure. 6 shows an execution of four GDAP operations that are not fully DAP. Every operation accesses a common hotspot such that it has a non-DAP part as well as a DAP one. As the non-DAP part is short (large k factor), the four operations can still execute concurrently. This represents the typical scenario resulting from adding a shared object to a set of DAP operations in order to obtain, for instance, a stronger liveness property.

In Fig. 3 we observe that operations which are GDAP of a higher order scale better than those of a lower order and can, in fact, perform identically to their fully DAP counterparts. In both experiments we increase the length of the NCAS operations while the non-DAP part remains constant. The result is

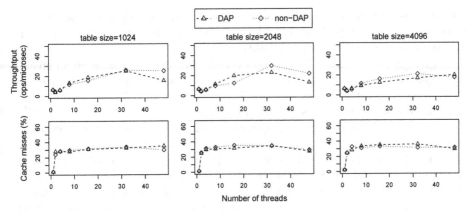

Fig. 7. Throughput and percentage of cache misses obtained when executing 10 % update operations on hashtables of different sizes and buckets of length 1 on the Opteron.

that longer operations scale better. Switching from length 2 to length 4 provides close to the same performance as the fully DAP version, while for length 8 and greater, the two are practically indistinguishable.

Although in most cases the fully DAP variant of an algorithm scales slightly better than a GDAP variant that is not fully DAP, in certain cases the latter can in fact outperform the former. As shown in Fig. 7, the performance gain obtained by adding an extra counter to our hashtable can be as high as 50 % for certain thread counts. In this scenario, the threads are executing 10 % update operations on a hashtable with buckets of length 1. We show results obtained using tables of size varying from 1024 to 4096 elements. The graphs show that, although the percentage of cache misses stays roughly the same between the DAP and GDAP variants, on some workloads the latter achieves better throughput even though it performs extra work.

8   Related Work

As concurrent algorithms become prevalent, knowing what properties to aim for in their design is crucial. In this paper, we contradict classical wisdom by showing that disjoint-access parallelism is neither necessary nor sufficient for ensuring scalability. Instead, we propose a new property, generalized disjoint-access parallelism that helps estimate how close a non-DAP algorithm is to a DAP one. Using this property, algorithm designers can build algorithms that scale similarly to DAP ones but are not subject to the same impossibility results.

The assumption that DAP is sufficient for scalability has been used both when building algorithms that promise good scalability, and as an assumption in proofs. Anderson and Moir [3] describe universal constructions that are expected to scale well due to being disjoint-access parallel. Kuznetsov and Ravi [16] explore the lower bounds on the number of synchronization operations that a transactional memory must perform in order to guarantee disjoint-access parallelism and the progressiveness liveness condition.

Although DAP seems to be the most accepted theoretical condition for ensuring scalability in practice, other works explore properties that are promising in this direction. Whether or not they are either necessary or sufficient for obtaining scalable concurrent programs remains uncertain.

Afek et al. [2] characterize an operation as having *d-local step complexity* if the number of steps performed by the operation in a given execution interval is bounded by a function of the number of primitives applied within distance d in the conflict graph of the given interval. They define an algorithm as having *d-local contention* if two operations access the same object only if their distance in the conflict graph of their joint execution interval is at most d. Ellen et al. [8] introduce the *obstruction-free step complexity* as the maximum number of steps that an operation needs to perform if no other processes are taking steps.

Imbs and Raynal [14] introduce a property called *help locality* that restricts which other operations can be helped by the current operation. They build upon this property to design an atomic snapshot that scales well, under the assumption that help locality is sufficient for ensuring scalability in practice. However, this assumption has not yet been tested and, similar to disjoint-access parallelism, may have less merit than it receives.

Roy et al. [18] show a tool that profiles concurrent programs giving information about critical sections such as the average time threads spend waiting for a lock and the amount of disjoint-access parallelism that can be exploited. Such a tool can potentially be modified in order to provide the order of GDAP of a concurrent program, helping algorithm designers understand if their scalability issues can be solved by attempting a fully DAP solution.

This paper should be regarded as a step to better understanding scalability. Theoretical conditions that ensure practical scalability are important but, unfortunately, disjoint-access parallelism is not a silver bullet in this regard. As further work, we plan to test other promising theoretical properties in hope to find one that guarantees practical scalability.

References

1. Perf @ONLINE. https://perf.wiki.kernel.org
2. Afek, Y., Merritt, M., Taubenfeld, G., Touitou, D.: Disentangling multi-object operations. In: PODC (1997)
3. Anderson, J.H., Moir, M.: Universal constructions for multi-object operations. In: PODC (1995)
4. Attiya, H., Hillel, E., Milani, A.: Inherent limitations on disjoint-access parallel implementations of transactional memory. In: SPAA (2009)
5. Attiya, H., Jennifer, W.: Distributed Computing: Fundamentals, Simulations and Advanced Topics, 2nd edn. Wiley, New York (2004)
6. Dragojević, A., Guerraoui, R., Kapalka, M.: Stretching transactional memory. In: PLDI (2009)

7. Ellen, F., Fatourou, P., Kosmas, E., Milani, A., Travers, C.: Universal constructions that ensure disjoint-access parallelism and wait-freedom. In: PODC (2012)
8. Fich, F.E., Luchangco, V., Moir, M., Shavit, N.N.: Obstruction-free step complexity: lock-free DCAS as an example. In: Fraigniaud, P. (ed.) DISC 2005. LNCS, vol. 3724, pp. 493–494. Springer, Heidelberg (2005)
9. Guerraoui, R., Kapalka, M.: On obstruction-free transactions. In: SPAA (2008)
10. Harris, T.L., Fraser, K., Pratt, I.A.: A practical multi-word compare-and-swap operation. In: Malkhi, D. (ed.) DISC 2002. LNCS, vol. 2508, pp. 265–279. Springer, Heidelberg (2002)
11. Hendler, D., Incze, I., Shavit, N., Tzafrir, M.: Flat combining and the synchronization-parallelism tradeoff. In: SPAA (2010)
12. Herlihy, M.: Wait-free synchronization. TOPLAS 13, 124–149 (1991)
13. Herlihy, M., Shavit, N.: The Art of Multiprocessor Programming. Morgan Kaufmann, San Mateo (2008)
14. Imbs, D., Raynal, M.: Help when needed, but no more: efficient read/write partial snapshot. JPDC 72, 1–12 (2012)
15. Israeli, A., Rappoport, L.: Disjoint-access-parallel implementations of strong shared memory primitives. In: PODC (1994)
16. Kuznetsov, P., Ravi, S.: On the cost of concurrency in transactional memory. In: Fernàndez Anta, A., Lipari, G., Roy, M. (eds.) OPODIS 2011. LNCS, vol. 7109, pp. 112–127. Springer, Heidelberg (2011)
17. Riegel, T., Felber, P., Fetzer, C.: A lazy snapshot algorithm with eager validation. In: Dolev, S. (ed.) DISC 2006. LNCS, vol. 4167, pp. 284–298. Springer, Heidelberg (2006)
18. Roy, A., Hand, S., Harris, T.: Exploring the limits of disjoint access parallelism. In: HotPar (2009)

Linearizability Is Not Always a Safety Property

Rachid Guerraoui[1] and Eric Ruppert[2]([⊠])

[1] EPFL, Lausanne, Switzerland
[2] York University, Toronto, Canada
ruppert@cse.yorku.ca

Abstract. We show that, in contrast to the general belief in the distributed computing community, linearizability, the celebrated consistency property, is not always a safety property. More specifically, we give an object for which it is possible to have an infinite history that is not linearizable, even though every finite prefix of the history is linearizable. The object we consider as a counterexample has infinite nondeterminism. We show, however, that if we restrict attention to objects with finite nondeterminism, we can use König's lemma to prove that linearizability is indeed a safety property. In the same vein, we show that the backward simulation technique, which is a classical technique to prove linearizability, is not sound for arbitrary types, but is sound for types with finite nondeterminism.

1 Introduction

One of the most challenging problems in concurrent and distributed systems is to build software objects that appear to processes using them as "perfect": always available and consistent. In particular, proving that implementations of such objects are correct can be very difficult.

To make the challenge more tractable, it is common to divide the difficulty into proving two properties: a *safety* and a *liveness* property [2,3]. In short, a safety property says "bad things should never happen" whereas a liveness property says "good things should eventually happen." Traditionally, in the context of building "perfect" shared objects, safety has been associated with the concept of *linearizability* [9] while liveness has been associated with a progress guarantee such as *wait-freedom* [8].

- **Linearizability:** Despite concurrent accesses to an object, the operations issued on that object should appear as if they are executed sequentially. In other words, each operation *op* on an object X should appear to take effect at some indivisible instant between the invocation and the response of *op*. This property, also called *atomicity*, transforms the difficult problem of reasoning about a concurrent system into the simpler problem of reasoning about one where the processes access each object one after another.
- **Wait-freedom:** No process p ever prevents any other process q from making progress when q executes an operation on any shared object X. This means

© Springer International Publishing Switzerland 2014
G. Noubir and M. Raynal (Eds.): NETYS 2014, LNCS 8593, pp. 57–69, 2014.
DOI: 10.1007/978-3-319-09581-3_5

that, provided it remains alive and kicking, q completes its operation on X regardless of the speed or even the failure of any other process p. Process p could be very fast and might be permanently accessing shared object X, or could have failed or been swapped out by the operating system while accessing X. None of these situations should prevent q from executing its operation.

Ensuring each of linearizability or wait-freedom alone is simple. The challenge is to ensure both. In particular, one could easily ensure linearizability using locks and mutual exclusion. But this would not guarantee wait-freedom: a process that holds a lock and fails can prevent others from progressing. One could also forget about linearizability and ensure wait-freedom by creating copies of the object that never synchronize: this would lead to different objects, one per process, defeating the sense of a shared object. So indeed the challenge is to design shared abstractions that ensure both linearizability and wait-freedom. But proving correctness can be made simpler if we could prove each property separately.

It was shown that properties of distributed systems can be divided into *safety* and *liveness* properties [2], each requiring specific kinds of proof techniques. So the general approach in proving the correctness of shared objects is that linearizability, being a safety property, requires techniques to reason about finite executions (such as backward simulation [13]), whereas wait-freedom, being a liveness property, requires another set of techniques to reason about infinite executions. The association between safety and linearizability on the one hand, and liveness and wait-freedom on the other, is considered a pillar in the theory of distributed computing.

This paper shows that, strictly speaking, this association is wrong for the most general definition of object type specifications. More specifically, we show that, in contrast to what is largely believed in the distributed computing literature, linearizability is not a safety property. This might be surprising because (a) it was often argued that linearizability is a safety property, *e.g.*, in [12], and (b) linearizability proofs have used techniques specific to safety properties, *e.g.*, backward simulation [13]. In fact, there is no real contradiction with our new result for the following reasons.

- To prove that linearizability is not a safety property, we exhibit an object, which we call the *countdown* object, and a non-linearizable history such that every finite prefix of the execution is linearizable. The object we consider has infinite nondeterminism, which might occur, for instance, in a distributed system that seeks to ensure fairness (as we discuss in Sect. 2.2). Interestingly, the execution we use in our proof is by a single process, so it demonstrates that other consistency conditions that are weaker than linearizability (such as sequential consistency) are also not safety properties for the countdown object.
- We show, however, that if we restrict attention to objects with finite nondeterminism, we can use König's lemma [10] to prove that linearizability is indeed a safety property. We thus highlight that, even if this was not always stated in

the past, claims that linearizability is a safety property, should assume finite nondeterminism.[1] Lynch's proof that linearizability is a safety property [12] applies only to the more restricted class of deterministic objects.

In the same vein, we show that the backward simulation technique, which is sometimes used to prove linearizability, is not sound for arbitrary types (if infinite nondeterminism is permitted). It is sound, however, for finite nondeterminism.

The rest of the paper is organized as follows. We describe our system model in Sect. 2. We recall the notion of linearizability in Sect. 3. In Sect. 4 we recall the concept of safety and give our counterexample that shows linearizability is not a safety property. Then we show in Sect. 5 that, if we restrict ourselves to objects with finite nondeterminism, linearizability becomes a safety property. We consider the implications for backward simulations in Sect. 6 and conclude the paper in Sect. 7.

2 System Model

We consider a system consisting of a finite set of n *processes*, denoted $p_1, \ldots, p_n$. Processes communicate by executing operations on *shared objects*. The execution of an operation op on an object X by a process p_i is modelled by two events, the invocation event denoted $inv[X.op$ by $p_i]$ that occurs when p_i invokes the operation, and the response event denoted $resp[X.res$ by $p_i]$ that occurs when the operation terminates and returns the response res. (When there is no ambiguity, we talk about *operations* where we should be talking about *operation executions*.)

2.1 Objects

An object has a unique identity and a type. Multiple objects can be of the same type. A type is defined by a sequential specification that consists of

- the set Q of possible states for an object of that type,
- the initial state $q_0 \in Q$,
- a set OPS of operations that can be applied to the object,
- a set RES of possible responses the object can return, and
- a transition relation $\delta \subseteq Q \times OPS \times RES \times Q$.

This specification describes how the object behaves if it is accessed by one operation at a time. If $(q, op, res, q') \in \delta$, it means that a possible result of applying operation op to an object in state q is that the object moves to state q' and returns the response res to the process that invoked op.

---

[1] For example, an erroneous claim is made in two recent papers [1,11] that explicitly permit nondeterministic objects and make no restriction that the nondeterminism of the objects should be finite. The latter paper states that "linearizability is a safety property, so its violation can be detected with a finite prefix of an execution history." Using the definitions given in that paper, this statement is false. However, this does not affect the correctness of that paper's main results because those results are about objects with finite nondeterminism.

2.2 Infinite Nondeterminism

- We say that an object is *deterministic* if, for all $q \in Q$ and $op \in OPS$, there is at most one pair (res, q') such that (q, op, res, q') is in the object's transition relation δ.
- An object has *finite nondeterminism* if, for all $q \in Q$ and $op \in OPS$, the set of possible outcomes $\{(res, q') : (q, op, res, q') \in \delta\}$ is finite.

Dijkstra [6] argued that infinite nondeterminism should not arise in computing systems. He showed, for example, the functionality of nondeterministically choosing an arbitrary positive integer cannot be implemented in a reasonable sequential programming language. Nevertheless, there is a significant literature on infinite nondeterminism. For example, Apt and Plotkin [4] observed that infinite nondeterminism can arise naturally in systems that guarantee fairness. Consider a system of two processes P and Q programmed as follows, using a shared boolean variable *Stop* that is initially false.

Process P :	Process Q :
$Stop :=$ true	$x := 1$
	do until *Stop*
	$\quad x := x + 1$
	end do
	print x

If these processes are run in a fair environment, where each process is guaranteed to be given infinitely many opportunities to take a step (but there is no bound on the relative speeds of the processes), Q will choose and print an arbitrary positive integer. Thus, at the right level of abstraction, this system implements a choice with infinite nondeterminism. In the context of shared-memory computing, objects with infinite nondeterminism have also occasionally arisen (*e.g.*, [14]).

2.3 Histories

A (finite or infinite) sequence of invocation and response events is called a *history* and this is how we model an execution. We assume that processes are *sequential*: a process executes (at most) one operation at a time. Of course, the fact that processes are (individually) sequential does not preclude different processes from concurrently invoking operations on the same shared object.

The total order relation on the set of events induced by H is denoted $<_H$. A history abstracts the real-time order in which the events occur. We assume that simultaneous (invocation or response) events do not affect one another, so that we can arbitrarily order simultaneous events.

A *local* history of p_i, denoted $H|p_i$, is a projection of H on process p_i: the subsequence H consisting of the events generated by p_i. Two histories H and H' are said to be *equivalent* if they have the same local histories, *i.e.*, for each process p_i, $H|p_i = H'|p_i$.

As we are interested only in histories generated by sequential processes, we focus on histories H such that, for each process p_i, $H|p_i$ is *well-formed*: it starts with an invocation, followed by a response (the matching response associated with the same object), followed by another invocation, and so on.

An operation is said to be *complete* in a history if the history includes both the events corresponding to the operation's invocation and its response. Otherwise, we say that the operation is *pending*. A history is *complete* if it has no pending operations and *incomplete* otherwise.

A history H induces an irreflexive partial order on its operations as follows. Let op and op' be two operations. Informally, operation op precedes operation op', if op terminates before op' starts. More precisely:

$$\left(op \rightarrow_H op'\right) \overset{\text{def}}{=} \left(resp[op] <_H inv[op']\right).$$

Two operations op and op' are said to *overlap* (we also say are *concurrent*) in a history H if neither $op \rightarrow_H op'$ nor $op' \rightarrow_H op$.

2.4 Sequential Histories

A history is *sequential* if its first event is an invocation, and then (1) each invocation event, except possibly the last, is immediately followed by the matching response event, and (2) each response event, except possibly the last, is immediately followed by an invocation event. A complete sequential history always ends with a response event. A history that is not sequential is said to be *concurrent*. Given that a sequential history S has no overlapping operations, the associated partial order $\rightarrow_S$ defined on its operations is actually a total order.

Let $S|X$ (S at X) denote the subsequence of history S made up of all the events involving object X. We say that a sequential history S is *legal* if, for each object X, the sequence $X.op_1, X.res_1, X.op_2, X.res_2, \ldots$ satisfies the sequential specification $(Q, q_0, OPS, RES, \delta)$ of X in the following sense: there exists $q_1, q_2, \ldots$ in Q such that $(q_{i-1}, op_i, res_i, q_i) \in \delta$ for all i.

3 Linearizability

Linearizability [9] basically requires that each operation on an object appears to execute at some indivisible point in time, also called the operation's *linearization point*, between the invocation and response of the operation. Linearizability provides the illusion that the operations issued by the processes on the shared objects are executed one after another.

We first define linearizability for complete histories H, *i.e.*, histories without pending operations, and then extend the definition to incomplete histories. A complete history H is *linearizable* if there is a "witness" history S such that:

1. H and S are equivalent,
2. S is sequential and legal, and
3. $\rightarrow_H \subseteq \rightarrow_S$.

This means that for a history H to be linearizable, there must exist a permutation S of H, which satisfies the following requirements. First, S has to be indistinguishable from H to any process. Second, S has to be sequential (interleaving the process histories at the granularity of complete operations) and legal (respecting the sequential specification of each object). Notice that, as S is sequential, $\rightarrow_S$ is a total order. Finally, S must also respect the real-time occurrence order of the operations as defined by $\rightarrow_H$. Such a sequential history S is called a *linearization* of H.

The definition of linearizability is extended to incomplete histories as follows. An incomplete history H is linearizable if H can be *completed*, *i.e.*, modified in such a way that every invocation of a pending operation is either removed or completed with a response event, so that the resulting (complete) history H' is linearizable. Intuitively, H' is obtained by adding response events to certain pending operations of H, as if these operations have indeed been completed, but also by removing invocation events from some of the pending operations of H. We require however that all complete operations of H are preserved in H'.

When proving that an algorithm implements a linearizable object, we need to prove that all histories generated by the algorithm are linearizable. A history H may allow for several different linearizations.

4 Linearizability Is Not a Safety Property

4.1 Safety

Intuitively, safety properties ensure that nothing "bad" ever happens. More specifically, a *safety property* is a set of histories that is non-empty, prefix-closed and limit-closed. Thus, a set P of histories is a safety property if it satisfies the following three conditions.

- P is *non-empty*: $P \neq \{\}$.
- P is *prefix-closed*: if $H \in P$, then for every prefix H' of H, $H' \in P$.
- P is *limit-closed*: for every infinite sequence $H_0, H_1, \ldots$ of histories, where each H_i is a prefix of H_{i+1} and each $H_i \in P$, the limit history $H = \lim_{i \to \infty} H_i$ is in P.

To ensure that a safety property P holds for a given implementation, it is thus enough to show that every *finite* history of the implementation is in P; an execution is in P if and only if each of its *finite* prefixes is in P. Indeed, every infinite history of an implementation is the limit of some sequence of ever-extending finite histories and thus should also be in P.

4.2 Counterexample

Theorem 1. *Linearizability is not a safety property.*

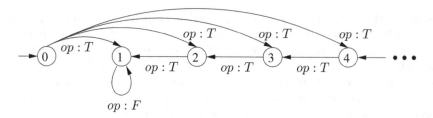

Fig. 1. The countdown object.

Proof. We define a type of object called a *countdown object*, which provides a single operation *op* that outputs T or F. The first invocation of *op* nondeterministically picks a positive integer k. The object returns T for the first k invocations of *op*. After that, it returns F for all remaining invocations of *op*. Formally, this type has the following sequential specification, which is illustrated in Fig. 1.

$$Q = \mathbb{N}$$
$$q_0 = 0$$
$$OPS = \{op\}$$
$$RES = \{T, F\}$$
$$\delta = \{(0, op, T, k) : k \geq 1\} \cup \{(1, op, F, 1)\} \cup \{(k, op, T, k-1) : k \geq 2\}$$

Consider the following infinite sequential history H that uses a single countdown object X.

$$inv[X.op \text{ by } p],$$
$$resp[X.T \text{ by } p],$$
$$inv[X.op \text{ by } p],$$
$$resp[X.T \text{ by } p],$$
$$inv[X.op \text{ by } p],$$
$$resp[X.T \text{ by } p],$$
$$\vdots$$

We first show that this history is not legal (and hence not linearizable). If we try to assign any positive integer state k to the object X after the first operation has been performed, then the states of the object after the next $k-1$ operations must be $k-1, k-2, k-3, \ldots, 1$. Thus, the $(k+1)$th invocation of *op* in the execution would have to return F. Since there is no way to assign states to the object consistent with all responses in H, we conclude that H is not legal.

Now consider any finite prefix H' of H. We show that H' is legal (and hence linearizable). Let k be the number of complete operations in H'. We can assign the sequence of states $k, k-1, \ldots, 2, 1$ to X. Note that $(0, op, T, k)$ and $(i, op, T, i-1)$ (for $2 \leq i \leq k$) are transitions of a countdown type, so this sequence of states satisfies the definition of legality for H'.

Let H_i be the prefix of H consisting of the first i complete operations. Then, for all i, H_i is linearizable and H_i is a prefix of H_{i+1}. However, $H = \lim_{i \to \infty} H_i$ is not linearizable. Thus, the property of being linearizable is not limit-closed, and linearizability is not a safety property for this object specification. $\square$

Remark 2. Because the execution used in the proof of Theorem 1 is a sequential execution, the argument in fact shows that even legality is not a safety property for the countdown object type, since the sequential execution is not legal but every prefix of it is. Moreover, since the execution in the proof is by a single process, it also demonstrates that other consistency conditions that are weaker than linearizability (such as sequential consistency) are also not safety properties for the countdown object.

5   When Linearizability Is a Safety Property

We now show that a slight generalization of König's (Infinity) Lemma enables us to show that linearizability, when restricted to objects with finite nondeterminism, is a safety property. König's Lemma can be formulated as follows.

Lemma 3. *(König's Lemma [10]). Let G be an infinite directed graph such that (1) each vertex of G has finite outdegree, (2) each vertex of G is reachable from some root vertex of G (a vertex with zero indegree), and (3) G has only finitely many roots. Then G has an infinite path with no repeated vertices starting from some root.*

Theorem 4. *Linearizability is a safety property for object types with finite non-determinism.*

Proof. Consider any object type with finite nondeterminism. The set of linearizable histories is non-empty, since the empty history (consisting of 0 events) is trivially linearizable. We show that the set of linearizable histories is prefix- and limit-closed.

Consider a linearizable history H. We show that any prefix H' of H is also linearizable. Let S be any linearization of H. Let sequential history S' be the shortest prefix of S that contains all complete operations of H'.

We claim that S' is a linearization of H'. We complete H' by appending responses that are present in S' but not in H' to the end of H' and removing operations that do not appear in S'. Note that only incomplete operations are removed from H' since all complete ones appear in S'. Let $\bar{H}'$ denote the resulting complete history.

First we show that complete histories S' and $\bar{H}'$ contain the same set of operations. Any operation in $\bar{H}'$ must also be in S' (since all operations not in S' are removed when forming $\bar{H}'$). To derive a contradiction, suppose that S' contains an operation op that does not appear in $\bar{H}'$. Since only operations that do not appear in S' were removed from H' to obtain $\bar{H}'$, op does not appear in H' either. Since S' is the shortest prefix of S that contains all complete operations of H', the last operation op' in S' must be a complete operation in H'. Thus, $op \neq op'$. Since op' is complete in H' and op does not appear in H', $op' <_H op$. But $op <_S op'$, contradicting the assumption that S is a linearization of H.

Since S' is a prefix of a legal history S, it is also legal. Moreover, it also respects the real-time order in $\bar{H}'$: if $op <_{\bar{H}'} op'$, then $op <_{S'} op'$ (otherwise, S would violate the real-time order in H). Since S and $\bar{H}'$ contain the same set of operations, S' respects the real-time order of $\bar{H}'$, and local histories are well-formed, S' is equivalent to $\bar{H}'$: local histories in S' and $\bar{H}'$ are identical.

So, S' is a linearization of H' and, thus, linearizability is prefix-closed.

To prove the limit-closed property, we consider an infinite sequence of ever-extending linearizable histories $H_0, H_1, H_2, \ldots$. Our goal is to show that $H = \lim_{i \to \infty} H_i$ is linearizable. We assume that H_0 is the empty history and each H_{i+1} is a one-event extension of H_i. (By prefix-closedness, each prefix of every H_i is linearizable, so there is no loss of generality in this assumption.)

Now we construct a directed graph $G = (V, E)$ as follows. Vertices of G are all tuples (H_i, S, W), where $i \in \mathbb{N}$, S is any linearization of H_i that ends with a *complete* operation present in H_i, and W is a sequence of states that witnesses the legality of S. There is a directed edge $((H_i, S, W), (H_j, S', W'))$ in G if and only if $j = i + 1$, S is a prefix of S' and W is a prefix of W'.

Note that for each H_i there is at least one vertex (H_i, S, W), since H_i is linearizable and if we remove all operations at the end of the linearization that are incomplete in H_i, we still have a linearization of H_i (the incomplete operations can also be removed from H_i to obtain a completion of H_i). Moreover, since S is necessarily legal, there exists a witness W for it. Thus, the graph G contains infinitely many vertices.

We use König's lemma to show that the resulting graph G contains an infinite path $(H_0, S_0, W_0), (H_1, S_1, W_1), \ldots$ and the limit $\lim_{i \to \infty} S_i$ is a linearization of the infinite limit history H. The legality of $\lim_{i \to \infty} S_i$ is witnessed by the infinite sequence of states $\lim_{i \to \infty} W_i$.

First we observe that for each vertex (H_{i+1}, S', W') (with $i \geq 0$), there is an edge into the vertex from some vertex (H_i, S, W). There are two cases to consider.

– The last operation op of S' is a complete operation in H_i. In this case, S' is also a linearization of H_i. Indeed, even if the last event of H_{i+1} is the invocation of a new operation op', this operation cannot appear in S': it can only appear before op in S' violating the real-time order in H_{i+1}. Thus, (H_i, S', W') is a vertex in G and there is an edge from it to (H_{i+1}, S', W').
– The last operation op of S' is not a complete operation in H_i. But since S' ends with an operation op that is complete in H_{i+1} and H_{i+1} extends H_i with one event only, we conclude that the last event of H_{i+1} is the response of op. Thus, H_i and H_{i+1} contain the same set of operations, except that op is incomplete in H_i. Let S be the longest prefix of S' that ends with a complete operation in H_i. Let W be the prefix of W' whose length corresponds is the number of operations in S'. Since W witnesses the legality of S, W' witnesses

the legality of S'. Also, only incomplete operations in H_i do not appear in S. Thus, S is a linearization of H_i and (H_i, S, W) is a vertex in G and there is an edge from it to (H_{i+1}, S', W').

It follows that the graph G has only one root vertex, (H_0, S_0, W_0), where H_0, S_0 and W_0 are empty sequences, and moreover that every vertex is reachable from this root.

Now we show that the outdegree of every vertex of G is finite. There are only finitely many operations in H_{i+1} and each linearization of H_{i+1} is a permutation of these operations, so there can only be finitely many linearizations S' of H_{i+1}. Moreover for any finite-length sequential history S' there can only be finitely many witnesses to the legality of S', since the number of possible states after any finite number of operations has been performed is finite. (This is where we use the assumption that the object's specification has finite nondeterminism.) Thus, there are only finitely many vertices of the form (H_{i+1}, S', W'). Since all outgoing edges of any vertex (H_i, S, W) are directed to vertices of the form (H_{i+1}, S', W'), the outdegree of every such vertex is also finite.

By Lemma 3, G contains an infinite path starting from the root vertex: $(H_0, S_0, W_0), (H_1, S_1, W_1), \ldots$. Let $S = \lim_{i \to \infty} S_i$ and $W = \lim_{i \to \infty} W_i$. First, note that W witnesses the legality of S. We argue now that the S is a linearization of the infinite history H. Let H' be the completion of H obtained by removing the incomplete operations of H that are not included in S and inserting into H response events for incomplete operations of H that are included in S. (The response events should be inserted in the order they occur in S and the response to an operation op should be inserted after the response to any operation that appears before op in S.) By construction, S is equivalent to H', and S respects the real-time order of H; otherwise there would be a vertex (H_i, S_i) such that S_i is not equivalent to H_i or violates the real-time order of H_i. Thus, S is indeed a linearization of H, which concludes the proof that linearizability is a safety property.   □

6   Backward Simulations

A backward simulation [13] is a technique that is sometimes used to show that an implementation of a shared object is linearizable (for example, [5,7]). A backward simulation from a system A to a system A' (which have state sets Q and Q', respectively) is a relation $bsr \subseteq Q \times Q'$ with the following properties.

1. For every state s of A, there is a state s' of A' such that $(s, s') \in bsr$.
2. If there is a transition α from state s_1 to state s_2 in A and $(s_2, s_2') \in bsr$ then there is a state s_1' and a sequence of transitions α' of A' such that $(s_1, s_1') \in bsr$, α' moves from state s_1' to s_2', and the sequence of externally observable events[2] is the same in α and α'.

---

[2] In the context of implementations of shared object of type T, observable events are just invocations and responses on the object of type T.

3. If q_0 is a possible initial state of A and $(q_0, q_0') \in bsr$ then q_0' is a possible initial state of A'.

If such a backward simulation exists from an implementation automaton to an abstract automaton that specifies correct linearizable behaviour, it is easy to prove that every finite history of the implementation is also a history of the abstract automaton, and hence linearizable. Intuitively, given a history H of the implementation A, we start from the final state of that history and find a matching state of the abstract automaton A' using property 1. Then, working backwards step by step, we build a history H' of A' by finding, for each transition of H, a sequence of transitions to prepend to H' using property 2. Finally, when we reach the beginning of H we observe, using property 3, that the history we have built could take place starting from an initial state of A'. Moreover, by construction the two histories have the same sequence of externally visible events.

Thus, if we can build a backward simulation from the implementation to the abstract automaton that specifies linearizable behaviour *and* if linearizability is a safety property, it follows that the implementation is linearizable. However, if linearizability is not a safety property, then the existence of the backward simulation does *not* necessarily imply that the implementation is linearizable. In fact, we can provide an example of an incorrect implementation of the countdown object where there is a backward simulation between the implementation and the abstract automaton.

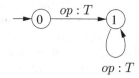

Fig. 2. An incorrect implementation of the countdown object.

Consider the following trivial (but incorrect) implementation of a countdown object: to perform an op on the countdown object, a process immediately returns T. One way to model this implementation is the automaton shown in Fig. 2. The reason that this implementation is incorrect is that it is possible for the implementation to return T forever in an infinite execution, something that is not permitted by the specification of the countdown object. Nevertheless, there is a backward simulation relation from the implementation to the countdown type. Let

$$bsr = \{(0, 0)\} \cup \{(1, k) : k \geq 1\}.$$

It is easy to verify that bsr satisfies the three properties that define a backward simulation relation using the following correspondence between actions.

α	s_2'	α'	External actions
$0 \to 1$	k, where $k \geq 1$	$0 \to k$	$op : T$
$1 \to 1$	k, where $k \geq 1$	$k + 1 \to k$	$op : T$

Thus, for objects with infinite nondeterminism, backward simulations are not necessarily a sound technique for proving linearizability (unless one can also prove that linearizability is a safety property for the object type considered). In view of Theorem 4, proving linearizability with a backward simulations *is* sound for any type with finite nondeterminism.

7   Concluding Remarks

For clarity, we have used the terms finite nondeterminism, rather than bounded nondeterminism (which is often used in the literature) because an object may have finite nondeterminism even when there is no bound B such that the number of possible responses to an operation is always bounded by B. For example, consider the *bag* object type, which stores a set of natural numbers and provides two operations: insert(k), which adds k to the set, and delete, which nondeterministically removes and returns an arbitrary element of the set. It has the following formal specification.

$$Q = \mathcal{P}(\mathbb{N})$$
$$q_0 = \{\}$$
$$OPS = \{\text{insert}(k) : k \in \mathbb{N}\} \cup \{\text{delete}\}$$
$$RES = \{ack, empty\} \cup \mathbb{N}$$
$$\delta = \{(S, \text{insert}(k), ack, S \cup \{k\}) : S \subseteq \mathbb{N}, k \in \mathbb{N}\} \cup$$
$$\{(S, \text{delete}, k, S - \{k\}) : S \subseteq \mathbb{N}, k \in S\} \cup \{(\{\}, \text{delete}, empty, \{\})\}$$

Although the number of nondeterministic choices available to a delete operation depends on the current state, and there is no *a priori* bound on this number, the bag object does have finite nondeterminism, so Theorem 4 says that linearizability *is* a safety property for the bag object.

We have shown in this paper that, strictly speaking, linearizability is not a safety property if infinite nondeterminism is permitted in the definition of object types. This points out the importance of considering carefully whether theorems proved about shared-memory systems apply to arbitrary nondeterministic object type specifications, or whether one should make the (often reasonable) restriction that object types must have finite nondeterminism. In particular, this shows that if linearizability is established by proving that every finite run is linearizable, for example by using a backward simulation, then there is an additional proof obligation to show that linearizability is a safety property for the particular type, for example by showing that the type specification has finite nondeterminism and then applying Theorem 4 of this paper. One open question raised by this work would be to give a precise characterization of the object types for which linearizability *is* a safety property.

Acknowledgements. The model section and definition of linearizability are based on lecture notes written by the first author with Michel Raynal and then with Petr Kuznetsov. The proof of Theorem 2 is inspired by a proof by Petr Kuznetsov, itself inspired by a proof by Nancy Lynch [12]. We thank Franck van Breugel for helpful discussions.

References

1. Adhikari, K., Street, J., Wang, C., Liu, Y., Zhang, S.J.: Verifying a quantitative relaxation of linearizability via refinement. In: Bartocci, E., Ramakrishnan, C.R. (eds.) SPIN 2013. LNCS, vol. 7976, pp. 24–42. Springer, Heidelberg (2013)
2. Alpern, B., Schneider, F.B.: Defining liveness. Inf. Process. Lett. **21**(4), 181–185 (1985)
3. Alpern, B., Schneider, F.B.: Recognizing safety and liveness. Distrib. Comput. **2**(3), 117–126 (1987)
4. Apt, K.R., Plotkin, G.D.: A cook's tour of countable nondeterminism. In: Even, S., Kariv, O. (eds.) Automata, Languages and Programming. LNCS, vol. 115, pp. 479–494. Springer, Heidelberg (1981)
5. Colvin, R., Groves, L., Luchangco, V., Moir, M.: Formal verification of a lazy concurrent list-based set algorithm. In: Ball, T., Jones, R.B. (eds.) CAV 2006. LNCS, vol. 4144, pp. 475–488. Springer, Heidelberg (2006)
6. Dijkstra, E.W.: On nondeterminacy being bounded. In: Dijkstra, E.W. (ed.) A Discipline of Programming, Chap. 9. Prentice-Hall, Englewood Cliffs (1976)
7. Doherty, S., Moir, M.: Nonblocking algorithms and backward simulation. In: Keidar, I. (ed.) DISC 2009. LNCS, vol. 5805, pp. 274–288. Springer, Heidelberg (2009)
8. Herlihy, M.P.: Wait-free synchronization. ACM Trans. Program. Lang. Syst. **13**(1), 123–149 (1991)
9. Herlihy, M.P., Wing, J.M.: Linearizability: a correctness condition for concurrent objects. ACM Trans. Program. Lang. Syst. **12**(3), 463–492 (1990)
10. König, D.: Über eine Schlussweise aus dem Endlichen ins Unendliche. Acta Litterarum ac Scientiarum Regiae Universitatis Hungaricae Francisco-Josephinae: Sectio Scientiarum Mathematicarum **3**, 121–130 (1927). also in chapter VI of Dénes König. Theory of Finite and Infinite Graphs, Birkhäuser, Boston, 1990
11. Liu, Y., Chen, W., Liu, Y.A., Sun, J., Zhang, S.J., Dong, J.S.: Verifying linearizability via optimized refinement checking. IEEE Trans. Softw. Eng. **39**(7), 1018–1039 (2013)
12. Lynch, N.: Distributed Algorithms, Chap. 13. Morgan Kaufmann, San Mateo (1996)
13. Lynch, N.A., Vaandrager, F.W.: Forward and backward simulations. Inf. Comput. **121**(2), 214–233 (1995)
14. Schenk, E.: The consensus hierarchy is not robust. In: Proceedings of 16th ACM Symposium on Principles of Distributed Computing, p. 279 (1997)

Fair Linking Mechanisms for Resource Allocation with Correlated Player Types

Agustín Santos[1], Antonio Fernández Anta[1(✉)], José A. Cuesta[2], and Luis López Fernández[3]

[1] IMDEA Networks Institute, Madrid, Spain
antonio.fernandez@imdea.org
[2] GISC, Mathematics Department, Universidad Carlos III, Madrid, Spain
[3] FUN-LAB, Universidad Rey Juan Carlos, Madrid, Spain

Abstract. Resource allocation is one of the most relevant problems in the area of Mechanism Design for computing systems. Devising algorithms capable of providing efficient and fair allocation is the objective of many previous research efforts. Usually, the mechanisms they propose use payments in order to deal with selfishness. Since using payments is undesirable in some contexts, a family of mechanisms without payments is proposed in this paper. These mechanisms extend the Linking Mechanism of Jackson and Sonnenschein introducing a generic concept of fairness with correlated preferences. We prove that these mechanisms have good incentive, fairness, and efficiency properties. To conclude, we provide an algorithm, based on the mechanisms, that could be used in practical computing environments.

Keywords: Linking mechanism · Fairness · Resource allocation

1 Introduction

The success of the Internet has made the problem of resource allocation to emerge in many versions like, for example, deciding which peer must receive bandwidth or disk in a file sharing P2P system [1], or deciding to which computational task some CPU is assigned in a collaborative distributed environment [2]. The problem may also appear with a negative formulation (i.e., instead of deciding who shall receive a resource, the problem is deciding who shall not receive it).

In all these scenarios, it is very important to conceive mechanisms that achieve efficient and fair resource allocation even when players present selfish or non-rational behavior. With that purpose, a number of interesting protocols and mechanisms based on Game Theory concepts [3,4] have been proposed.

This research was supported in part by the Comunidad de Madrid grant S2009TIC-1692, Spanish MICINN/MINECO grants FIS2011-22449 (PRODIEVO) and TEC2011-29688-C02-01 (E2Net), and National Natural Science Foundation of China grant 61020106002.

© Springer International Publishing Switzerland 2014
G. Noubir and M. Raynal (Eds.): NETYS 2014, LNCS 8593, pp. 70–83, 2014.
DOI: 10.1007/978-3-319-09581-3_6

In such works, it is often assumed that players can transfer their utilities (i.e., use payments). However, there are many systems in which this assumption is not realistic. Recently, some mechanisms without payments have been proposed, like those of Procaccia and Tennenholtz [5], or the seminal work of Jackson and Sonnenschein [6,7] in which a new type of mechanism (called *Linking Mechanism*) is proposed. A Linking Mechanism, instead of offering incentives or payments to players, limits the spectrum of players' responses to a probability distribution known by the game designer. The objective of this paper is to explore and extend Linking Mechanisms, introducing a wide spectrum of fairness concepts, while preserving all the original properties.

State of the Art. Mechanism Design has been gaining increasing popularity in distributed computing during the last few years (see, e.g., [8–10]). Even though the mechanisms proposed in these works are interesting, they are usually based on payment systems. Deploying such payment system in practice is often difficult. For this reason, mechanisms without payments have also been proposed. Related literature could be found in economics on cooperation [11,12] or similar problems in P2P systems such as reputation [13] and artificial currencies [14]. The work closest to our own, and in which we have based our proposal, is the *Linking Mechanism* proposed by Jackson and Sonnenschein [6,7]. Related to this work, Engelmann and Grimm [15] presents experimental research on linking mechanisms. An algorithm called QPQ (Quid Pro Quo) [16] has been proposed as an application of this kind of mechanisms to distribute task executions fairly among independent players.

QPQ reflects the main idea behind the concept of linking mechanism: when a game consists of multiple instances of the same basic decision problem (e.g., saying yes or no, choosing among a number of discrete options), it is possible to define selfishness-resistant algorithms by restricting the players' responses to a given distribution. Hence, in that case, the frequency with which a player declares a particular decision is established beforehand. Based on this, QPQ presents quite relevant features as the fact of not requiring payments, the flexibility on the definitions of the utility functions of the players, its applicability in iterative (i.e. repeated) games, the lack of central control authority, etc. While QPQ presents some very interesting properties, it only guarantees fairness and efficiency when users behave independently on each other. Nevertheless, this does not need to be the case in real environments, where users may have correlated preferences. The problem of fairness among players has been widely analyzed in the game theory literature and a wide range of fairness concept has been proposed, but, as far as we know, there is no fair linking mechanisms when players have correlated preferences. This motivates the research proposed in this paper.

Contributions. Our contributions are twofold. On the one hand, we have extended the idea of Linking Mechanism introducing fairness, while preserving desirable properties, like efficiency, truthful reporting, incentive compatibility, etc. On the other hand, we propose an algorithm based on these mechanisms that we expect to be used in practical scenarios.

In our model, fairness is a key element introduced to compensate current sacrifices in future iterations. Due to the large number of notions of fairness that could be defined, it is difficult to find a general model that encompasses any approach. Fairness is, in general, an elusive concept that can be seen from many different perspectives. In this work we have proposed a generic fairness definition, which we hope will serve as a reference to wider models. Hence, our contribution is clear: to the best of our knowledge, no other previous research work has offered a linking mechanism providing fair and efficient decisions.

In addition, from a theoretical perspective, we contribute to the progress of the state-of-the-art by proposing a mathematical framework suitable for proving all claimed algorithmic properties. This framework is inspired on previous work on theoretical economics but, as far as we know, it has never been adapted to the specific peculiarities of distributed computing (at least not to solve the resource allocation problem). This technique has proven to be extremely powerful for our specific problem, but it can be re-used in other scenarios with similar assumptions.

Based on the theoretical results, we propose a realization of the mechanism suitable for being implemented as an iterative game in real distributed environments. Unlike in the original linking mechanism, this algorithm does not need to know the probability distribution of the players' responses. We show that this realization does not require central entities and that its computational cost is affordable for current state of the art networks and devices. In addition, through simulations, we confirm the stability of the algorithm demonstrating that few iterations on a repeated game are enough for making the mechanism to converge to a fair equilibrium even when the players' distributions are strongly correlated.

To illustrate the application of this mechanism in a real environment, consider a P2P system used for computation to which requests arrive continuously. When a request arrives, the computational cost of processing it at a given node of the system will depend on the load of the node. Our mechanism could be used to enforce that all nodes process the same proportion of requests, while the total computational cost is minimized.

2   Model and Definitions

We start by presenting the usual mathematical framework for mechanism design and then we formally define the specific problem we face in this paper.

Mechanism Design Concepts. The following provides the usual theoretic framework that will be later applied to our problem. We assume that there are n players. The set of players is $N = \{1, 2, \ldots, n\}$. Players are risk-neutral. The alternative or outcome set of the game played is D. In a general setting, D could be defined over $\Delta(N)^1$, but in this paper we define $D = N$ so that the outcome $d \in D$ is the player to whom the resource will be allocated.

---

[1] We denote by $\Delta(S)$ the set of all probability distribution over some set S.

Prior to making the collective choice in the game, each player privately observes her preferences over the alternatives in D. This is modeled by assuming that player i privately observes a parameter or signal θ_i that determines her preferences. (For instance, in resource allocation, θ_i could represent the value player i assigns to the resource.) For a given player i, we say that θ_i is the player type. The set of possible types of player i is Θ_i. We denote by $\theta = (\theta_1, \theta_2, \ldots, \theta_n)$ the vector of player types. The set of all possible vectors is $\Theta = \Theta_1 \times \Theta_2 \times \ldots \Theta_n$. We denote by θ_{-i} the vector obtained by removing θ_i from θ.

We denote by $\Pi = \Delta(\Theta)$ the set of all probability distributions over Θ. It is assumed that there is a common prior distribution $\pi \in \Pi$ that is shared by all the players. We denote by $\pi_i \in \Delta(\Theta_i)$ the marginal probability of θ_i. We define $\beta_i(\theta_{-i}|\theta_i)$ as the conditional probability distribution of θ_{-i} given θ_i. That is, for any possible type $\theta_i \in \Theta_i$, $\beta_i(\cdot|\theta_i)$ specifies a probability distribution over the set Θ_{-i} representing what player i would believe about the types of the other players if her own type were θ_i. Beliefs $(\beta_i)_{i \in N}$ are *consistent*, since individual belief functions β_i can all be derived from the common prior π. This implies that $\pi(\theta_{-i}|\theta_i) = \beta_i(\theta_{-i}|\theta_i)$.

Individual players have preferences over outcomes, which are represented by a utility function $u_i(d, \theta_i) \in \mathbb{R}$ defined over all $d \in D$ and $\theta_i \in \Theta_i$.

The set of outcomes D, the set of players N, the type sets in Θ, the common prior distribution $\pi \in \Pi$, and the payoff functions $u_i, i \in N$ are assumed to be *common knowledge* among all the players. The game rules defined by a specific mechanism are also common knowledge. However, the specific value θ_i observed by player i is *private information* of player i.

A strategy for the player i is any map $\sigma_i : \Theta_i \to \Delta(\Theta_i)$, where $\sigma_i(\hat{\theta}_i|\theta_i)$ is the conditional probability that the player reports $\hat{\theta}_i$ when her true type is θ_i. A reporting strategy σ_i is *truthful* if for every pair $(\hat{\theta}_i, \theta_i)$, $\sigma_i(\hat{\theta}_i|\theta_i) = 1$ if $\hat{\theta}_i = \theta_i$ and 0 otherwise. As usually done, we will use $\hat{\theta}_i$ to denote the reported type and θ_i the actual type.

Given that the prior distribution π is known, player i can not change it. Hence, we say that a player i has a *limited strategy space*, since her strategy can not change the beliefs of other players. Intuitively, player i has a limited strategy space if beliefs over reports are the same as actual beliefs.

For a given Bayesian mechanism $\langle \Theta, g \rangle$ we shall write $q_i(\cdot|\theta_i)$ for player i's interim probability density function on D conditional on player i's type being θ_i.

In this paper, we are looking for a mechanism $\langle \Theta, g \rangle$, where $g(\cdot)$ is the decision function, without utility transfers (payments) and that implements some social choice function f under some equilibrium when the induced game is Bayesian. In addition, we introduce fairness as a key tool to compensate or reward players. We call this kind of mechanisms as *Quid Pro Quo Mechanisms* (QPQ).

Fairness. In our model, we use fairness as a very abstract concept. For us, fairness is the property of balancing in expectation some game parameters (modelled with a real function) among all players. Our model was originally built with two examples in mind: *fairness in utility* ("players have same expected utility") and *fairness in assignment* ("same expected number of assignments"). But these two examples are just special cases of our model. Additionally, we have contemplated the possibility that some scenarios require allocations other than equiproportional; or than the game must be constrained to several fairness concepts at the same time. All of this is modelled introducing a set of functions $\eta_{i,l} : \theta \to \mathbb{R}$ and ratios $\delta_{i,l}$, all defined for each player $i \in N$ and for each fairness concept $l = 1, \cdots, m$ (m is the number of fairness concepts). The function $\eta_{i,l}$ represents a fairness concept. For instance, for *fairness in assignment* this function could be defined as $\eta_{i,l}(\theta) = 1$. Similarly, *fairness in utility* is applied when $\eta_{i,l}(\theta) = \theta_i$. On the other hand, $\delta_{i,l}$ is the ratio for player i when fairness l is applied. Typically, this ratio is $\delta_{i,l} = \frac{1}{n}$. Then, formally, our concept of fairness is defined as follows.

Definition 1 (Fairness). *Given functions $\eta_{i,l} : \Theta \to \mathbb{R}$, and values $\delta_{i,l}$, we say that a mechanism $\langle \Theta, g \rangle$ is fair (or η-fair) when, for all $i \in N$ and $l = 1, \cdots, m$,*

$$\int_{\Theta} \eta_{i,l}(\theta) q_i(\theta) \, d\pi(\theta) = \delta_{i,l} \sum_{j \in N} \int_{\Theta} \eta_{j,l}(\theta) q_j(\theta) \, d\pi(\theta) \tag{1}$$

In this paper, we deal mathematically with this general concept of fairness, but for the algorithm and simulations we used a particular concept of fairness, where players will have *equal number* of allocated resources (in expectation).

Resource Allocation Problem. We now formally define the problem we study in this work. Intuitively, the problem is like a repeated single-unit auction, where the mechanism that decides how to allocate the resource in each auction is a QPQ mechanism. Hence there are no payments and the allocation must satisfy a notion of fairness.

The problem of resource allocation is a tuple $\langle R, N, \Theta \rangle$ where, N and Θ are as defined above, and $R = \{r_1, r_2, \ldots\}$ is the ordered set of resources that have to be allocated by the system over time. Resources are received by the system in their order in R, they are independent among them, and the system must allocate resource r_k to a single player before receiving resource r_{k+1}. R is assumed to be infinite.

As was mentioned previously, in this problem the outcome set is $D = N$, where an outcome of $d \in D$ for resource r_k means that r_k is allocated to player d. In [16], we have proposed a QPQ algorithm that implements this function when the type of players follow mutually independent distributions. As in that work, we assume here that the type of each player is normalized using a *Probability Integral Transform* (PIT), so that it takes real values in the interval $[0, 1]$ and follows a uniform distribution within that support. Hence, we assume that $\Theta_i = [0, 1]$. Finally, as mentioned, we assume that players have a limited space strategy (i.e., π is known a priori and cannot be changed by the players).

The social choice function (scf) $g(\cdot)$ we are looking for is one that optimizes the social utility restricted by fairness conditions. The social choice function must be the solution to the following equation,

$$\max_{g} \left\{ \sum_{i \in N} \int_{\Theta} u_i(d(\theta), \theta_i) \, q_i(\theta) \, d\pi(\theta) \right\}$$

s.t., (2)

$$\int_{\Theta} \eta_{i,l}(\theta) q_i(\theta) \, d\pi(\theta) = \delta_{i,l} \sum_{j \in N} \int_{\Theta} \eta_{j,l}(\theta) q_j(\theta) \, d\pi(\theta), l = 1, \cdots, m$$

As an example, we study the fairness concept where each player i will receive a *proportional number of resources* δ_i. Hence, we obtain that the scf is the solution of the following equation.

$$\max_{g} \left\{ \sum_{i \in N} \int_{\Theta} u_i(d, \theta_i) \, q_j(\theta) \, d\pi(\theta) \right\}$$

s.t. (3)

$$\int_{\Theta} q_j(\theta) \, d\pi(\theta) = \delta_i, \forall i \in N.$$

Another fairness concept that we study as an instance of this framework is *players with proportional utility*. Under this fairness concept every player will obtain a proportional expected utility. The equations are similar in this case.

$$\max_{g} \left\{ \sum_{i \in N} \int_{\Theta} u_i(d, \theta_i) \, q_j(\theta) \, d\pi(\theta) \right\}$$

s.t. (4)

$$\int_{\Theta} u_i(d, \theta_i) \, q_j(\theta) \, d\pi(\theta) = \delta_i \sum_{j \in N} \int_{\Theta} u_j(d, \theta_j) \, q_j(\theta) \, d\pi(\theta), \forall i \in N.$$

Without loss of generality, we can define the utility of a player i as follows,

$$u_i(d, \theta_i) = \begin{cases} \theta_i & \text{if } d = i, \\ 0 & \text{otherwise.} \end{cases}$$

(5)

In this paper, we are interested in dynamic mechanisms where truth-telling is a Bayesian equilibrium of the static QPQ mechanism. In that case we call the QPQ mechanism Bayesian incentive compatible. That means that a player obtains a higher utility when reporting truthfully.

3   The Fair Quid Pro Quo Mechanism

With the above definitions, we now derive QPQ Mechanisms that implement the social choice functions given by Eqs. 3 and 4 under equilibrium, as special cases of the solution to Eq. 2.

Theorem 1. *The QPQ Mechanism that implements the social function 2 with η-fairness is a set of functions $\psi = (\psi_1, \cdots \psi_n)$ that defines a line $y = \psi_i(x)$ for each player i with deterministic assignment $d = g_\psi(\theta) = \operatorname*{argmax}_{i \in N}(\psi_i(\theta))$ (except at some points where the decision is indifferent).*

Proof. The problem we aim to solve is to find the decision function g that maximizes

$$\int_\Theta \sum_{i \in N} \theta_i \, q_i(\theta) \, d\pi(\theta) \tag{6}$$

under the constraints given in Eq. 2. Using Lagrange multipliers, this is tantamount to maximizing the functional

$$\mathcal{F}[q] \equiv \int_\Theta \sum_{i \in N} \theta_i \, q_i(\theta) \, d\pi(\theta) + \sum_{k \in N} \sum_{l=1}^m \lambda_{k,l} \int_\Theta \left\{ \eta_{k,l}(\theta) q_k(\theta) - \delta_{k,l} \sum_{j \in N} \eta_{j,l}(\theta) \, q_j(\theta) \right\} d\pi(\theta), \tag{7}$$

which can be rewritten

$$\mathcal{F}[q] = \int_\Theta \sum_{i \in N} \psi_i(\theta) q_i(\theta) \, d\pi(\theta), \tag{8}$$

where

$$\psi_i(\theta) \equiv \theta_i + \sum_{l=1}^m \lambda_{i,l} \, \eta_{i,l}(\theta) - \sum_{k \in N} \sum_{l=1}^m \lambda_{k,l} \, \delta_{k,l} \, \eta_{i,l}(\theta). \tag{9}$$

Since $0 \le q_i(\theta) \le 1$ and $\sum_{i \in N} q_i(\theta) = 1$ for all $\theta \in \Theta$, then for each $\theta \in \Theta$,

$$\sum_{i \in N} \psi_i(\theta) q_i(\theta) \le \psi_j(\theta) \tag{10}$$

if $j \in N$ is such that $\psi_j(\theta) > \psi_k(\theta)$ for all $k \ne j$. The upper bound is reached if, and only if, for that value of θ we have $q_j(\theta) = 1$ and $q_k(\theta) = 0$ for all $k \ne j$.

If, on the other hand, $j_1, \ldots, j_r$ are such that $\psi_{j_1}(\theta) = \cdots = \psi_{j_r}(\theta) > \psi_k(\theta)$ for all $k \ne j_1, \ldots, j_r$, then the upper bound is $\psi_{j_1}(\theta)$, but this time is reached for any choice of the functions $q_i(\theta)$ such that $q_{j_1}(\theta) + \cdots + q_{j_r}(\theta) = 1$ and $q_k(\theta) = 0$ for all $k \ne j_1, \ldots, j_r$.   □

For convenience, we build the decision function of our mechanism introducing a *transformation function* $\psi : \Theta \to \mathbb{R}^n$ that returns a vector of n real values. The decision function is then obtained as $d = g(\theta) = g_\psi = \operatorname*{argmax}_{i \in N}(\psi_i(\theta))$. We say that ψ determines the "decision rule" or "decision function". Our main theorem give us insight into what can we expect about the set of functions ψ. Given our definition of $\psi_i(\theta)$ we can derive some intuition about the decision function. The theorem tells us that we can restrict our attention to deterministic solutions except when $\psi_i(\theta) = \psi_j(\theta), i, j \in N$. At these points, the decision is indifferent. The above theorem also gives us an optimality result.

Corollary 2. *Assume that all players are honest, mechanism M defined using the decision function* $d = \underset{i \in N}{\text{argmax}} \, (\psi_i(\theta))$ *maximizes the utility of the system subject to fairness constraints.*

Finally, when fairness is symmetric in the sense that each player has the same fairness function, then each ψ_i depends only on the player's profile θ_i and therefore $\psi_i(\theta_i, \theta_{-i})$ could be reduced to $\psi_i(\theta_i)$. This last aspect allows us to state the following corollary.

Corollary 3. *When fairness is symmetric in the sense of* $\eta_i(\theta) = \eta(\theta_i) \, \forall i \in N$, *and players have limited space strategy, then the probability* q_i *depends only on the player's value, that is* $q_i(\theta) = q_i(\theta_i)$.

Proof. The proof follows from the definition of $\psi_i(\theta)$ and therefore the decision function could be reduced to $d = \underset{i \in N}{\text{argmax}} \, (\psi_i(\theta_i))$. As beliefs can not be changed by the strategy of others players, the probability $q_i(\theta)$ is only defined as a function of θ_i. □

Revisiting our particular cases of fairness defined as equal-number of resources (Eq. 3) and equal number of utility (Eq. 4) we can check that the solutions for ψ are in both cases straight lines. When fairness is defined as equal-number of resources (Eq. 3), $\psi_i(\theta)$ becomes

$$\psi_i(\theta) \equiv \theta_i + \lambda_i - \sum_{k=1}^{n} \lambda_k \delta_k, \tag{11}$$

and therefore $\psi(\theta_i) = \theta_i + \lambda_i - \sum_{k=1}^{n} \lambda_k \delta_k$.

This solution has a very nice property that was already observed in our original work (QPQ with independent players). The mechanism designer could aggregate players when studying a single player. The mechanism designer can see the game as player i against the system formed by all other players ($j \in N, j \neq i$). In this case, player i has to compute just two values for λ, her own value λ_i and the aggregate value $\lambda_j = \sum_{k=1}^{n} \lambda_k \delta_k$. That is: $\psi(\theta_i) = \theta_i + \lambda_i - \lambda_j$, or even simpler: $\psi(\theta_i) = \theta_i + \lambda$. if we redefine λ as a new single real parameter that represents $\lambda_i - \sum_{k=1}^{n} \lambda_k \delta_k$.

This confirms that the decision function is a straight line where the parameter λ determines the point at which the line crosses the y-axis. And this is true for all players.

On the other hand, when fairness is defined as a function of utility (Eq. 4), our ψ function could be defined using

$$\psi_i(\theta) \equiv \theta_i \left(1 + \lambda_i - \sum_{k=1}^{n} \lambda_k \delta_k\right), \tag{12}$$

and therefore $\psi(\theta_i) = \theta_i \left(1 + \lambda_i - \sum_{k=1}^{n} \lambda_k \delta_k\right)$.

Again, the decision function is a straight line where λ determines the slope. Aggregating players, the above solution could be reduced to $\psi(\theta_i) = (1 + \lambda_i - \frac{1}{n}\lambda_j)$, or $\psi(\theta_i) = \lambda \, \theta_i$.

Properties. The Fair QPQ Mechanism with Correlated players (M_{fair}) has the following properties:

1. M_{fair} is (ex-ante) **individual-rational**. This means that the expected utility of a player is at least its expected outside utility.
2. M_{fair} is not **allocative-efficient**, but assign tasks efficiently subject to equal number of tasks for each player. This property is a clear conclusion from Corollary 2.
3. There is no incentive for any of the players to lie about or hide their private information from the other players. Players will report truthfully in a Bayesian equilibrium. We said that M_{fair} is Bayesian incentive compatible. This property prevents selfish players from obtaining a benefit by misbehaving.

The two first properties are quite evident. The last property follows from Theorem 4.

Theorem 4. *When players have limited space strategy, and fairness is symmetric in the sense that $\eta_i(\theta) = \eta(\theta_i) \; \forall i \in N$, then M_{fair} is Bayesian incentive compatible.*

Proof. For the sake of contradiction, let us suppose this proposition is false. Hence, there is some set of assignments for which, if i is not honest, she will obtain more utility in expectation.

From Corollary 3, this holds for any strategy of the aggregate player j, and in particular when all its players are honest. Hence, we can consider in the rest of the proof that the rest of $n - 1$ players behave honestly.

Additionally, using the same corollary, we know that every player, $j \neq i \in N$, will obtain the same expected utility (independently whether i lies or not),

$$\int_{\Theta} u_j(d, \theta_j) \, q_j(\theta) \, d\pi(\theta) = \int_{\Theta} u_j(d, \theta_j) \, \hat{q}_j(\theta) \, d\hat{\pi}(\theta)$$

Now we can define a new mechanism M that assigns a task to player i (when i is honest and declares θ_i) with the same probability as the original QPQ assigns the task to the player i when she declares a false value $\hat{\theta}_i$. Then, $q_i(\theta_i) = \hat{q}_i(\hat{\theta})$. Note this new mechanism conserves the same fairness constraints as the original one. However, if the above were true, QPQ would not be optimal, since a mechanism that reproduces the same decisions under i lying (in presence of honest players) would different (lower) utility. Clearly, this is in contradiction of optimality of QPQ. Therefore, the best strategy for a player (the one optimizing her normalized utility) is to be honest. □

4   Practical QPQ Algorithm

After describing the different ingredients of our solution, we are able to propose an application of our mechanism. Due to space restrictions, we will only discuss an algorithm for a particular case. We propose an algorithm where the resource

---

Algorithm 1. QPQ Correlated mechanism (code for node i)

1: Estimate the preference θ_i
2: Publish the normalized value $\bar{\theta}_i = PIT(\theta_i)$
3: Wait to receive the normalized values $\bar{\theta}_j$ from the other players
4: **for all** $j \in N$ **do**
5:     **if** not $GoF\_Test(\bar{\theta}_j, Historic)$ **then**
6:         $\bar{\theta}_j \leftarrow Random(\bar{\theta}_{-j}, Historic)$
7:     **end if**
8: **end for**
9: $Historic \leftarrow Historic \cup \{\bar{\theta}\}$
10: Let $d = \underset{j \in N}{\operatorname{argmax}} \{\psi_j(\bar{\theta}_j)\}$
11: **if** $d = i$ **then**
12:     Resource is assigned to node i
13: **end if**
14: Update $\lambda_j, \forall j \in N$: $\lambda_{k+1,j} = \lambda_{k,j} + \epsilon_k(T_{k,j} - 1/n)$.

---

allocation achieves fairness in the number of resources allocated to each player. This algorithm could be extended to other fairness concepts. The details can be observed in Algorithm 1.

In the algorithm, $T_{k,j}$ denotes the percentage of decisions assigned to player j, computed at round k. As it can be observed, for each round, each player estimates her own value and publishes it. Publication means broadcasting a message with the value to all players (although any other means of distribution, like shared memory, can be used). By assumption, a player sends its value before it receives any of the others (concurrency, which implies that they do not depend from each other), and all of the values are correctly received at each player (reliability). Then, the algorithm assigns the resource to the player that publishes the highest value modified by a particular ψ_k.

Acceptance Test. We are assuming that players are reporting values using a uniform distribution. If their original distribution is not the uniform, we apply here the same normalization transformation proposed in [16] based on the *Probability Integral Transform* (PIT). Given the properties of the PIT, the idea is that any player applying correctly the PIT on her real type distribution, must generate a uniform distribution on the unit interval on her published normalized values. Hence, from the point of view of the mechanism designer, the problem consists on determining whether these published values follow or not that uniform distribution. There are a wide range of tests that allow checking that. These tests are called Goodness-of-Fit or GoF tests.

Continuing with this argument, we propose to implement the acceptance test of our algorithm by using some GoF test on the declared transformed sequence of values published by the player. Whenever a player is honest and she declares the values by applying the PIT transformation on her own distribution, these values will be uniformly distributed in the unit interval. In that case (with high probability) the GoF tests will accept the samples. More importantly, this process has an error which tends to zero when the number of samples (rounds) increases for any reasonable value of the threshold. For the study of our analytical results, we assume that GoF tests are perfect and this error is zero.

A tremendous amount of GoF tests have been proposed in the scientific literature. We propose to use the Kolmogorov-Smirnov (KS) test [17, 18] test as the GoF test of QPQ. In contrast to our previous work with independent players [16], in this case it is necessary to add a second test. The goal for this new test is to check if a player is trying to modify the joint distribution. For our work, we have used the "Copula" R-Cran package. We note that no approach is always the best.

Punishment. In the case that a dishonest player tried to lie, one possible strategy is to generate increasing $\hat{\theta}$ values, so that the PIT transformed values are close to the unit. However, this type of behavior is quickly detected by the test. In that case, the question is how to establish a punishment. Inspired on previous works on linking mechanisms, the proposal is to reject the value declared by the player and generate a new random value according to the join prior distribution.

Practical computation of λ. The above solution reduces the problem to finding the value of λ that adjusts the tasks performed by players. In principle, we can ask the players to declare the joint distribution and calculate that parameter accordingly. But in general, we should not expect to find an analytical equation. That is, it is possible that π does not have an analytical expression, or even if it exists, players must estimate it empirically. There are multiple methods for π estimation, both parametric and nonparametric. The major difficulty with these systems is the convergence speed making it necessary a large number of samples. There is a relationship between the dimension of the feature and the number of samples needed. In our case, the dimension would be given by the number of players. Fortunately, each player can compute the QPQ mechanism using just only two dimensions (itself and the aggregate system).

However, players do not need to know the joint density function π, they only need to know the function $T(\cdot)$ that indicates the number of tasks performed given a parameter λ. We denote by $T(\lambda)$ the number of tasks that run the player when the decision value ψ is determined by the parameter λ. Again, we can not expect an analytic form for T. But under the right assumptions, we can approximate λ using stochastic approximation methods. Due to the characteristics of the transformation function and noting how it influences the number of tasks, we can expect that the function $T(\lambda)$ is continuous and decreasing (or increasing in the direction of λ). That is, there is always a value of λ for each percentage of desired tasks. Our proposal is to approximate λ by a sequence $\lambda_0, \lambda_1, \lambda_2, \lambda_3, \cdots \rightarrow \lambda$ constructed using a stochastic approximation method. The best known method is perhaps the Robbins-Monro method [19] although not the only one. Then, our algorithm must compute, for each iteration k,

$$\lambda_{k+1} = \lambda_k + \epsilon_k(T_k - 1/n). \tag{13}$$

Where T_k is an estimation of the average number of tasks performed by the player and where ϵ_k is a sequence of values that satisfies $\epsilon_k > 0$, $\epsilon_k \to 0$, $\sum_k \epsilon_k = \infty$. Note that, in order to estimate T_k we don't need to store previous samples and memory consumption is low.

Simulations. By performing simulations, we have checked various aspects of our proposal. Mainly, we wondered how Robbins-Monro algorithm performs in time. We have simulated several alternatives for the generation of the sequence of values ϵ_k. In our simulation we have used two methods: $\epsilon_k = 1/k$ and $\epsilon_k = \frac{1}{log(k)+k}$. The first one is the original proposal of Robbins-Monro's work. With this sequence, our experiments produce some oscillations in the λ estimation and the speed of convergence was far from ideal. We found better results with the second approach. Figure 1 presents an experiment with three players, the first two are correlated and the third one is independent. Without our algorithm, the independent player will obtain less utility than the two other players. On the other hand, with our proposal, fairness is achieved and every player will have a proportional number of assignments.

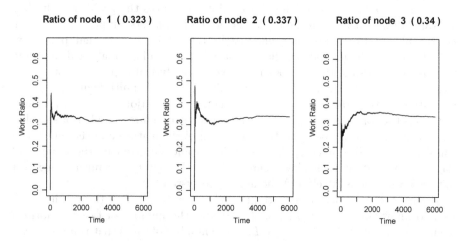

Fig. 1. Evolution of work ratio (number of tasks) with QPQ.

5   Conclusions and Future Work

In this paper we have created a novel scheme capable of providing efficient resource allocation in distributed systems even in the presence of selfish correlated players. We have shown that, for a general notion of fairness, the mechanism can be proved to perform efficiently and to maintain the incentive of players to participate. In addition, we have proposed a specific realization of the mechanism as an algorithm implementable in real distributed environments with affordable computational and communication costs. This algorithm is susceptible of being used in repeated task allocations given that our simulations demonstrate its rapid convergence, which open new horizons for systems based on open systems for distributed collaborative tasks execution.

Despite this, the authors consider necessary to extend the current research in several directions. First, the model requires knowledge on the number of players that participate. We may find scenarios where this is not reasonable, e.g., scenarios in which several players "hide" and play the game with a single identity, which may resulting on the mechanism not achieving fairness. Second, it would be important to analyze the problem when more flexible space strategies are possible. One of our main assumptions has been to consider that correlations are fixed and that players are not able to alter them through their strategies. This assumption is reasonable when information is private and the mechanism is designed in such a way that players cannot make their declared (true or false) values on an iteration dependent on the values of others at the same iteration. However, there are many real-live scenarios where players may be able to share their values making more complex interdependent strategies possible. This would break the properties of our proposed algorithm.

References

1. Jun, S., Ahamad, M.: Incentives in BitTorrent induce free riding. In: Proceedings of the 2005 ACM SIGCOMM Workshop on Economics of Peer-to-Peer Systems. P2PECON '05, pp. 116–121. ACM, New York (2005)
2. Ahmad, I., Ranka, S., Khan, S.: Using game theory for scheduling tasks on multicore processors for simultaneous optimization of performance and energy. In: IEEE International Symposium on Parallel and Distributed Processing, IPDPS 2008, pp. 1–6. IEEE (2008)
3. Bell, M.G.: A game theory approach to measuring the performance reliability of transport networks. Transp. Res. Part B: Methodol. **34**, 533–545 (2000)
4. Srivastava, V., Neel, J., Mackenzie, A.B., Menon, R., Dasilva, L.A., Hicks, J.E., Reed, J.H., Gilles, R.P.: Using game theory to analyze wireless ad hoc networks. IEEE Commun. Surv. Tutor. **7**, 46–56 (2005)
5. Procaccia, A.D., Tennenholtz, M.: Approximate mechanism design without money. In: Proceedings of the 10th ACM Conference on Electronic Commerce, pp. 177–186. ACM (2009)
6. Jackson, M.O., Sonnenschein, H.F.: The linking of collective decisions and efficiency. Microeconomics 0303007, EconWPA (2003)
7. Jackson, M.O., Sonnenschein, H.F.: Overcoming incentive constraints by linking decisions. Econometrica **75**, 241–257 (2007)
8. Papadimitriou, C.H.: Games, algorithms, and the internet. In: Srinivasan, S., Ramamritham, K., Kumar, A., Ravindra, M.P., Bertino, E., Kumar, R., (eds.) WWW, pp. 5–6. ACM (2011)
9. Jackson, M.: Mechanism theory (2003). http://web.stanford.edu/~jacksonm/mechtheo.pdf
10. Jackson, M.O.: A crash course in implementation theory. Working papers 1076, Division of the Humanities and Social Sciences, California Institute of Technology (1999)

11. Kandori, M.: Social norms and community enforcement. Rev. Econ. Stud. **59**, 63–80 (1992)
12. Ellison, G.: Cooperation in the prisoner's dilemma with anonymous random matching. Rev. Econ. Stud. **61**, 567–588 (1994)
13. Kamvar, S.D., Schlosser, M.T., Garcia-Molina, H.: The Eigentrust algorithm for reputation management in P2P networks. In: Proceedings of the 12th International Conference on World Wide Web, pp. 640–651. ACM (2003)
14. Friedman, E.J., Halpern, J.Y., Kash, I.: Efficiency and nash equilibria in a scrip system for P2P networks. In: Proceedings of the 7th ACM Conference on Electronic Commerce, pp. 140–149. ACM (2006)
15. Engelmann, D., Grimm, V.: Mechanisms for efficient voting with private information about preferences. Econ. J. **122**, 1010–1041 (2012)
16. Santos Méndez, A., Fernández Anta, A., López Fernández, L.: Quid pro quo: a mechanism for fair collaboration in networked systems. PLOS ONE (2013), See CoRR abs/1207.6045 (2012, in press)
17. Kolmogorov, A.N.: Sulla determinazione empirica di una legge di distribuzione. Giornale dellIstituto Italiano degli Attuari **4**, 83–91 (1933)
18. Smirnov, N.V.: On the estimation of the discrepancy between empirical curves of distribution for two independent samples. Bull. Moscow Univ. **2**, 3–16 (1939)
19. Robbins, H., Monro, S.: A stochastic approximation method. Ann. Math. Stat. **22**, 400–407 (1951)

Iterative Approximate Consensus
in the Presence of Byzantine Link Failures

Lewis Tseng[1][✉] and Nitin Vaidya[2]

[1] Department of Computer Science, University of Illinois at Urbana-Champaign,
Champaign, USA
ltseng3@illinois.edu
[2] Department of Electrical and Computer Engineering,
University of Illinois at Urbana-Champaign, Champaign, USA
nhv@illinois.edu

Abstract. This paper explores the problem of reaching approximate consensus in synchronous point-to-point networks, where each directed link of the underlying communication graph represents a communication channel between a pair of nodes. We adopt the *transient Byzantine link failure* model [15,16], where an omniscient adversary controls a subset of the *directed* communication links, but the nodes are assumed to be *fault-free.*

Recent work has addressed the problem of reaching approximate consensus in incomplete graphs with Byzantine *nodes* using a *restricted class* of iterative algorithms that maintain only a small amount of memory across iterations [12,21,23,24]. This paper addresses approximate consensus in the presence of Byzantine *links*. We extend our past work [21,23] that provided exact characterization of graphs in which the iterative approximate consensus problem in the presence of Byzantine *node* failures is solvable. In particular, we prove a *tight* necessary and sufficient condition on the underlying communication graph for the existence of iterative approximate consensus algorithms under *transient Byzantine link* model [15,16].

1 Introduction

Approximate consensus can be related to many distributed computations in networked systems, such as data aggregation [10], decentralized estimation [17], and flocking [9]. Extensive work has addressed the problem in the presence of *Byzantine nodes* [11] in complete networks [1,6] and arbitrary directed networks [12,21,23]. This paper consider the problem of tolerating Byzantine link failures [2,15,16,18].

This research is supported in part by National Science Foundation award CNS 1329681. Any opinions, findings, and conclusions or recommendations expressed here are those of the authors and do not necessarily reflect the views of the funding agencies or the U.S. government.

© Springer International Publishing Switzerland 2014
G. Noubir and M. Raynal (Eds.): NETYS 2014, LNCS 8593, pp. 84–98, 2014.
DOI: 10.1007/978-3-319-09581-3_7

We consider synchronous point-to-point networks, where each directed link of the underlying communication graph represents a communication channel between a pair of nodes. The link failures are modeled using a *transient Byzantine link* failure model (formal definition in Sect. 2) [15,16], in which different sets of link failures may occur at different times. We consider the problem in arbitrary directed graphs using a *restricted class* of iterative algorithms that maintain only a small amount of memory across iterations, e.g., the algorithms do not require the nodes to have a knowledge of the entire network topology. Such iterative algorithms are of interest in networked systems in which nodes have only constrained power or memory, e.g., large-scale sensor systems, since the iterative algorithms have low complexity and do not rely on global knowledge [12]. In particular, the iterative algorithms have the following properties:

- **Initial state** of each node is equal to a real-valued *input* provided to that node.
- **Termination:** The algorithm terminates in finite number of iterations.
- **Validity:** After each iteration of the algorithm, the state of each node must stay in the *convex hull* of the states of all the nodes at the end of the *previous* iteration.
- **ϵ-agreement:** For any $\epsilon > 0$, when the algorithm terminates, the difference between the outputs at any pair of nodes is guaranteed to be within ϵ.

Main Contribution. This paper extends our recent work on approximate consensus under node failures [21,23]. The main contribution is identifying a *tight* necessary and sufficient condition for the graphs to be able to reach approximate consensus under *transient Byzantine link* failure models [15,16] using restricted iterative algorithms; our proof of correctness follows a structure previously used in our work to prove correctness of other consensus algorithms in incomplete networks [21,24]. The use of matrix analysis is inspired by the prior work on non-fault-tolerant consensus (e.g., [3,8,9]). For lack of space, the proofs of most claims in the paper are omitted here. Further details can be found in [22].

Related Work. Approximate consensus has been studied extensively in synchronous as well as asynchronous systems. Bertsekas and Tsitsiklis explored reaching approximate consensus without failures in a dynamic network, where the underlying communication graph is time-varying [3]. Dolev et al. considered approximate consensus in the presence of *Byzantine nodes* in both synchronous and asynchronous systems [6], where the network is assumed to be a clique, i.e., a complete graph. Subsequently, for complete graphs, Abraham et al. proposed an algorithm to achieve approximate consensus with *Byzantine nodes* in asynchronous systems using optimal number of nodes [1].

Recent work has addressed approximate consensus in incomplete graphs with faulty *nodes* [12,21,23]. References [21,23] and reference [12] showed exact characterizations of graphs in which the approximate consensus problem is solvable in the presence of Byzantine nodes and malicious nodes, respectively. Malicious fault is a restricted type of Byzantine fault in which every node is forced to send an identical message to all of its neighbors [12].

Much effort has also been devoted to the problem of achieving consensus in the presence of link failures [2,4,15,16,18]. Charron-Bost and Schiper proposed a HO (Heard-Of) model that captures both the link and node failures at the same time [4]. However, the failures are assumed to be benign in the sense that no corrupted message will ever be received in the network. Santoro and Widmayer proposed the *transient* Byzantine link failure model: a different set of links can be faulty at different time [15,16]. They characterized a necessary condition and a sufficient condition for undirected networks to achieve consensus in the transient link failure model; however, the necessary and sufficient conditions do not match: the necessary and sufficient conditions are specified in terms of node degree and edge-connectivity,[1] respectively. Subsequently, Biely et al. proposed another link failure model that imposes an upper bound on the number of faulty links incident to each node [2]. As a result, it is possible to tolerate $O(n^2)$ link failures with n nodes in the new model. Under this model, Schmid et al. proved lower bounds on number of nodes, and number of rounds for achieving consensus [18]. However, incomplete graphs were not considered in [2,18].

For consensus problem, it has been shown that (i) an undirected graph of $2f + 1$ node-connectivity[2] is able to tolerate f Byzantine nodes [7]; and (ii) an undirected graph of $2f + 1$ edge-connectivity is able to tolerate f Byzantine links [16]. Independently, researchers showed that $2f + 1$ node-connectivity is both necessary and sufficient for the problem of information dissemination in the presence of either f faulty nodes [20] or f *fixed* faulty links [19].[3]

Link failures have also been addressed under other contexts, such as distributed method for wireless control network [14], reliable transmission over packet network [13], and estimation over noisy links [17].

2 System Model

Communication model: The system is assumed to be *synchronous*. The communication network is modeled as a simple *directed* graph $G = (\mathcal{V}, \mathcal{E})$, where $\mathcal{V} = \{1, \ldots, n\}$ is the set of n nodes, and $\mathcal{E}$ is the set of directed edges between the nodes in $\mathcal{V}$. With a slight abuse of terminology, we will use the terms *edge* and *link* interchangeably in our presentation. In a simple graph, there is at most one directed edge from any node i to any other node j (But our results can be extended to multi-graphs). We assume that $n \geq 2$, since the consensus problem for $n = 1$ is trivial. Node i can transmit messages to node j if and only if the directed edge (i, j) is in $\mathcal{E}$. Each node can send messages to itself as well; however, for convenience, we exclude *self-loops* from set $\mathcal{E}$. That is, $(i, i) \notin \mathcal{E}$ for $i \in \mathcal{V}$.

---

[1] A graph $G = (\mathcal{V}, \mathcal{E})$ is said to be k-edge connected, if $G' = (\mathcal{V}, \mathcal{E} - X)$ is connected for all $X \subseteq \mathcal{E}$ such that $|X| < k$.

[2] A graph $G = (\mathcal{V}, \mathcal{E})$ is said to be k-node connected, if $G' = (\mathcal{V} - X, \mathcal{E})$ is connected for all $X \subseteq \mathcal{V}$ such that $|X| < k$.

[3] Unlike the "transient" failures in our model, the faulty links are assumed to be fixed throughout the execution of the algorithm in [19].

For each node i, let N_i^- be the set of nodes from which i has incoming edges. That is, $N_i^- = \{ j \mid (j,i) \in \mathcal{E} \}$. Similarly, define N_i^+ as the set of nodes to which node i has outgoing edges. That is, $N_i^+ = \{ j \mid (i,j) \in \mathcal{E} \}$. Since we exclude self-loops from $\mathcal{E}$, $i \notin N_i^-$ and $i \notin N_i^+$. However, we note again that each node can indeed send messages to itself. Similarly, let E_i^- be the set of incoming links incident to node i. That is, E_i^- contains all the links from nodes in N_i^- to node i, i.e., $E_i^- = \{ (j,i) \mid j \in N_i^- \}$.

Fault Model. We consider the transient Byzantine *link* failure model [15,16] for iterative algorithms in directed network. All nodes are assumed to be *fault-free*, and only send a single message on each outgoing edge in each iteration. A link (i,j) is said to be faulty *in a certain iteration* if the message sent by node i is different from the message received by node j in that iteration, i.e., the message from i to j is corrupted. Note that in our model, it is possible that link (i,j) is faulty while link (j,i) is fault-free.[4] In every iteration, up to f links may be faulty, i.e., at most f links may deliver corrupted messages or drop messages. Note that different sets of link failures may occur in different iterations.

A faulty link may tamper or drop messages. Also, the faulty links may be controlled by a single omniscient adversary. The adversary is assumed to have a complete knowledge of the execution of the algorithm, including the states of all the nodes, contents of the messages exchanged, the algorithm specification, and the network topology.

3   IABC Algorithms

In this section, we describe the structure of the *Iterative Approximate Byzantine Consensus* (IABC) algorithms of interest, and state conditions that they must satisfy. The IABC structure is identical to the one in our prior work on node failures [21, 23, 24].

Each node i maintains state v_i, with $v_i[t]$ denoting the state of node i at the *end* of the t-th iteration of the algorithm ($t \geq 0$). Initial state of node i, $v_i[0]$, is equal to the initial *input* provided to node i. At the *start* of the t-th iteration ($t > 0$), the state of node i is $v_i[t-1]$. We assume that the input at each node is lower bounded by a constant μ and upper bounded by a constant U. The iterative algorithm may terminate after a number of iterations that is a function of μ and U. μ and U are assumed to be known a priori.

The IABC algorithms of interest will require each node i to perform the following three steps in iteration t, where $t > 0$.

---

[4] For example, the described case is possible in wireless network, if node i's transmitter is broken while node i's receiver and node j's transmitter and receiver all function correctly.

1. *Transmit step:* Transmit current state, namely $v_i[t-1]$, on all outgoing edges (to nodes in N_i^+).
2. *Receive step:* Receive values on all incoming edges (from nodes in N_i^-). Denote by $r_i[t]$ the vector of values received by node i from its neighbors. The size of vector $r_i[t]$ is $|N_i^-|$. The values sent in iteration t are received in the same iteration. If a faulty link drops (discards) a message, it is assumed to have some default value.
3. *Update step:* Node i updates its state using a transition function T_i as follows. T_i is a part of the specification of the algorithm, and takes as input the vector $r_i[t]$ and state $v_i[t-1]$.

$$v_i[t] = T_i \left(\; r_i[t] \, , \; v_i[t-1] \; \right) \tag{1}$$

Finally, the output is set to the state at termination.

The following properties must be satisfied by an IABC algorithm in the presence of up to f Byzantine faulty links in every iteration:

- **Termination:** the algorithm terminates in finite number of iterations.
- **Validity:** $\forall t > 0$, and $\forall i \in V$, $\min_{j \in V} v_j[t-1] \leq v_i[t] \leq \max_{j \in V} v_j[t-1]$.
- **ϵ-agreement:** If the algorithm terminates after t_{end} iterations, then

$$\forall i, j \in V, |v_i[t_{end}] - v_j[t_{end}]| < \epsilon.$$

For a given communication graph $G = (V, \mathcal{E})$, the objective in this paper is to identify the necessary and sufficient conditions in graph G for the existence of a *correct* IABC algorithm (i.e., an algorithm satisfying the above properties).

4   Necessary Condition

For a correct iterative approximate consensus algorithm to exist under transient Byzantine link failures, the graph $G = (V, \mathcal{E})$ must satisfy the necessary condition proved in this section. We first define relations $\Rightarrow$ and $\not\Rightarrow$ introduced in our prior work [23], and a condition on the graph based on $\Rightarrow$.

Definition 1. *For non-empty disjoint sets of nodes A and B in $G' = (V', \mathcal{E}')$, $A \Rightarrow B$ in G' iff there exists a node $i \in B$ that has at least $f+1$ incoming links from nodes in A, i.e., $|\{(j,i) \mid j \in A, \ (j,i) \in \mathcal{E}\}| > f$; $A \not\Rightarrow B$ iff $A \Rightarrow B$ is not true.*

Condition P: Consider graph $G = (V, \mathcal{E})$. Denote by F a subset of $\mathcal{E}$ such that $|F| \leq f$. Let sets L, C, R form a partition of V, such that both L and R are non-empty. Then, in $G' = (V, \mathcal{E} - F)$, at least one of the two conditions below must be true: (i) $C \cup R \Rightarrow L$ or (ii) $L \cup C \Rightarrow R$.

Theorem 1. *Suppose that a correct IABC algorithm exists for $G = (V, \mathcal{E})$. Then G satisfies Condition P.*

Proof. The proof is by contradiction. Let us assume that a correct IABC algorithm exists in $G = (\mathcal{V}, \mathcal{E})$, and for some node partition L, C, R of $\mathcal{V}$ and a subset $F \subseteq \mathcal{E}$ such that $|F| \leq f$, $C \cup R \not\Rightarrow L$ and $L \cup C \not\Rightarrow R$ in $G' = (\mathcal{V}, \mathcal{E}')$, where $\mathcal{E}' = \mathcal{E} - F$. Thus, for any $i \in L$, $|\{(k, i) \mid k \in C \cup R, (k, i) \in \mathcal{E} - F\}| \leq f$. Similarly, for any $j \in R$, $|\{(k, j) \mid k \in L \cup C, (k, j) \in \mathcal{E} - F\}| \leq f$.

Also assume that all the links in F (if F is non-empty) are faulty, and the rest of the links are fault-free in every iteration. Note that the nodes are not aware of the identity of the faulty links.

Consider the case when (i) each node in L has initial input m, (ii) each node in R has initial input M, such that $M > m + \epsilon$, and (iii) each node in C, if C is non-empty, has an input in the interval $[m, M]$. Define m^- and M^+ such that $m^- < m$ and $M < M^+$.

In the *Transmit Step* of iteration 1 in the IABC algorithm, each node k, sends to nodes in N_k^+ value $v_k[0]$; however, some values sent via faulty links may be tampered. Suppose that the messages sent via the faulty links in F (if non-empty) are tampered in the following way: (i) if the link is an incoming link to a node in L, then $m^- < m$ is delivered to that node; (ii) if the link is an incoming link to a node in R, then $M^+ > M$ is delivered to that node; and (iii) if the link is an incoming link to a node in C, then some arbitrary value in interval $[m, M]$ is delivered to that node. This behavior is possible since links in F are Byzantine faulty by assumption.

Consider any node $i \in L$. Recall that E_i^- is the set of all the incoming links at node i. Let E_i' be the subset of links in E_i^- from the nodes in $C \cup R$, i.e.,

$$E_i' = \{(j, i) \mid j \in C \cup R, (j, i) \in \mathcal{E}\}.$$

Since $|F| \leq f$, $|E_i^- \cap F| \leq f$. Moreover, by assumption $C \cup R \not\Rightarrow L$; thus, $|E_i'| \leq f$, and we have $|E_i' - F| \leq |E_i'| \leq f$. Node i will then receive m^- via the links in $E_i^- \cap F$ (if non-empty) and values in $[m, M]$ via the links in $E_i' - F$, and m via the rest of the links, i.e., links in $E_i^- - E_i' - F$.

Consider the following two cases:

- Both $E_i^- \cap F$ and $E_i' - F$ are non-empty:
  In this case, recall that $|E_i^- \cap F| \leq f$ and $|E_i' - F| \leq f$. From node i's perspective, consider two possible scenarios: (a) links in $E_i^- \cap F$ are faulty, and the other links are fault-free, and (b) links in $E_i' - F$ are faulty, and the other links are fault-free.

  In scenario (a), from node i's perspective, all the nodes may have sent values in interval $[m, M]$, but the faulty links have tampered the message so that m^- is delivered to node i. According to the validity property, $v_i[1] \geq m$. On the other hand, in scenario (b), all the nodes may have sent values m^- or m, where $m^- < m$; so $v_i[1] \leq m$, according to the validity property. Since node i does not know whether the correct scenario is (a) or (b), it must update its state to satisfy the validity property in both cases. Thus, it follows that $v_i[1] = m$.

– At most one of $E_i^- \cap F$ and $E_i' - F$ is non-empty:
Recall that by assumption, $\left| E_i^- \cap F \right| \leq f$ and $\left| E_i' - F \right| \leq f$. Since at most one of the set is non-empty, $\left| (E_i^- \cap F) \cup (E_i' - F) \right| \leq f$. From node i's perspective, it is possible that the links in $(E_i^- \cap F) \cup (E_i' - F)$ are all faulty, and the rest of the links are fault-free. In this situation, all the nodes have sent m to node i, and therefore, $v_i[1]$ must be set to m as per the validity property.

Thus, $v_i[1] = m$ for each node $i \in L$. Similarly, we can show that $v_j[1] = M$ for each node $j \in R$.

Now consider the nodes in set C, if C is non-empty. All the values received by the nodes in C are in $[m, M]$; therefore, their new state must also remain in $[m, M]$, as per the *validity* property.

The above discussion implies that, at the end of iteration 1, the following conditions hold true: (i) state of each node in L is m, (ii) state of each node in R is M, and (iii) state of each node in C is in the interval $[m, M]$. These conditions are identical to the initial conditions listed previously. Then, by a repeated application of the above argument (proof by induction), it follows that for any $t \geq 0$, (i) $v_i[t] = m$ for all $i \in L$; (ii) $v_j[t] = M$ for all $j \in R$; and (iii) $v_k[t] \in [m, M]$ for all $k \in C$.

Since both L and R are non-empty, the ϵ-*agreement* property is not satisfied. A contradiction. □

Theorem 1 shows that *Condition P* is necessary. However, *Condition P* is not intuitive. Below, we state an equivalent condition *Condition S* that is easier to interpret. To facilitate the statement, we introduce the notions of "source component" and "link-reduced graph" using the following three definitions. The link-reduced graph is analogous to the concept introduced in our prior work on node failures [21,23,24].

Definition 2. Graph decomposition ([5])**.** *Let H be a directed graph. Partition graph H into non-empty strongly connected components, $H_1, H_2, \cdots, H_h$, where h is a non-zero integer dependent on graph H, such that*

– *every pair of nodes within the same strongly connected component has directed paths in H to each other, and*
– *for each pair of nodes, say i and j, that belong to two different strongly connected components, either i does not have a directed path to j in H, or j does not have a directed path to i in H.*

Construct a graph H^d wherein each strongly connected component H_k above is represented by vertex c_k, and there is an edge from vertex c_k to vertex c_l if and only if the nodes in H_k have directed paths in H to the nodes in H_l.
It is known that the decomposition graph H^d is a directed *acyclic* graph [5].

Definition 3. Source component. *Let H be a directed graph, and let H^d be its decomposition as per Definition 2. Strongly connected component H_k of H is said to be a* source component *if the corresponding vertex c_k in H^d is <u>not</u> reachable from any other vertex in H^d.*

Definition 4. Link-Reduced Graph. *For a given graph* $G = (V, \mathcal{E})$ *and* $F \subset \mathcal{E}$, *a graph* $G_F = (V, \mathcal{E}_F)$ *is said to be a* link-reduced graph, *if* $\mathcal{E}_F$ *is obtained by first removing from* $\mathcal{E}$ *all the links in* F, *and then at each node, removing up to* f *other incoming links in* $\mathcal{E} - F$.

Note that for a given $G = (V, \mathcal{E})$ and a given F, multiple link-reduced graphs G_F may exist. Now, we state *Condition S* based on the concept of link-reduce graphs:

Condition S: Consider graph $G = (V, \mathcal{E})$. For any $F \subseteq \mathcal{E}$ such that $|F| \leq f$, every link-reduced graph G_F obtained as per Definition 4 must contain exactly one *source component.*

Now, we present a key lemma below. The proof is omitted for lack of space. This proof, and the other omitted proofs in the paper are presented in [22].

Lemma 1. Condition P *is equivalent to* Condition S.

An alternate interpretation of *Condition S* is that in every link-reduced graph G_F, non-fault-tolerant iterative consensus must be possible. We will use this intuition to prove that *Condition S* is sufficient in Sect. 6. Then, by Lemma 1, *Condition P* is also sufficient.

4.1   Useful Properties

Suppose $G = (V, \mathcal{E})$ satisfies *Condition P* and *Condition S*. We provide two lemmas below to state some properties of $G = (V, \mathcal{E})$ that are useful for analyzing the iterative algorithm presented later. The proofs are presented in [22].

Lemma 2. *Suppose that graph* $G = (V, \mathcal{E})$ *satisfies* Condition S. *Then, in any link-reduced graph* $G_F = (V, \mathcal{E}_F)$, *there exists a node that has a directed path to all the other nodes in* V.

Lemma 3. *For* $f > 0$, *if graph* $G = (V, \mathcal{E})$ *satisfies* Condition P, *then each node in* V *has in-degree at least* $2f + 1$, *i.e., for each* $i \in V$, $\left|N_i^-\right| \geq 2f + 1$.

5   Algorithm 1

We will prove that there exists a correct IABC algorithm – particularly Algorithm 1 below – that satisfies the termination, validity and ϵ-agreement properties provided that the graph $G = (V, \mathcal{E})$ satisfies *Condition S*. This implies that *Condition P* and *Condition S* ares also sufficient. Algorithm 1 has the iterative structure described in Sect. 3, and it is similar to algorithms that were analyzed in prior work as well [21, 23] (although correctness of the algorithm under the necessary condition – *Conditions P* and *S* – has not been proved previously).

Algorithm 1

---

1. *Transmit step:* Transmit current state $v_i[t-1]$ on all outgoing edges.
2. *Receive step:* Receive values on all incoming edges. These values form vector $r_i[t]$ of size $|N_i^-|$. If a faulty incoming edge drops the message, then the message value is assumed to be equal to the state at node i, i.e., $v_i[t-1]$.
3. *Update step:* Sort the values in $r_i[t]$ in an increasing order (breaking ties arbitrarily), and eliminate the smallest and largest f values. Let $N_i^*[t]$ denote the set of nodes from whom the remaining $|N_i^-| - 2f$ values in $r_i[t]$ were received. Note that as proved in Lemma 3, each node has at least $2f + 1$ incoming neighbors if $f > 0$. Thus, when $f > 0$, $|N_i^*[t]| \geq 1$. Let w_j denote the value received from node $j \in N_i^*[t]$, and for convenience, define $w_i = v_i[t-1]$. Observe that if the link from $j \in N_i^*[t]$ is fault-free, then $w_j = v_j[t-1]$.
Define
$$v_i[t] = T_i(r_i[t], v_i[t-1]) = \sum_{j \in \{i\} \cup N_i^*[t]} a_i\, w_j \qquad (2)$$

where
$$a_i = \frac{1}{|N_i^*[t]| + 1} = \frac{1}{|N_i^-| + 1 - 2f}$$

The "weight" of each term on the right-hand side of (2) is a_i. Note that $|N_i^*[t]| = |N_i^-| - 2f$, and $i \notin N_i^*[t]$ because $(i,i) \notin \mathcal{E}$. Thus, the weights on the right-hand side add to 1. Also, $0 < a_i \leq 1$.

Termination: Each node terminates after completing iteration t_{end}, where t_{end} is a constant defined later in Equation (9). The value of t_{end} depends on graph $G = (\mathcal{V}, \mathcal{E})$, constants U and μ defined earlier in Sect. 3 and parameter ϵ in ϵ-agreement property.

---

6 Sufficiency (Correctness of Algorithm 1)

We will prove that given a graph $G = (\mathcal{V}, \mathcal{E})$ satisfying *Condition S*, Algorithm 1 is correct, i.e., Algorithm 1 satisfies *termination, validity, ϵ-agreement* properties. Therefore, *Condition S* and *Condition P* are proved to be sufficient. We borrow the matrix analysis from the work on non-fault-tolerant consensus [3,8,9]. The proof below follows the same structure in our prior work on node failures [21,24]; however, such analysis has not been applied in the case of link failures.

In the rest of the section, we assume that $G = (\mathcal{V}, \mathcal{F})$ satisfies *Condition S* and *Condition P*. We first introduce standard matrix tools to facilitate our proof. Then, we use transition matrix to represent the *Update* step in Algorithm 1, and show how to use these tools to prove the correctness of Algorithm 1 in $G = (\mathcal{V}, \mathcal{F})$.

6.1   Matrix Preliminaries

In the discussion below, we use boldface upper case letters to denote matrices, rows of matrices, and their elements. For instance, $\mathbf{A}$ denotes a matrix, $\mathbf{A}_i$ denotes the i-th row of matrix $\mathbf{A}$, and $\mathbf{A}_{ij}$ denotes the element at the intersection of the i-th row and the j-th column of matrix $\mathbf{A}$.

Definition 5. *A vector is said to be* stochastic *if all the elements of the vector are non-negative, and the elements add up to 1. A matrix is said to be* row stochastic *if each row of the matrix is a stochastic vector.*

When presenting matrix products, for convenience of presentation, we adopt the "backward" product convention below, where $a \leq b$,

$$\Pi_{i=a}^{b}\mathbf{A}[i] = \mathbf{A}[b]\mathbf{A}[b-1]\cdots\mathbf{A}[a] \tag{3}$$

For a row stochastic matrix $\mathbf{A}$, coefficients of ergodicity $\delta(\mathbf{A})$ and $\lambda(\mathbf{A})$ are defined as follows [25]:

$$\delta(\mathbf{A}) = \max_j \max_{i_1,i_2} |\mathbf{A}_{i_1 j} - \mathbf{A}_{i_2 j}|$$

$$\lambda(\mathbf{A}) = 1 - \min_{i_1,i_2} \sum_j \min(\mathbf{A}_{i_1 j}, \mathbf{A}_{i_2 j})$$

Lemma 4. *For any p square row stochastic matrices $\mathbf{A}(1), \mathbf{A}(2), \ldots, \mathbf{A}(p)$,*

$$\delta(\Pi_{u=1}^{p}\mathbf{A}(u)) \leq \Pi_{u=1}^{p}\lambda(\mathbf{A}(u))$$

Lemma 4 is proved in [8]. Lemma 5 below follows from the definition of $\lambda(\cdot)$.

Lemma 5. *If all the elements in any one column of matrix $\mathbf{A}$ are lower bounded by a constant γ, then $\lambda(\mathbf{A}) \leq 1 - \gamma$. That is, if $\exists g$, such that $\mathbf{A}_{ig} \geq \gamma$ $\forall i$, then $\lambda(\mathbf{A}) \leq 1 - \gamma$.*

It is easy to show that $0 \leq \delta(\mathbf{A}) \leq 1$ and $0 \leq \lambda(\mathbf{A}) \leq 1$, and that the rows of $\mathbf{A}$ are all identical iff $\delta(\mathbf{A}) = 0$. Also, $\lambda(\mathbf{A}) = 0$ iff $\delta(\mathbf{A}) = 0$.

6.2   Correctness of Algorithm 1

Denote by $v[0]$ the column vector consisting of the initial states at all nodes. The i-th element of $v[0]$, $v_i[0]$, is the initial state of node i. Denote by $v[t]$, for $t \geq 1$, the column vector consisting of the states of all nodes at the end of the t-th iteration. The i-th element of vector $v[t]$ is state $v_i[t]$.

For $t \geq 1$, define $F[t]$ to be the set of all faulty links in iteration t. Recall that link (j, i) is said to be faulty in iteration t if the value received by node i is different from what node j sent in iteration t. Then, define N_i^F as the set of all nodes whose outgoing links to node i are faulty in iteration t, i.e.,[5]

---

[5] N_i^F may be different for each iteration t. For simplicity, the notation does not explicitly represent this dependence.

$$N_i^F = \{j \mid j \in N_i^-, \ (j,i) \in F[t]\}.$$

Now we state a key lemma. In particular, Lemma 6 allows us to use results for non-homogeneous Markov chains to prove the correctness of Algorithm 1. The proof is presented in [22].

Lemma 6. *The* Update *step in iteration* t $(t \geq 1)$ *of Algorithm 1 at the nodes can be expressed as*

$$v[t] = \boldsymbol{M}[t]v[t-1] \tag{4}$$

where $\boldsymbol{M}[t]$ *is an* $n \times n$ *row stochastic transition matrix with the following property: there exist* N_i^r, *a subset of incoming neighbors at node* i *of size at most* f,[6] *and a constant* β $(0 < \beta \leq 1)$ *that depends only on graph* $G = (\mathcal{V}, \mathcal{E})$ *such that for each* $i \in \mathcal{V}$, *and for all* $j \in \{i\} \cup (N_i^- - N_i^F - N_i^r)$,

$$\boldsymbol{M}_{ij}[t] \geq \beta.$$

Matrix $\boldsymbol{M}[t]$ is said to be a <u>transition matrix</u> for iteration t. As the lemma states above, $\boldsymbol{M}[t]$ is a row stochastic matrix. The proof of Lemma 6 shows how to construct a suitable row stochastic matrix $\boldsymbol{M}[t]$ for each iteration t (presented in [22]). $\boldsymbol{M}[t]$ depends not only on t but also on the behavior of the faulty links in iteration t.

Theorem 2. *Algorithm 1 satisfies the* Termination, Validity, *and* ϵ-agreement *properties.*

Proof. Sects. 6.3–6.5 provide the proof that Algorithm 1 satisfies the three properties for iterative approximate consensus in the presence of Byzantine links. This proof follows a structure used to prove correctness of other consensus algorithms in our prior work [21,24]. □

6.3   Validity Property

Observe that $\boldsymbol{M}[t+1](\boldsymbol{M}[t]v[t-1]) = (\boldsymbol{M}[t+1]\boldsymbol{M}[t])v[t-1]$. Therefore, by repeated application of (4), we obtain for $t \geq 1$,

$$v[t] = (\Pi_{u=1}^t \boldsymbol{M}[u])v[0] \tag{5}$$

Since each $\boldsymbol{M}[u]$ is row stochastic as shown in Lemma 6, the matrix product $\Pi_{u=1}^t \boldsymbol{M}[u]$ is also a row stochastic matrix. Thus, (5) implies that the state of each node i at the end of iteration t can be expressed as a convex combination of the initial states at all the nodes. Therefore, the validity property is satisfied.

---

[6] Intuitively, N_i^r corresponds to the links removed in some link-reduced graph. Thus, the superscript r in the notation stands for "removed." Also, N_i^r may be different for each t. For simplicity, the notation does not explicitly represent this dependence.

6.4   Termination Property

Algorithm 1 terminates after t_{end} iterations, where t_{end} is a finite constant depending only on $G = (\mathcal{V}, \mathcal{E}), U, \mu$, and ϵ. Recall that U and μ are defined as upper and lower bounds of the initial inputs at all nodes, respectively. Therefore, trivially, the algorithm satisfies the termination property. Later, using (9), we define a suitable value for t_{end}.

6.5 ϵ-Agreement Property

Denote by R_F the set of all the link-reduced graph of $G = (\mathcal{V}, \mathcal{E})$ corresponding to some faulty link set F. Let

$$r = \sum_{F \subset \mathcal{E},\ |F| \leq f} |R_F|$$

Note that r only depends on $G = (\mathcal{V}, \mathcal{E})$ and f, and is a finite integer.

Consider iteration t ($t \geq 1$). Recall that $F[t]$ denotes the set of faulty links in iteration t. Then for each link-reduced graph $H[t] \in R_{F[t]}$, define connectivity matrix $\mathbf{H}[t]$ as follows, where $1 \leq i, j \leq n$:

– $\mathbf{H}_{ij}[t] = 1$, if either $j = i$, or edge (j, i) exists in link-reduced graph H;
– $\mathbf{H}_{ij}[t] = 0$, otherwise.

Thus, the non-zero elements of row $\mathbf{H}_i[t]$ correspond to the incoming links at node i in the link-reduced graph $H[t]$, or the self-loop at i. Observe that $\mathbf{H}[t]$ has a non-zero diagonal.

Based on *Condition S* and Lemmas 2 and 6, we can show the following key lemmas. The omitted proofs are presented in [22].

Lemma 7. *For any $H[t] \in R_{F[t]}$, and $k \geq n$, $\mathbf{H}^k[t]$ has at least one non-zero column, i.e., a column with all elements non-zero.*

Then, Lemma 7 can be used to prove the following lemma.

Lemma 8. *For any $z \geq 1$, at least one column in the matrix product $\Pi_{t=u}^{u+rn-1} \mathbf{H}[t]$ is non-zero.*

For matrices $\mathbf{A}$ and $\mathbf{B}$ of identical dimension, we say that $\mathbf{A} \leq \mathbf{B}$ iff $\mathbf{A}_{ij} \leq \mathbf{B}_{ij}$ for all i, j. Lemma below relates the transition matrices with the connectivity matrices. Constant β used in the lemma below was introduced in Lemma 6.

Lemma 9. *For any $t \geq 1$, there exists a link-reduced graph $H[t] \in R_{F[t]}$ such that $\beta \mathbf{H}[t] \leq M[t]$, where $\mathbf{H}[t]$ is the connectivity matrix for $H[t]$.*

Let us now define a sequence of matrices $\mathbf{Q}(i)$, $i \geq 1$, such that each of these matrices is a product of rn of the $\mathbf{M}[t]$ matrices. Specifically,

$$\mathbf{Q}(i) = \Pi_{t=(i-1)rn+1}^{irn} \mathbf{M}[t] \tag{6}$$

From (5) and (6) observe that

$$v[krn] = \left(\Pi_{i=1}^{k} \mathbf{Q}(i) \right) v[0] \tag{7}$$

Based on (7), Lemmas 6, 8, and 9, we can show the following lemma.

Lemma 10. *For $i \geq 1$, $\mathbf{Q}(i)$ is a row stochastic matrix, and*

$$\lambda(\mathbf{Q}(i)) \leq 1 - \beta^{rn}.$$

Let us now continue with the proof of ϵ-agreement. Consider the coefficient of ergodicity $\delta(\Pi_{u=1}^{t}\mathbf{M}[u])$.

$$
\begin{aligned}
\delta(\Pi_{u=1}^{t}\mathbf{M}[u]) &= \delta\left(\left(\Pi_{u=(\lfloor \frac{t}{rn} \rfloor)rn+1}^{t}\mathbf{M}[u] \right) \left(\Pi_{u=1}^{\lfloor \frac{t}{rn} \rfloor}\mathbf{Q}(u) \right) \right) && \text{by definition of } \mathbf{Q}(u) \\
&\leq \lambda\left(\Pi_{u=(\lfloor \frac{t}{rn} \rfloor)rn+1}^{t}\mathbf{M}[u] \right) \left(\Pi_{u=1}^{\lfloor \frac{t}{rn} \rfloor}\lambda(\mathbf{Q}(u)) \right) && \text{by Lemma 4} \\
&\leq \Pi_{u=1}^{\lfloor \frac{t}{rn} \rfloor}\lambda(\mathbf{Q}(u)) && \text{because } \lambda(\cdot) \leq 1 \\
&\leq (1 - \beta^{rn})^{\lfloor \frac{t}{rn} \rfloor} && \text{by Lemma 10} \tag{8}
\end{aligned}
$$

Observe that the upper bound on right side of (8) depends only on graph $G = (\mathcal{V}, \mathcal{E})$ and t, and is independent of the input states, and the behavior of the faulty links. Moreover, the upper bound on the right side of (8) is a non-increasing function of t. Define t_{end} as the smallest positive integer such that the right hand side of (8) is smaller than $\frac{\epsilon}{n \max(|U|,|\mu|)}$. Recall that U and μ are defined as the upper and lower bound of the inputs at all nodes. Thus,

$$\delta(\Pi_{u=1}^{t_{end}}\mathbf{M}[u]) \leq (1 - \beta^{rn})^{\lfloor \frac{t_{end}}{rn} \rfloor} < \frac{\epsilon}{n \max(|U|,|\mu|)} \tag{9}$$

Recall that β and r depend only on $G = (\mathcal{V}, \mathcal{E})$. Thus, t_{end} depends only on graph $G = (\mathcal{V}, \mathcal{E})$, and constants U, μ and ϵ.

By construction, $\Pi_{u=1}^{t}\mathbf{M}[u]$ is an $n \times n$ row stochastic matrix. Let $\mathbf{M}^{*} = \Pi_{u=1}^{t}\mathbf{M}[u]$. We omit time index $[t]$ from the notation $\mathbf{M}^{*}$ for simplicity. From (5), we have $v_j[t] = \mathbf{M}_j^{*}v[0]$. That is, the state of any node j can be obtained as the product of the j-th row of $\mathbf{M}^{*}$ and $v[0]$. Now, consider any two nodes j, k. By simple algebraic manipulation (the omitted steps are presented in [22]), we have

$$
\begin{aligned}
|v_j[t] - v_k[t]| &= \left| \Sigma_{i=1}^{n}\mathbf{M}_{ji}^{*}v_i[0] - \Sigma_{i=1}^{n}\mathbf{M}_{ki}^{*}v_i[0] \right| \\
&\leq \Sigma_{i=1}^{n} \left| \mathbf{M}_{ji}^{*} - \mathbf{M}_{ki}^{*} \right| \ |v_i[0]| \\
&\leq \Sigma_{i=1}^{n}\delta(\mathbf{M}^{*}) \ |v_i[0]| \\
&\leq n\delta(\Pi_{u=1}^{t}\mathbf{M}[u]) \ \max(|U|,|\mu|) \tag{10}
\end{aligned}
$$

Therefore, by (9) and (10), we have

$$|v_j[t_{end}] - v_k[t_{end}]| < \epsilon \tag{11}$$

Since the output of the nodes equals its state at termination (after t_{end} iterations). Thus, (11) implies that Algorithm 1 satisfies the ϵ-agreement property.

7 Summary

This paper explores approximate consensus problem under transient Byzantine link failure model. We address a particular class of iterative algorithms in arbitrary directed graphs, and prove the *tight* necessary and sufficient condition for the graphs to be able to solve the approximate consensus problem in the presence of Byzantine links iteratively.

References

1. Abraham, I., Amit, Y., Dolev, D.: Optimal resilience asynchronous approximate agreement. In: Higashino, T. (ed.) OPODIS 2004. LNCS, vol. 3544, pp. 229–239. Springer, Heidelberg (2005)
2. Biely, M., Schmid, U., Weiss, B.: Synchronous consensus under hybrid process and link failures. Theor. Comput. Sci. **412**(40), 5602–5630 (2011)
3. Bertsekas, D.P., Tsitsiklis, J.N.: Parallel and Distributed Computation: Numerical Methods. Optimization and Neural Computation Series. Athena Scientific, Belmont (1997)
4. Charron-Bost, B., Schiper, A.: The Heard-Of model: computing in distributed systems with benign faults. Distrib. Comput. **22**(1), 49–71 (2009)
5. Dasgupta, S., Papadimitriou, C., Vazirani, U.: Algorithms. McGraw-Hill Higher Education, Boston (2006)
6. Dolev, D., Lynch, N.A., Pinter, S.S., Stark, E.W., Weihl, W.E.: Reaching approximate agreement in the presence of faults. J. ACM **33**(3), 499–516 (1986)
7. Fischer, M.J., Lynch, N.A., Merritt, M.: Easy impossibility proofs for distributed consensus problems. In: PODC '85. ACM (1985)
8. Hajnal, J.: Weak Ergodicity in non-homogeneous Markov chains. Proc. Cambridge Philos. Soc. **54**, 233–246 (1958)
9. Jadbabaie, A., Lin, J., Morse, A.: Coordination of groups of mobile autonomous agents using nearest neighbor rules. IEEE Trans. Autom. Control **48**(6), 988–1001 (2003)
10. Kempe, D., Dobra, A., Gehrke, J.: Gossip-based computation of aggregate information. In: IEEE Symposium on Foundations of Computer Science, October 2003
11. Lamport, L., Shostak, R., Pease, M.: The Byzantine generals problem. ACM Trans. Program. Lang. Syst. **4**(3), 382–401 (1982)
12. LeBlanc, H.J., Zhang, H., Koutsoukos, X., Sundaram, S.: Resilient asymptotic consensus in robust networks. IEEE J. Sel. Areas Commun. **31**(4), 766–781 (2013)
13. Lun, D.S., Médard, M., Koetter, R., Effros, M.: On coding for reliable communication over packet networks. Phys. Commun. **1**(1), 3–20 (2008)
14. Pajic, M., Sundaram, S., Le Ny, J., Pappas, G.J., Mangharam, R.: Closing the loop: A simple distributed method for control over wireless networks. In: International Conference on Information Processing in Sensor Networks (2012)
15. Santoro, N., Widmayer, P.: Time is not a healer. In: Monien, B., Cori, R. (eds.) STACS 89. LNCS, vol. 349, pp. 304–313. Springer, Heidelberg (1989)
16. Santoro, N., Widmayer, P.: Agreement in synchronous networks with ubiquitous faults. Theor. Comput. Sci. **384**(2–3), 232–249 (2007)
17. Schizas, I.D., Ribeiro, A., Giannakis, G.B.: Consensus in ad hoc WSNs with noisy links- Part I: distributed estimation of deterministic signals. IEEE Trans. Sig. Process. **56**(1), 350–364 (2008)

18. Schmid, U., Weiss, B., Keidar, I.: Impossibility results and lower bounds for consensus under link failures. SIAM J. Comput. **38**(5), 1912–1951 (2009)
19. Sundaram, S., Revzen, S., Pappas, G.: A control-theoretic approach to disseminating values and overcoming malicious links in wireless networks. Automatica **57**(9), 2308–2311 (2012)
20. Sundaram, S., Hadjicostis, C.N.: Distributed function calculation via linear iterative strategies in the presence of malicious agent. IEEE Trans. Autom. Control **56**(7), 1495–1508 (2011)
21. Tseng, L., Vaidya, N.: Iterative approximate Byzantine consensus under a generalized fault model. In: Frey, D., Raynal, M., Sarkar, S., Shyamasundar, R.K., Sinha, P. (eds.) ICDCN 2013. LNCS, vol. 7730, pp. 72–86. Springer, Heidelberg (2013)
22. Tseng, L., Vaidya, N.H.: Iterative approximate consensus in the presence of Byzantine link failures. Technical report, UIUC (2014). http://www.crhc.illinois.edu/wireless/papers/ByzantineLink.pdf
23. Vaidya, N.H., Tseng, L., Liang, G.: Iterative approximate Byzantine consensus in arbitrary directed graphs. In: PODC '12. ACM (2012)
24. Vaidya, N.H.: Iterative Byzantine vector consensus in incomplete graphs. In: Chatterjee, M., Cao, J., Kothapalli, K., Rajsbaum, S. (eds.) ICDCN 2014. LNCS, vol. 8314, pp. 14–28. Springer, Heidelberg (2014)
25. Wolfowitz, J.: Products of indecomposable, aperiodic, stochastic matrices. Proc. Am. Math. Soc. **14**, 733–737 (1963)

Practically Self-stabilizing Paxos Replicated State-Machine

Peva Blanchard[1]([✉]), Shlomi Dolev[2], Joffroy Beauquier[1], and Sylvie Delaët[1]

[1] LRI, Paris-Sud XI University, Orsay, France
{blanchard,jb,delaet}@lri.fr
[2] Department of Computer Science,
Ben-Gurion University of the Negev, 84105 Beer-Sheva, Israel
dolev@cs.bgu.ac.il

Abstract. We present the first (practically) self-stabilizing replicated state machine for asynchronous message passing systems. The scheme is based on a variant of the Paxos algorithm and ensures that starting from an arbitrary configuration, the replicated state-machine eventually exhibits the desired behaviour for a long enough execution regarding all practical considerations.

1 Introduction

To provide a highly reliable system, a common approach is to replicate a state-machine over many servers (replicas). From the system's client point of view, the replicas implement a unique state-machine which acts in a sequential manner. This problem is related to the Consensus problem. Indeed, if all the replicas initially share the same state and if they execute the same requests in the same order, then the system is coherent from the client's point of view. In other words, we can picture the system as a sequence of Consensus instances that decide on the request to execute at each step. In an asynchronous message-passing system prone to crash failures, solving a single consensus instance has been proven impossible [10]. This hinders the possibility of a state-machine replication protocol.

Lamport, however, has provided an algorithmic scheme, namely Paxos [14, 15], that partially satisfies the requirements of state-machine replication in the following sense. The safety property (two processes cannot decide to execute different requests for the same step) is always guaranteed. On the other hand, the liveness property (every non-crashed process eventually decides) requires additional assumptions, usually any means to elect a unique leader for a long enough period of time. Note that the original formulation [15] presented Paxos as a (partial) solution to the Consensus problem, but its actual purpose is to

Partially supported by Deutsche Telekom, Rita Altura Trust Chair in Computer Sciences, Israeli Internet Association, Israeli Ministry of Science, Lynne and William Frankel Center for Computer Sciences, and Israel Science Foundation (grant number 428/11).

© Springer International Publishing Switzerland 2014
G. Noubir and M. Raynal (Eds.): NETYS 2014, LNCS 8593, pp. 99–121, 2014.
DOI: 10.1007/978-3-319-09581-3_8

implement a replicated state-machine. Since then, many improvements have been proposed, e.g., Fast Paxos [17], Generalized Paxos [16], Byzantine Paxos [18], and the study of Paxos has become a subject of research on its own. The extreme usefulness of such an approach is proven daily by the usage of this technique by the very leading companies [5].

Unfortunately, none of these approaches deal with the issue of transient faults. A transient fault may put the system in a completely arbitrary configuration. In the context of replicated state-machine, the consequences (among many other unanticipated scenarios) may be the following: (a) the states of the replica are incoherent, (b) the replicas never execute the same requests in the same order, (c) the replicas are blocked even if the usual liveness conditions (e.g., unique leader) are satisfied. The issues (a) and (b) hinder the linearizability of the state-machine, whereas the issue (c) hinders the liveness of the state-machine.

A self-stabilizing system is able to recover from any transient fault after a finite period of time. In other words, after any transient fault, a self-stabilizing system ensures that eventually the replicas have coherent states, execute the same requests in the same order and progress is achieved when the liveness conditions are satisfied.

Nevertheless, completing this goal is rather difficult. One of the main ingredients of any Paxos-based replicated state-machine algorithm is its ability to distinguish old and new messages. At a very abstract level, one uses natural numbers to timestamp data, i.e., each processor is assumed to have an infinite memory. At a more concrete level, the processes have a finite memory, and the simplest timestamp structure is given by a natural number bounded by some constant 2^b (b-bits counter). Roughly speaking, this implies that the classic Paxos-based replicated state-machine approach is able to distinguish messages in a window of size 2^b.

This constant is so large that it is sufficient for any practical purposes, as long as transient faults are not considered. For example, if a 64-bits counter is initialized to 0, incrementing the counter every nanosecond will last about 500 years before the maximum value is reached; this is far greater than any concrete system's timescale. But, a transient fault may corrupt the timestamps (e.g., counters set to the maximum value) and, thus, lead to replicas executing requests in different order or being permanently blocked although the usual liveness related conditions (e.g., unique leader) are satisfied.

This remark leads to a realistic form of self-stabilizing systems, namely *practically self-stabilizing systems*. Roughly speaking, after any transient fault, a practically self-stabilizing system is ensured to reach a finite segment of execution during which its behavior is correct, this segment being "long enough" relatively to some predefined timescale. We give details in Sect. 2.

In this paper, we provide a new bounded timestamp architecture and describe the core of a practically self-stabilizing replicated state-machine, in an asynchronous message passing communication environment prone to crash failures.

Related work. If a process undergoes a transient fault, then one can model the process behaviour as a Byzantine behaviour. In [4], Castro and Liskov present a concrete[1] replicated state-machine algorithm that copes with Byzantine failures. Lamport presents in [18] a Byzantine tolerant variant of Paxos which has some connections with Castro and Liskov's solution. Note, however, that in both cases, the number of Byzantine processes must be less than one third of the total number of processes. This is related to the impossibility of a Byzantine tolerant solution to Consensus where more than one third of the system are Byzantine. The approach of self-stabilization is comprehensive, rather than addressing specific fault scenarios (risking to miss a scenario), and thus is somehow orthogonal to Byzantine fault tolerance. The issue of bounded timestamp system has been studied in [6,12], but these works do not deal with self-stabilization. The first work, as far as we know, on a self-stabilizing timestamp system is presented in [1], but it assumes communications based on a shared memory. In [2,9], the authors present the notion of practically stabilizing algorithm and provide an implementation of practically self-stabilizing replicated state machine using shared memory, and the message passing implementation of a practically self-stabilizing single-write multi-reader atomic register. Doing so, they introduce a self-stabilizing timestamp system. However, their approach assumes that a single processor (the writer) is responsible for incrementing timestamps and stabilization is conditional on such write executions. Our timestamp system is a generalization which allows many processors to increment timestamps. A first formulation of the present work has been given in [3].

The paper starts with a background and description of techniques and correctness in a nutshell. Then we turn to a more formal and detailed description.

2   Overview

In this section, we define the Replicated State-Machine (RSM) problem and give an overview of the Paxos algorithm. In addition, we give arguments for the need of a self-stabilizing algorithm that would solve the Replicated State-Machine Problem. Doing so, we investigate the recently defined kind of self-stabilizing behaviour, namely the *practically self-stabilizing* behaviour, and also briefly present the core idea of our algorithm.

Replicated State-Machine. Replicated State-Machine (RSM) aims at providing a reliable service to clients. From the client point of view, it is only required that the RSM acts as a correct sequential machine, and that every client request eventually gets a response. Formally, the problem is defined by the two following properties: *(Safety)* every execution yields a history of client requests and responses that is linearizable [11], *(Liveness)* in this history, every request has a corresponding response.

Original Paxos. Although the original Paxos algorithm [15] has been formulated as a (partial) solution to the Consensus problem, its actual purpose is to

---

[1] In their paper, "practical" is not related to our notion of practical self-stabilization.

implement a RSM. Hence, in the following, our presentation of Paxos will include aspects related to the RSM problem.

The original Paxos algorithm allows to implement a RSM property in an asynchronous complete network of processors communicating by message-passing such that less than half of the processors are prone to crash failures. Precisely, the safety of the RSM is always guaranteed, whereas the liveness is guaranteed if some conditions (e.g., unique leader) are satisfied. We refer to these conditions as the *liveness conditions*. The algorithm uses unbounded integers and also assumes that the system starts in a consistent initial configuration.

If it were possible to elect a unique leader in the system, then implementing a replicated state-machine would be easy: this leader receives the client requests, chooses an order, and tells the other processors. But, since the leader may crash (no more leader), and since it is impossible to reliably detect the crashes (many leaders at the same time), a take-over mechanism is required. To do so, the Paxos algorithm defines three roles: *proposer* (or *leader*), *acceptor* and *learner*.

Basically, a proposer is a willing-to-be leader. It receives requests from clients, orders them (using a step number s, natural number) and proposes them to the acceptors. The acceptor accepts a request for a step s according to some specific rules discussed below. A request can be decided on for step s when a majority of acceptors have accepted it in step s. Finally, the learner learns when some request has been accepted by a majority of acceptors for some step and decides accordingly. The learner has a local copy of the state-machine, and it applies the decided requests in an increasing step order.

There are many possible mappings of these roles to the processors of a concrete system. In our case, we assume that every processor is both an acceptor and a learner. We also assume that some unreliable failure detector elects some processors; the elected processors, in addition to their other roles, become proposers.

To deal with the presence of many proposers, the Paxos algorithm uses ballot numbers[2] (unbounded natural numbers). Every proposer can create new ballot numbers (two proposers include their identifiers to produce mutually distinct ballot numbers). Every acceptor records a ballot number which roughly represents the proposer it is attached to. When a processor becomes a proposer, it executes the following *prepare phase* or *phase 1*. It creates a new ballot number t, and tries to recruit a majority of acceptors by broadcasting its ballot number (*p1a* message) and waiting for replies (*p1b*) from a majority. An acceptor adopts the ballot number t (i.e., is recruited by the proposer) only if its previously adopted ballot number is strictly smaller. In any case, it replies to the proposer. If the proposer does not manage to recruit a majority of acceptors, it increments its ballot number and tries again.

An acceptor α adds to its *p1b* reply, the lastly accepted request $accepted_\alpha[s]$ for each step s (if any), along with the corresponding ballot number at the time of acceptance. Thanks to this data, at the end of the prepare phase, the proposer

---

[2] These ballot numbers are not used to indexed the requests like the step numbers above.

knows the advancement of a majority of acceptors, and can compute requests to propose which do not interfere with possibly previous proposals. It selects, for each step s, the most recent (by referring to the ballot numbers of the accepted requests) accepted request, and if there are no such requests, it can pick any requests it has personally received from clients.

Then for each step s for which the proposer has a request to propose, the proposer executes the following *accept phase* or *phase 2*. The proposer broadcasts to the acceptors a $p2a$ message containing its ballot number t, the step s, and the proposed request p. An acceptor accepts this request for step s if the ballot number t is greater than or equal to its previously adopted ballot number, and acknowledges the proposer. If the proposer sees an acceptor with a greater ballot number, it reexecutes phase 1. Otherwise, it receives positive answers from a majority of acceptors, and it tells the learners to decide on the request for the corresponding step.

Phase 2 can be thought as the "normal case" operation. When a proposer is unique, each time it receives a request from a client, it assigns to it a step number and tell the acceptors. Phase 1 is executed when a processor becomes a proposer. Usually, a processor becomes a proposer when it detects the crash of the previous proposer, e.g., according to some unreliable failure detector. Phase 1 serves as a "take-over" mechanism: the new proposer recruits a majority of acceptors and records, for each of them, their lastly accepted requests. In order for the proposer to make sure that these lastly accepted requests are accepted by a majority of acceptors, it executes phase 2 for each corresponding step.

The difficulty lies in proving that the safety property holds. Indeed, since the failure detection is unreliable, many proposers may be active simultaneously. Roughly speaking, the safety correctness is given by the claim that once a proposer has succeeded to complete phase 2 for a given step s, the chosen request is not changed afterwards for step s. Ordering of events in a common processor that answers two proposers yields the detailed argument, and the existence of such a common processor stems from the fact that any two majorities of acceptors always have non-empty intersection. The liveness property, however, is not guaranteed. A close look at the behaviour of Paxos shows why it is so. Indeed, since every proposer tries to produce a ballot number that is greater than the ballot numbers of a majority of acceptor, two such proposers may execute many unsuccessful phases 1. Intuitively though, if there is a single proposer in the system during a long enough period of time, then requests are eventually decided on, and progress of the state-machine is ensured.

Practically Self-Stabilizing Replicated State-Machine. As we pointed out in the previous section, the Paxos algorithm uses unbounded integers to timestamp data (ballot and step numbers). In practice, however, every integer handled by the processors is bounded by some constant 2^b where b is the integer memory size. Yet, if every integer variable is initialized to a very low value, the time needed for any such variable to reach the maximum value 2^b is actually way larger than any reasonable system's timescale. For instance, counting from 0 to 2^{64} by incrementing every nanosecond takes roughly 500 years to complete. Such a long sequence is said to be practically infinite. This leads to the following important remark from which the current work stems. *Assuming that the integers are theoretically unbounded is reasonable only when it is ensured, in practice, that every counter is initially set to low values, compared to the maximum value. In particular, any initialized execution of the original Paxos algorithm with bounded integers is valid as long as the counters are not exhausted.*

In the context of self-stabilization, a transient fault may hinder the system in several ways as explained in the introduction. First, it can corrupt the states of the replicas or alter messages leading to incoherent replicas states. Second, and most importantly, a transient fault may also corrupt the variables used to timestamp data (e.g., ballot or step number) in the processors memory or in the communication channels, and set them to a value close to the maximum value 2^b. This leads to an infinite suffix of execution in which the State-Machine Replication conditions are never jointly satisfied. This issue is much more worrying than punctual breakings of the State-Machine Replication specifications.

Intuitively though, if one can manage to get every integer variable to be reset to low values at some point in time, then there is consequently a finite execution (ending with ballot or step number reaching the maximum value 2^b) during which the system behaves like an initialized original Paxos-based State-Machine Replication execution that satisfies the specifications. Since we use bounded integers, we cannot prove the safe execution to be infinite (just like the original Paxos cannot), but we can prove that this safe execution is as long as counting from 0 to 2^b, which is as long as the length of an initialized and safe execution assumed in the original Paxos prior to exhausting the counters. This is what we call a *practically self-stabilizing* behaviour.

More formally, a finite execution is said to be practically infinite when it contains a causally ordered (Lamport's happen-before relation [13]) chain of events of length greater than 2^b. We then formulate the *Practically Self-Stabilizing Replicated State-Machine* (PSS-RSM) specification as follows: *(Safety)* Every infinite execution contains a practically infinite segment that yields a linearizable history of client requests and responses, *(Liveness)* In this history, every request has a corresponding response.

Tag System. Our algorithm uses a new kind of timestamping architecture, namely a tag system, to deal with the overflow of integer variables. We first describe a simpler tag system that works when there is a single proposer, before adapting it to the case of multiple proposers.

One of the key ingredient of Paxos is the possibility for a proposer to increment its ballot number t. We start with t being a natural number between 0 and a large constant 2^b, namely a bounded integer. Assume, for now, that there is a single proposer in the system. With an arbitrary initial configuration, some processors may have ballot numbers set to the maximum 2^b, thus the proposer will not be able to produce a greater ballot number. To cope with this problem, we redefine the ballot number to be a couple $(l\ t)$ where t is a bounded integer (the integer ballot number), and l a label, which is not an integer but whose type is explicited below. We simply assume that it is possible to increment a label, and that two labels are comparable. The proposer can increment the integer variable t, or increment the label l and reset the integer variable t to zero. Now, if the proposer manages to produce a label that is greater than every label of the acceptors, then right after everything is as if the (integer part of the) ballot numbers of the processors have all started from zero, and, intuitively, we get a practically infinite execution that looks like an initialized one. To do so, whenever the proposer notices an acceptor label which is not less than or equal to the proposer current label (such an acceptor label is said to cancel the proposer label), it records it in a history of canceling labels and produces a label greater than every label in its history.

Obviously, the label type cannot be an integer. Actually, it is sufficient to have some finite set of labels along with a comparison operator and a function that takes any finite (bounded by some constant) subset of labels and produces a label that is greater than every label in this subset. Such a device is called a finite labeling scheme (see Sect. 3).

In the case of multiple proposers, the situation is a bit more complicated. Indeed, in the previous case, the single proposer is the only processor to produce labels, and thus it manages to produce a label greater than every acceptor label once it has collected enough information in its canceling label history. If multiple proposers were also producing labels, none of them would be ensured to produce a label that every other proposer will use. Indeed, the first proposer can produce a label l_1, and then a second proposer produces a label l_2 such that $l_1 \prec l_2$. The first proposer then sees that the label l_2 cancels its label and it produces a label l_3 such that $l_2 \prec l_3$, and so on.

To avoid such interferences between the proposers, we elaborate on the previous scheme as follows. Instead of being a couple (l, t) as above, a ballot number will be a couple (v, t) where t is the integer ballot number, and v is a tag, i.e., a vector of labels indexed by the identifiers of the processors. We assume that the set of identifiers is totally ordered. A proposer μ can only create new labels in the entry μ of its tag. By recording enough of the labels that cancel the label in the entry μ, μ is able to produce a greatest label in the entry μ; therefore the entry μ becomes a valid entry (it has a greatest label) that can be used by other proposers. In order for the different processors to agree on which valid entry to use, we simply impose that each of them uses the valid entry with the smallest identifier.

Finally, in the informal presentation above, we presented the tag system as a means to deal with overflows of ballot numbers, but the same goes for overflows of any other kind of ever increasing (but bounded) sort of variables. In particular, in any implementation of Paxos, the processors record the sequence of executed requests (which is related to the step number); our tag system also copes with overflows of this kind of data.

3   System Settings

Model. All the basic notions we use (state, configuration, execution, asynchrony, ...) can be found in, e.g., [7,19]. Here, the model we work with is given by a system of **n** *asynchronous processors* in a *complete communication network*. Each communication channel between two processors is a *bidirectional asynchronous communication channel of finite capacity* **C** [8]. Every processor has a unique identifier and the set Π of identifiers is totally ordered. If α and β are two processor identifiers, the couple (α, β) denotes the communication channel between α and β. A *configuration* is the vector of states of every processor and communication channel. If γ is a configuration of the system, we note $\gamma(\alpha)$ (resp. $\gamma(\alpha, \beta)$) for the state of the processor α (resp. the communication channel (α, β)) in the configuration γ. We informally[3] define an *event* as the sending or reception of a message at a processor or as a local state transition at a processor. Given a configuration, an event induces a transition to a new configuration. An *execution* is denoted by a sequence of configurations $(\gamma_k)_{0 \le k < T}$, $T \in \mathbb{N} \cup \{+\infty\}$ related by such transitions[4]. A *local execution* at processor λ is the sequence of states obtained as the projection of an execution on λ.

We consider transient and crash faults only. The effect of a transient fault is to corrupt the state of some processors and/or communication channels; but it does not corrupt the memory where the program is located[5]. As usual in self-stabilization, it is assumed that all the basic services related to message transmission (in particular identifiers) are reliable. Also, we only consider the suffix of execution after the last transient fault; though crash faults may occur in this suffix. This amounts to assume that the initial configuration of every execution is arbitrary and at most **f** processors are prone to crash failures.

A *quorum* is any set of at least **n** − **f** processors. The maximum number of crash failures **f** satisfies **n** $\geq$ 2 · **f** + 1. Thus, there always exists a responding majority quorum and any two quorums have a non-empty intersection. We also use the "happened-before" strict partial order introduced by Lamport [13]. In our case, we note $e \rightsquigarrow f$ and we say that e happens before f, or f happens after[6] e. Each processor plays the role of a proposer, acceptor and learner. A proposer can be active or inactive[7]. We simply assume that at least one processor acts as a proposer infinitely often. This proposer is not required to be unique in order for our algorithm to stabilize. A unique proposer is required only for the liveness of the state-machine (Sect. 6). Finally, we fix a state-machine $\mathcal{M}$, and each processor has a local copy of $\mathcal{M}$. A *request* corresponds to a transition of the state-machine. We assume that the machine $\mathcal{M}$ has a predefined initial state.

Data Structures. Given a positive integer $\mathfrak{b}$, a $\mathfrak{b}$-bounded integer, or simply a bounded integer, is any non-negative integer less than or equal to $2^{\mathfrak{b}}$. A *finite labeling scheme* is a 4-tuple $\overline{\mathscr{L}} = (\mathscr{L}, \prec, d, \nu)$ where $\mathscr{L}$ is a finite set whose elements are called *labels*, $\prec$ is a partial relation on $\mathscr{L}$ that is irreflexive ($l \not\prec l$)

---

[3] For a formal definition, refer to, e.g., [7,19].

[4] For sake of simplicity, the events and the transitions are omitted.

[5] This would create Byzantine processes, and is outside of our scope.

[6] Note that the sentences "f happens after e" and "e does not happen before f" are not equivalent.

[7] How a proposer becomes active can be modeled by a the output of a failure detector.

and antisymmetric ($\not\exists(l, l')\ l \prec l' \wedge l' \prec l$), d is an integer, namely the *dimension* of the labeling scheme, and ν is the *label increment function*, i.e., a function that maps any finite set A of at most d labels to a label $\nu(A)$ such that for every label l in A, we have $l \prec \nu(A)$. We denote the reflexive closure of $\prec$ by $\preccurlyeq$. The definition of a finite labeling scheme imposes that the relation $\prec$ is not transitive. Hence, it is not a preorder relation. Given a label l, a *canceling label* for l is a label cl such that $cl \not\preccurlyeq l$. See [2] for a concrete construction of finite labeling scheme of any dimension.

A *tag* is a vector $v[\mu] = (l\ cl)$ where $\mu \in \Pi$ is a processor identifier, l is a label, cl is either the null symbol $\bot$, the overflow symbol ∞ or a canceling label for l. The entry μ in v is said to be *valid* when the corresponding canceling field is null, $v[\mu].cl = \bot$. If v has at least one valid entry, we denote by $\chi(v)$ the *first valid entry of* v, i.e., the smallest identifier μ such that $v[\mu]$ is valid. If v has no valid entry, we set $\chi(v) = \omega$ where ω is a special symbol (not in Π). Given two tags v and v', we note $v \prec v'$ when either $\chi(v) > \chi(v')$ or $\chi(v) = \chi(v') = \mu \neq \omega$ and $v[\mu].l < v'[\mu].l$. We note $v \simeq v'$ when $\chi(v) = \chi(v') = \mu$ and $v[\mu] = v'[\mu]$. We note $v \preccurlyeq v'$ when either $v \prec v'$ or $v \simeq v'$.

A *fifo label history* H of size d, is a vector of size d of labels along with an operator $+$ defined as follows. Let $H = (l_1, \ldots, l_d)$ and l be a label. If l does not appear in H, then $H + l = (l, l_1, \ldots, l_{d-1})$, otherwise $H + l = H$. We define the *tag storage limit* $\mathbf{K}$ and the *canceling label storage limit* $\mathbf{K}^{cl}$ by $\mathbf{K} = \mathbf{n} + \mathbf{C}\frac{\mathbf{n(n-1)}}{2}$ and $\mathbf{K}^{cl} = (\mathbf{n} + 1)\mathbf{K}$.

4   The Algorithm

In this section, we describe the Practically Self-Stabilizing Paxos algorithm. In its essence, our algorithm is close to the Paxos scheme except for some details. First, in the original Paxos, the processors decide on a unique request for each step s. In our case, there is no actual step number, but the processors agree on a growing sequence of requests of size at most 2^b as in [16] (see Remark 1 below). Second, our algorithm includes tag related data to cope with overflows.

The variables are presented in Algorithm 1. The clients are not modeled here; we simply assume that each active proposer α can query a stream $queue_\alpha$ to get a client request to propose. The variables are divided in three sections corresponding to the different Paxos roles: proposer, acceptor, learner. In each section, some variables are marked as Paxos variables[8] while the others are related to the tag system.

The message flow is similar to Paxos. When a proposer λ becomes active, it executes a prepare phase (phase 1), trying to recruit a majority of acceptors. An acceptor α is recruited if the proposer ballot number is (strictly) greater than its own ballot number. In this case, it adopts the ballot number. It also replies (positively or negatively) to the leader with its latest accepted sequence of requests $accepted_\alpha$ along with the corresponding (integer) ballot number. After

---

[8] They come from the original formulation of Paxos.

recruiting a quorum of acceptors, the proposer λ records the latest sequence (w.r.t. the associated integer ballot numbers) of requests accepted by them in its variable proposed $proposed_\lambda$. If this phase 1 is successful, the proposer λ can execute accept phases (phase 2) for each request received in $queue_\lambda$. For each such request r, the proposer λ appends r to its variable $proposed_\lambda$, and tell the acceptors to accept $proposed_\lambda$. An acceptor accepts the proposal $proposed_\lambda$ when the two following conditions are satisfied: (1) the proposer's ballot number is greater than or equal to its own ballot number, and (2) if the ballot integer associated with the lastly accepted proposal is equal to the proposer's ballot integer, then $proposed_\lambda$ is an extension of the lastly accepted proposal. Roughly speaking, this last condition avoids the acceptor to accept an older (hence shorter) sequence of request. In any case, the acceptor replies (positively or negatively) to the proposer. The proposer λ plays the role of a special learner in the sense that it waits for positive replies from a quorum of acceptors, and, sends the corresponding decision message. The decision procedure when receiving a decision message is similar to the acceptation procedure (reception of a $p2a$ message), except that if the acceptor accepts the proposal, then it also learns (decides on) this proposal and execute the corresponding new requests.

We now describe the treatment of the variables related to the tag system. Anytime a processor α (as an acceptor, learner or proposer) with tag v_α receives a message with a tag v', it updates the canceling label fields before comparing them, i.e., for any μ, if $v_\alpha[\mu].l$ (or $v_\alpha[\mu].cl$) is a label that cancels $v'[\mu].l$, or $v_\alpha[\mu].cl = \infty$ is the overflow symbol, then the field $v'[\mu].cl$ is updated accordingly[9], and vice versa. Also, if the processor α notices an overflow in its own variables (e.g. its ballot integer, or one of the request sequence variables, has reached the upper bound), it sets the overflow symbol ∞ in the canceling field of the first valid entry of the tag. If after such an update, the label $v_\alpha[\alpha].l$ is canceled, then the corresponding canceling label is added to H_α^{cl} as well as the label $v_\alpha[\alpha].l$, and $v_\alpha[\alpha].l$ is set to the new label $\nu(H_\alpha^{cl})$ created from the labels in H_α^{cl} with the label increment function. The purpose of H_α^{cl} is to record enough canceling labels for the proposer to produce a greatest label. In addition, if, after the update, it appears that $v_\alpha \preccurlyeq v'$, then α adopts the tag v', i.e., it copies the content of the first valid entry $\mu = \chi(v')$ of v' to the same entry in v_α (assuming $\mu < \alpha$). Doing so, it also records the previous label in v_α in the label history $H_\alpha[\mu]$. If there is a label in $H_\alpha[\mu]$ that cancels $v_\alpha[\mu].l$, then the corresponding field is updated accordingly. The purpose of $H_\alpha[\mu]$ is to avoid cycle of labels in the entry μ of the tag. Recall that the comparison between labels is not a preorder. In case $\mu = \alpha$, then α uses the label increment function on H_α^{cl} to produce a greater label as above.

We say that there is an *epoch change* in the tag v_λ if either the first valid entry $\chi(v_\lambda)$ has changed, or the first valid entry has not changed but the corresponding label has changed. Whenever there is an epoch change in the tag v_λ the processor cleans the Paxos related variables. For a proposer λ, this means that the proposer

---

[9] i.e., the field $v'[\mu].cl$ is set to $v_\alpha[\mu].(l \text{ or } cl)$. In case, there is a canceling label and the overflow symbol, the canceling label is preferred.

ballot integer t_λ^p is reset to zero, the proposed requests $proposed_\lambda$ to the empty sequence; in addition, the proposer proceeds to a new prepare phase. For an acceptor (and learner) α, this means that the acceptor ballot integer is reset to zero, the sequences $accepted_\alpha$ and $learned_\alpha$ are reset to the empty sequence, and the local state q_α^* is reset to the predefined initial state of the state-machine.

The pseudo-code in Algorithms 2 and 3 sums up the previous description. Note that, the predicate $(v_\alpha, t_\alpha) < (v_\lambda, t_\lambda)$ (resp. $(v_\alpha, t_\alpha) \leq (v_\lambda, t_\lambda)$) means that either $v_\alpha \prec v_\lambda$, or $v_\alpha \simeq v_\lambda$ and $t_\alpha < t_\lambda$ (resp. $t_\alpha \leq t_\lambda$).

Remark 1. Note that, in our algorithm, the replicas agree on growing sequences of requests, of length at most 2^b. Our goal in this paper is not to provide an optimized solution, but to pave the way to it. Yet, a means to control the length of the sequences would be to replace a prefix of request sequence by the state reached from the initial state when applying the prefix. Then the replicas can agree on (possibly conflicting) states by the latest found in a quorum.

Algorithm 1. Variables at processor α

---

1 (tag system)
2   v_α : tag
3   canceling label history, H_α^{cl} : fifo history of size $(\mathbf{K}+1)\mathbf{K}^{cl}$
4   for each $\mu \in \Pi$, label history, $H[\mu]$: fifo history of size $\mathbf{K}$
5 (proposer)
6   client requests, $queue_\alpha$: queue (read-only)
7   [Paxos] proposer ballot integer, t_α^p : bounded integer
8   [Paxos] proposed requests, $proposed_\alpha$: requests sequence of size $\leq 2^b$
9 (acceptor)
10   [Paxos] acceptor ballot integer, t_α^a : bounded integer
11   [Paxos] accepted requests, $accepted_\alpha = (t, seq)$: t bounded integer, seq
          requests sequence of size $\leq 2^b$
12 (learner)
13   [Paxos] learned requests, $learned_\alpha$: requests sequence of size $\leq 2^b$
14   [Paxos] local state, q_α^* : state of the state-machine

---

5   Proofs

Due to lack of space, proofs are only sketched. More details can be found in [3].

5.1   Tag Stabilization

Definition 1 (Interrupt). *Let λ be any processor (as a proposer, or an acceptor) and consider a local subexecution $\sigma = (\gamma_k(\lambda))_{k_0 \leq k \leq k_1}$ at λ. We denote by v_λ^k the λ's tag in $\gamma_k(\lambda)$. We say that an interrupt has occurred at position k in the local subexecution σ when one of the following happens*

Algorithm 2. Prepare phase (Phase 1)

1	Processor λ becomes a proposer:	22	
2	increment t_λ	23	Processor α receives $p1a$ message from λ:
3	**if** t_λ *reaches* 2^b **then**	24	update canceling fields in (v_α, v_λ)
4	set $v_\lambda[\chi(v_\lambda)].cl$ to ∞	25	**if** $(v_\alpha, t_\alpha) < (v_\lambda, t_\lambda)$ **then**
5	update the entry $v_\lambda[\lambda]$ with H^{cl}	26	adopt v_λ, t_λ
	if it is invalid	27	**if** *epoch change in* v_α **then**
6	clean the proposer Paxos variables	28	clean Paxos variables
7	broadcast $\langle p1a, v_\lambda, t_\lambda, \lambda \rangle$	29	reply to λ, $\langle p1b, v_\alpha, t_\alpha, accepted_\alpha, \alpha \rangle$
8	collect replies R from some quorum Q	30	
9	update (if necessary) the tag v_λ and		
	the label histories		
10	**if** *no epoch change in* v_λ *and all replies*		
	are positive **then**		
11	order R with lexicographical order		
	$(accepted_\alpha.t, |accepted_\alpha.seq|)$		
12	$proposed_\lambda \leftarrow accepted_\alpha.seq$ the		
	maximum in R (break ties if necessary)		
13	**if** *proposed*$_\lambda$ *has reached max length*		
	then		
14	set $v_\lambda[\chi(v_\lambda)].cl$ to ∞		
15	update the entry $v_\lambda[\lambda]$ with H^{cl} if		
	it is invalid		
16	clean the Paxos variables		
17	repeat phase 1		
18	**else**		
19	**if** *epoch change in* v_λ **then**		
20	clean the Paxos variables		
21	repeat phase 1		

- $\mu < \lambda$, type $[\mu, \leftarrow]$: *the first valid entry moves to μ such that $\mu = \chi(v_\lambda^{k+1}) < \chi(v_\lambda^k)$, or the first valid entry does not change but the label does, i.e., $\mu = \chi(v_\lambda^{k+1}) = \chi(v_\lambda^k)$ and $v_\lambda^k[\mu].l \neq v_\lambda^{k+1}[\mu].l$.*
- $\mu < \lambda$, type $[\mu, \rightarrow]$: *the first valid entry moves to μ such that $\mu = \chi(v_\lambda^{k+1}) > \chi(v_\lambda^k)$.*
- type $[\lambda, \infty]$: *the first valid entry is the same but there is a change of label in the entry λ due to an overflow of one of the Paxos variables; we then have $\chi(v_\lambda^{k+1}) = \chi(v_\lambda^k) = \lambda$ and $v_\lambda^k[\lambda].l \neq v_\lambda^{k+1}[\lambda].l$.*
- $[\lambda, cl]$: *the first valid entry is the same but there is a change of label in the entry λ due to the canceling of the corresponding label; we then have $\chi(v_\lambda^{k+1}) = \chi(v_\lambda^k) = \lambda$ and $v_\lambda^k[\lambda].l \neq v_\lambda^{k+1}[\lambda].l$.*

For each type $[\mu, *]$ ($\mu \leq \lambda$) of interrupt, we denote by $\|[\mu, *]\|$ the total number (possibly infinite) of interrupts of type $[\mu, *]$ that occur during the local subexecution σ.

If there is an interrupt like $[\mu, \leftarrow]$, $\mu < \lambda$, occurs at position k, then necessarily there is a change of label in the field $v_\lambda[\mu].l$ (due to the adoption of received tag). In addition, the new label l' is greater than the previous label l, i.e., $l \prec l'$. Also note that, if $\chi(v_\lambda^k) = \lambda$, the proposer λ never copies the content of the entry λ

Algorithm 3. Accept phase (Phase 2) and Decision

---

1 Once λ gets requests in $queue_\lambda$:
2   append requests to $proposed_\lambda$
3   broadcast $\langle p2a, v_\lambda, t_\lambda, proposed_\lambda \rangle$
4   collect replies R from some quorum Q
5   update (if necessary) the tag v_λ
      and the label histories
6   **if** *no epoch change in v_λ and*
        all replies are positive **then**
7   broadcast $\langle dec, v_\lambda, t_\lambda, proposed_\lambda \rangle$
8   **else**
9   **if** *epoch change in v_λ* **then** clean
          the Paxos variables
10   proceed to phase 1
11

12 Processor α receives $p2a$ or dec message
      from λ:
13   update canceling fields in (v_α, v_λ)
14   **if** $(v_\alpha, t_\alpha) \leq (v_\lambda, t_\lambda)$ **then**
15   adopt v_λ, t_λ
16   **if** *epoch change in v_α* **then**
          clean the Paxos variables
17   **if** $accepted_\alpha.t < t_\lambda$ *or*
          $accepted_\alpha.seq$ *is a prefix of*
          $proposed_\lambda$ **then**
18   accept $(t_\lambda, proposed_\lambda)$
19   **if** *it is a dec message* **then**
20   learn $proposed_\lambda$
21   update q_α^* by executing
            the new requests
22   **if** *it is a p2a message* **then**
23   reply to λ, $\langle p2b, v_\alpha, t_\alpha,$
          $accepted_\alpha, \alpha \rangle$

24

---

of a received tag, say v', to the entry λ of its tag, even if $v_\lambda^k[\lambda].l \prec v'[\lambda].l$. New labels in the entry λ are only produced with the label increment function applied to the union of the current label and the canceling label history H_λ^{cl}.

Definition 2 (Epoch). *Let λ be a processor. An epoch σ at λ is a maximal (for the inclusion of local subexecutions) local subexecution at λ such that no interrupts occur at any position in σ except for the last position. By the definition of an interrupt, all the tag's values within a given epoch σ at λ have the same first valid entry, say μ, and the same corresponding label, i.e., for any two processor states that appear in σ, the corresponding tag values v and v' satisfies $\chi(v) = \chi(v') = \mu$ and $v[\mu].l = v'[\mu].l$. We denote by μ_σ and l_σ the first valid entry and the corresponding label common to all the tag values in σ.*

Definition 3 (h-Safe Epoch). *Consider an execution E and a processor λ. Let Σ be a subexecution in E such that the local subexecution $\sigma = \Sigma(\lambda)$ is an epoch at λ. Let γ^* be the configuration of the system right before the subexecution Σ, and h be a bounded integer. The epoch σ is said to be h-safe when the interrupt at the end of σ is due to an overflow of one of the Paxos variables. In addition, for every processor α (resp. communication channel (α, β)), for every tag x in $\gamma^*(\alpha)$ (resp. $\gamma^*(\alpha, \beta)$), if $x[\mu_\sigma].l = l_\sigma$ then any corresponding integer variables (ballot integers, or lengths of request sequences) have values less than or equal to h.*

If there is an epoch σ at processor λ such that $\mu_\sigma = \lambda$ and λ has produced the label l_σ, then necessarily, at the beginning of σ, the Paxos variables have been reset. However, other processors may already be using the label l_σ with, for example, arbitrary ballot integer value. Such an arbitrary value may be the cause of the overflow interrupt at the end of σ. The definition of a h-safe epoch ensures that the epoch is truly as long as counting from h to 2^b.

Since a processor λ always checks that the entry $v_\lambda[\lambda]$ is valid (updating with $\nu(H_\lambda^{cl})$ if necessary), it is now assumed, unless stated explicitly, that we always have $\chi(v_\lambda) \leq \lambda$.

Consider a configuration γ and a processor identifier μ. Let $S(\gamma)$ be the set of every tag present either in a processor memory or in some message in a communication channel, in the configuration γ. Let $S^{cl}(\mu, \gamma)$ be the set of labels l such that either l is the value of the label field $x[\mu].l$ for some tag x in $S(\gamma)$, or l appears in the label history $H_\alpha[\mu]$ of some processor α, in the configuration γ. Then, we have $|S(\gamma)| \leq \mathbf{K}$ and $|S^{cl}(\mu, \gamma)| \leq \mathbf{K}^{cl}$. In particular, the number of label values $x[\mu].l$ with x in $S(\gamma)$ is less than or equal to $\mathbf{K}$.

Lemma 1 (Cycle of Labels). *Consider a subexecution E, a processor λ and an entry $\mu < \lambda$ in the tag variable v_λ. The label value in $v_\lambda[\mu].l$ can change during the subexecution E and we denote by $(l^i)_{1 \leq i \leq T+1}$ for the sequence of successive distinct label values that are taken by the label $v_\lambda[\mu].l$ in the entry μ during the subexecution E. We assume that the first T labels $l^1, \ldots, l^T$ are different from each other, i.e., for every $1 \leq i < j \leq T$, $l^i \neq l^j$. If $T > \mathbf{K}$, then at least one of the label l^i has been produced[10] by the processor μ during E. If $T \leq \mathbf{K}$ and $l^{T+1} = l^1$, then when the processor λ adopts the label l^{T+1} in the entry μ of its tag v_λ, the entry μ becomes invalid.*

Proof (Sketch). This stems from the fact that in any configuration there are at most $\mathbf{K}$ different tags in the system, and that λ records the last $\mathbf{K}$ label values of the entry μ of its tag. □

Lemma 2 (Counting the Interrupts). *Consider an infinite execution E_∞ and let λ be a processor identifier such that every processor $\mu < \lambda$ produces labels finitely many times. Consider an identifier $\mu < \lambda$ and any processor $\rho \geq \lambda$. Then, the local execution $E_\infty(\rho)$ at ρ induces a sequence of interrupts such that $\|[\mu, \leftarrow]\| \leq R_\mu = (J_\mu + 1) \cdot (\mathbf{K} + 1) - 1$ where J_μ is the number of times the processor μ has produced a label since the beginning of the execution.*

Proof (Sketch). Assume the contrary. Then there are $R_\mu + 1$ successive distinct label values in the field $v_\rho[\mu].l$, $l^1 \prec \cdots \prec l^{R_\mu+1}$. We can divide this sequence in $J_\mu + 1$ segments of length $\mathbf{K} + 1$. Due to the previous lemma, there is one segment containing a cycle of labels of length $\leq \mathbf{K}$; this is a contradiction since ρ records the last $\mathbf{K}$ labels in $H_\rho[\mu]$. □

Theorem 1 (Existence of a 0-Safe Epoch). *Consider an infinite execution E_∞ and let λ be a processor such that every processor $\mu < \lambda$ produces labels finitely many times. We denote by $|\lambda|$ the number of identifiers $\mu \leq \lambda$, J_μ for the number of times a proposer $\mu < \lambda$ produces a label and we define*

$$T_\lambda = \left(\sum_{\mu < \lambda} R_\mu + 1\right) \cdot (|\lambda| + 1) \cdot (\mathbf{K}^{cl} + 1) \cdot (\mathbf{K} + 1) \tag{1}$$

---

[10] Precisely, it has invoked the label increment function to update the entry μ of its tag v_μ.

where $R_\mu = (J_\mu + 1) \cdot (\mathbf{K} + 1) - 1$. *Assume that there are more than* T_λ *interrupts at processor* λ *during* E_∞ *and consider the concatenation* $E_c(\lambda)$ *of the first* T_λ *epochs,* $E_c(\lambda) = \sigma^1 \ldots \sigma^{T_\lambda}$. *Then* $E_c(\lambda)$ *contains a 0-safe epoch.*

Proof (Sketch). The bound given by the previous lemma and successive applications of the pigeonhole principle yield a segment $E_2(\lambda)$ of $(\mathbf{K}^{cl} + 1)(\mathbf{K} + 1)$ successive epochs with interrupts like $[\lambda, \infty]$ and $[\lambda, cl]$ only. If there is in E_2 a segment E_3 of $\mathbf{K} + 1$ successive epochs with interrupts like $[\lambda, \infty]$ only, λ must have a created a label that was not present in the system; and the corresponding epoch is 0-safe. Otherwise, there is at least $\mathbf{K}^{cl} + 1$ interrupts like $[\lambda, cl]$. This implies that λ has collected all the possible canceling labels. At the end, it produces a greatest label, and the corresponding epoch is necessarily 0-safe. $\square$

Note that the epoch found in the proof is not necessarily the unique 0-safe epoch in $E_c(\lambda)$. The idea is only to prove that there exists a practically infinite epoch. If the first epoch σ at λ ends because the corresponding label l_σ in the entry μ_σ gets canceled, but lasts a practically infinite long time, then this epoch can be considered, from an informal point of view, safe. One could worry about having only very "short" epochs at λ due to some inconsistencies (canceling labels or overflows) in the system. Theorem 1 shows that every time a "short" epoch ends, the system somehow loses one of its inconsistencies, and, eventually, the proposer λ reaches a practically infinite epoch. Note also that a 0-safe epoch and a 1-safe or a 2-safe epoch are, in practice, as long as each other. Indeed, any h-safe epoch with h very small compared to 2^b can be considered practically infinite. Whether h can be considered very small depends on the concrete timescale of the system. Besides, every processor α always checks that the entry α is valid. Doing so the processor α still works to find a "winning" label for its entry α. In that case, if the entry μ becomes invalid, then the entry α is ready to be used, and a safe epoch can start without waiting any longer.

5.2   Safety

To prove the safety property within a subexecution, we have to focus on the events that correspond to deciding a proposal, e.g., (v, t, p) at processor α (v being a tag, t a ballot integer, p a sequence of requests). Such an event may be due to corrupted messages in the communication channels an any stage of the Paxos algorithm. Indeed, a proposer computes the proposal it will send in its phase 2 thanks to the replies it has received at the end of its phase 1. Hence, if one of these messages is corrupted, then the safety might be violated. However, there is a finite number of corrupted messages since the capacity of the communication channels is finite. To formally deal with these issues, we define the notion of scenario that corresponds to specific chain of events involved in the Paxos algorithm. Consider a subexecution $E = (\gamma_k)_{k_0 \leq k \leq k_1}$. A *scenario* in E is a sequence $U = (U_i)_{0 \leq i < I}$ where each U_i is a collection of events in E. In addition, every event in U_i happens before every event in U_{i+1}.

Definition 4 (Phase Scenario). *Consider a proposer ρ, an acceptor α, quorums S and Q of acceptors, a tag v, a ballot integer t, and a sequence of requests p.*

A phase 1 scenario is defined as follows. The proposer ρ broadcasts a message p1a containing the tag v, and ballot integer t. Every acceptor in the quorum S receives this message and adopts[11] the tag v. Every processor α in the quorum S replies to the proposer ρ a p1b message telling they adopted the couple (v,t), and containing the last proposal they accepted. These messages are received by ρ. We denote this scenario by $\rho \xrightarrow{p1a} (S,v,t) \xrightarrow{p1b} \rho$.

A phase 2 scenario with acceptance is defined as follows. The proposer ρ broadcasts a p2a message containing the tag v, the ballot integer t, and the proposed sequence of requests p. The acceptor α accepts the proposal (v,t,p). We denote this scenario by $\rho \xrightarrow{p2a} (\alpha,v,t,p)$.

A phase 2 scenario with quorum acceptance is defined as follows. The proposer ρ broadcasts a p2a message containing the tag v, the ballot integer t, and the proposed sequence of requests p. Every acceptor in the quorum Q accepts the proposal (v,t,p). Every acceptor α in the quorum Q sends to the proposer ρ a p2b message telling that it has accepted the proposal (v,t,p). The proposer ρ receives these messages. We denote this scenario by $\rho \xrightarrow{p2a} (Q,v,t,p) \xrightarrow{p2b} \rho$.

A phase 2 scenario with decision is defined as follows. The proposer ρ broadcasts a p2a message containing the tag v, the ballot integer t, and the proposed sequence of requests p. Every acceptor in the quorum Q accepts the proposal (v,t,p). Every acceptor α in the quorum Q sends to the proposer ρ a p2b message telling that it has accepted the proposal (v,t,p). The proposer ρ receives these messages. The proposer ρ sends a decision message containing the proposal (v,t,p). The processor α receives this message, accepts and decides on the proposal (v,t,p). We denote this scenario by $\rho \xrightarrow{p2a} (Q,v,t,p) \xrightarrow{p2b} \rho \xrightarrow{dec} (\alpha,v,t,p)$.

In all the previous cases, we say that the phase scenarios are conducted by *the proposer ρ and* use the ballot *(v,t).*

Definition 5 (Simple Acceptation Scenario). *A simple acceptation scenario is the concatenation of a phase 1 scenario, followed by a finite number of phase 2 scenarios with quorum acceptation, and ending with a phase 2 scenario with either acceptation, or decision; all the phase scenarios being conducted by the same proposer ρ, and using the same ballot (v,t). Let S be the quorum of acceptors in the phase 1 scenario, p be the sequence of requests accepted (or decided on) in the last event of the scenario, and α be the corresponding acceptor. If the last phase scenario is a phase scenario with acceptation, then we denote the simple acceptation scenario by $\rho \xrightarrow{p1a} (S,v,t) \rightsquigarrow \rho \xrightarrow{p2a} (\alpha,v,t,p)$. If the last phase scenario is a phase scenario with decision, then we denote the simple acceptation scenario by $\rho \xrightarrow{p1a} (S,v,t) \rightsquigarrow \rho \xrightarrow{p2a} (Q,v,t,p) \xrightarrow{p2b} \rho \xrightarrow{dec} (\alpha,v,t,p)$.*

---

[11] Recall that this means the acceptor, say α, copies the entry $v[\chi(v)]$ in the entry $v_\alpha[\chi(v)]$.

When we want to indicate that both cases are possible, we simply denote the simple acceptation scenario by $(\rho, S, v, t) \rightsquigarrow (\alpha, v, t, p)$.

A simple acceptation scenario is simply a basic execution of the Paxos algorithm that leads a processor to either accept a proposal, or decide on a proposal (accepting it by the way).

Definition 6 (Fake Message). *Given a subexecution* $E = (\gamma_k)_{k_0 \leq k \leq k_1}$, *a fake message relative to the subexecution* E, *or simply a fake message, is a message that is in the communication channels in the first configuration* γ_{k_0} *of the subexecution* E.

This definition of fake messages comprises the messages at the beginning of E that were not sent by any processor, but also messages produced in the prefix of execution that precedes E.

Definition 7 (Fake Phase Scenario). *Consider a proposer* ρ, *an acceptor* α, *quorums* S *and* Q *of acceptors, a tag* v, *a ballot integer* t, *and a sequence of requests* p. *Fix a subexecution* E. *A fake phase scenario relative to* E *is one of the following scenario.*

(Fake phase 1 scenario) *The proposer* ρ *sends a p1a message with ballot* (v, t). *It receives positive replies from a quorum* S, *one of these replies at least being fake (i.e. it was not actually sent by an acceptor). We denote this fake phase scenario by* $\rho \xrightarrow{p1a} (S, v, t) \xrightarrow{fake\ p1b} \rho$.

(Fake phase 2 scenario with acceptation) *The acceptor* α *receives a fake p2a with proposal* (v, t, p) *that seems to come from the processor* ρ. *The acceptor* α *accepts the proposal. We denote this scenario by* $\rho \xrightarrow{fake\ p2a} (\alpha, v, t, p)$.

(Fake phase 2 scenario with quorum acceptation) *The proposer* ρ *sends a p2a message with proposal* (v, t, p). *The proposer* ρ *receives positive replies from a quorum* Q, *one of these replies, at least, being fake. Then* ρ *sends a decision message with proposal* (v, t, p) *to the acceptor* α, *and* α *decides accordingly. We denote this scenario by* $\rho \xrightarrow{p2a} (Q, v, t, p) \xrightarrow{fake\ p2b} \rho \xrightarrow{dec} (\alpha, v, t, p)$.

(Fake phase 2 scenario with decision) *The acceptor* α *receives a fake decision message with proposal* (v, t, p) *which seems to come from the proposer* ρ. *The acceptor* α *decides accordingly. We denote this scenario by* $\rho \xrightarrow{fake\ dec} (\alpha, v, t, p)$.

Definition 8 (Simple Fake Acceptation Scenario). *A simple fake acceptation scenario is either a fake phase 2 scenario with acceptation, a fake phase 2 scenario with quorum acceptation, a fake phase 2 scenario with decision, or the concatenation of a fake phase 1 scenario, followed by a finite number of (non-fake) phase 2 scenarios with quorum acceptation, and ending with a (non-fake) phase 2 scenario with either an acceptation, or a decision; all the scenarios being conducted by the same proposer* ρ, *and using the same ballot* (v, t). *We often denote this kind of scenarios by* fake $\rightsquigarrow (\alpha, v, t, p)$ *where* (α, v, t, p) *refers to the last acceptation (or decision) event.*

A simple fake acceptation scenario is somehow similar to a simple acceptation scenario except for the fact that at least one fake message (relative to the given subexecution) is involved during the scenario.

Definition 9 (Composition). *Consider two simple scenarios*

$$U = X \rightsquigarrow (\alpha_1, v_1, t_1, p_1)$$
$$V = (\rho_2, S_2, v_2, t_2) \rightsquigarrow (\alpha_2, v_2, t_2, p_2)$$

where $X = fake$ or $X = (\rho_1, S_1, v_1, t_1)$ such that the following three conditions are satisfied. (1) The processor α_1 belongs to S_2 (2) Let e_2 be the event that corresponds to α_1 sending a p1b message in scenario V. Then the event "α_1 accepts the proposal (v_1, t_1, p_1)" from U is the last acceptation event before e_2 occurring at α_1. In addition, the proposer ρ_2 selects the proposal (t_1, p_1) as the highest-numbered proposal at the end of the Paxos phase 1. In particular, p_1 is a prefix of p_2, i.e., $p_1 \sqsubset p_2$. (3) All the tags involved share the same first valid entry, the same corresponding label.

Then the composition of the two simple scenarios is the concatenation the scenarios U and V. This scenario is denoted by $X \rightsquigarrow (\alpha_1, v_1, t_1, p_1) \rightarrow (\rho_2, S_2, v_2, t_2) \rightsquigarrow (\alpha_2, v_2, t_2, p_2)$. Note also that the ballot integer is strictly increasing along the simple scenarios (Fig. 1).

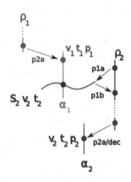

Fig. 1. Composition of scenarios - Time flows downward, straight lines are local executions, arrows represent messages.

Definition 10 (Acceptation Scenario). *Given a subexecution E, an acceptation scenario is the composition U of simple acceptation scenarios $U_1, \ldots, U_r$ where U_1 is either a simple acceptation scenario or a simple fake acceptation scenario relative to E, whereas the other are real (i.e. non-fake) simple acceptation scenarios. We denote it by $X \rightsquigarrow (\alpha_1, v_1, t_1, p_1) \rightarrow (\rho_2, S_2, v_2, t_2) \rightsquigarrow (\alpha_2, v_2, t_2, p_1) \ldots (\rho_r, S_r, v_r, t_r) \rightsquigarrow (\alpha_r, v_r, t_r, p_r)$ where X is either fake or some (ρ_1, S_1, v_1, t_1).*

An acceptation scenario whose first simple scenario is not fake relative to E is called real acceptation scenario relative to E. *An acceptation scenario whose first simple scenario is fake relative to E is called* fake acceptation scenario relative to E.

Given an acceptation event or a decision event, there is always at least one way to trace back the scenario that has lead to this event. If one of these scenarios involve a fake message, then we cannot control the safety property. Besides, all the tags involved share the same first valid entry μ and the same corresponding label l. Also, the ballot integer value, as well as the sequence of requests, is increasing along the acceptation scenario; i.e., if $i < j$, then $t_i < t_j$ and $p_i \sqsubset p_j$.

Definition 11 (Fake event). *Consider an event e that corresponds to some processor accepting a proposal, let U be the simple acceptation scenarios that ends with the event e. The event e is said to be* fake *relative to a subexecution E if U is a fake simple acceptation scenario relative to E. The event e is said to be* real *relative to E otherwise.*

Definition 12 (Simple Scenario Characteristic). *The* characteristic *of a simple acceptation scenario U with tag v, ballot integer t, is the tuple $char(U) = (\chi(v), v[\chi(v)].l, t)$.*

Definition 13 (Observed Zone). *Consider an execution E. Let λ be a proposer and let Σ be a subexecution such that the local execution $\sigma = \Sigma(\lambda)$ at λ is a h-safe epoch. We denote by F the suffix of the execution that starts with Σ. Assume that λ hears from at least two quorums during its epoch σ. Let Q^0, Q^f be the first and last quorums respectively whose messages are processed by the proposer λ during σ. For each processor α in Q^0 (resp. Q^f), we denote by $e^0(\alpha)$ (resp. $e^f(\alpha)$) the event that corresponds to α sending to λ a message received in the phase that corresponds to Q^0 (resp. Q^f).*

The zone observed *by λ during the epoch σ, namely $Z(F, \lambda, \sigma)$, is the set of acceptation scenarios relative to F described as follows. An acceptation scenario relative to F belongs to $Z(F, \lambda, \sigma)$ if and only if it ends with a real acceptation (or decision) event (relative to F) that does not happen after the end of σ and it contains a real simple acceptation scenario $U = (\rho, S, v, t) \rightsquigarrow (\beta, v, t, p)$ such that there exists an acceptor α in $S \cap Q^0 \cap Q^f$ at which the event $e^0(\alpha)$ happens before the event e that corresponds to sending a p1b message in U, and the event e happens before the event $e^f(\alpha)$ (cf. Fig. 2).*

The observed zone models a globally defined time period during which we will prove, under specific assumptions, the safety property (cf. Theorem 3).

Lemma 3 (Epoch and Cycle of Labels). *Consider an execution E. Let λ be a processor and consider a subexecution Σ such that the local execution $\sigma = \Sigma(\lambda)$ is an epoch at λ. We denote by F the suffix of the execution E that starts with Σ. Consider a processor ρ and a finite subexecution G in F as follows: G starts in Σ and induces a local execution $G(\rho)$ at ρ such that it starts and ends with the first valid entry of the tag v_ρ being equal to μ_σ and containing the label l_σ,*

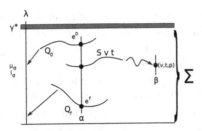

Fig. 2. Scenario $(\rho, S, v, t) \rightsquigarrow (\beta, v, t, p)$ in $Z(F, \lambda, \sigma)$ - Time flows downward, straight lines are local executions, curves are send/receive events, arrows represent messages.

and the label field in the entry $v_\rho[\mu_\sigma]$ undergoes a cycle of labels during $G(\rho)$. Assume that, if $\mu_\sigma < \lambda$, the processor μ_σ does not produce any label during G. Then $\mu_\sigma = \lambda$ and the last event of σ happens before the last event of $G(\rho)$.

Proof. By Lemma 1, since the entry $v_\rho[\lambda]$ remains valid after the readoption of the label l at the end of $G(\rho)$, the proposer μ_σ must have produced some label l' during G (hence $\mu_\sigma = \lambda$) that was received by ρ during G. Necessarily, the production of l' happens after the last event of σ at λ, thus the last event of $G(\rho)$ at ρ also happens after the last event of σ at λ. □

Theorem 2 (Safety - Weak Version). *Consider an execution E. Let λ be a processor and let Σ be a subexecution such that the local execution $\sigma = \Sigma(\lambda)$ at λ is an h-safe epoch. We denote by F the suffix of the execution that starts with Σ. Consider the two simple scenarios $U_1 = \rho_1 \xrightarrow{p1a} (S_1, v_1, t_1) \rightsquigarrow \rho_1 \xrightarrow{p2a} (Q_1, v_1, t_1, p_1) \xrightarrow{p2b} \rho_1 \xrightarrow{dec} (\alpha_1, v_1, t_1, p_1)$ and $U_2 = (\rho_2, S_2, v_2, t_2) \rightsquigarrow (\alpha_2, v_2, t_2, p_2)$ with characteristics $(\mu_\sigma, l_\sigma, t_1)$ and $(\mu_\sigma, l_\sigma, t_2)$ respectively.*
We denote by e_i' the acceptation event $(\alpha_i, v_i, t_i, p_i)$. Assume that the events e_1 and e_2 occur in F and that $h \le t_1 \le t_2$. In addition, assume that, if $\mu_\sigma < \lambda$, then the processor μ_σ does not produce any label during F. We then have two cases: (a) If $t_1 = t_2$, then either $p_1 \sqsubseteq p_2$, or $p_2 \sqsubseteq p_1$, or the last event of σ happens before one of the event e_1 or e_2. (b) If $t_1 < t_2$, then $p_1 \sqsubseteq p_2$ or the last event of σ happens before one of the event e_1 or e_2.

Proof (Sketch). We assume that both events e_1 and e_2 do not happen after the last event of σ and we prove the result. We denote by γ^* the configuration right before the subexecution Σ. We prove the result by induction on the value of t_2.

(*Bootstrapping*). We first assume that $t_2 = t_1$. Recall the ballot integers include the identifiers of the proposer, hence $\rho_1 = \rho_2$. If $p_1 \not\sqsubseteq p_2$ and $p_2 \not\sqsubseteq p_1$, then ρ_1 has sent two $p2a$ messages with different proposals and the same ballot. Let e and f be the events corresponding to these two sendings. None of the events e and f occurs in the execution prefix A, otherwise, since e_1 and e_2 occur in F, the configuration γ^* would contain a ballot (x, t) with $x[\mu_\sigma].l = l_\sigma$ and $t \ge h$; this is a contradiction since σ is h-safe. We will refer to this argument as the *safe epoch* argument. Hence, e and f occur in F. The fact that $p_1 \not\sqsubseteq p_2$ and

$p_2 \not\sqsubseteq p_1$ implies that there must be a cycle of labels in the entry $v_{\rho_1}[\mu_\sigma]$ between the e and f. By Lemma 3, this implies that the last event of σ happens before the event e_1 or e_2; this is a contradiction. We will refer to this argument as the *cycle of label* argument. Hence, $p_1 \sqsubseteq p_2$ or $p_2 \sqsubseteq p_1$.

(Induction). Now, $t_1 < t_2$ and we assume the result holds for every value t such that $t_1 \leq t < t_2$. Pick some acceptor β in $Q_1 \cap S_2$. From its point of view, there are two events f_1 and f_2 at β that respectively correspond to the acceptance of the proposal (v_1, t_1, p_1) in the scenario U_1 (reception of a *p2a* message), and the adoption of the ballot (v_2, t_2) in the scenario U_2 (reception of a *p1a* message).

First, the events f_1 and f_2 occur in the suffix F (same argument as in bootstrapping). Since $t_1 < t_2$, by the *cycle of labels* argument, f_1 happens before f_2. The *p1b* message the acceptor β has sent contains a non-null lastly accepted proposal (t, p) such that $t_1 \leq t < t_2$ and $p_1 \sqsubseteq p$. Otherwise, the *cycle of labels* argument would show (again) a contradiction.

Now, the proposer ρ_2 receives a set of proposals from the acceptors of the quorum S_2, including at least one non-null proposal from β. Then, it selects among the replies, the accepted proposal (t_c, p_c) with the highest ballot integer, and highest request sequence length (lexicographical order). Since ρ_2 has received the proposal (t, p) from β, we then have $h \leq t_1 \leq t \leq t_c < t_2$ and $(t, |p|) \leq (t_c, |p_c|)$ (lexicographically).

Let β_c be the proposer in S_2 which has sent to ρ_2 the proposal (t_c, p_c) in the *p1b* message. By the *safe epoch* argument, there is an event f_c in F that corresponds to β_c accepting the proposal (t_c, p_c). Consider the simple acceptation scenario V_c that ends with f_c, and let $char(V_c) = (\mu_c, l_c, t_c)$ be its characteristic. Since f_c is the last acceptation event before β_c replies to ρ_2 (with a *p1a* message), we must have $(\mu_c, l_c) = (\mu_\sigma, l_\sigma)$; otherwise, the accepted variable $accepted_{\beta_c}$ would have been cleared (epoch change at β_c), and β_c would have not sent the non-null proposal (t_c, p_c) to ρ_2. Because of the *safe epoch* argument, V_c cannot be a fake simple acceptation scenario; thus V_c is a real simple acceptation scenario.

By applying the induction hypothesis to V_c, and since f_c cannot happen after the last event of σ (otherwise e_2 would also happen after it), we have two cases. The case (A) $t_1 = t_c$. Then $p_1 \sqsubseteq p_c$ or $p_c \sqsubseteq p_1$. But, the fact that $(t, |p|) \leq (t_c, |p_c|)$ (lexicographically) and $p_1 \sqsubseteq p$ implies that $|p_c| \geq |p| \geq |p_1|$, and thus $p_1 \sqsubseteq p_c$. The case (B) $t_1 < t_c$. But then $p_1 \sqsubseteq p_c$.

In all cases, we have $p_1 \sqsubseteq p_c$. But, we also have $p_c \sqsubseteq p_2$ (scenario U_2), hence $p_1 \sqsubseteq p_2$. □

Corollary 1. *Consider an execution E. Let λ be a processor and let Σ be a subexecution such that the local execution $\sigma = \Sigma(\lambda)$ at λ is an h-safe epoch. We denote by F the suffix of the execution that starts with Σ.*

Consider two decision events $e_i = (\alpha_i, v_i, t_i, p_i)$, $i = 1, 2$, such that $\chi(v_i) = \mu_\sigma$, $v_i[\mu_\sigma].l = l_\sigma$ and $t_i \geq h$. Assume that both events e_1 and e_2 are real decision events relative to F. In addition, assume that, if $\mu_\sigma < \lambda$, then the processor μ_σ does not produce any label during F. Then either $p_1 \sqsubseteq p_2$, $p_2 \sqsubseteq p_1$ or the last event of σ happens before one of the event e_1 or e_2.

Theorem 3 (Safety). *Consider an execution E, a proposer λ proposer and a subexecution Σ such that the local execution $\sigma = \Sigma(\lambda)$ at λ is a h-safe epoch for some bounded integer h. We denote by F the suffix of execution that starts with Σ. Assume that the observed zone $Z(F, \lambda, \sigma)$ is defined and that, if $\mu_\sigma < \lambda$, then the processor μ_σ does not produce any label during F. Consider two scenarios U_1 and U_2 in $Z(F, \lambda, \sigma)$ ending with acceptation events $e_1 = (\alpha_1, v_1, t_1, p_1)$ and $e_2 = (\alpha_2, v_2, t_2, p_2)$. Let $\mu_i = \chi(v_i)$ and $l_i = v_i[\mu_i]$, $i = 1, 2$, and assume that $\mu_\sigma \leq \min(\mu_1, \mu_2)$ and $t_1, t_2 \geq h$. Then $(\mu_1, l_1) = (\mu_2, l_2) = (\mu_\sigma, l_\sigma)$, and $p_1 \sqsubseteq p_2$ or $p_2 \sqsubseteq p_1$.*

Proof (Sketch). The definition of the observed zone imply that $(\mu_1, l_1) = (\mu_2, l_2) = (\mu_\sigma, l_\sigma)$ because the corresponding scenarios has been "seen" by λ during its epoch. Then the previous corollary applies.   □

In the case $\mu_\sigma < \lambda$, assuming that μ_σ does not produce any label during F means that the proposer λ should be the live processor with the lowest identifier. To deal with this issue, one can use a failure detector.

6   Self-stabilizing Failure Detector

Liveness in Paxos is not guaranteed unless there is a unique proposer. The original Paxos algorithm assumes that the choice of a distinguished proposer is done through an external module. In the sequel, we present an implementation of a self-stabilizing failure detector that works under a partial synchronism assumption. Note that this assumption is strong enough to implement an eventual perfect failure detector, but such a failure detector is not mandatory for our tag system to stabilize. This brief section simply explains how a *self-stabilizing* implementation can be done; which is, although not difficult, not obvious either. Each processor α has a vector L_α indexed by the processor identifiers; each entry $L_\alpha[\mu]$ is an integer whose value is comprised between 0 and some predefined maximum constant W. Every processor α keeps broadcasting a heartbeat message $\langle hb, \alpha \rangle$ containing its identifier (e.g., by using [7,8]). When the processor α receives a heartbeat from processor β, it sets the entry $L_\alpha[\beta]$ to zero, and increments the value of every entry $L_\alpha[\rho]$, $\rho \neq \beta$ that has value less than W. The detector output at processor α is the list F_α of every identifier μ such that $L_\alpha[\mu] = W$. In other words, the processor α assesses that the processor β has crashed if and only if $L_\alpha[\beta] = W$.

(*Interleaving of Heartbeats*). *For any two live processors α and β, between two receptions of heartbeat $\langle hb, \beta \rangle$ at processor α, there are strictly less than W receptions of heartbeats from other processors.* Under this condition, for every processor α, if the processor β is alive, then eventually the identifier β does not belong to the list F_α. A distinguished proposer ρ can be defined as follows: $\rho = \min(\mu; \ L_\rho[\mu] < W)$.

References

1. Abraham, U.: Self-stabilizing timestamps. Theor. Comput. Sci. **308**(1–3), 449–515 (2003)
2. Alon, N., Attiya, H., Dolev, S., Dubois, S., Potop-Butucaru, M., Tixeuil, S.: Pragmatic self-stabilization of atomic memory in message-passing systems. In: Défago, X., Petit, F., Villain, V. (eds.) SSS 2011. LNCS, vol. 6976, pp. 19–31. Springer, Heidelberg (2011)
3. Blanchard, P., Dolev, S., Beauquier, J., Delaët, S.: Self-stabilizing Paxos. CoRR, abs/1305.4263 (2013)
4. Castro, M., Liskov, B.: Practical byzantine fault tolerance. In: Proceedings of the Third Symposium on Operating Systems Design and Implementation, OSDI'99, Berkeley, CA, USA, pp. 173–186. USENIX Association (1999)
5. Chandra, T.D., Griesemer, R., Redstone, J.: Paxos made live: an engineering perspective. In: Proceedings of the Twenty-Sixth Annual ACM Symposium on Principles of Distributed Computing, PODC'07, New York, USA, pp. 398–407. ACM (2007)
6. Dolev, D., Shavit, N.: Bounded concurrent time-stamping. SIAM J. Comput. **26**(2), 418–455 (1997)
7. Dolev, S.: Self-stabilization. MIT Press, Cambridge (2000)
8. Dolev, S., Hanemann, A., Schiller, E.M., Sharma, S.: Self-stabilizing end-to-end communication in (bounded capacity, omitting, duplicating and non-FIFO) dynamic networks. In: Richa, A.W., Scheideler, C. (eds.) SSS 2012. LNCS, vol. 7596, pp. 133–147. Springer, Heidelberg (2012)
9. Dolev, S., Kat, R.I., Schiller, E.M.: When consensus meets self-stabilization. J. Comput. Syst. Sci. **76**, 884–900 (2010)
10. Fischer, M.J., Lynch, N.A., Paterson, M.S.: Impossibility of distributed consensus with one faulty process. J. ACM **32**, 374–382 (1985)
11. Herlihy, M.P., Wing, J.M.: Linearizability: a correctness condition for concurrent objects. ACM Trans. Program. Lang. Syst. **12**(3), 463–492 (1990)
12. Israeli, A., Li, M.: Bounded time-stamps. Distrib. Comput. **6**(4), 205–209 (1993)
13. Lamport, L.: Time, clocks, and the ordering of events in a distributed system. Commun. ACM **21**(7), 558–565 (1978)
14. Lamport, L.: The part-time parliament. ACM Trans. Comput. Syst. **16**(2), 133–169 (1998)
15. Lamport, L.: Paxos made simple. ACM SIGACT News **32**(4), 18–25 (2001)
16. Lamport, L.: Generalized consensus and Paxos. Technical report MSR-TR-2005-33, Microsoft Research (2005)
17. Lamport, L.: Fast Paxos. Distrib. Comput. **19**(2), 79–103 (2006)
18. Lamport, L.: Byzantizing Paxos by refinement. In: Peleg, D. (ed.) Distributed Computing. LNCS, vol. 6950, pp. 211–224. Springer, Heidelberg (2011)
19. Lynch, N.A.: Distributed Algorithms. Morgan Kaufmann Publishers Inc., San Francisco (1996)

An Architecture for Automatic Scaling of Replicated Services

Leonardo Aniello[1,2]([✉]), Silvia Bonomi[1,2], Federico Lombardi[1,2],
Alessandro Zelli[2], and Roberto Baldoni[1,2]

[1] Cyber Intelligence and Information Security Research Center,
University of Rome "La Sapienza", Via Ariosto 25, 00185 Rome, Italy
[2] Department of Computer, Control, and Management Engineering
"Antonio Ruberti", University of Rome "La Sapienza",
Via Ariosto 25, 00185 Rome, Italy
{aniello,bonomi,lombardi,zelli,baldoni}@dis.uniroma1.it

Abstract. Replicated services that allow to scale dynamically can adapt to requests load. Choosing the right number of replicas is fundamental to avoid performance worsening when input spikes occur and to save resources when the load is low. Current mechanisms for automatic scaling are mostly based on fixed thresholds on CPU and memory usage, which are not sufficiently accurate and often entail late countermeasures. We propose Make Your Service Elastic (MYSE), an architecture for automatic scaling of generic replicated services based on queuing models for accurate response time estimation. Requests and service times patterns are analyzed to learn and predict over time their distribution so as to allow for early scaling. A novel heuristic is proposed to avoid the flipping phenomenon. We carried out simulations that show promising results for what concerns the effectiveness of our approach.

Keywords: Automatic scaling · Performance modeling · Traffic forecasting · QoS compliance · Resource-saving

1 Introduction

While designing a replicated service to deliver target response time for a fixed workload is easily achievable by properly tuning the number and the specifics of replicas, it becomes really challenging for highly variable loads. Methods based on *over-provisioning* allow to cope with load peaks but entail huge waste of resources, which translates in to money loss. Nevertheless, *under-provisioning* systematically fails in delivering required performance when input spikes occur. The actual alternative to static provisioning is rendering the service *elastic*, so that it can adapt to fluctuating workloads by changing the number of replicas (*configuration*) on the fly. Such a functionality is called *auto scaling*. Amazon Web Services (http://aws.amazon.com) and Google App Engine (https://appengine.google.com) are among

© Springer International Publishing Switzerland 2014
G. Noubir and M. Raynal (Eds.): NETYS 2014, LNCS 8593, pp. 122–137, 2014.
DOI: 10.1007/978-3-319-09581-3_9

the most relevant XaaS providers offering the possibility to reconfigure at runtime. Both allow to define policies that trigger a reconfiguration on the basis of the variation of a set of off-the-shelf and custom metrics, like memory usage and CPU utilization.

This kind of solutions has two main issues. One concerns the difficulty to find an accurate relationship between the value of monitored metrics and the configuration needed to meet latency requirements. Indeed, an effective model should be employed in order to find the proper relationship between gathered measures and expected performance. The other regards the timeliness in reacting to load variations: spotting a problematic situation when it is already occurring brings temporary Quality of Service (QoS) violations, while reacting late to a load drop causes the same problems of over-provisioning. The reaction delay also includes the time required for the new configuration to be ready, which comprises additional factors like replica activation time and state transfer time.

One additional challenge of designing elastic solutions is the cost of elasticity, i.e. the cost that the service provider pays to activate/deactivate a replica like, for example, the bandwidth used to transfer the state from an active replica to a new one, the energy used to keep replicas running with low utilization and the tradeoff between buying the infrastructure or just renting it. Usually, such costs occur each time that the system moves from one configuration to another and they may grow up if the *flipping phenomenon* (i.e. a sequence of activation and deactivation of replicas) is not properly mastered.

We propose a solution aimed at facing these issues. We designed the *Make Your Service Elastic* module (MYSE) for the automatic horizontal scaling of a replicated service. By monitoring input requests patterns and the service times delivered by the replicated service, the MYSE module learns over time through neural networks how input load and service times vary, and produces estimations to enable early decisions about reconfiguration. A queuing model of the replicated service is used to compute the expected response time given the current configuration (number of replicas) and the distributions of both input requests and service times. A novel graph-based heuristic called *Flipping-reducing Scaling Heuristic* is employed that leverages this model to find the minimum number of replicas required to achieve the target performance and to reduce as much as possible the flipping phenomenon.

We carried out simulations by using a real dataset containing the requests to a website over the time. The results showed high accuracy in input traffic prediction and good effectiveness in taking proper scaling decisions. These promising outcomes of the MYSE module validation have driven us to start its real implementation on Amazon Web Services. With reference to the related work (see Sect. 2), the novelty of MYSE consists in (i) combining together traffic forecasting, done through artificial neural networks, and performance estimation through queuing models, and (ii) addressing the problem of flipping by employing the innovative Flipping-reducing Scaling Heuristic.

The rest of the paper is organized as follows: related works are presented in Sect. 2; Sect. 3 describes the MYSE architecture; Sect. 4 reports the preliminary

results obtained from simulations and Sect. 5 outlines how the work is going
to continue.

2 Related Work

According to a recent survey [19], there are several works on automatic scaling of
elastic applications in the cloud. This survey proposes the following classification
of the auto-scaling techniques existing in literature, on the basis of the approach
they employ.

- **Static, threshold-based policies.** The configuration is changed according
  to a set of *rules*, some for scaling out and others for scaling in [9,14,15,20].
  This is a completely *reactive* approach that is currently used by most of the
  cloud providers.
- **Reinforcement learning.** It is an automatic decision-making technique to
  learn online the performance model of the target system without any a priori
  knowledge. Such continuous learning is used to choose the best scaling decision
  according to the goals of decreasing response time and saving resources [3,10,
  26,30].
- **Queuing theory.** The target system is modeled using techniques coming from
  the queuing theory with the aim of estimating its performance given a small
  set of parameters, like input rate and service time, that can be monitored at
  runtime [30–32,36].
- **Control theory.** It is used to automate the management of scaling decisions through the employment of a feedback or feed-forward controller module
  whose objective is to meet performance requirements by adjusting the configuration of the target system [1,5,24,25,34]. Feedback controllers correct
  their behavior by taking into account the error reported by the target system
  through a *gain parameter* that can be adapted dynamically. Feed-forward controllers are based on model predictive control (MPC) and aim at forecasting
  the future behavior of the system. The relationship between the input (the
  workload) and the output (the configuration to adopt) is embedded into the
  transfer function, which can be implemented in several ways (i.e., smoothing
  spline, Kalman filter, Fuzzy model).
- **Time-series analysis.** It can be used to spot recurring patterns of the workload over time, in order to forecast future workload so as to come to a scaling
  decision early. Several techniques can be used like averaging methods, regression and neural networks [6–8,13,16–18,21,27,29].

The limitations of an approach based on static, threshold-based rules lies in
its reactive nature: it only takes action after the recognition of a situation that
requires scaling, and during the time needed for the scaling to complete either
the system provides poor performance or resources are wasted. This problem can
be addressed by using time-series analysis in order to forecast how the workload
is likely to change over time so as to enable scaling decisions in advance and
consequently avoid transient periods where the system is not properly configured.

The drawbacks of the techniques based on reinforcement learning are the excessive length of the training phase before reaching a point where it becomes effective, and the difficulty to adapt to workloads that change quickly.

Using control theory can actually be a valid choice, but choosing the right gain parameter is hard. In fact, considering a fixed gain parameter, its tuning is hard and cannot be adjusted at runtime; on the contrary, using an adaptive parameter, that is changed according to the workload, is likely to introduce flipping.

The employment of queuing models to estimate performance can turn out to be not reliable enough because the hard assumptions it requires could be not valid in a real scenario. Nevertheless, we chose to model the replicated service using a queue model because it doesn't require a long training as reinforcement learning does instead.

In addition to the works cited in the survey, also others employ a proactive approach for auto-scaling as we do, but none combines together traffic forecasting through artificial neural networks, and performance estimation through queuing models. Ghanbari et al. [12] present an auto-scaling approach based on MPC that aims both to meet SLA and save resources by framing the problem as an MPC problem. Moore et al. [22] describe an elasticity framework composed by two controllers operating in a coordinated manner: one works reactively on the basis of static rules and the other uses a time-series forecaster (based on support vector machines) and two Naive Bayes models to predict both the workload and the target system performance.

For what concerns how the flipping phenomenon is dealt with in literature, the survey [19] reports that such an issue is addressed in some of the threshold-based works by setting two distinct thresholds: one for scaling out and another for scaling in, so as to have a "tolerance band" that can absorb part of the oscillations. The survey also advises to set so called *calm periods* during which scaling decisions are suspended. Our approach is based on the concept of calm periods, as suggested in the survey, but is more refined as the length of such period is adapted on the basis of the amount of flipping experienced so far.

3   MYSE Architecture

Figure 1 shows how the MYSE module is expected to be integrated with the target service. We assume that a Configuration Manager module is available to receive external commands that update the configuration.

We modeled the service as a queuing system with s servers [11]. Without loss of generality, we considered that replicas are homogeneous (i.e. they have the same computational capabilities and can be used interchangeably) and a single class of service. The basic idea is to consider the replicated service as a black box and monitor requests patterns over time to identify the relevant characteristics of input traffic so as to properly reconfigure the service through the Configuration Manager. To this aim, we assume that replicated service instances export, as performance metrics, their service times. This allows us to follow the black box approach as in [2,33] by considering only observable parameters.

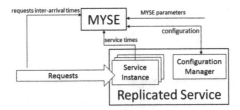

Fig. 1. Integration of MYSE module with target replicated service.

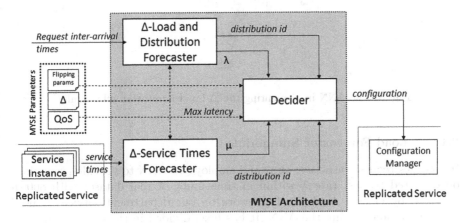

Fig. 2. MYSE internal structure.

Monitoring requests arrival and service times over time enables to predict their probability distribution. The queuing model is then used to compute the expected latency in serving a single request, which can be compared to given QoS requirements to figure out whether the compliance is actually achieved. The same queuing model is employed to derive the minimum configuration allowing to meet the QoS and, at the same time, to avoid wasting resources. We employed four Artificial Neural Networks (ANNs), two ANNs to learn how request rate and request distribution vary over time, and other two to learn how service times and their distribution vary over time. In this way, we can conveniently update the configuration early enough to avoid temporary performance worsening or resource under-utilization. The timeline of these predictions is provided externally (Δ parameter).

Figure 2 details the submodules of MYSE. The Δ-*Load and Distribution Forecaster* is in charge of learning and forecasting request rate and request distribution (it includes Δ-*Load Forecaster* and Δ-*Distribution Forecaster* submodules). The Δ-*Service Times Forecaster* looks at service time patterns to extract the distribution of service times and its mean μ. The *Decider* determines the suitable configuration to meet QoS on the basis of the inputs supplied by the other two submodules and of the *Flipping Parameters* (see Sect. 3.4). Single submodules are described below.

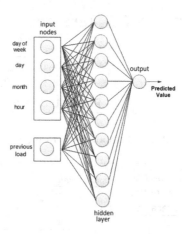

Fig. 3. The ANN implementing the Δ-Load Forecaster submodule.

3.1 Δ-Load Forecaster Submodule

It analyzes request rates over time and employs an ANN to provide predictions on expected request rate λ within Δ time units. A real dataset with 8000 h provided by Google Analytics framework on our department services is used for training and testing the ANN. It has been divided in three parts: 70 % for training, 15 % for validation and 15 % for test using a k-fold cross validation with $k = 10$ in order to choose the right ANN parameters and address overfitting. We normalized the input parameters with the *Max-Min Normalization* $[0, 1]$ and employed the *Backpropagation Algorithm* [28] for learning, with a sigmoid as activation function. A general method to set the network parameters doesn't exist, so we empirically fixed *learning rate* and *momentum* (to 0.3 and 0.5, respectively), by executing several tests aimed at trading off the recognition error with the exposure to overfitting.

Several guidelines are available for choosing the number of hidden layers and nodes for obtaining good generalization and low overfitting. One hidden layer is sufficient to approximate any complex nonlinear functions to any desired accuracy. We implemented several ANNs to find out the best one, and it turned out to be the one with four input nodes for the date (day, day of the week, month, hour) and one input node for the current traffic. Again, we chose the number of hidden nodes empirically (as also suggested in [35]) and we found out that using 11 hidden neurons gives the best performances. The output node simply represents the predicted traffic values. Figure 3 shows the final architecture of the ANN used in the Δ-Load forecaster.

We also carried out some simulations to check how long it takes for the ANN to be properly trained as the number of backpropagation iterations varies. The obtained results show that using up to 100 iterations allows to keep the training time below 1.2 s.

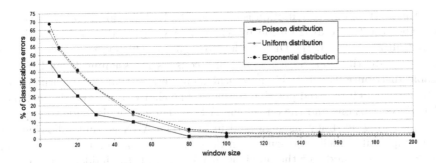

Fig. 4. Classification error in the Δ-Distribution Recognized while increasing the window size.

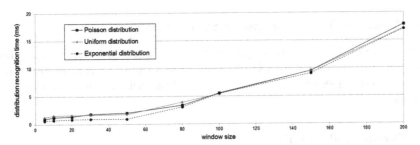

Fig. 5. Time needed by the Δ-Distribution Recognized to get the estimation of the distribution type by varying the window size. This experiment has been executed on an Intel Core 2 2.00 GHz, 2 GB RAM.

3.2 Δ-Distribution Forecaster Submodule

It is composed by two parts, the *Distribution Recognizer* and the *Distribution Forecaster*; it analyzes requests inter-arrival times to produce predictions on request distribution Δ time units ahead. The Distribution Recognizer estimates the best-fitting continuous or discrete distribution by analyzing a set of samples given in input, which represent the requests inter-arrival times. These samples are analyzed with a fixed-length sliding window. We computed that the length has to be at least 80 samples to get an estimation error lower than or equal to 5 % (see Fig. 4); on the other hand, Fig. 5 gives evidence that obtaining an estimation latency below 5 ms requires 80 samples or less.

The estimation of distribution parameters is made by using the *maximum-likelihood estimation method* [23]. This result is then used to perform "goodness-of-fit" tests, such as the *chi-squared test* (for discrete distributions, i.e. Poisson) and *Kolmogorov-Smirnov test* (for continuous distributions, i.e. Normal), for discriminating among distinct distributions [4]. In the current implementation, the submodule is able to recognize and classify the following distributions: Poisson, Uniform and Exponential. Obviously, in case the real distribution of the samples doesn't correspond to any of those recognized by the Distribution Recognizer, then the most similar distribution is chosen. The Distribution Forecaster is able to predict the future distribution by using an ANN trained by taking as input the output produced by the Distribution Recognizer, which is an encoding of the recognized distribution. Such an encoding consists in assigning to each recognizable distribution a distinct numerical identifier, so that the identifiers are distanced enough to avoid possible conflicts. The choice to use two distinct parallel ANNs (this one and the one of the Δ-Load Forecaster) is made to improve the forecasting accuracy, as suggested in [35]. The ANN is built following the same empirical guidelines discussed in Sect. 3.1: it has as input four nodes for the date and one node for the previous distribution id, 150 hidden neurons and one output for the forecasted distribution. The learning rate is fixed to 0.9 and momentum to 0.4, while the other parameters are the same derived in Sect. 3.1.

3.3 Δ-Service Times Forecaster Submodule

It takes as input the service times provided by the replicated service and produces as output the estimation of their distribution and the mean μ of service times. The same techniques employed for the Δ-Load and Distribution Forecaster are used here.

3.4 Decider Submodule

The submodule computes the minimum configuration for guaranteeing QoS compliance in service provisioning (i.e. the latency in the specific case). It takes as input the latency threshold specified in the QoS, the predictions on request distribution (distribution id and λ), the predictions on the distribution of service times (distribution id and μ) and the *Flipping parameters*, which are the tuning parameters of the Flipping-reducing Scaling Heuristic, described in detail later in this section. The Decider submodule first applies the well-known queuing model techniques to compute the expected latency T in the current configuration (i.e. with s replicas), given the request rate and the service times provided by the forecasters. Then, it applies the Flipping-reducing Scaling Heuristic to decide whether scaling out (in case QoS is violated), scaling in (in case a configuration with less replicas can still guarantee QoS compliance) or keeping the current configuration.

The Flipping-Reducing Scaling Heuristic. If QoS compliance can be achieved with the current configuration (with s replicas), then the algorithm evaluates if switching off replicas still makes it possible to satisfy QoS requirements. It computes the maximum number n of replicas that can be removed without violating the QoS, and moves from a configuration with s servers to a configuration with $s - n$. On the contrary, if the expected latency is higher than QoS threshold, then the algorithm computes the minimum number n of replicas to activate in order to comply with the QoS, and moves from a configuration with s servers to a configuration with $s + n$. Highly variable traffic and prediction errors can make the configuration oscillate very often, introducing a lot of overhead due to frequent activation/deactivation of replicas. This phenomenon is referred to as *flipping*, and we dealt with it by introducing a *cost function* that prevents the algorithm from moving back in a certain configuration in case such configuration was set too recently.

To this aim, we defined an edge-weighted directed graph $G = (V, E, w(e, t))$ where (i) the set of vertex V represents all the possible configurations (i.e. number of active replicas) i.e. $V = \{1, 2, 3, \ldots s_{max}\}$, (ii) there exists an edge between any pair of vertexes (iii) for any edge $e_{s,s'} \in E$ the edge weight $w(e_{s,s'}, t)$ represents the cost of moving from the configuration s to the configuration s' at the current time t.

The cost function is defined as $w(e_{s,s'}, t) = FlippingCost \cdot flipping\%$, where *FlippingCost* is one of the Flipping parameters, while $flipping\%$ is computed as the number of the flippings detected from the beginning divided by the number of heuristic executions. The detection of a flipping is triggered when two scaling decisions in opposite directions (i.e., a scaling out and a scaling in) are executed within a configurable window (the *FlippingWindow*, another Flipping Parameter). In this way, the $flipping\%$ decreases in time in case no flipping occurs. When the algorithm moves from the configuration s to the configuration s' at time t, the edge $e_{s,s'}$ is assigned with the value $w(e_{s,s'}, t)$. Then, such weight is decreased linearly in time until it comes back to 0. The transition from a configuration s to a configuration s' is allowed at time t only if $w(e_{s,s'}, t) = 0$. The flipping phenomenon is very likely to involve additional costs because of the high number of machine activations. On the other hand, forcing to keep a certain configuration for a period of time regardless of the load can raise temporary over-provisioning and/or under-provisioning, and both lead to increased costs. The *FlippingCost* parameter is indeed aimed at tuning such a tradeoff, on the basis of both the real costs of replica activation and QoS violation, and the expected variability of the input traffic.

We evaluated the effectiveness in avoiding the flipping phenomenon by carrying out a simulation that compares the behavior of the heuristic that uses the cost function with a heuristic that doesn't put any cost on the edges (i.e., $FlippingCost = 0$). We set *FlippingCost* to 15000 and *FlippingWindow* to 100 s. The results shown in Fig. 6 give evidence that our heuristic is successful, indeed it manages to keep the configuration fixed during the intervals when the other oscillates instead. It is to note that at the beginning the algorithm actually introduces flipping, but this is due to the fact the no flipping was occurred before, so $flipping\%$ is zero, yet.

4   Simulations

In this section we describe a set of simulations aimed at assessing the effectiveness of the proposed architecture. In particular, we first evaluated the ability of the Δ-Load Forecaster and Δ-Distribution Forecaster to adapt to different types of loads and then we evaluated globally the goodness of the approach by evaluating the evolution of the configurations in time. In all these simulations, Δ is fixed to one hour.

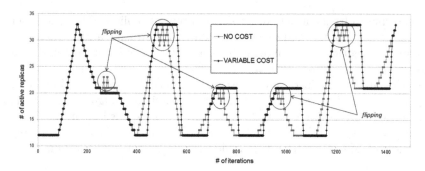

Fig. 6. A comparison between the heuristic employing a cost function and another one that doesn't use any cost function. Over time, it is shown that putting costs on the edges allows to limit the flipping phenomenon.

Evaluation of the Δ-Load Forecaster. In this experiments, we used a real dataset including one year of statistics collected through the Google Analytics framework on our Department services. In order to show the adaptation to changes in the load pattern, this dataset has been integrated with a synthetic one. In particular, starting from the real Google Analytics dataset, we appended five days of the same dataset that has been scaled (amplified), and a sine function. We didn't simulate the Service Times Estimator because of the unavailability of traces describing service times over time, but we considered it as fixed and known to the Decider Module. Anyway, we believe that the effectiveness of the results obtained for the Δ-Load and Distribution Forecaster can also hold for this module, since the employed techniques are the same. In order to make the ANN really adaptive to traffic changes, online learning is employed as follows. We store the training set in a fixed-length sliding window containing the last 100 inputs, and at each new input the ANN is trained using all the inputs in the window (by executing 100 iterations of the backpropagation algorithm, as explained in Sect. 3.1). Figure 7 shows the comparison between the real number of requests over time and the predictions. As we can see, the predictions follow the real pattern and converge quite quickly after a request pattern change. The weekly *Root Mean Square Error* (RMSE) of predictions is 4 %, and the *Mean Average Error* (MAE) is 3 %.

Evaluation of the Δ-Distribution Forecaster. We evaluated the capability of this module to recognize a distribution by using a synthetic dataset where the distribution of inter-arrival times changes very often over time, from Uniform to Poisson and viceversa. We measured the number of iterations required to correctly recognize distribution changes, where one iteration corresponds to the analysis of the samples of a single window, whose length was fixed to 80 samples (see Sect. 3.2). The results showed that 62 iterations are required on average to detect the transition from Uniform to Poisson, and 30 are needed instead for the opposite transition. Since the window slides at each sample, these results

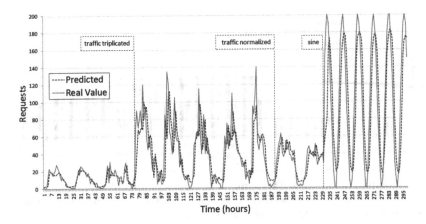

Fig. 7. Comparison between dataset traffic and forecaster predictions. The instants in time are indicated where traffic pattern changes: from normal to triplicated, to normal again and finally to a sine function with amplitude 100 is used.

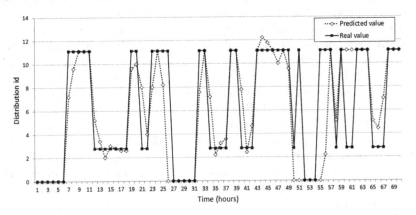

Fig. 8. Comparison between real and predicted request arrival distributions. Three distributions are recognizable: Uniform (id = 0), Exponential (id = 3) and Poisson (id = 11). The average error in 72 h is 3%

indicate that distribution changes can be recognized before the window gets totally renewed.

We also evaluated the predictive accuracy of the ANN, by comparing real and forecasted request distributions over time. Three distinct distributions are recognized, each mapped to distinct ids chosen so that classification errors get minimized. We modified the dataset used for the evaluation of the Δ-Load Forecaster in such a way that the distribution of inter-arrival times changes very often over time among the recognizable distributions. Figure 8 shows that predictions are notably accurate (3% error over 3 days).

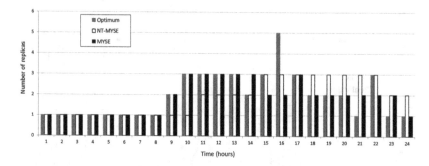

Fig. 9. Comparison between the number of replicas requested by MYSE and NT-MYSE, together with the indication of the optimum, that is the minimum number of replicas required to meet QoS requirements.

Evaluation of the Overall Architecture. This evaluation is aimed to highlight the relevant added value of employing traffic predictions for correctly issuing resource provisioning. The dataset used here is the Google Analytics one. Figure 9 shows how the number of requested replicas varies over time on a hour-basis during a whole day. These results have been obtained by simulating three distinct scenarios: (i) the optimal configuration, that is the minimum number of replicas required to meet QoS requirements, (ii) the configuration produced without the contributions of Δ-Load and Distribution Forecaster, referred to as *Non-Trained MYSE* (NT-MYSE) and (iii) the configuration requested by the complete MYSE module. In the simulation of NT-MYSE, the Decider is fed with traffic details that are produced in real-time by the Distribution Recognizer on the basis of the current traffic only.

Until 8:00 the traffic is stable and both the approaches behave correctly, then traffic begins changing and the use of predictions shows its effectiveness by contributing to generate configurations that are nearer to the optimum compared to NT-MYSE approach. Another important advantage of employing predictions is rendering the system more robust to unexpected peaks. This can be seen by observing the effect of the isolated peak occurring at 16:00 (a peak in the number of the optimal number of replicas corresponds to a peak in traffic load): NT-MYSE is biased by such occurrence and hereafter keeps to over-provision, while MYSE correctly recognizes it as an outlier. We quantified numerically the error of each approach by averaging over the entire day the number of replicas above (over-provisioning) and below (QoS violation) the optimum. NT-MYSE provided on average 0.29 replicas in excess and 0.33 replicas less than the minimum required, for a total of 0.62. MYSE allows on average to over-provision 0.13 replicas (55 % more accurate) and under-provision 0.21 replicas (36 % more accurate), that is a total error of 0.34 replicas (45 % more accurate).

5   Conclusions and Future Directions

Avoiding both performance worsening and over-provisioning for replicated services is the goal of the architecture we propose in this work and, according to the results obtained by the simulations we carried out, we believe that forecasting requests and service times, and carefully modeling how performance gets affected, are the proper building blocks for achieving that objective. We claim that this approach is novel within the context of auto-scaling works. An additional original contribution concerns the Flipping-reducing Heuristic, which allows to address the problems due to quick oscillations in the load. Along this line, we are carrying on this work by exploring distinct directions.

At the time of this writing we are deploying the MYSE architecture on Amazon Web Services in order to concretely assess strengths and weaknesses of the model. Once a target service for the prototype implementation is chosen, we will be able to provide both a validation of the MYSE module and the specification of the analytical model for the actual service in order to compare the results. The deployment of MYSE in a real cloud infrastructure will allow to estimate the delays due to replicas activation/deactivation, which will contribute to the accuracy of the model itself. Another important aspect we want to investigate is the economics behind this elastic model. What is the best model to price the elastic replication system? Who are the customers for this kind of service? The answers to these questions depend on the definition of a precise cost model that can help to identify the market sectors where such replication mechanism could be beneficial.

Finally, we are investigating how to make the MYSE architecture completely non-intrusive, i.e., so that the MYSE module does not need any information provided by the replicated service, such as the service times. This would enable and ease its employment in a wider range of applications.

Acknowledgments. This work has been partially supported by the TENACE PRIN Project (n. 20103P34XC) funded by the Italian Ministry of Education, University and Research and by the academic project C26A133HZY funded by the University of Rome "La Sapienza".

References

1. Ali-Eldin, A., Tordsson, J., Elmroth, E.: An adaptive hybrid elasticity controller for cloud infrastructures. In: 2012 IEEE Network Operations and Management Symposium (NOMS), pp. 204–212 (2012)
2. Baldoni, R., Lodi, G., Montanari, L., Mariotta, G., Rizzuto, M.: Online black-box failure prediction for mission critical distributed systems. In: Ortmeier, F., Lipaczewski, M. (eds.) SAFECOMP 2012. LNCS, vol. 7612, pp. 185–197. Springer, Heidelberg (2012)

3. Barrett, E., Howley, E., Duggan, J.: Applying reinforcement learning towards automating resource allocation and application scalability in the cloud. Concurrency Comput.: Pract. Experience **25**(12), 1656–1674 (2013)
4. Biswas, S., Ahmad, S., Molla, M.K.I., Hirose, K., Nasser, M.: Kolmogorov-smirnov test in text-dependent automatic speaker identification. Eng. Lett. **16**(4), 469–472 (2008)
5. Bodík, P., Griffith, R., Sutton, C., Fox, A., Jordan, M., Patterson, D.: Statistical machine learning makes automatic control practical for internet datacenters. In: Proceedings of the 2009 Conference on Hot Topics in Cloud Computing, Hot-Cloud'09. USENIX Association, Berkeley (2009)
6. Cardosa, M., Chandra, A.: Resource bundles: using aggregation for statistical large-scale resource discovery and management. IEEE Trans. Parallel Distrib. Syst. **21**(8), 1089–1102 (2010)
7. Caron, E., Desprez, F., Muresan, A.: Forecasting for cloud computing on-demand resources based on pattern matching. Research RR-7217, Inria (2010)
8. Chen, G., He, W., Liu, J., Nath, S., Rigas, L., Xiao, L., Zhao, F.: Energy-aware server provisioning and load dispatching for connection-intensive internet services. In: Proceedings of the 5th USENIX Symposium on Networked Systems Design and Implementation (NSDI), pp. 337–350. USENIX Association (2008)
9. Dutreilh, X., Rivierre, N., Moreau, A., Malenfant, J., Truck, I.: From data center resource allocation to control theory and back. In: 2010 IEEE 3rd International Conference on Cloud Computing (CLOUD), pp. 410–417 (2010)
10. Dutreilh, X., Kirgizov, S., Melekhova, O., Malenfant, J., Rivierre, N., Truck, I.: Using reinforcement learning for autonomic resource allocation in clouds: towards a fully automated workflow. In: The Seventh International Conference on Autonomic and Autonomous Systems, ICAS 2011, Venice/Mestre, Italy, pp. 67–74 (2011)
11. Garlan, D., Cheng, S.W., Schmerl, B.: Increasing system dependability through architecture-based self-repair. In: de Lemos, R., Gacek, C., Romanovsky, A. (eds.) Architecting Dependable Systems. LNCS, vol. 2677, pp. 61–89. Springer, Heidelberg (2003)
12. Ghanbari, H., Simmons, B., Litoiu, M., Barna, C., Iszlai, G.: Optimal autoscaling in a iaas cloud. In: Proceedings of the 9th International Conference on Autonomic Computing, ICAC '12, pp. 173–178. ACM, New York (2012)
13. Gong, Z., Gu, X., Wilkes, J.: Press: predictive elastic resource scaling for cloud systems. In: 2010 International Conference on Network and Service Management (CNSM), pp. 9–16 (2010)
14. Han, R., Guo, L., Ghanem, M., Guo, Y.: Lightweight resource scaling for cloud applications. In: 2012 12th IEEE/ACM International Symposium on Cluster, Cloud and Grid Computing (CCGrid), pp. 644–651 (2012)
15. Hasan, M., Magana, E., Clemm, A., Tucker, L., Gudreddi, S.: Integrated and autonomic cloud resource scaling. In: 2012 IEEE Network Operations and Management Symposium (NOMS), pp. 1327–1334 (2012)
16. Huang, J., Li, C., Yu, J.: Resource prediction based on double exponential smoothing in cloud computing. In: 2012 2nd International Conference on Consumer Electronics, Communications and Networks (CECNet), pp. 2056–2060 (2012)
17. Iqbal, W., Dailey, M.N., Carrera, D., Janecek, P.: Adaptive resource provisioning for read intensive multi-tier applications in the cloud. Future Gener. Comput. Syst. **27**(6), 871–879 (2011)
18. Islam, S., Keung, J., Lee, K., Liu, A.: Empirical prediction models for adaptive resource provisioning in the cloud. Future Gener. Comput. Syst. **28**(1), 155–162 (2012)

19. Lorido-Botrán, T., Miguel-Alonso, J., Lozano, J.A.: Auto-scaling techniques for elastic applications in cloud environments. Research EHU-KAT-IK, Department of Computer Architecture and Technology, UPV/EHU (2012)
20. Maurer, M., Brandic, I., Sakellariou, R.: Enacting SLAs in clouds using rules. In: Jeannot, E., Namyst, R., Roman, J. (eds.) Euro-Par 2011, Part I. LNCS, vol. 6852, pp. 455–466. Springer, Heidelberg (2011)
21. Mi, H., Wang, H., Yin, G., Zhou, Y., Shi, D., Yuan, L.: Online self-reconfiguration with performance guarantee for energy-efficient large-scale cloud computing data centers. In: 2010 IEEE International Conference on Services Computing (SCC), pp. 514–521 (2010)
22. Moore, L.R., Bean, K., Ellahi, T.: Transforming reactive auto-scaling into proactive auto-scaling. In: Proceedings of the 3rd International Workshop on Cloud Data and Platforms, CloudDP '13, pp. 7–12. ACM, New York (2013)
23. Myung, I.J.: Tutorial on maximum likelihood estimation. J. Math. Psychol. **47**(1), 90–100 (2003)
24. Padala, P., Hou, K.Y., Shin, K.G., Zhu, X., Uysal, M., Wang, Z., Singhal, S., Merchant, A.: Automated control of multiple virtualized resources. In: Proceedings of the 4th ACM European Conference on Computer Systems, EuroSys '09, pp. 13–26. ACM, New York (2009)
25. Park, S.M., Humphrey, M.: Self-tuning virtual machines for predictable escience. In: Proceedings of the 2009 9th IEEE/ACM International Symposium on Cluster Computing and the Grid, CCGRID '09, pp. 356–363. IEEE Computer Society, Washington, DC (2009)
26. Rao, J., Bu, X., Xu, C.Z., Wang, L., Yin, G.: Vconf: a reinforcement learning approach to virtual machines auto-configuration. In: Proceedings of the 6th International Conference on Autonomic Computing, ICAC '09, pp. 137–146. ACM, New York (2009)
27. Roy, N., Dubey, A., Gokhale, A.: Efficient autoscaling in the cloud using predictive models for workload forecasting. In: 2011 IEEE International Conference on Cloud Computing (CLOUD), pp. 500–507 (2011)
28. Rumelhart, D.E., Hinton, G.E., Williams, R.J.: Learning internal representations by error propagation. Technical report, DTIC Document (1985)
29. Shen, Z., Subbiah, S., Gu, X., Wilkes, J.: Cloudscale: elastic resource scaling for multi-tenant cloud systems. In: Proceedings of the 2nd ACM Symposium on Cloud Computing, SOCC '11, pp. 5:1–5:14. ACM, New York (2011)
30. Tesauro, G., Jong, N.K., Das, R., Bennani, M.N.: A hybrid reinforcement learning approach to autonomic resource allocation. In: Proceedings of the 2006 IEEE International Conference on Autonomic Computing, ICAC '06, pp. 65–73. IEEE Computer Society, Washington, DC (2006)
31. Urgaonkar, B., Shenoy, P., Chandra, A., Goyal, P., Wood, T.: Agile dynamic provisioning of multi-tier internet applications. ACM Trans. Auton. Adapt. Syst. **3**(1), 1:1–1:39 (2008)
32. Villela, D., Pradhan, P., Rubenstein, D.: Provisioning servers in the application tier for e-commerce systems. In: Twelfth IEEE International Workshop on Quality of Service, IWQOS 2004, pp. 57–66 (2004)
33. Williams, A.W., Pertet, S.M., Narasimhan, P.: Tiresias: black-box failure prediction in distributed systems. In: IPDPS, pp. 1–8 (2007)
34. Xu, J., Zhao, M., Fortes, J., Carpenter, R., Yousif, M.: On the use of fuzzy modeling in virtualized data center management. In: Fourth International Conference on Autonomic Computing, ICAC '07, pp. 25–25 (2007)

35. Zhang, G., Patuwo, B.E., Hu, M.Y.: Forecasting with artificial neural networks: the state of the art. Int. J. Forecast. **14**(1), 35–62 (1998)
36. Zhang, Q., Cherkasova, L., Smirni, E.: A regression-based analytic model for dynamic resource provisioning of multi-tier applications. In: Proceedings of the Fourth International Conference on Autonomic Computing, ICAC '07, pp. 27–36. IEEE Computer Society, Washington, DC (2007)

CEP4CMA: Multi-layer Cloud Performance Monitoring and Analysis via Complex Event Processing

Afef Mdhaffar[1,2]($\boxtimes$), Riadh Ben Halima[2], Mohamed Jmaiel[2], and Bernd Freisleben[1]

[1] Department of Mathematics and Computer Science, University of Marburg, Hans-Meerwein-Str. 3, 35032 Marburg, Germany
{mdhaffar,freisleb}@informatik.uni-marburg.de
[2] National School of Engineers, University of Sfax, B.P. 1173, Sfax, Tunisia
{riadh.benhalima,mohamed.jmaiel}@enis.rnu.tn

Abstract. This paper presents a multi-layer monitoring and analysis approach for Cloud computing environments based on the methodology of Complex Event Processing (CEP). Instead of having to manually specify continuous queries on monitored event streams, CEP queries are derived from analyzing the correlations between monitored metrics across multiple Cloud layers. The results of our correlation analysis allow us to reduce the number of monitored parameters and enable us to perform a root cause analysis to identify the causes of performance-related problems. The derived analysis rules are implemented as queries in a CEP engine. The results of several experiments demonstrate the benefits of the proposed approach in terms of precision and recall in comparison with threshold-based methods. They also show the accuracy of our approach in identifying the causes of performance-related problems.

1 Introduction

In a Cloud computing environment with many resources, many applications and many concurrent users, performance degradations are quite likely to occur and rather the norm than the exception. Thus, it is necessary to monitor the performance of Cloud computing environments to detect performance problems and analyze their causes.

Today's Cloud computing environments are typically based on a layered architecture consisting of infrastructure, platform and software layers. Most of the existing Cloud monitoring and analysis approaches have been designed to separately work for only one of these layers [1–6] and thus do not consider the interactions between these layers.

However, monitoring events and analyzing their correlations across layers is very promising to improve the quality of the analysis, especially in terms of identifying the causes of performance degradations. On the other hand, a multi-layer monitoring and analysis approach generates a huge volume of data. Thus, an analysis could be quite slow and could consume a lot of storage space.

© Springer International Publishing Switzerland 2014
G. Noubir and M. Raynal (Eds.): NETYS 2014, LNCS 8593, pp. 138–152, 2014.
DOI: 10.1007/978-3-319-09581-3_10

This paper presents a novel multi-layer monitoring and analysis approach for Cloud computing environments. Our approach offers accurate diagnosis and does not require any storage space for recording monitored events. It is based on Complex Event Processing (CEP) [7], an approach to realize publish-subscribe systems. It can be used to monitor, process and analyze elementary events to deduce complex events describing the state of the monitored system. CEP performs continuously running queries on streams of monitored events. The queries usually have to be specified manually, which typically is a quite challenging task. The novelty of our approach is that the CEP queries are derived from a comprehensive analysis of the relationships between monitored metrics across Cloud layers. The correlations between the monitored metrics on different Cloud layers are obtained via a set of experiments and well known statistical methods. The results of our correlation study allow us to reduce the number of monitored parameters. Furthermore, they are used to perform a Root Cause Analysis (RCA) to identify the causes of performance-related problems [8]. The derived analysis rules are implemented as queries in the CEP engine used in our approach.

To evaluate our proposal, several experiments have been conducted. The first group of experiments investigates the quality of our analysis approach in terms of precision and recall. The results indicate that the proposed approach offers better precision and recall than threshold-based methods. The second set of experiments illustrates the accuracy of our approach in identifying failed components and the causes of performance degradations.

The paper is organized as follows. Section 2 discusses related work. In Sect. 3, the multi-layer monitoring and analysis approach is presented. Our experimental results are described in Sect. 4. Section 5 concludes the paper and outlines areas for future research.

2   Related Work

Monalytics [1] is a large scale monitoring and analysis approach for Cloud services. It focuses on monitoring a Cloud infrastructure (Infrastructure-as-a-Service (IaaS)) and virtualized systems. The authors define different deployment topologies between monitoring brokers and analysis agents: centralized, distributed and hierarchical. The topologies are represented as graphs and can be managed at runtime. Monalytics monitors CPU and memory utilization. It is integrated into the Xen virtualization infrastructure. PCMONS [2] is a monitoring architecture for an IaaS Cloud. It makes use of open source monitoring tools such as Nagios. The challenge of this work is to deal with the majority of Cloud technologies. An integration layer that makes PCMONS easy to install in Cloud platforms such as OpenNebula and Eucalyptus is presented. C-Meter [3] is a performance analysis framework for Cloud computing. It is an extension of Grenchmark: a Grid tool, allowing performance tests in Grid computing environments. C-Meter manages virtual resources allocation, according to the state of the virtual machines. Contrary to our approach, Monalytics [1], PCMONS [2] and C-Meter [3] are limited to the IaaS layer only, and do not take into account monitoring data from higher layers (i.e., Platform-as-a-Service (PaaS) and Software-as-a-Service (SaaS) layers). HOLMES [4] is a monitoring architecture for data centers, based on CEP. The defined CEP queries get the observed data of the monitoring sensors as inputs, process them and generate alarms when an anomaly is detected. The used monitoring sensors act at the infrastructure layer. This means that HOLMES is not able to detect anomalies related to higher layers. Moreover, HOLMES uses straightforward analysis rules that analyze only a single category of parameters. The proposed analysis rules are mostly based on pre-defined thresholds. Thus, this analysis is not able to accurately identify the source of an anomaly, due to the lack of relevant analyzed metrics. In contrast, our approach allows us to analyze multiple Cloud layers while exploiting the correlations between metrics across Cloud layers, without using pre-defined thresholds. Cohen et al. [9] present a three-layer analysis approach for web services. It is based on the use of Tree-Augmented Bayesian Networks (TAN). The used TANs model the correlations between the Service Level Objective (SLO) and the resource usage. The proposal can be used (1) to detect SLO violations via simple comparisons with pre-defined thresholds; and (2) to identify the cause of a violation via the use of correlations between the different monitored metrics. The TANs (modeling correlations) are deduced from historical data that were previously collected and stored in a separate database. This means that a training period is necessary for the execution of this approach. During this training period, the system is unable to identify the cause of a violation. Moreover, it is hard to apply this approach in the context of Cloud computing due to the large volume of data that has to be stored. EbAT [10] is an online detection method of Cloud computing anomalies. It is based on the calculation of a multi-level entropy. It analyzes distributions of metrics instead of individual metrics. To ensure accuracy, EbAT needs a storage space to keep historical data. In contrast to [10] and [9], our approach does not require a database for storing monitored data, thanks to the use of CEP. Sarkar et al. [5] present a self-healing architecture for a PaaS Cloud. Its analysis module is based on two main components: an Event Aggregation and Correlation System (EACS) and an Automated Incident Management System (AIMS). The EACS is in charge of receiving events from the monitoring module. It stores events received within a window of time. Then, it performs aggregation, correlation and suppression of events. Subsequently, a filtering activity is performed. It decides about events that should be sent to the AIMS. The latter detects performance incidents. Correlations, in this work, are determined by the aggregation operations. These just decide about the relevant events to observe and do not aim to extract relationships between collected metrics. Mi et al. [6] have proposed a performance analysis approach, called Magnifier. It allows to detect Cloud failures, while identifying their prime causes. Magnifier is based on a hierarchical analysis. Therefore, it is able to detect performance degradations layer by layer, separately. The detection procedure is based on a basic threshold comparison. In contrast to [5] and [6], our approach exploits the relationships between the Cloud metrics across Cloud layers and is not based on thresholds.

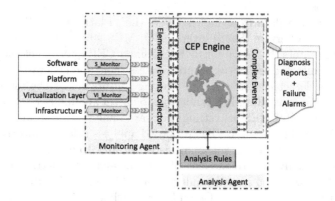

Fig. 1. The architecture of CEP4CMA

3   Multi-layer Monitoring and Analysis in Clouds

In this section, our multi-layer monitoring and analysis approach for Cloud environments based on CEP is presented. We call it CEP4CMA for "**C**omplex **E**vent **P**rocessing for **C**loud **M**onitoring and **A**nalysis".

3.1   The Architecture

Figure 1 shows the architecture of CEP4CMA. It consists of two main components: a multi-layer monitoring agent and a CEP-based analysis agent.

The multi-layer monitoring agent relies on four monitoring components. The first component, **PI_Monitor**, operates on the physical infrastructure layer and collects performance-related parameters on this layer. The second component, **VI_Monitor**, operates on the virtualization layer and measures the virtual infrastructure parameters. The third component, **P_Monitor**, acts on the platform layer and collects platform metrics. The fourth component, **S_Monitor**, gathers metrics pertinent to the software layer.

PI_Monitor, VI_Monitor, P_Monitor and S_Monitor send collected data to the **Elementary Events Collector (EVC)**. The EVC transfers all monitored data to the CEP-based analysis agent of CEP4CMA. The analysis agent takes as inputs the elementary events that correspond to the observed parameters of the monitoring agent. These events are then processed and analyzed by the CEP engine, via the use of our analysis rules. The conducted analysis is used to detect performance degradations. It generates diagnosis reports and triggers alarms when a performance degradation is detected. The monitoring and the analysis agents are described in detail below.

3.2   The Monitoring Agent

Our monitoring agent has been designed to leverage the results of existing monitoring tools that typically operate on a single Cloud layer (e.g., [2,11–13]).

Thus, the four components of our monitoring agent described above make use of existing sensors, as discussed below.

PI_Monitor monitors the physical infrastructure layer and gathers metrics related to the consumption of hardware resources, such as the CPU usage of the physical cores, the waiting and blocked times spent by virtual machines to access the physical disk, the memory consumption etc. It is installed on the privileged domain (Dom0) with direct access to the XEN hypervisor, the virtualization technology used in our work. PI_Monitor makes use of a set of existing sensors: Xenmon [14], Ganglia[1] [11], IoStat[2] and MpStat[3]. Xenmon collects information about the CPU, such as the blocked times, the waiting times and the number of executions (i.e. number of times a domain was scheduled to run [14]) per second. Ganglia mainly gathers information about the state of resources, such as disk and memory consumption. Moreover, it measures the network link quality. IoStat measures disk transactions, such as the I/O requests to the physical disk. It is running in the privileged domain (Dom0) that has direct access to the physical disk. Finally, MpStat gathers the software and hardware interrupts of Dom0.

VI_Monitor operates on the virtualization layer and monitors virtual machines. It is installed on each virtual machine. VI_Monitor makes use of Ganglia, MpStat and IoStat. Ganglia collects CPU, RAM, disk and network metrics of the virtual machines, such as the used swap space and the throughput of the network (BytesIn and BytesOut). MpStat measures the CPU steal of virtual machines, reflecting the time spent by the VM waiting for the hypervisor's tasks. IoStat gathers information about the number of read and written pages of the considered virtual machine.

P_Monitor operates on the platform layer and gathers corresponding data. For this purpose, we have developed the JVMSensor tool dealing with Java Virtual Machine (JVM) monitoring. JVMSensor measures JVM platform metrics, such as the CPU time of the running threads, the heap memory and the number of loaded classes. JVMSensor is based on the Jconsole tool[4].

S_Monitor operates on the software layer and collects performance-related parameters of Cloud services at the SaaS layer. It makes use of AOP4CSM, a monitoring tool based on aspect-oriented programming developed in our previous work [12]. S_Monitor measures the execution, communication and response times of SaaS Cloud services.

PI_Monitor, VI_Monitor, P_Monitor and S_Monitor make use of basic TCP/IP sockets to send collected data to the Elementary Event Collector. It should be pointed out that there are typically two methods to monitor VMs: (1) from inside the VMs via installing a monitoring tool; (2) from outside via introspection [15], using, e.g., LibVMI[5]. We use the first option in this paper. This makes VI_Monitor suitable to all kinds of VMs, and independent of the hypervisor.

---

[1] http://www.ganglia.sourceforge.net
[2] http://www.linux.die.net/man/1/iostat
[3] http://www.linux.die.net/man/1/mpstat
[4] http://www.openjdk.java.net/tools/svc/jconsole/
[5] https://code.google.com/p/vmitools/

3.3   The Analysis Agent

An important component of our architecture is the analysis agent. It is used to detect performance degradations, while identifying their causes and the corresponding layers (physical infrastructure, virtual infrastructure, platform and software). Our analysis agent is based on CEP and makes use of a set of cross-layer analysis rules (i.e., queries) implemented in a CEP engine. We use Esper[6], an open source CEP engine. It is written in JAVA and implements rules as EPL (Event Processing Language) queries. The used analysis rules are defined on the basis of relationships between the monitored parameters across Cloud layers.

In particular, extracting relationships (i.e., correlations) between metrics has two main benefits. First, it allows us to reduce the number of monitored parameters, since analyzing two "highly" correlated metrics gives the same result as analyzing one of these two metrics. Second, the relationships are very useful to define the analysis rules. Consequently, we can rapidly detect a performance degradation (thanks to the reduced number of observed metrics) and accurately identify its layer and its cause (thanks to the intelligent analysis rules).

Relationships Between Cloud Layers: To identify the relationships between Cloud layers, we followed two steps. First, we theoretically examined the interactions between metrics across Cloud layers. Second, we conducted several experiments in order to verify the theoretically obtained relationships. The conducted experiments are based on 2 steps: (1) monitor the different Cloud parameters and (2) compute the correlation between them, via different statistical indicators such as the correlation and the multiple correlation coefficients. Our experiments have been performed on several samples. The sample size depends on the scenario. It varies between 20 and 100 data points[7]. They are partitioned into three groups. The first group of experiments consists of measuring two metrics in normal conditions (without generating any load) and calculating the correlation coefficient. According to its value, we deduce the relationship between the two metrics [16]. The second group of experiments deals with the case when there are more than two related metrics. The related metrics are monitored in normal conditions and the multiple correlation coefficient between them is computed [17]. We use the G*Power[8] [18] tool to compute the multiple correlation coefficient. The last group of experiments consists in generating load with respect to the first parameter and observing its effects on the second one. If both increase, decrease or inversely vary together, this means that they are related.

Since in this step we deal with correlation experiments, we use a small testbed to isolate the studied metrics and easily identify their relationships. The testbed for the correlation experiments consists of one physical node with 1 GB of RAM and 100 GB of disk, running under the Debian operating system. Xen 4.1 was chosen as the virtualization technology to administer virtual machines through

---

[6] http://esper.codehaus.org/

[7] A data point represents one measurement of the studied metric.

[8] http://www.psycho.uni-duesseldorf.de/abteilungen/aap/gpower3/

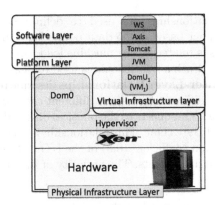

Fig. 2. Testbed for correlation experiments

its hypervisor and its privileged domain Dom0 [19]. Moreover, it manages access to the hardware resources, such as the disk and the memory, via Dom0 and the hypervisor. The testbed for the correlation experiments has a Cloud architecture with four layers. The hardware resources, Xen, its hypervisor and Dom0 constitute the physical infrastructure layer. The virtual infrastructure layer is composed of the DomU virtual machines. The used platform layer consists of the Java Virtual Machine (JVM) with Apache Tomcat as a web server. Under Tomcat, the Axis engine is deployed to manage web services (WS). The Axis engine and the web services constitute the software layer (see Fig. 2).

To extract relationships between the monitored metrics in a theoretical study, we classified the monitored metrics according to two criteria: the layer of a metric (e.g., the infrastructure layer) and the category of a metric (e.g., the CPU category). Thus, we have four groups of relationships:

- **Intra-Category, Intra-Layer Relationships** describe relationships between metrics belonging to the same layer and the same category. The majority of these relationships are used to reduce the number of parameters. For example, we experimentally confirmed that the CPU time of a running thread is related to its *waited count* by calculating the correlation coefficient (0.9) of the two parameters for 50 data points. Such a relationship allows us to reduce the number of monitored parameters. It is sufficient to monitor only one of the two metrics, since they describe the same information.
- **Intra-Category, Inter-Layer Relationships** describe relationships between metrics belonging to the same category. They are used to define the analysis rules. For example, an experiment based on 30 data points has shown that the CPU time of a Java thread is related to the *CPU user time* of its virtual machine, since the corresponding correlation coefficient is equal to 0.5. This observation allows us to deduce the cause of a VM CPU performance-related problem.
- **Inter-Category, Intra-Layer Relationships** describe relationships between metrics belonging to the same Cloud layer. They are useful to reduce the number of observed metrics if this reduction does not affect the quality of the analysis.

Otherwise, these relationships are used to define the analysis rules. For example, an experiment based on 65 data points has shown that the number of running processes is related to the machine load, since the correlation coefficient is equal to 0.9. Such a relationship is used to define the analysis rules.

– **Inter-Category, Inter-Layer Relationships** describe relationships between metrics belonging to different layers and different categories, such as the relationship between the I/O requests to the physical disk and the number of Bytes In and the number of Bytes Out. This relationship is illustrated by calculating the multiple correlation coefficient (0.8) of the I/O disk requests and Bytes In and Bytes Out for 30 data points. The majority of such relationships are used in our analysis rules.

Next, we present the proposed analysis rules, the associated Fishbone diagrams and their implementation as continuous queries in the CEP engine.

The Analysis Rules: The definition of analysis rules is based on the extracted relationships between Cloud metrics, while adopting a **R**oot **C**ause **A**nalysis (RCA) method [8]. RCA is an analytic approach that helps analysts to diagnose crisis situations, while identifying the cause of failures [8]. It is the process that allows to discover what happened, why it happened and how to prevent / solve it [8]. The extracted correlations can be used by RCA methods, since they are augmented by "extra" knowledge. The fishbone (also called cause-effect) diagram is a visual method that follows the RCA approach to detect failures and identify their causes. In this paper, we use fishbone diagrams to perform Cloud performance analysis. Thus, we start our analysis by stating the trivial causes of a performance degradation. Starting the analysis by studying such evident causes is necessary, but not sufficient to give accurate information about the nature of a degradation. Figure 3 presents a high level view of our fishbone diagram.

As shown in Fig. 3, the first step of the analysis only states trivial causes of a performance-related problem (degradation of the communication (Tcom) and execution (Texec) times), such as network congestion, high resource (Disk, CPU, memory) consumption and high load. Stopping the analysis in this step could lead, in some cases, to wrong results, due to the interaction between Cloud metrics. This is the reason why it is necessary to continue the analysis of these evident causes. For instance, this first analysis (see Fig. 3) shows that a communication time degradation is always related to a network congestion (low throughput). However, expanding this branch on the basis of the extracted relationships demonstrates that such a degradation could also be related to a huge number of requests to the physical disk (see Fig. 4). Actually, our correlation study has indicated that the number of requests to the physical disk (I/O Req) is related to the network characteristics (Bytes In/Out)[9].

Each elementary branch of the cause-effect diagram is an analysis rule. It is composed of a set of symptoms and a diagnosis report. An analysis rule is analytically

---

[9] A complete version of our fishbone diagram can be found at http://www.redcad.org/members/mdhaffar/cep4cma/Fishbone.html.

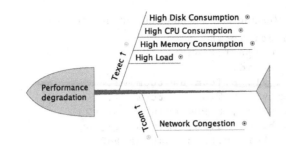

Fig. 3. Cause-effect diagram: a high level view

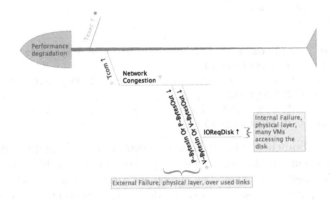

Fig. 4. Cause-effect diagram: analysis of a communication time degradation

represented by $\mathbf{R}(S_1, S_2, .. , S_3 // D)$, where R is the rule; $S_1, S_2, .. , S_3$ are the observed symptoms, and D is the deduced diagnosis report.

For instance, the first part of the cause-effect diagram, showing the communication time analysis (see Fig. 4) is translated into two analysis rules R_1 (see Formula (1)) and R_2 (see Formula (2)).

$$
\begin{aligned}
R_1(Tcom \uparrow, P - BytesIn \downarrow Or P - BytesOut \downarrow \\
//External\ Failure, \\
Physical\ layer, \\
over - used\ links)
\end{aligned}
\tag{1}
$$

$$
\begin{aligned}
R_2(Tcom \uparrow, V - BytesIn \downarrow Or V - BytesOut \downarrow, \\
IOReqDisk \uparrow // \\
Internal\ Failure, \\
Physical\ layer, \\
Many\ VMs\ accessing\ the\ disk)
\end{aligned}
\tag{2}
$$

These rules are implemented within the CEP engine (Esper). Listing 1.1 presents the implementation of the rule R_1, called query in the Esper language.

Listing 1.1. The implementation of the rule R_1

```
select * from JoinTcomB
match_recognize (partition by IP
measures A.IP as id,
A.Tcom as tcom_v1, B.Tcom as tcom_v2,
C.Tcom as tcom_v3, D.Tcom as tcom_v4,
A.PBytesIn as bi_v1, B.PBytesIn as bi_v2,
C.PBytesIn as bi_v3, D.PBytesIn as bi_v4,
A.PBytesOut as bo1, B.PBytesOut as bo2,
C.PBytesOut as bo3, D.PBytesOut as bo4,
A.TimeValue as TVBegin,
D.TimeValue as TVEnd
pattern (A B C D)
define
B as B.Tcom > A.Tcom and ((B.PBytesOut < A.PBytesOut) or (B.
    PBytesIn < A.PBytesIn)),
C as C.Tcom > B.Tcom and ((C.PBytesOut < B.PBytesOut) or (C.
    PBytesIn < B.PBytesIn)),
D as D.Tcom > C.Tcom and ((D.PBytesOut < C.PBytesOut) or (D.
    PBytesIn < C.PBytesIn)))
```

Translating the branches of the fishbone diagram into CEP queries allows us to ensure an easy and scalable implementation of our approach, in contrast to traditional RCA-based approaches. The implementation of the analysis rules is based on the use of patterns that are used to detect the different symptoms. They describe, in the majority of our rules, the variation of the Cloud parameters and trigger alarms when this variation lasts for N successive observations. The minimum value of N is calculated based on the definition of a performance degradation. In our case, a performance degradation is a continuous decrease of the performance parameters. In other words, we consider that the Cloud suffers from a performance degradation, if it will still suffer from this degradation in the next instant of time. This means that we need to observe symptoms at least two times. Thus, the minimum value of N is equal to 2. However, N depends also on the Cloud provider requirements. Actually, if the provider requires a fast detection and does not care about false alarms, then 2 is the best value of N. If the provider does not care about the detection time and cares about the number of false alarms, then N should be strictly greater than 2. To find the optimal N in our case, we measured the number of false alarms while varying N from 2 to 5. Our experiments have illustrated that 3 is the best value of N, since it eliminates false alarms.

4   Experimental Results

This section describes our Cloud testbed. Furthermore, it presents the conducted experiments to evaluate our approach.

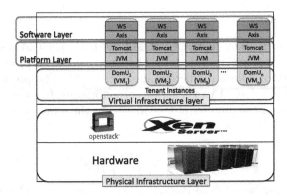

Fig. 5. The cloud environment testbed

4.1 Testbed

Figure 5 depicts the layered architecture of the private Cloud environment used in our experiments. It consists of 9 physical machines: a Cloud controller and 8 compute nodes. They host our virtual machines (instances).

The Ubuntu Server 12.04 TLS is used as the operating system for the physical machines. Each physical machine has a 64-bit CPU, with 250 GB of disk. The Cloud controller and six compute nodes have 16 GB of RAM. The seventh compute node has 12 GB of RAM, and the last one has 8 GB of RAM. The Xen Server is the used virtualization technology. The open source Cloud software OpenStack[10] (Folsom release) has been deployed in order to upload Cloud images and launch instances. Based on the Ubuntu Cloud image, we build our image. It includes our monitoring agent. This image has been uploaded into our OpenStack Cloud platform. For testing purposes and to show the feasibility of the proposed analysis rules, we launched, via OpenStack horizon, 80 VM instances. Each instance has 1 virtual CPU and 1 GB of RAM, with 10 GB of disk. A Java Virtual Machine (JVM) and an Apache Tomcat web server are running on all instances. Moreover, the Axis engine is deployed on every Tomcat, in order to manage web services. The deployed web services compute the factorial of a given number. Our testbed environment has a typical Cloud architecture, since it makes use of OpenStack and is composed of the four principal Cloud layers (physical infrastructure, virtual infrastructure, platform and software layers). The physical infrastructure layer is composed of the physical resources, Xen server and OpenStack. The 80 VM instances constitute the virtual infrastructure layer. The JVM and the Tomcat web server are the main components of the platform layer. The software layer is composed of Axis and its related web services. Our analysis agent is installed on a dedicated machine, called Cloud Analyzer. It is running under an Ubuntu Server 12.04 TLS. The Cloud Analyzer machine has a 64-bit CPU, with 4 GB of RAM and 140 GB of disk. It receives monitoring data and processes analysis rules to detect performance degradations.

---

[10] http://www.openstack.org/

4.2   Experiments

Precision/Recall: To evaluate CEP4CMA, we compare it to baseline analysis methods in terms of precision and recall. These two metrics are often used to investigate the quality of failure prediction approaches [20]. The precision expresses the probability of CEP4CMA to generate correct alarms. It is determined by calculating the ratio of the number of true alarms to the number of all alarms (see Formula 3):

$$Precision = \frac{TP}{TP + FP} \ [20] \tag{3}$$

where TP is the number of True Positive (correct alarms); and FP is the number of False Positive (false alarms).

The recall is defined as the ratio of correct alarms to the number of true failures (see Formula 4). It reflects the probability of detecting true failures:

$$Recall = \frac{TP}{TP + FN} \ [20] \tag{4}$$

where FN is the number of False Negative (missing alarms).

We have chosen threshold-based detection approaches as our baseline methods. They allow us to detect a performance-related problem by comparing a Cloud parameter value to a fixed threshold. We use an'oracle'-based approach [10] to set a threshold's value. It consists of (1) monitoring the corresponding parameters during a training period, and (2) calculating the lowest and highest 1 % of the extracted values, while considering them as outliers. The acceptable range is then taken between the lowest and the highest 1 % of the values [10]. We compared CEP4CMA to 3 different threshold-based approaches. The first one is an I/OReq-based method. It checks whether the I/OReq value is in the acceptable range, to decide about the Cloud state. The second one, similar to the first one, is based on the CPU usage metric. The third approach combines the two previous methods. It analyzes the Cloud state according to the values of I/OReq and CPU usage.

First, we injected 30 I/O failures, via dbench, and compared CEP4CMA to the I/OReq-based method. The results of this first experiment show that CEP4CMA is better than the I/OReq-based method, in terms of precision and recall. Actually, CEP4CMA achieves a precision of 89 %, while the I/OReq-based approach's precision is 57 %. Moreover, the recall of CEP4CMA is 83 %, while the I/OReq-based approach achieves a recall of 53 %. Thus, CEP4CMA outperforms the I/OReq-based method by a precision and recall improvement of 56.1 % and 56.6 %, respectively.

Second, we injected 30 CPU failures, via sysbench[11], and evaluated the precision and the recall of CEP4CMA and the CPU-based approach. Our experimental results show that CEP4CMA achieves better precision (86 %) than the CPU-based approach (72 %). Thus, the improvement of precision is around 18.5 %.

---

[11] Sysbench is a multi-threaded benchmark tool. It allows us to evaluate OS parameters by injecting different kinds of load: http://sysbench.sourceforge.net/docs/.

Furthermore, the recall of CEP4CMA is about 83 %. It outperforms the CPU-based method by an improvement of 56 %. In fact, the recall of the CPU-based method is 53 %.

Third, we compared CEP4CMA to the combined approach (based on I/OReq and CPU thresholds). For this purpose, we injected 60 failures: 50 % of them are I/O failures (i.e. injected via dbench); and the remaining 50 % are CPU failures (i.e., injected via sysbench). In this scenario, we noticed that CEP4CMA achieves a precision of 87 % and a recall of 83 %. The precision of the combined approach is about 34 %, while its recall is around 53 %. This means that CEP4CMA is also better than the combined approach: It improves the precision by 157 % and outperforms the recall by an improvement of 56 %. Thus, the recall improvement is similar for the three conducted experiments. This implies that the three threshold-based approaches have almost the same capabilities in detecting true failures. Using two parameters, in the case of the combined approach, does not make a big difference. Actually, CEP4CMA still achieves the same improvements, when compared to the combined approach. On the other hand, we observed that the combined approach does not reach better results in terms of precision. Indeed, using two threshold comparisons increases the number of false alarms. This is why CEP4CMA outperforms the combined approach by an improvement of 157 %, in terms of precision. An experimental comparison of CEP4CMA with other related approaches will be performed in future work.

Accuracy of the Diagnosis: To demonstrate the accuracy of the diagnosis reports generated by CEP4CMA, we injected 4 different failures and observed the returned outputs. First, we generated I/O load on the physical machine "compute05", via the benchmark dbench. In this scenario, we observed that CEP4CMA raised two alarms: the first one indicates that a degradation of the execution time has happened on one of the VMs, belonging to "compute05", due to a high I/O load. The second alarm identified a degradation of the communication time on another VM, also hosted by "compute05". It indicated again that the failure was caused by a high I/O load. This demonstrates that CEP4CMA was able to correctly identify the failed VMs and the failure's cause. Second, we injected a Java memory failure. To this end, we implemented a benchmark that consumes a lot of memory. When we started running this benchmark on one of our VMs, CEP4CMA raised an alarm while accurately identifying the failed VM and the cause of the failure. It indicated that the failure was caused by an increase of the Java heap memory. Third, we used the Hping3[12] benchmark to saturate the network links. Hping3 is a networking tool that allows us to send TCP/IP packets and could generate a Denial-of-Service (DoS) attack when used with the flood option. In this scenario, CEP4CMA accurately identified the failed physical node. It was also able to deduce the cause of the failure: a network failure. Fourth, we injected a CPU failure via sysbench. CEP4CMA raised an alarm, when sysbench was running on one of the VMs. It correctly identified the failed VM and the failure's cause (high CPU load).

---

[12] http://linux.die.net/man/8/hping3

5   Conclusion

This paper presented a multi-layer monitoring and analysis approach for Cloud computing environments, called CEP4CMA. It is based on using a CEP engine to continuously run queries on streams of monitored events across Cloud layers. In contrast to other approaches where the queries must be written manually, we derive them from the results of a theoretical and experimental analysis of the relationships of monitored metrics on different Cloud layers and follow a root cause analysis approach. The conducted experiments have demonstrated the benefits of CEP4CMA in terms of precision and recall, in comparison with threshold-based methods. Furthermore, our experimental results have shown that the proposed analysis rules are suitable for the diagnosis of Cloud environments, in the sense that they generate an accurate diagnosis report.

There are several directions for future work. First, it is interesting to design a distributed analysis architecture based on cooperating CEP engines (possibly in a hierarchical fashion) to efficiently process different analysis rules. Second, additional experiments, based on known benchmarks, will be conducted in large-scale Clouds. Finally, the extracted relationships of the monitored events can be used to perform other kinds of analysis, such as security analysis. Detected anomalies could then be related to security intrusions.

Acknowledgments. This work is partly supported by the German Ministry of Education and Research (BMBF) and the German Academic Exchange Service (DAAD).

References

1. Kutare, M., Eisenhauer, G., Wang, C., Schwan, K., Talwar, V., Wolf, M.: Monalytics: online monitoring and analytics for managing large scale data centers. In: Proceedings of the 7th International Conference on Autonomic Computing, pp. 141–150. ACM (2010)
2. De Chaves, S.A., Uriarte, R.B., Westphall, C.B.: Toward an architecture for monitoring private clouds. IEEE Commun. Mag. **49**, 130–137 (2011)
3. Yigitbasi, N., Iosup, A., Epema, D., Ostermann, S.: C-meter: a framework for performance analysis of computing clouds. In: Proceedings of the 9th IEEE/ACM International Symposium on Cluster Computing and the Grid, pp. 472–477. IEEE (2009)
4. Dos Teixeira, P.H.S., Clemente, R.G., Kaiser, R.A., Vieira Jr., D.A.: HOLMES: an event-driven solution to monitor data centers through continuous queries and machine learning. In: Proceedings of the 4th ACM International Conference On Distributed Event-Based Systems, pp. 216–221. ACM (2010)
5. Sarkar, S., Mahindru, R., Hosn, R.A., Vogl, N., Ramasamy, H.V.: Automated incident management for a platform-as-a-service cloud. In: Proceedings of the 11th USENIX Conference on Hot Topics in Management of Internet, Cloud, and Enterprise Networks and Services, USENIX Association, pp. 1–6 (2011)
6. Mi, H., Wang, H., Yin, G., Cai, H., Zhou, Q., Sun, T., Zhou, Y.: Magnifier: online detection of performance problems in large-scale cloud computing systems. In: Proceedings of the 11th IEEE International Conference on Services Computing, pp. 418–425. IEEE (2011)

7. Cugola, G., Margara, A.: Processing flows of information: from data stream to complex event processing. ACM Comput. Surv. **44**(3), 1–62 (2012)
8. Bhaumik, S.: Root cause analysis in engineering failures. Trans. Indian Inst. Met. **63**, 297–299 (2010)
9. Cohen, I., Goldszmidt, M., Kelly, T., Symons, J.: Correlating instrumentation data to system states: a building block for automated diagnosis and control. In: Proceedings of the 6th Symposium on Operating Systems Design and Implementation, pp. 231–244 (2004)
10. Wang, C., Talwar, V., Schwan, K., Ranganathan, P.: Online detection of utility cloud anomalies using metric distributions. In: 12th IEEE/IFIP Network Operations and Management Symposium, pp. 96–103. IEEE (2010)
11. Massie, M.L., Chun, B.N., Culler, D.E.: The ganglia distributed monitoring system: design, implementation, and experience. Parallel Comput. **30**, 817–840 (2004)
12. Mdhaffar, A., Halima, R.B., Juhnke, E., Jmaiel, M., Freisleben, B.: AOP4CSM: an aspect-oriented programming approach for cloud service monitoring. In: Proceedings of the 11th IEEE International Conference on Computer and Information Technology, pp. 363–370. IEEE Press (2011)
13. Rabkin, A.: Chukwa: a large-scale monitoring system. In: Cloud Computing and its Applications, pp. 1–5 (2008)
14. Gupta, D., Gardner, R., Cherkasova, L.: XenMon: QoS monitoring and performance profiling tool. Technical report, HP Labs (2005)
15. Nance, K.L., Bishop, M., Hay, B.: Virtual machine introspection: observation or interference? IEEE Secur. Priv. **6**(5), 32–37 (2008)
16. Taylor, R.: Interpretation of the correlation coefficient: a basic review. J. Diagn. Med. Sonogr. **6**, 35–39 (1990)
17. Crocker, D.C.: Some interpretations of the multiple correlation coefficient. Am. Stat. **26**, 31–33 (1972)
18. Faul, F., Erdfelder, E., Buchner, A., Lang, A.G.: Statistical power analyses using G*Power 3.1: tests for correlation and regression analyses. Behav. Res. Methods **41**, 1149–1160 (2009)
19. von Hagen, W.: Professional Xen Virtualization. Wiley, Indianapolis (2008)
20. Salfner, F., Lenk, M., Malek, M.: A survey of online failure prediction methods. ACM Comput. Surv. **42**(3), 1–42 (2010)

Hardness of Firewall Analysis

Ehab S. Elmallah[1]([✉]) and Mohamed G. Gouda[2]

[1] Department of Computing Science, University of Alberta,
Edmonton T6G 2E8, Canada
elmallah@ualberta.ca
[2] Department of Computing Science,
University of Texas at Austin, Austin, TX 78712, USA
gouda@cs.utexas.edu

Abstract. We identify 13 problems whose solutions can significantly enhance our ability to design and analyze firewalls and other packet classifiers. These problems include the firewall equivalence problem, the firewall redundancy problem, the firewall verification problem, and the firewall completeness problem. The main result of this paper is to prove that every one of these problems is NP-hard. Our proof of this result is interesting in the following way. Only one of the 13 problems, the so called slice probing problem, is shown to be NP-hard by a reduction from the well-known 3-SAT problem. Then, the remaining 12 problems are shown to be NP-hard by reductions from the slice probing problem. The negative results of this paper suggest that firewalls designers may need to rely on SAT solvers to solve instances of these 13 problems or may be content with probabilistic solutions of these problems.

Keywords: Firewalls · Packet classifiers · Logical analysis · Equivalence · Redundancy · Verification · Completeness · 3-SAT · NP-hard

1 Introduction

A firewall is a packet filter that is placed at a point where a private computer network is connected to the rest of the Internet [14]. The firewall intercepts each packet that is exchanged between the private network and the Internet, examines the fields of the packet headers, and makes a decision either to discard the packet or accept it and allow it to proceed on its way. The decision that a firewall makes to discard or accept a packet depends on two factors:

1. The values of the fields in the packet headers.
2. The sequence of rules in the firewall that are specified by the firewall designer.

A firewall rule consists of a predicate and a decision, which is either accept or discard. When the firewall receives a packet, the firewall searches its sequence of rules for the first rule, whose predicate is satisfied by the values of the fields in the packet headers, and then applies the decision of this rule to the packet.

© Springer International Publishing Switzerland 2014
G. Noubir and M. Raynal (Eds.): NETYS 2014, LNCS 8593, pp. 153–168, 2014.
DOI: 10.1007/978-3-319-09581-3_11

Note that there are three sets of packets that are associated with each firewall: (1) the set of packets that are discarded by the firewall, (2) the set of packets that are accepted by the firewall, and (3) the set of packets that are neither discarded nor accepted by the firewall. This third set is usually empty.

The task of designing, verifying, and analyzing a firewall (especially one with thousands of rules, as usually is the case) is not an easy one [9,11,16]. Performing this task properly usually requires solving thousands of instances of the following problems:

1. **Firewall Verification:**
   Show that a given firewall discards or accepts a given set of packets.
2. **Firewall Implication:**
   Show that a given firewall discards (or accepts, respectively) every packet that is discarded (or accepted, respectively) by another given firewall.
3. **Firewall Equivalence:**
   Show that two given firewalls discard or accept the same set of packets.
4. **Firewall Adequacy:**
   Show that a given firewall discards or accepts at least one packet.
5. **Firewall Redundancy:**
   Show that a given discard (or accept, respectively) rule in a given firewall can be removed from the firewall without changing the set of packets that are discarded (or accepted, respectively) by the firewall.
6. **Firewall Completeness:**
   Show that any given firewall discards or accepts every packet.

Efficient algorithms for solving these six problems can benefit the design, verification, and analysis of firewalls. For example, consider the next three scenarios that occur frequently during the design phase, verification phase, and analysis phase of firewalls.

Scenario 1. A firewall designer designs a firewall that is required to accept some specified sets of packets and to discard other specified sets of packets. After the firewall design is completed, the designer needs to verify that indeed the designed firewall accepts every set of packets that it should accept and discards every set of packets that it should discard. Thus, the designer needs to apply an algorithm, that solves the above firewall verification problem, on the designed firewall. Moreover, if the verification shows that the firewall discards a set of packets that should be accepted or accepts a set of packets that should be discarded, then the designer needs to modify the designed firewall and repeat the verification.

Scenario 2. A firewall can be designed through a series of refinement steps that proceeds as follows. Initially, the firewall is designed to accept all packets. Then at each refinement step, the designer modifies the firewall slightly to make the firewall discard one more set of packets (that the firewall is required to discard). To check the correctness of each refinement step, the designer needs to apply an algorithm, that solves the above firewall implication problem, to check that indeed the firewall at the end of the refinement step discards every packet that is discarded by the firewall at the beginning of the refinement step.

Scenario 3. After a firewall designer completes the design of a firewall, the designer needs to identify the redundant rules in the designed firewall and remove them from the firewall. (Note that removing the redundant rules from a firewall does not affect the sets of packets that are discarded by or accepted by the firewall.) To identify the redundant rules in the designed firewall, the designer needs to apply an algorithm that solves the above firewall redundancy problem, to check whether each rule in the firewall is redundant.

Recognizing the importance of these problems (to the task of designing, verifying, and analyzing firewalls), many researchers have attempted to develop efficient algorithms that can solve these problems in polynomial time. But the efforts of these researchers (including the authors of the current paper) have failed to develop polynomial algorithms for solving any of these problems. And the time complexity of the best known algorithm to solve any of these problems remains exponential.

In this paper, we show that in fact each one of these problems is NP-hard! This paper is the first to show that any significant problem related to the logical analysis of firewalls is NP-hard. Note that the paper not only proves that one or two of these problems are NP-hard but it also proves that many of these problems are NP-hard.

The rest of this paper is organized as follows. In Sect. 2, we formally define the four main concepts of firewalls, namely fields, packets, rules, and firewalls. In Sect. 3, we formally state 13 problems related to the logical analysis of firewalls. In Sects. 4–10, we prove that each one of the 13 problems in Sect. 3 is NP-hard. Then in Sect. 11, we outline three research directions that can still enhance our ability to design and analyze firewalls, in light of these negative results. Concluding remarks are in Sect. 13.

2   Fields, Packets, Rules, and Firewalls

In this section, we define the four main concepts of firewalls: fields, packets, rules, and firewalls. We start our presentation by introducing the concept of a field.

A *field* is a variable whose value is taken from a nonempty interval of consecutive integers. This interval is called the domain of the field. A nonempty interval X of consecutive integers can be written as a pair $[y, z]$, where y is the smallest integer in interval X, z is the largest integer in X, and X contains only every integer that is neither smaller than y nor larger than z. Note that if X is $[y, y]$, then X contains only one integer, y.

In this paper, we assume that each packet has d fields, named $f_1, f_2, \cdots$, and f_d. The domain of each field f_j is denoted $D(f_j)$. (Examples of the d fields in a packet are the source IP address of the packet, the destination IP address of the packet, the transport protocol of the packet, the source port number of the packet, and the destination port number of the packet.)

Formally, a *packet* p is a tuple $(p_1, \cdots, p_d)$ of d integers, where each integer p_j is taken from the domain $D(f_j)$ of field f_j.

A *rule* in a firewall consists of two parts, a $< predicate >$ and a $< decision >$. A rule is usually written as

$$< predicate > \rightarrow < decision >$$

The $< predicate >$ of a rule is a conjunction of d conjuncts of the form:

$$((f_1 \in X_1) \wedge \cdots \wedge (f_d \in X_d))$$

where each f_j is a field, each X_j is a nonempty interval of consecutive integers taken from the domain $D(f_j)$ of field f_j, and '$\wedge$' is the logical AND operator. The value of each conjunct $(f_j \in X_j)$ is true iff the value of field f_j is taken from the interval X_j.

The $< decision >$ of a rule is either discard or accept. A rule whose decision is discard is called a discard rule and a rule whose decision is accept is called an accept rule. A packet $(p_1, \cdots, p_d)$ is said to *match* a rule of the form:

$$((f_1 \in X_1) \wedge \cdots \wedge (f_d \in X_d)) \rightarrow < decision >$$

iff the predicate $((p_1 \in X_1) \wedge \cdots \wedge (p_d \in X_d))$ is true.

A *firewall* is a sequence of rules. A firewall F is said to discard (or accept, respectively) a packet p iff F has a discard (or accept, respectively) rule rl such that the following two conditions hold: **(a)** packet p matches rule rl, and **(b)** packet p does not match any rule that precedes rule rl in firewall F.

A firewall F is said to ignore a packet p iff p matches no rule in F. It follows that for any firewall F and any packet p, exactly one of the following three statements holds: **(a)** F accepts p, **(b)** F discards p, or **(c)** F ignores p.

Two firewalls F and F' are said to be equivalent iff for every packet p, exactly one of the following three statements holds: **(a)** both F and F' accept p, **(b)** both F and F' discard p, or **(c)** both F and F' ignore p.

A packet is said to match a firewall F iff the packet matches at least one rule in F. A firewall F is called *complete* iff every packet matches F. A rule of the form:

$$((f_1 \in X_1) \wedge \cdots \wedge (f_d \in X_d)) \rightarrow < decision >$$

is called an ALL rule iff each interval X_j is the whole domain $D(f_j)$ of field f_j. Note that every packet matches each ALL rule. Thus, each firewall that has an ALL rule is complete.

A *property* of a firewall has the same form as a rule in a firewall:

$$((f_1 \in X_1) \wedge \cdots \wedge (f_d \in X_d)) \rightarrow < decision >$$

where each f_j is a field, each X_j is a nonempty interval of consecutive integers taken from the domain $D(f_j)$ of field f_j, and $< decision >$ is either discard or accept. A property whose decision is discard is called a discard property, and a property whose decision is accept is called an accept property. A discard property of the form:

$$((f_1 \in X_1) \wedge \cdots \wedge (f_d \in X_d)) \rightarrow discard$$

is said to discard a packet $(p_1, \cdots, p_d)$ iff the predicate $((p_1 \in X_1) \wedge \cdots \wedge (p_d \in X_d))$ is true. Similarly, an accept property of the form:

$$((f_1 \in X_1) \wedge \cdots \wedge (f_d \in X_d)) \rightarrow accept$$

is said to accept a packet $(p_1, \cdots, p_d)$ iff the predicate $((p_1 \in X_1) \wedge \cdots \wedge (p_d \in X_d))$ is true. A firewall F is said to satisfy a property pr iff one of the following two conditions holds.

(a) pr is a discard property and each packet that is discarded by pr is discarded by F.

(b) pr is an accept property and each packet that is accepted by pr is accepted by F.

We end this section by identifying two special classes of firewalls, named discard slices and accept slices. Later in this paper we show that two problems concerning these two special firewall classes are NP-hard. From the fact that these two problems are NP-hard, we show that many problems concerning the design and analysis of general firewalls are also NP-hard. A firewall that consists of zero or more accept rules followed by an ALL discard rule is called a *discard* slice. Similarly, a firewall that consists of zero or more discard rules followed by an ALL accept rule is called an *accept* slice.

3   Firewall Analysis

In this section we identify 13 problems that need to be solved in order to carry out the logical analysis of firewalls. As discussed below, these problems include firewall verification, firewall implication, and firewall equivalence. Later, we show that each one of these 13 problems is NP-hard. These results indicate that the logical analysis of firewalls is hard, at least theoretically from an asymptotic worst case analysis perspective.

The 13 problems that we identify in this section can be classified into 7 classes: Problems of Slice Probing, Problems of Firewall Adequacy, Problems of Firewall Verification, Problems of Firewall Implication, Problems of Firewall Equivalence, the Problem of Firewall Redundancy, and the Problem of Firewall Completeness.

Problems of Slice Probing. There are two Slice Probing problems, which we denote SP-D and SP-A. These two problems are defined as follows.

SP-D: Probing of Discard Slices:
Design an algorithm that takes as input a discard slice S and determines whether S discards at least one packet.

SP-A: Probing of Accept Slices:

Design an algorithm that takes as input an accept slice S and determines whether S accepts at least one packet.

Problems of Firewall Adequacy: There are two Firewall Adequacy problems, which we denote FA-D and FA-A. These two problems are defined as follows.

FA-D: Discard-Adequacy of Firewalls:

Design an algorithm that takes as input a firewall F and determines whether F discards at least one packet.

FA-A: Accept-Adequacy of Firewalls:

Design an algorithm that takes as input a firewall F and determines whether F accepts at least one packet.

The Problem of Firewall Completeness: The Firewall Completeness problem, which we denote FC, is defined as follows:

FC: Completeness of Firewalls:

Design an algorithm that takes as input a firewall F and determines whether every packet is either discarded or accepted by F.

Problems of Firewall Verification: There are two Firewall Verification problems, which we denote FV-D and FV-A. These two problems are defined as follows.

FV-D: Discard-Verification of Firewalls:

Design an algorithm that takes as input a firewall F and a discard property pr and determines whether every packet that is discarded by pr is also discarded by F.

FV-A: Accept-Verification of Firewalls:

Design an algorithm that takes as input a firewall F and an accept property pr and determines whether every packet that is accepted by pr is also accepted by F.

Problems of Firewall Implication: There are two Firewall Implication problems, which we denote FI-D and FI-A. These two problems are defined as follows.

FI-D: Discard-Implication of Firewalls:

Design an algorithm that takes as input two firewalls F_1 and F_2 and determines whether every packet that is discarded by F_1 is also discarded by F_2.

FI-A: Accept-Implication of Firewalls:

Design an algorithm that takes as input two firewalls F_1 and F_2 and determines whether every packet that is accepted by F_1 is also accepted by F_2.

Problems of Firewall Redundancy: There are two Firewall Redundancy problems, which we denote FR-D and FR-A. These two problems are defined as follows.

FR-D: Discard-Redundancy of Firewalls:

Design an algorithm that takes as input a firewall F and a discard rule rl in F and determines whether the two firewalls F and $F \setminus rl$ discard the same set of packets, where $F \setminus rl$ is the firewall that is obtained after removing rule rl from firewall F.

FR-A: Accept-Redundancy of Firewalls:

Design an algorithm that takes as input a firewall F and an accept rule rl in F and determines whether the two firewalls F and $F \setminus rl$ accept the same set of packets, where $F \setminus rl$ is the firewall that is obtained after removing rule rl from firewall F.

Problems of Firewall Equivalence: There are two Firewall Equivalence problems, which we denote FE-D and FE-A. These two problems are defined as follows.

FE-D: Discard-Equivalence of Firewalls:

Design an algorithm that takes as input two firewalls F_1 and F_2 and determines whether F_1 and F_2 discard the same set of packets.

FE-A: Accept-Equivalence of Firewalls:

Design an algorithm that takes as input two firewalls F_1 and F_2 and determines whether F_1 and F_2 accept the same set of packets.

4   Hardness of the Slice Probing

In this section, we show that the first Slice Probing problem SP-D is NP-hard by a reduction from the 3-SAT problem. We then show that the Slice Probing problems SP-A is NP-hard by a reduction from SP-D. For convenience, we state the 3-SAT problem next

3-SAT:

Design an algorithm that takes as input a Boolean formula BF of the form $BF = C_1 \wedge C_2 \wedge \cdots \wedge C_n$ where each clause C_k is a disjunction of 3 literals taken from the set of Boolean variables $\{v_1, \cdots, v_d\}$, and determines whether BF is satisfiable (i.e. determines whether there is an assignment of Boolean values to the variables $\{v_1, \cdots, v_d\}$ that makes BF true).

The 3-SAT problem is known to be NP-hard [8]. This means that the time complexity of any algorithm that solves this problem is very likely to require exponential time of $O(n \times 2^d)$, where n is the number of clauses and d is the number of variables in the Boolean formula BF.

(To date, progress in solving the 3-SAT problem has resulted in both deterministic and randomized algorithms with reduced complexity. For example, in

[5] the authors present a deterministic algorithm that runs in $O(1.473^n)$ time, and in [10] the authors present a randomized algorithm that runs in $O(1.32113^n)$ time on average.)

Next, we describe a polynomial translation of any instance of the 3-SAT problem to an instance of the SP-D problem such that any solution of the 3-SAT instance yields a solution of the SP-D instance and vice versa. The existence of this polynomial translation indicates that the SP-D problem is NP-hard and that the time complexity of any algorithm that solves this problem is very likely to be exponential. Translating an instance of 3-SAT to an instance of SP-D proceeds as follows:

1. The 3-SAT instance is defined by a Boolean formula BF and the SP-D instance is defined by a discard slice S.
2. Each Boolean variable v_j that occurs in formula BF is translated to a field f_j in slice S.
3. The domain of values for each variable v_j is the set $\{false, true\}$ and the domain of values for each field f_j is the set $\{0, 1\}$. Value false of each variable v_j is translated to value 0 of the corresponding field f_j. Similarly, value true of each variable v_j is translated to value 1 of the corresponding field f_j.
4. Each clause C_k in formula BF is translated to an accept rule R_k in slice S as follows. First, if the literal v_j occurs in clause C_k, then the conjunct $(f_j \in [0, 0])$ occurs in the predicate of rule R_k. Second, if the literal $\overline{v_j}$ occurs in clause C_k, then the conjunct $(f_j \in [1, 1])$ occurs in the predicate of rule R_k. Third, if no literal of v_j occurs in clause C_k, then the conjunct $(f_j \in [0, 1])$ occurs in the predicate of rule R_k.
5. Add an ALL discard rule at the bottom of slice S.

From this translation, an assignment of values $(\mathrm{val}(v_1), \cdots, \mathrm{val}(v_d))$ makes a clause C_k true iff the corresponding packet $(\mathrm{val}(f_1), \cdots, \mathrm{val}(f_d))$ does not match the corresponding accept rule R_k. Thus, we draw the following two conclusions:

(1) If there is an assignment of values $(val(v_1), \cdots, val(v_d))$ that makes the Boolean formula BF true, then the corresponding packet $(val(f_1), \cdots, val(f_d))$ does not match any of the accept rules in the discard slice S and matches only the last ALL discard rule. In other words, if the Boolean formula BF is satisfiable, then the discard slice S discards at least one packet.
(2) If the discard slice S discards at least one packet, then the Boolean formula BF is satisfiable.

Therefore, any solution of the 3-SAT instance yields a solution of the SP-D instance and vice versa. This completes our proof of the following theorem.

Theorem 1. Problem SP-D is NP-hard.

Having established that problem SP-D is NP-hard, we can now use this problem to establish that problem SP-A is also NP-hard.

Theorem 2. Problem SP-A is NP-hard.

Proof. We describe a polynomial translation of any instance of the SP-D problem to an instance of the SP-A problem such that any solution of the SP-D instance yields a solution of the SP-A instance and vice versa. Translating an instance of SP-D to an instance of SP-A proceeds as follows:

1. An instance of SP-D is defined by a discard slice S.
2. Replacing every discard (or accept, respectively) decision in S by an accept (or discard, respectively) decision yields an accept slice denoted S'.
3. The accept slice S' defines an instance of SP-A.

From this translation, packet p is discarded by slice S iff packet p is accepted by slice S'. Thus, we draw the following two conclusions:

(1) If slice S discards at least one packet, then slice S' accepts at least one packet.
(2) If slice S' accepts at least one packet, then slice S discards at least one packet.

Therefore, any solution of the SP-D instance yields a solution of the SP-A instance and vice versa.

5   Hardness of Firewall Adequacy

In this section, we employ problem SP-D, which we have shown to be NP-hard in the previous section, to show that the two Firewall Adequacy problems FA-D and FA-A are also NP-hard. First, we assert that the FA-D problem is NP-hard (by a reduction from the SP-D problem). Then we assert that the FA-A problem is NP-hard (by a reduction from the FA-D problem). We omit proofs (due to space limitation), and refer the reader to the details in [7].

Theorem 3. Problem FA-D is NP-hard.

Theorem 4. Problem FA-A is NP-hard.

6   Hardness of Firewall Completeness

In this section, we employ problem SP-D, which we have shown to be NP-hard in Sect. 4, to show that the Firewall Completeness problem FC is NP-hard.

Theorem 5. Problem FC is NP-hard.

Proof: We describe a polynomial translation of any instance of the SP-D problem to an instance of the FC problem such that any solution of the SP-D instance yields a solution of the FC instance and vice versa. Translating an instance of SP-D to an instance of FC proceeds as follows:

1. An instance of SP-D is defined by a discard slice S.
2. Let F denote the firewall that results from removing the last (ALL discard) rule from slice S.
3. Firewall F, which consists entirely of accept rules, defines an instance of FC.

From this translation, we conclude that the discard slice S discards at least one packet iff firewall F is not complete (i.e., F ignores at least one packet.) Therefore, any solution of the SP-D instance yields a solution of the FC instance and vice versa.

7   Hardness of Firewall Verification

In this section, we employ problem SP-A, which we have shown to be NP-hard in Sect. 4, to show that the two Firewall Verification problems, namely FV-D and FV-A, are also NP-hard. First, we show that the FV-D problem is NP-hard by a reduction from the SP-A problem. Then we assert that the FV-A problem is NP-hard (by a reduction from the FV-D problem).

Theorem 6. Problem FV-D is NP-hard.

Proof. We describe a polynomial translation of any instance of the SP-A problem to an instance of the FV-D problem such that any solution of the SP-A instance yields a solution of the FV-D instance and vice versa. Translating an instance of SP-A to an instance of FV-D proceeds as follows:

1. An instance of SP-A is defined by an accept slice S.
2. Because each accept slice is a special case of a firewall, the accept slice S can be viewed as a firewall denoted F.
3. Firewall F and the ALL discard property pr together define an instance of FV-D.

From this translation, we conclude that the accept slice S accepts at least one packet iff this packet is discarded by property pr and not discarded by Firewall F. Therefore, any solution of the SP-A instance yields a solution of the FV-D instance and vice versa.

We omit the proof of the next theorem; the details are presented in [7].

Theorem 7. Problem FV-A is NP-hard.

8   Hardness of Firewall Implication

In this section, we employ problem FV-D, which we have shown to be NP-hard in the previous section, to show that the two Firewall Implication problems, namely FI-D and FI-A, are also NP-hard. First, we show that the FI-D problem is NP-hard by a reduction from the FV-D problem. Then we assert that the FI-A problem is NP-hard (by a reduction from the FI-D problem).

Theorem 8. Problem FI-D is NP-hard.

Proof. We describe a polynomial translation of any instance of the FV-D problem to an instance of the FI-D problem such that any solution of the FV-D instance yields a solution of the FI-D instance and vice versa. Translating an instance of FV-D to an instance of FI-D proceeds as follows:

1. An instance of FV-D is defined by a firewall F and a discard property pr.
2. Because each property is a special case of a firewall, the discard property pr can be viewed as a firewall denoted F'.
3. The two firewalls F and F' together define an instance of FI-D.

From this translation, we conclude that every packet that is discarded by property pr is discarded by firewall F iff every packet that is discarded by firewall F' is discarded by firewall F. Therefore, any solution of the FV-D instance yields a solution of the FI-D instance and vice versa.

We omit the proof of the next theorem; the details are presented in [7].

Theorem 9. Problem FI-A is NP-hard.

9   Hardness of Firewall Redundancy

In this section, we employ problem FV-D, which we have shown to be NP-hard in Sect. 7, to show that the two Firewall Redundancy problems FR-D and FR-A are also NP-hard. First, we show that the FR-D problem is NP-hard by a reduction from the FV-D problem. Then, we assert that the FR-A problem is NP-hard (by a reduction from the FR-D problem).

Theorem 10. Problem FR-D is NP-hard.

Proof. We describe a polynomial translation of any instance of the FV-D problem to an instance of the FR-D problem such that any solution of the FV-D instance yields a solution of the FR-D instance and vice versa. Translating an instance of FV-D to an instance of FR-D proceeds as follows:

1. An instance of FV-D is defined by a firewall F and a discard property pr.
2. Because each property can be viewed as a rule, the discard property pr can be viewed as a discard rule denoted rl. Let F' denote the firewall that results from placing rule rl at the top of firewall F. (Note that firewall F is the same as firewall $F' \setminus rl$.)
3. Firewall F' and its top (discard) rule rl together define an instance of FR-D.

From this translation, we conclude that every packet that is discarded by the discard property pr is discarded by firewall F iff the two firewalls F and F' discard the same set of packets. Therefore, any solution of the FV-D instance yields a solution of the FR-D instance and vice versa.

We omit the proof of the next theorem; the details are presented in [7].

Theorem 11. Problem FR-A is NP-hard.

10   Hardness of Firewall Equivalence

In this section, we rely on the NP-hardness of the FR-D problem, which is established in the previous section, to show that the two Firewall Equivalence problems FE-D and FE-A are also NP-hard. First, we assert that the FE-D problem is NP-hard (by a reduction from the FR-D problem). Then, we assert that the FE-A problem is NP-hard (by a reduction from the FE-D problem). We omit proofs (due to space limitation), and refer the reader to the details in [7].

Theorem 12. Problem FE-D is NP-hard.

Theorem 13. Problem FE-A is NP-hard.

11   Where We Go from Here

Figure 1 shows an outline of our proof, presented in the five Sects. 4–10, that each one of the 13 problems in Sect. 3 is NP-hard. This proof outline is a directed graph where each node represents one problem and where each directed edge from node P to node P' indicates that problem P' is shown to be NP-hard by a reduction from problem P. Note that in this graph, each node P has exactly one incoming edge labeled by a number k to indicate that the NP-hardness of problem P is proven in Theorem k.

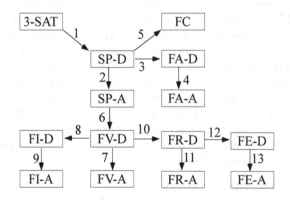

Fig. 1. Hardness reductions between 13 firewall analysis problems

From this proof outline, each one of the 13 problems is shown to be NP-hard by an ultimate reduction from the 3-SAT problem. As mentioned in Sect. 4, the time complexity of any algorithm that solves the 3-SAT problem is very likely to be of $O(n \times 2^d)$, where n is the number of clauses in the Boolean formula and d is the number of Boolean variables in the Boolean formula.

Thus, assuming that the firewall fields are all binary, the time complexity of any algorithm that solves any of the 13 problems in Sect. 3 is very likely to be of

$O(n \times 2^d)$, where n is the number of rules in a firewall, and d is the number of bits that are checked by the firewall rules in the headers of every packet. For most firewalls, n is at most 2000 rules, and d is at most 120 bits. Therefore, assuming that the firewall fields are all binary, the time complexity of any algorithm that solves any of the 13 problems in Sect. 3 is very likely to be of $O(2000 \times 2^{120})$.

At first, this large time complexity may discourage many researchers from trying to solve any of the 13 problems in Sect. 3. But it turns out that researchers can take advantage of the following three techniques in order to avoid this large complexity in many practical situations.

1. Using SAT-Solvers:
As discussed in [17], each instance of the 13 problems in Sect. 3 can be translated into an instance of the SAT problem and then can be easily solved (in many practical situations) using any of the available SAT-solvers, such as Minisat [6].

Indeed the experimental results reported in [17] are impressive. For example, it is shown that many instances of the Firewall Equivalence problem, the Firewall Implication problem, and the Firewall Redundancy problem can all be solved using the Minisat solver [6] and the firewall generator Classbench [15]. More importantly, solving each of these problem instances, which involves one or two firewalls of about 2,000 rules each, takes less than 5 s.

2. Adopting Integer Fields:
The large time complexity of $O(2000 \times 2^{120})$ for solving any of the 13 problems in Sect. 3 is based on our assumption that the firewalls in these problems have a large number (around 120) of Boolean fields. Technically, this assumption can be replaced by assuming that the firewalls in these problems have a small number (around 5) of integer fields. Adopting this new assumption, it is shown in [1,2,4,12,13] that there are algorithms, whose time complexity is of $O(n^{e+1})$, that solve the Slice Probing problem, the Firewall Verification problem, and the Firewall Redundancy problem. In this case, n is the number of rules in a firewall and e is the number of integer fields that are checked by the firewall rules in the headers of every packet. For most firewalls, n is at most 2000 rules, and e is at most 5 integer fields. Therefore, the time complexity of any algorithm that solves any of the 13 problems in Sect. 3 is very likely to be of $O(2000^6)$ which is much smaller than $O(2000 \times 2^{120})$.

3. Accepting Probabilistic Solutions:
The large time complexity of $O(n^{e+1})$ for any algorithm to solve any of the 13 problems in Sect. 3 is based on the implicit requirement that the algorithm be deterministic. It is possible to drastically reduce this time complexity if one is willing to accept probabilistic algorithms that solve these problems.

For example, a probabilistic algorithm for solving the Firewall Verification problem is proposed in [3]. This algorithm determines whether any given firewall satisfies any given property. The time complexity of this algorithm is optimally linear of $O(n \times e)$, where n is the number of rules in the given firewall and e is the number of integer fields that are checked by the firewall rules in the headers of each packet. The only problem of this algorithm is that sometimes

when the algorithm returns a determination that the given firewall satisfies the given property, the returned determination is incorrect. A large simulation study showed that the probability of an incorrect determination is negligible.

12   Related Work

The importance of the logical analysis and verification of firewalls has been recognized since the year 2000 [14]. This recognition has led early on to some attempts to identify configuration errors and vulnerabilities in firewalls that were in operation at the time [9,11,16]. These early attempts, though useful in practice, did not develop into a mature theory for the logical analysis and verification of firewalls.

Later on, a robust and full theory for the logical analysis and verification of firewalls was developed [1,2,4,12,13]. The objective of this theory was to design efficient algorithms that can solve: firewall equivalence problems [12], firewall redundancy problems [1,13], and firewall verification problems [2,4].

It turns out that the time complexity of each algorithm that was designed in this theory is exponential! Yet until the current paper, no one was able to prove that any problem in this theory is NP-hard. The current paper not only proves that one or two problems in this theory are NP-hard but it also proves that many problems in the theory are NP-hard.

The fact, that the time complexity of all algorithms in the theory of logical analysis of firewalls is exponential, was alarming. This alarm led researchers to propose two new research directions. First, some researchers proposed to design probabilistic algorithms for solving the problems in the theory [2]. Second, other researchers proposed to rely on SAT solvers to solve the problems in the theory [6,17]. The results in the current paper will undoubtedly bolster and add credence and significance to these new research directions, as discussed in Sect. 11.

13   Concluding Remarks

In this paper, we identified 13 important problems related to the analysis of firewalls and showed that each one of these problems is NP-hard. This means that the time complexity of any algorithm that can solve any of these problems is very likely to be exponential. Our proofs of these NP-hardness results were based on reductions from the relatively new problem of Slice Probing. This fact confirms the central role that the Slice Probing problem plays in the analysis of firewalls. Future research in the analysis of firewalls should be mindful of this problem.

Some of the 13 problems discussed in this paper can be shown to be NP [8]. Examples of these problems are the Slice Probing problems. The remaining problems can be shown to be co-NP [8]. Example of these problems are the Firewall Implications problems. It is possible to think of other problems related to the analysis of firewalls and show that these problems are also NP-hard by reductions from the 13 problems in Sect. 3. For example consider the following problem

> **Firewall Exclusion:** Show that if any given firewall discards (or accepts, respectively) a packet, then another given firewall does not discard (or does not accept, respectively) the same packet.

We believe that this problem can be shown to be NP-hard by a reduction from the Firewall Implication problem. In Sect. 11, we pointed out three research directions that can be pursued in order to enhance our ability to design and analyze firewalls, in light of the NP-hardness results in this paper.

References

1. Acharya, H.B., Gouda, M.G.: Firewall verification and redundancy checking are equivalent. In: Proceedings of the 30th IEEE International Conference on Computer Communication (INFOCOM), pp. 2123–2128 (2011)
2. Acharya, H.B., et al.: Projection and division: linear space verification of firewalls. In: Proceedings of the 30th International Conference on Distributed Computing Systems (ICDCS), pp. 736–743 (2010)
3. Acharya, H.B., et al.: Linear-time verification of firewalls. In: Proceedings of the 17th IEEE International Conference on Network Protocols (ICNP), pp. 133–140 (2009)
4. Al-Shaer, E., Marrero, W., El-Atawy, A., Elbadawi, K.: Network configuration in a box: towards end-to-end verification of network reachability and security. In: 17th IEEE International Conference on Network Protocols (ICNP), pp. 123–132 (2009)
5. Brueggemann, T., Kern, W.: An improved deterministic local search algorithm for 3-SAT. Theoret. Comput. Sci. **329**(13), 303–313 (2004)
6. Eén, N., Sörensson, N.: An extensible SAT-solver. In: Giunchiglia, E., Tacchella, A. (eds.) SAT 2003. LNCS, vol. 2919, pp. 502–518. Springer, Heidelberg (2004)
7. Elmallah, E.S., Gouda, M.G.: Hardness of firewall analysis. Technical Report TR13-08, University of Alberta, Edmonton, Alberta, Canada T6G 2E8. http:// hdl.handle.net/10402/era.36864 (2013). Accessed April 2014
8. Garey, M.R., Johnson, D.S.: Computers and Intractability: A Guide to the Theory of NP-Completeness. W.H. Freeman, San Francisco (1979)
9. Hoffman, D., Yoo, K.: Blowtorch: a framework for firewall test automation. In: Proceedings of the 20th IEEE/ACM international Conference on Automated Software Engineering, ASE '05, pp. 96–103 (2005)
10. Iwama, K., Seto, K., Takai, T., Tamaki, S.: Improved randomized algorithms for 3-SAT. In: Cheong, O., Chwa, K.-Y., Park, K. (eds.) ISAAC 2010, Part I. LNCS, vol. 6506, pp. 73–84. Springer, Heidelberg (2010)
11. Kamara, S., Fahmy, S., Schultz, E., Kerschbaum, F., Frantzen, M.: Analysis of vulnerabilities in internet firewalls. Comput. Secur. **22**(3), 214–232 (2003)
12. Liu, A.X., Gouda, M.G.: Diverse firewall design. IEEE Trans. Parallel Distrib. Syst. **19**, 1237–1251 (2008)
13. Liu, A.X., et al.: Complete redundancy removal for packet classifiers in TCAMs. IEEE Trans. Parallel Distrib. Syst. **21**, 424–437 (2010)
14. Mayer, A., Wool, A., Ziskind, E.: Fang: a firewall analysis engine. In: IEEE Symposium on Security and Privacy, pp. 177–187 (2000)

15. Taylor, D., Turner, J.: Classbench: a packet classification benchmark. IEEE/ACM Trans. Networking **15**(3), 499–511 (2007)
16. Wool, A.: A quantitative study of firewall configuration errors. Computer **37**(6), 62–67 (2004)
17. Zhang, S., Mahmoud, A., Malik, S., Narain, S.: Verification and synthesis of firewalls using SAT and QBF. In: 20th IEEE International Conference on Network Protocols (ICNP), pp. 1–6 (2012)

Privacy-Preserving Distributed Collaborative Filtering

Antoine Boutet[1]([✉]), Davide Frey[1], Rachid Guerraoui[2], Arnaud Jégou[1], and Anne-Marie Kermarrec[1]

[1] INRIA Rennes, Rennes, France
{antoine.boutet,davide.frey,arnaud.jegou,Anne-marie.kermarrec}@inria.fr
[2] EPFL, Lausanne, Switzerland
rachid.guerraoui@epfl.ch

Abstract. We propose a new mechanism to preserve privacy while leveraging user profiles in distributed recommender systems. Our mechanism relies on (i) an original obfuscation scheme to hide the exact profiles of users without significantly decreasing their utility, as well as on (ii) a randomized dissemination protocol ensuring differential privacy during the dissemination process.

We compare our mechanism with a non-private as well as with a fully private alternative. We consider a real dataset from a user survey and report on simulations as well as planetlab experiments. We dissect our results in terms of accuracy and privacy trade-offs, bandwidth consumption, as well as resilience to a censorship attack. In short, our extensive evaluation shows that our twofold mechanism provides a good trade-off between privacy and accuracy, with little overhead and high resilience.

1 Introduction

Collaborative Filtering (CF) leverages interest similarities between users to recommend relevant content [19]. This helps users manage the ever-growing volume of data they are exposed to on the Web [8]. But it also introduces a trade-off between ensuring user privacy and enabling accurate recommendations. Decentralized collaborative filtering partially addresses this trade-off by removing the monopoly of a central entity that could commercially exploit user profiles. However, it introduces new privacy breaches: users may directly access the profiles of other users. Preventing these breaches is the challenge we address in this paper. We do so in the context of a news-oriented decentralized CF system.

We propose a twofold mechanism: (i) an obfuscation technique applied to user profiles, and (ii) a randomized dissemination protocol satisfying a strong notion of privacy. Each applies to one of the core components of a decentralized user-based CF system: clustering and dissemination. Clustering consists in building an interest-based topology, implicitly connecting users with similar preferences: it computes the similarity between profiles, capturing the opinions of users on the items they have been exposed to. The dissemination protocol propagates the items along the resulting topology.

© Springer International Publishing Switzerland 2014
G. Noubir and M. Raynal (Eds.): NETYS 2014, LNCS 8593, pp. 169–184, 2014.
DOI: 10.1007/978-3-319-09581-3_12

Our obfuscation scheme prevents user machines from exchanging their exact profiles while constructing the interest-based topology. We compute similarities using coarse-grained obfuscated versions of user profiles that reveal only the least sensitive information. To achieve this, we associate each disseminated item with an *item profile*. This profile aggregates information from the profiles of users that liked an item along its dissemination path. This reflects the interests of the portion of the network the item has traversed, gathering the tastes of a community of users that have liked similar items. We use this information to construct filters that identify the least sensitive parts of user profiles: those that are the most popular among users with similar interests. Albeit lightweight, our *obfuscation* scheme prevents any user from knowing, with certainty, the exact profile of another user. Interestingly, we achieve this without significantly hampering the quality of recommendation: the obfuscated profile reveals enough information to connect users with similar interests.

Our dissemination protocol ensures differential privacy [9]. Differential privacy bounds the probability of the output of an algorithm to be sensitive to the presence of information about a given entity—the interests of a user in our context—in the input data. We obtain differential privacy by introducing randomness in the dissemination of items. This prevents malicious players from guessing the interests of a user from the items she forwards.

We compare our mechanism with a non-private baseline as well as with an alternative solution that applies differential privacy to the entire recommendation process. We consider a real dataset from a user survey and report on simulations as well as planetlab experiments. We dissect our results in terms of accuracy and privacy trade-offs, bandwith consumption, as well as resilience to a censorship attack. Our extensive evaluation shows that our twofold mechanism provides a good trade-off between privacy and accuracy. For instance, by revealing only the least sensitive 30 % of a user profile, and by randomizing dissemination with a probability of 0.3, our solution achieves an F1-Score (trade-off between precision and recall) of 0.58, against a value of 0.59 for a solution that discloses all profiles, and a value of 0.57 for the differentially private alternative in a similar setting. Similarly, malicious users can predict only 26 % of the items in a user's profile with our solution, and as much as 70 % when using the differentially private one. In addition, our mechanism is very resilient to censorship attacks, unlike the fully differentially private approach.

2 Setting

We consider a decentralized news-item recommender employing user-based collaborative filtering (CF). Its architecture relies on two components: *user clustering* and *item dissemination*. We aim to protect users from *privacy threats*.

User clustering aims at identifying the k nearest neighbors of each user[1]. It maintains a dynamic interest-based topology consisting of a directed graph

---

[1] We use the terms 'node' and 'user' interchangeably to refer to the pair 'user/machine'.

$G(U, E)$, where vertices, $U = u_1, u_2, u_3, ...u_n$, correspond to users, and edges, $E = e_1, e_2, e_3, ...e_n$, connect users that have the most similar opinions about a set of items $I = i_1, i_2, ..., i_m$. The system is decentralized: each node records the interests of its associated user, u, in a *user profile*, a vector of tuples recording the opinions of the user on the items she has been exposed to. Each such tuple $P_u = < i, v, t >$ consists of an item identifier, i, a score value, v, and a timestamp, t, indicating when the opinion was recorded. Profiles track the interests of users using a sliding window scheme: each node removes from its profile all the tuples that are older than a specified *time window*. This allows the interest-based topology to quickly react to emerging interests while quickly forgetting stale ones. We focus on systems based on binary ratings: a user either *likes* or *dislikes* an item. The interest-based topology exploits two gossip protocols running on each node. The lower-layer random-peer-sampling (RPS) [22] protocol ensures connectivity by maintaining a continuously changing random graph. The upper-layer clustering protocol [6,23] starts from this random graph and quickly provides each node with its k closest neighbors according to a similarity metric. Several similarity metrics have been proposed [21], we use the Jaccard index in this paper.

Item dissemination exploits the above clustering scheme to drive the dissemination. When a user generates a new item or receives an item she likes, the associated node assumes that this is an interesting item for other users with similar interests. It thus forwards the item to its neighbors in the interest-based topology. If, instead, the user marks an item as *dislike*, the node drops it.

Privacy Threats. While decentralization removes the prying eyes of *Big-Brother* companies, it leaves those of curious users who might want to discover the personal tastes of others. In the decentralized item recommender considered, malicious nodes can extract information in two ways: (i) from the profiles they exchange with other nodes (profiles contain information about the interests of users); and (ii) from the predictive nature of the dissemination (a node sends an item only when it likes it). We consider the Honest-But-Curious adversary model [11] where malicious nodes can collude to predict interests from received profiles but cannot cheat in the protocol. In Sect. 6.6, we also consider attackers modifying their obfuscated profiles to control their location in the interest-based topology (*i.e.* their clustering views).

3 Obfuscation Protocol

Our first contribution is an obfuscation protocol that protects user profiles by (i) aggregating their interests with those of similar users, and (ii) revealing only the least sensitive information to other users. For clarity, this Section describes a simplified version of our obfuscation protocol. Section 4 completes this description with features required by our differentially-private dissemination scheme. Figure 1 gives an overview of the complete protocol. For space reason, we omit the pseudocode of the algorithms (available in [5]).

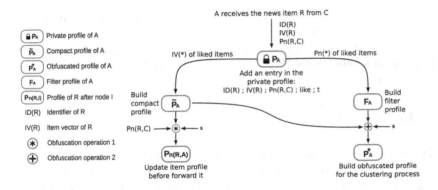

Fig. 1. Simplified information flow through the protocol's data structures.

3.1 Overview

Our protocol relies on random indexing, an incremental dimension reduction technique [14,24]. To apply it in our context, we associate each item with an *item vector*, a random signature generated by its source node. An *item vector* consists of a sparse d-dimensional bit array. To generate it, the source of an item randomly chooses $b << d$ distinct array positions and sets the corresponding bits to 1. It then attaches the *item vector* to the item before disseminating it.

Nodes use item vectors when recording information about items in their obfuscated profiles. Let us consider a node A that receives an item R from another node C. Figure 1 depicts the data flow through the protocol's data structures. When receiving R, node A records whether it likes or dislikes the item in its *private profile*. A node never shares its private profile. It only uses it as a basis to build an *obfuscated profile* whenever it must share interest information with other nodes in the clustering process. Nodes remove the items whose timestamps are outside the latest *time window*. This ensures that all profiles reflect the current interests of the corresponding nodes.

Let us now assume that A receives an item R and likes it. After updating its private profile, A updates the item profile of R before forwarding it to other nodes. This corresponds to the operations on the left branch of Fig. 1. A extracts the items it has liked from its *private profile* and combines the corresponding item vectors into a data structure called *compact profile*. This introduces some uncertainty because different sets of liked items may result in the same *compact profile*. Then A updates the *item profile* of R. This consists of a bitmap that aggregates the compact profiles of the nodes that liked R. To update it, A combines its own *compact profile* and R's old *item profile*. This makes R's *item profile* an obfuscated summary of the interests of the nodes that like R.

The right branch of Fig. 1 shows how a node, A, builds its *obfuscated profile* when required by the clustering process. First, A creates a *filter profile* that aggregates the information contained in the *item profiles* of the items it liked. Then, it uses this filter to identify the bits from its *compact profile* that will appear in its *obfuscated profile*. These consist of the most popular bit positions among the nodes that liked the same items as A did. This has two advantages. First, using the most popular bits makes A's *obfuscated profile* likely to overlap with those of similar nodes. Second, these bits carry less information than less popular ones, which makes them preferable in terms of privacy.

3.2   Profile Updates

Private Profile.   A node updates its private profile whenever it generates a new item or receives an item from another node. In either case, the node inserts a new tuple into its private profile. This tuple contains the item identifier, its timestamp (indicating when the item was generated), a score (1 if the node liked the item, 0 otherwise), its item vector, and the item profile upon receipt. Locally generated items count as liked and have an empty "item profile upon receipt".

Compact Profile.   Unlike private profiles, which contain item identifiers and their associated scores, the compact profile stores liked items in the form of a d-dimensional bit array. As shown in Fig. 1, a node uses the compact profile both to update the item profile of an item it likes and to compute its obfuscated profile when exchanging clustering information with other nodes. In each of these two cases, the node computes a fresh compact profile as the bitwise OR of the item vectors of all the liked items in its private profile.

This on demand computation allows the compact profile to take into account only the items associated with the current *time window*. It is in fact impossible to remove an item from an existing compact profile. The reason is that the compact profile provides a first basic form of obfuscation of the interests of a user through bit collisions: a bit at 1 in the compact profile of a node may in fact result from any of the liked items whose vectors have the corresponding bit set.

Compact profiles bring two clear benefits. First, the presence of bit collisions makes it harder for attackers to identify the items in a given profile. Second, the fixed and small size of bit vectors limits the size of the messages exchanged by the nodes in the system. As evaluated in Sect. 6.7, this drastically reduces the bandwidth cost of our protocol.

Item Profile.   A node never reveals its compact profile. Instead, it injects part of it into the item profiles of the items it likes. Consequently, the item profile of an item aggregates the interests of the users that liked the item along its dissemination path. A parameter s controls how much information from the compact profile nodes include in the item profile.

Let n be a node that liked an item R. When receiving R for the first time, n computes its compact profile as described above. Then, before forwarding R, n builds an integer vector as the bit-by-bit sum of R's item profile and n's own compact profile. Each entry in this vector has a value in $\{0, 1, 2\}$: node n chooses the s vector positions with the highest values, breaking ties randomly, and creates a fresh profile for item R by setting the corresponding bits to 1 and the remaining ones to 0. Finally, when n generates the profile for a new item, it simply sets to 1 the values of s bits from those that are set in its compact profile. This update process ensures that the item profile of each forwarded item always contains s bits with value 1.

Filter Profile. Nodes compute their filter profiles whenever they need to exchange clustering information with other nodes. Unlike the other profiles associated with nodes, this profile consists of a vector of integer values and does not represent the interests of a user. Rather it captures the interests of the community of users that have liked similar items. A node computes the value at each position in its filter profile by summing the values of the bits in the corresponding position in the profiles of liked items. This causes the filter profile to record the popularity of each bit within a community of nodes that liked similar items.

Obfuscated Profiles. As shown in Fig. 1, a node builds its obfuscated profile by filtering the contents of its compact profile through the filter profile. This yields a bit vector that captures the most popular bits in the node's community and thus hides the node's most specific and unique tastes. The node selects the s positions that have the highest values in its filter profile, breaking ties randomly, and sets the corresponding bits in the obfuscated profile to the values they have in its compact profile. It then sets all the remaining bits in the obfuscated profile to 0.

4   Randomized Dissemination

An attacker can discover the opinions of a user by observing the items she forwards (Sect. 2). We address this vulnerability through our second contribution: a differentially-private randomized dissemination protocol.

The key idea of our protocol is to randomize the forwarding decision: a node that likes an item drops it with probability pf, while a node that does not like it forwards it with the same pf. This prevents an attacker from acquiring certainties about a user's interests by observing which items she forwards. However, the attacker could still learn something from the content of the associated *item profiles* (nodes modify the item profiles of the items they like). To ensure that the whole dissemination protocol does not expose any non-differentially-private information, we therefore randomize not only forwarding actions, but also the *item profiles* associated with forwarded items. This requires us to modify the protocol described in Sect. 3 as follows.

First, we modify the *private profile*. For each item, not only do we store whether the node liked or disliked it, but we also add a new field: the *randomized decision*. This field stores the forwarding decision taken as a result of the randomization process (1 for forward and 0 for drop).

We then introduce a new *randomized compact profile* (as shown in Fig. 2). The node fills this profile analogously to the compact profile but it uses the *randomized decision* instead of its actual opinion on the item. The node iterates through all the items for which the randomized decision is 1 and integrates their item vectors into the *randomized compact profile* using the same operations described for the non-randomized one.

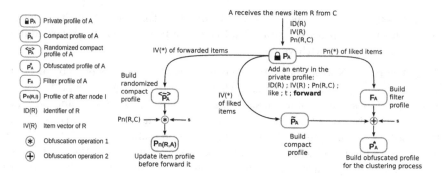

Fig. 2. Complete information flow through the protocol's data structures.

Finally, the node updates the *item profile* of an item when it decides to forward it as a result of randomization, regardless of whether it likes it or not. Moreover, the node performs this update as described in Sect. 3.2 except that the node uses its *randomized compact profile* instead of its *compact profile*. Nodes still use their non-randomized *compact profile* when choosing their neighbors. In this case, they compare their *compact profile* with the *obfuscated profiles* of candidate neighbors.

The above modifications guarantee that the actual content of the *compact profile* never leaks during dissemination. This guarantees that our dissemination protocol is *differentially private* [9]. Roughly speaking, a randomized algorithm $\mathcal{A}$ is ϵ-differentially private if it produces approximately the same output when applied to two neighboring datasets [10] (*i.e.* which differ on a single element). In the context of dissemination, the datasets to randomize are vectors of user opinions. For space reasons, we omit the proofs, which can be found in [5].

This algorithm bounds the amount of information an observer gets when receiving an item from a user. Instead of knowing with certainty that the user liked the item, the observer knows that the user liked it with probability $1 - pf$. However, this does not make our solution differentially private. The dissemination component is, but it only ensures ϵ-differential privacy when a user expresses her opinion about an item, not when she generates a new one. In the latter case the user always forwards the item.

5   Experimental Setup

Dataset. We conducted a survey on 200 news items involving 120 colleagues and relatives. We selected news items from a set of RSS feeds illustrating various topics. We exposed each of them to our test users and gathered their opinions (like/dislike). This provided us with a small but *real* dataset of users exposed to exactly the same news items. To scale out our system, we generated 4 instances of each user and news item in the experiments. While this may introduce a bias, it does so for both our mechanism and the two solutions we compare against.

Alternatives. We compare our approach with the following alternatives.

Cleartext profile (CT): This solution does not provide any privacy mechanism. This baseline implements the decentralized CF solution presented in Sect. 2 where user profiles are exchanged in clear during the clustering process.

Differentially private approach (2-DP): This alternative, denoted by 2-DP in the following, uses the *randomized compact profile* both for clustering and for dissemination. In other words, it applies randomization during the entire recommendation process. In particular, nodes leverage their randomized compact profiles to compute their clustering views. Every time a user expresses an opinion about an item, 2-DP inverses it with probability pd: this results in a differentially private clustering protocol and a differentially private dissemination protocol.

2-DP extends the privacy guarantee provided by our dissemination protocol to the management of interest profiles. Section 6.6 shows that 2-DP remains more vulnerable to censorship attacks than our solution.

Recommendation Quality. We evaluate recommendation using *recall* and *precision*. Both measures are in $[0, 1]$. A recall of 1 means that all interested users have received the item. Yet, a trivial way to ensure a recall of 1 is to send all news items to all users, potentially generating spam. Precision captures the level of spam: a precision of 1 means that all news items reach only users that are interested in them. The F1-Score captures the trade-off between these two metrics [21] as their harmonic mean.

Overhead. We evaluate the overhead of the system in terms of the network traffic it generates. For simulations, we compute the total number of sent messages. For our implementation, we instead measure the average consumed bandwidth. A key parameter that determines network traffic is the *fanout* of the dissemination protocol, *i.e.* the number of neighbors from the interest-based overlay to which nodes forward each item.

Privacy. We measure privacy as the ability of a system to hide the profile of a user from other users. We capture it by means of two metrics. The first evaluates to what extent the obfuscated profile is close to the real one by measuring the overlap rate between the two using the Jaccard index. The second measures the fraction of items present in a compact profile out of those that can be predicted by analyzing the presence of item vectors in the corresponding obfuscated profile. As item vectors are public, malicious users can leverage them to guess contents of the obfuscated profiles of other users, thereby inferring their interests.

6   Performance Evaluation

We evaluate the ability of our solution to achieve efficient information dissemination while protecting the profiles of its users. We consider both simulations, and a real implementation deployed on PlanelLab. In both cases, we randomly select the source of each item among all users. We refer to our solution as OPRD (Obfuscation Profile and Randomized Dissemination) in the following.

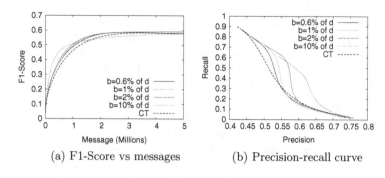

(a) F1-Score vs messages   (b) Precision-recall curve

Fig. 3. Impact of compacting the profiles (various b-to-d ratios)

6.1 Compacting Profiles

As explained in Sect. 3.2, our solution associates each item with a (sparse) item vector containing b 1's out of d possible positions. When a user likes an item, we add the corresponding item vector to her compact profile by performing a bitwise OR with the current profile. The ratio between b and d affects the probability of having two items sharing bits at 1 in their vectors, which in turn affects the accuracy of the similarity computation between users. Figure 3 evaluates its effect on performance.

Figure 3a shows the values of the F1-Score depending on network traffic for various values of the b-to-d ratio. The points in each curve correspond to a range of fanout values, the fanout being the number of neighbors to which a user forwards an item she likes: the larger the fanout the higher the load on the network. Figure 3b shows instead the corresponding precision-recall curve. Again, each curve reflects a range of fanout values: the larger the fanout, the higher the recall, and the lower the precision.

Interestingly, the larger the b-to-d ratio, the bigger the difference between our solution and CT. With a low b-to-d ratio, it is unlikely for any two item vectors to contain common bits at 1. As a result, the performance of our solution closely mimics that of CT. When the b-to-d ratio increases, the number of collisions between item vectors—cases in which two distinct item vectors have common bits at 1—also increases. This has two interesting effects on performance.

The first is that the F1-Score increases faster with the fanout and thus with the number of messages: the $b = 10\%$ curve climbs to an F1-Score of 0.4 with less than $400k$ messages. The curve on Fig. 3b shows that this results from a higher recall for corresponding precision values (bump in the $b = 10\%$ curve). The high probability of collisions between item vectors results in some user profiles being similar even though they do not contain many common items. This leads to a topology in which users are less clearly clustered, and in which the items can be disseminated more easily, which explains the high recall value.

The second effect is that the maximum F1-Score attained by the protocol with a large b-to-d ratio (to the right of Fig. 3a) stabilizes at lower values. Figure 3b clarifies that this results from a lower maximum recall, as indicated

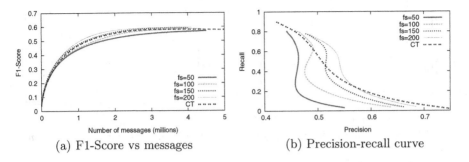

(a) F1-Score vs messages   (b) Precision-recall curve

Fig. 4. Impact of filtering sensitive information (various filter sizes, fs)

by the left endpoints of the curves corresponding to high values of b. The artificial similarities caused by a large b—advantageous with small fanout values (small number of messages)—also create false clusters that ultimately inhibit the dissemination of items to large populations of users. This effect is even more prominent with values of b that set a vast majority of the bits in compact profiles to 1 (not shown in the plot).

In the following, we set d to 500 and b to 5 for our evaluations. The values assigned to b and d should be computed depending on the expected number of items per user profile. Explanations about the computation of these values are outside of the scope of this paper, but are similar to those that relate the number of hash functions and the size of a bloom filter [20].

6.2   Filtering Sensitive Information

In our solution, the size of the filter defines how much information from the compact profile appears in the obfuscated profile. The larger the filter, the more the revealed information. Figure 4a depicts the F1-Score as a function of the number of messages. The performance increases with the size of the filter. Figure 4b shows that this variation comes from the fact that precision strongly decreases when the filter size decreases.

6.3   Randomizing the Dissemination

We now evaluate the impact of randomizing the dissemination process in addition to the obfuscation protocol evaluated above (the previous results were obtained without randomization). Figure 5a shows the F1-Score for our solution using a filter size of 200 and several values for pf. Performance decreases slightly as we increase the amount of randomness (for clarity, we only show $pf = 0$ and $pf = 0.5$, the other curves being in between). Figure 5b shows that increasing pf results mostly in a decrease in precision.

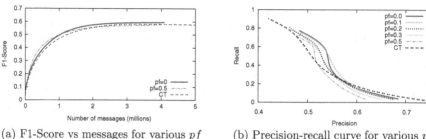

(a) F1-Score vs messages for various pf (b) Precision-recall curve for various pf

Fig. 5. Impact of obfuscating profiles and randomizing dissemination ($fs = 200$)

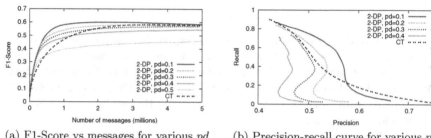

(a) F1-Score vs messages for various pd (b) Precision-recall curve for various pd

Fig. 6. Impact of the randomization for 2-DP

6.4   Evaluating 2-DP

2-DP reverses the opinions of users with a probability, pd, that affects both the construction of user profiles and the dissemination process. This differs from our solution in which only the dissemination is randomized.

Figure 6a shows the F1-Score of 2-DP versus network traffic for various values of pd. Performance strongly increases at low fanout values for $dp = 0.1$, but decreases for larger values. A small amount of randomness proves beneficial and allows the protocol to disseminate items more effectively with a low fanout. This effect, however, disappears at high fanouts. Very high values of pd on the other hand cause a drastic decrease in the F1-Score. Figure 6b shows that increasing randomness leads to a strong decrease in precision.

Figure 7 compares the F1-Score of OPRD using a filter of size of 200 and a pf value of 0.3, with that of CT and 2-DP using a pd of 0.3. We observe that above $2M$ messages, our solution provides slightly better F1-Score values than 2-DP. Overall, however, the best performances of the two approaches are comparable. In the following, we show that this is not the case for their ability to protect user profiles.

6.5   Privacy Versus Accuracy

We evaluate the trade-off between privacy, measured as the ability to conceal the exact profiles of users, and accuracy for both OPRD and 2-DP. OPRD controls

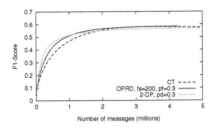

Fig. 7. OPRD vs 2-DP: F1-Score vs number of messages

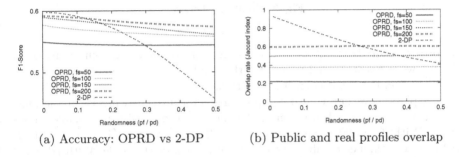

(a) Accuracy: OPRD vs 2-DP   (b) Public and real profiles overlap

Fig. 8. Randomness vs performance and level of privacy

this trade-off with two parameters: the size of the filter, and the probability pf. 2-DP controls it by tuning the probability pd to switch the opinion of the user.

Figure 8a compares their recommendation performance by measuring the F1-Score values for various filter sizes. The x-axis represents the evolution of the probabilities pf, for our solution, and pd, for 2-DP. We show that the F1-Score of 2-DP decreases faster than ours. The F1-Score of 2-DP with a pd of at least 0.2 is smaller than that of our solution with a filter size greater than 100. In addition, revealing the most popular 10 % of the compact profile ($fs = 50$) yields similar performance as 2-DP with $pd \geq 0.3$.

Figure 8b measures the level of privacy as the overlap rate (computed with the Jaccard index) between the compact profile and the obfuscated profile: lower overlap rate implies more privacy. As our randomized dissemination protocol hardly impacts the obfuscated profile, our results are almost independent of pf. 2-DP sees instead its similarity decrease with increasing pd. With $pd = 0.3$, 2-DP yields an overlap rate of about 0.55 with an F1-Score (from Fig. 8a) of 0.55. Our approach, on the other hand yields the same overlap rate with a filter size between $150 < fs < 200$, which corresponds to an F1-Score value of about 0.57.

Figure 9, instead, assesses privacy by measuring if the items in a user's real profile can be predicted by an attacker that analyzes the user's public profile. Note that in 2-DP, the real profile is the one that would exist without random perturbations. We evaluate this aspect by measuring the recall and the precision of predictions. Prediction recall measures the fraction of correctly predicted items out of those in the compact profile. Prediction precision measures the fraction

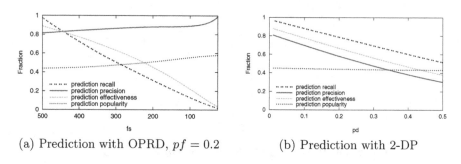

(a) Prediction with OPRD, $pf = 0.2$ (b) Prediction with 2-DP

Fig. 9. Profile prediction

of correct predictions out of all the prediction attempts. For our solution, in Fig. 9a, we use a $pf = 0.2$ to control the randomized dissemination, and vary the filter size. For 2-DP (Fig. 9b), we instead vary pd.

The plots show that while our approach is subject to fairly precise predictions, these cover only a small fraction of the compact profile with reasonable values of fs. With $fs = 200$, the prediction recall is of about 30 %. In contrast, 2-DP exposes a higher number of items from the compact profile. With $pd = 0.2$ the prediction recall is 0.8 with a prediction precision of 0.6. The curves for prediction effectiveness, computed as F1-Score values, highlight our approach's ability to strike an advantageous balance between privacy and recommendation performance. The two plots also show the average popularity of the predicted items. We observe that when the filter size decreases, the correctly predicted items are among the most popular ones, which are arguably the least private.

6.6   Resilience to a Censorship Attack

We illustrate the resilience of our obfuscation protocol against censorship by implementing a simple eclipse attack [18]. A coalition of censors mirrors the (obfuscated) profile of a target node in order to populate its clustering view. This is turn isolates it from the remaining nodes since its only neighbors are all censors. If the user profiles are exposed in clear, the profile of the censors matches exactly that of the target node: this gives censors a very high probability to enter its view. Once the censors have fully populated the target node's view, they simply intercept all the messages sent by the target node, preventing their dissemination. We evaluate the efficiency of this attack with two metrics: the poisoning rate of the target's clustering view by attackers; and the fraction of honest nodes (*e.g.* not censors) reachable by the target when it sends an item.

We ran this attack for each user in the dataset. The x-axis represents the users in the experiment sorted by their sensitivity to the attack. Figure 10a and b depict the results obtained with a cluster size of 50, and 50 censors (we observe similar results independently of the cluster size). In addition, this experiment uses a filter of 125 and $pf = 0.2$ for our solution, and $pd = 0.2$ for 2-DP. We can clearly see that 2-DP is not effective in preventing censorship attacks: only

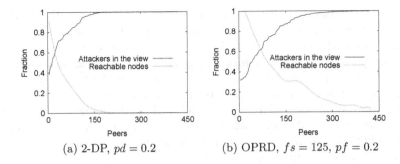

(a) 2-DP, $pd = 0.2$ (b) OPRD, $fs = 125$, $pf = 0.2$

Fig. 10. Resilience to censorship

150 nodes have a poisoning rate lower than 1. This is because 2-DP computes similarities using the randomized compact profile, which it also shares with other users. Therefore 2-DP exhibits exactly the same vulnerability as CT. The censors can trivially match the profile of the target node.

Our approach is more resilient to this censorship attack. It is difficult for censors to intercept all messages sent by the target and only a third of the nodes have a fully poisoned clustering view. The obfuscated profile only reveals the least sensitive information to other nodes: censors only mirror a coarse-grained sub part of the target node's profile. Consequently, their profiles are more likely to resemble those of users with correlated interests than to match the target profile. Figure 8b confirms this observation by showing the overlap between obfuscated and compact profiles. The resilience of OPRD is driven by the size of the obfuscation filter, the smaller the filter, the more resilient the protocol.

6.7   Bandwidth Consumption

We also conducted experiments using our prototype with 215 users running on approximately 110 PlanetLab nodes in order to evaluate the reduction of network cost resulting from the compactness of our profiles. The results in terms of F1-Score, recall, and precision closely mimic those obtained with our simulations and are therefore omitted. The bandwidth cost associated with our obfuscated solution (not depicted for space reason) is about one third of that of the solution based on cleartext profiles [5].

7   Related Work

Privacy is important in many applications. Several approaches [2,17] use randomized distortion techniques to preserve the privacy of sensitive data. However, [13,15] show that random distortion can seriously compromise privacy. Instead of adding randomness to user profiles, our solution uses coarse-grained profiles that reveal only the least sensitive information. The changes we apply to profiles are thus not random, but they depend on the interests of users. This makes it harder to separate privacy sensitive information from the introduced distortion.

Some authors [1] designed a statistical measure of privacy based on differential entropy. However, it is difficult to evaluate its meaning and its impact on sensitive data. Differential privacy was considered in [9,12]. In a distributed settings, [4] proposed a differentially private protocol to measure the similarity between peers. While this solution works well with static profiles, its differential privacy is not preserved when profiles are dynamic as in recommendation systems. In addition, still in the context of recommendation systems, [16] highlights the trade-off between privacy and accuracy.

Other approaches [7] exploit homomorphic encryption in a P2P environment to secure multi-party computation techniques. Similarly, [3] proposes an architecture for privacy preserving CF by replacing the single server providing the service with a coalition of trusted servers.

8   Concluding Remarks

The motivation of this work is to make distributed CF resilient to privacy and censorship attacks without jeopardizing the quality of recommendation. We proposed a mechanism that relies on two components: (i) an obfuscation scheme revealing only the least sensitive information in the profiles of users, and (ii) a randomization-based dissemination protocol ensuring differential privacy during the dissemination. We showed the viability of our mechanism by comparing it with a non-private and a fully (differentially) private alternative. However, many questions remain open. In particular, evaluating the fundamental trade-offs between privacy, resilience to censorship, and recommendation quality constitutes an interesting research direction.

References

1. Agrawal, D., Aggarwal, C.C.: On the design and quantification of privacy preserving data mining algorithms. In: PODS (2001)
2. Agrawal, R., Srikant, R.: Privacy-preserving data mining. In: SIGMOD (2000)
3. Ahmad, W., Khokhar, A.: An architecture for privacy preserving collaborative filtering on web portals. In: IAS (2007)
4. Alaggan, M., Gambs, S., Kermarrec, A.-M.: BLIP: non-interactive differentially-private similarity computation on bloom filters. In: Richa, A.W., Scheideler, C. (eds.) SSS 2012. LNCS, vol. 7596, pp. 202–216. Springer, Heidelberg (2012)
5. Boutet, A., Frey, D., Guerraoui, R., Jégou, A., Kermarrec, A-.M.: Privacy-preserving distributed collaborative filtering. Technical report RR-8253, INRIA, March 2013
6. Boutet, A., Frey, D., Guerraoui, R., Jégou, A., Kermarrec, A.-M.: WhatsUp Decentralized Instant News Recommender. In: IPDPS (2013)
7. Canny, J.: Collaborative filtering with privacy via factor analysis. In: SIGIR (2002)
8. Das, A.S., Datar, M., Garg, A., Rajaram, S.: Google news personalization: scalable online collaborative filtering. In: WWW (2007)

9. Dwork, C.: Differential privacy: a survey of results. In: Agrawal, M., Du, D.-Z., Duan, Z., Li, A. (eds.) TAMC 2008. LNCS, vol. 4978, pp. 1–19. Springer, Heidelberg (2008)

10. Dwork, C., McSherry, F., Nissim, K., Smith, A.: Calibrating noise to sensitivity in private data analysis. In: Halevi, S., Rabin, T. (eds.) TCC 2006. LNCS, vol. 3876, pp. 265–284. Springer, Heidelberg (2006)

11. Goldreich, O.: Cryptography and cryptographic protocols. Distrib. Comput. **16**, 177–199 (2003)

12. Haeberlen, A., Pierce, B.C., Narayan, A.: Differential privacy under fire. In: SEC (2011)

13. Huang, Z., Du, W., Chen, B.: Deriving private information from randomized data. In: SIGMOD (2005)

14. Kanerva, P., Kristoferson, J., Holst, A.: Random indexing of text samples for latent semantic analysis. In: CCSS (2000)

15. Kargupta, H., Datta, S., Wang, Q., Sivakumar, K.: On the privacy preserving properties of random data perturbation techniques. In: ICDM (2003)

16. Machanavajjhala, A., Korolova, A., Sarma,A.D.: Personalized social recommendations: accurate or private. In: VLDB (2011)

17. Polat, H., Du, W.: Svd-based collaborative filtering with privacy. In: SAC (2005)

18. Singh, A., Castro, M., Druschel, P., Rowstron, A.: Defending against eclipse attacks on overlay networks. In: SIGOPS (2004)

19. Su, X., Khoshgoftaar, T.M.: A survey of collaborative filtering techniques. Adv. Artif. Intell. (2009)

20. Tarkoma, S., Rothenberg, C.E., Lagerspetz, E.: Theory and practice of bloom filters for distributed systems. IEEE Commun. Surv. Tutorials **14**, 131–155 (2012)

21. van Rijsbergen, C.J.: Information Retrieval. Butterworth, London (1979)

22. Voulgaris, S., Gavidia, D., van Steen, M.: Cyclon: inexpensive membership management for unstructured p2p overlays. J. Netw. Syst. Manage. **13**, 197–217 (2005)

23. Voulgaris, S., van Steen, M.: Epidemic-style management of semantic overlays for content-based searching. In: Cunha, J.C., Medeiros, P.D. (eds.) Euro-Par 2005. LNCS, vol. 3648, pp. 1143–1152. Springer, Heidelberg (2005)

24. Wan, M., Jönsson, A., Wang, C., Li, L., Yang, Y.: A random indexing approach for web user clustering and web prefetching. In: Cao, L., Huang, J.Z., Bailey, J., Koh, Y.S., Luo, J. (eds.) PAKDD Workshops 2011. LNCS, vol. 7104, pp. 40–52. Springer, Heidelberg (2012)

A Scalable P2P RIA Crawling System
with Partial Knowledge

Khaled Ben Hafaiedh[1,3]($\boxtimes$), Gregor von Bochmann[1,3],
Guy-Vincent Jourdan[1,3], and Iosif Viorel Onut[2,3]

[1] School of Electrical Engineering and Computer Science,
University of Ottawa, Ottawa, ON, Canada
hafaiedh.khaled@uottawa.ca, {bochmann,gvj}@eecs.uottawa.ca
[2] R&D IBM Security AppScan® Enterprise, Ottawa, ON, Canada
vioonut@ca.ibm.com
[3] Software Security Research Group, Ottawa, Canada
http://ssrg.site.uottawa.ca/

Abstract. Rich Internet Applications are widely used as they are inter-active and user friendly. Automated tools for crawling Rich Internet Applications have become needed for many reasons such as content indexing or testing for correctness and security. Due to the large size of RIAs, distributed crawling has been introduced to reduce the amount of time required for crawling. However, having one controller may result in a performance bottleneck resulting from a single database simulta-neously accessed by many crawlers. It may also be vulnerable to com-plete data loss if a node failure occurs at the storage unit. We present a distributed decentralized scheme for crawling large-scale RIAs capable of partitioning the search space among several controllers in which the information is partially stored, which allows for fault tolerance and for the scalability of the system. Our results are significantly better than for non-distributed crawling, and outperforms the distributed crawling using one coordinator.

Keywords: Rich Internet Applications · Web crawling · Web applica-tion modeling · Graph exploration · Distributed crawling · P2P networks

1 Introduction

As the web has evolved towards dynamic content, modern web technologies gave birth to interactive and more responsive applications, referred to as Rich Internet Applications [4], which combine client-side scripting with new features such as AJAX (Asynchronous JavaScript and XML) [2,6], allowing the client to asyn-chronously modify the currently displayed page. Exploring a RIA is referred to as *event-based crawling*. Automated *event-based crawling* [3] automatically explores all events by traveling each of the possible user-interactions within the given page, where each page is represented by its Document Object Model (DOM) [12].

© Springer International Publishing Switzerland 2014
G. Noubir and M. Raynal (Eds.): NETYS 2014, LNCS 8593, pp. 185–199, 2014.
DOI: 10.1007/978-3-319-09581-3_13

In the context of RIAs, a study [1] has been conducted in a centralized environment to store states within a single coordinator. This central hub has the responsibility of partitioning the task of crawling RIAs among multiple crawlers. We address the scalability and resilience problems when crawling RIAs by distributing states in a P2P network composed of multiple coordinators, where each coordinator maintains a list of states and is associated with a set of crawlers.

The proposed decentralized architecture for crawling RIAs is challenging for two reasons: (1) Crawlers may have to go through a path of ordered states before exploring a new transition. If the states are partitioned among multiple coordinators, it is unsuitable to communicate with all coordinators that are associated with the states in this path. (2) Traversing a long path before executing a new state is costly. Some coordination between the coordinators needs to be performed to allow crawlers to execute new transitions while the length of the path to reach each of these transitions is minimized.

To our knowledge, crawling large-scale RIAs over P2P networks while minimizing the cost (number of event executions), where coordinators maintain a partial knowledge of the application model has not been investigated yet. We make the following contributions:

- The distribution of responsibilities for the states among multiple coordinators in the underlying P2P network, where each coordinator maintains a portion of the application model, and a high number of crawlers are associated with each coordinator, which allows for scalability.
- Defining and comparing different knowledge sharing schemes for efficiently crawling RIAs in the P2P network.

The rest of this paper is organized as follows: Sect. 2 gives an overview of the distributed RIA crawling. Section 3 introduces the distributed P2P Architecture for Crawling RIAs with partial knowledge. The decentralized distributed greedy strategy and the P2P crawling protocol are also described. Section 4 introduces different knowledge sharing schemes for efficiently crawling RIAs. Finally, Sect. 5 describes the results of our simulation study and compares the efficiency of our exploration mechanisms. A conclusion is provided in the end of the paper with some future directions for improvements.

2   Overview of the Distributed Decentralized RIA Crawling

2.1   Traditional Web Crawling

The typical interaction between client and server in a traditional web application consists of sending a request for a URL so that the corresponding web page is returned in response. Thus, each web page is identified by its URL. Crawling a traditional web application consists of finding all its URLs [10]. Improving both scalability and efficiency of crawling traditional web applications may be achieved by partitioning the task of the crawl among multiple crawlers in a distributed network. Distributed crawling allows each crawler to explore only a portion of the search space by contacting one or more units, which are responsible for storing and distributing the graph exploration task, referred to as the coordinator.

Different approaches have been used to concurrently crawl traditional web applications [7]. In a centralized environment, a single unit is responsible for storing a list of the newly discovered URLs and gives the instruction of loading each unexplored URL to an idle crawler [10]. An alternative has been proposed in a P2P [8] network in order to partition URLs among several coordinators by means of a Distributed Hash Table (DHT) [5,14] where each coordinator maintains a portion of the application model so that there is no single point of failure.

2.2   RIA Crawling with One Single Crawler

In contrast to traditional web applications where each state represents a single URL, states represent the distinct pages within the same URL in a RIA model [3], while transitions illustrate the possible ways to move from one page to another. Consequently, a graph with a high number of states can be derived for each single URL in a RIA. Formally speaking, the task of crawling a RIA consists of finding all distinct states for each seed URL [3], where the initial state corresponds to the initial page that is reached from loading the seed URL. The triple $(SourceState, event, DestinationState)$ describes a transition in the RIA model, and $event$ describes a possible user-interaction within a source state and leading to a destination state. The basic greedy strategy with a single crawler consists of exploring an event from the current state if there is any unexplored event. Otherwise, the crawler executes an unexplored event from another state by either performing a reset, i.e. returning to the initial state and retracing the steps that lead to this state [4], or by using a shortest path algorithm [13] to find the closest state with an unexecuted event without necessarily performing a reset.

2.3   Distributed Centralized RIA Crawling

A distributed centralized scheme [1] for crawling RIAs has been recently introduced with the aim of reducing the required amount of time to crawl RIAs, by allowing multiple crawlers to crawl a given RIA simultaneously. In this system, all states are maintained by a single entity, the coordinator. This entity is responsible for storing information about the new discovered states including the unexecuted events on each state. All crawlers are associated with the single coordinator. That is, each crawler may retrieve the required graph information by communicating with the single coordinator, and then executes a single unexecuted event from its current state if such an event exists, or may move to another state with some unexecuted events based on the information available in the database. A shortest path algorithm is performed by the coordinator to find the closest state with an unexecuted event of a given crawler.

However, maintaining the states within a single unit may be problematic for the following reasons: (1) Scalability: Preliminary analysis of experimental results [1] have shown that a coordinator can support up to only 20 crawlers without becoming overloaded. (2) Fault tolerance: A failure occurring within this unit may result in the entire loss of the graph under exploration.

2.4   Distributed Decentralized RIA Crawling

In this paper, we propose a P2P chordal ring structure [9] that is composed of multiple coordinators that are dispersed over the P2P network as shown in Fig. 1. Moreover, a set of crawlers is associated with each coordinator, where crawlers and coordinators are independent processes running on different computers.

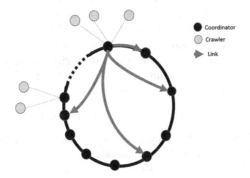

Fig. 1. Distribution of states and crawlers among coordinators: Each state is associated with one coordinator, and each crawler gets access to all coordinators through a single coordinator it is associated with.

3   Distributed P2P Architecture for Crawling RIAs with Partial Knowledge

3.1   The Decentralized Distributed Greedy Strategy

In the P2P environment, states are partitioned among the coordinators. The coordinator responsible for storing the information about a state is contacted when a crawler reaches a new state. For each request, the coordinator returns in response a single event to execute on this state.

However, if there is no event to execute on the current state of a visiting crawler, the coordinator associated with this state may look for another state with an unexecuted event among all states it is responsible for. Notice that maintaining a possible path from the initial state to a target state within the coordinator is necessary in RIA crawling as coordinators must be able to tell each visiting crawler how to reach a particular state starting from the initial state.

3.2   Protocol Description

Data-Structures

- **State**: This represents a state of the application and has the following variables:
  - Integer *stateID*: The identifier of this state.
  - Set $<$ *Transition* $>$ *myTransitions*: The set of transitions that can be executed from this state.
  - (initial URL, Sequence $<$ *Transition* $>$) *path*: A pair of the initial URL and a sequence of transitions describing a path to this state from the initial state.
- **Transition**: This represents a transition of the application and has the following variables:
  - Enumeration *status*: (*unexecuted, assigned, executed*):
    1. *unexecuted*: This is the initial status of the transition.
    2. *assigned*: A transition is assigned to a crawler.
    3. *executed*: The transition has been executed.
  - Integer *eventID*: The identifier of the JavaScript event on this transition.
  - Integer *destStateID*: The identifier of the destination State of this transition. It is null if its status is not *executed*.

Processes: We describe the processes involved during the crawl.

- **Crawler**: Crawlers are only responsible for executing JavaScript events in a RIA. Each crawler has the following variables:
  - Address *myAddress*: The address of the crawler.
  - Address *myCoordinator*: The address of the coordinator that is associated with this crawler.
- **Coordinator**: Coordinators are responsible for storing states and coordinating the crawling task. Each coordinator has the following variables:
  - Address *myAddress*: The address of the coordinator.
  - Set $<$ *State* $>$ *myDiscoveredStates*: The discovered states that belong to this coordinator.
  - String *URL*: The seed URL to be loaded when a reset is performed.

Exchanged Messages. The following section describes the different type of messages that are exchanged between controllers and crawlers during the crawl. Each message type has the form *(destination, source, messageInformation)*

- **destination:** This identifies the destination process. It is either an address, or an identifier, as follows:
  - **AdressedByAddress**: This is when a message is sent directly to a known destination process.
  - **AdressedByKey**: It is a message forwarded to the appropriate process using the DHT look-up based on the given identifier in the P2P network.
- **source:** It maintains the address of the sending process.
- **messageInformation:** It consists of the message type and some parameters that represents the content of the message.

Message Types. We classify the message type with respect to the *message Information* included in each message:

- **Sent from a crawler to a coordinator**:
  - **StateInfo(State currentState)**: This is to inform the coordinator about the current state of the crawler. The message is addressed by key using the ID of the crawler's current state, allowing the coordinator for finding an event to execute.
  - **AckJob(Transition executedTransition)**: Upon receiving an acknowledgment, the coordinator updates the list of unexecuted events by setting the status of the newly executed event to *executed*. The destination state of this transition is updated accordingly.
  - **RequestJob(State currentState)**: *RequestJob* is a message sent by an idle crawler looking for a job after having received an ExecuteEvent message without an event to be executed. This message is forwarded around the ring until a receiving coordinator finds an unexecuted event, or the same message is received back by the coordinator that is associated with this crawler, leading to entering the termination phase [11].
- **Sent from a coordinator to a crawler**:
  - **Start(URL)**: Initially, each crawler establishes a session with its associated coordinator. The coordinator sends a Start message in response to the crawler to start crawling the RIA.
  - **ExecuteEvent((initial URL, Sequence $< Transition >$) path)**: This is an instruction to a crawler to execute a given event. The message includes the execution path, i.e. the ordered transitions to be executed by the crawler, where the last transition in the list contains the event to be executed. Furthermore, the message may contain a *URL*, which is used to tell the crawler that a reset is required before processing the *executionPath*. The following four cases are considered:
    * Both the URL and the *path* are NULL: There is no event to execute in the scope of the coordinator.
    * The URL is NULL but the *path* consists of one single transition: There is an event to execute from the current state of the crawler.
    * The URL is NULL but the *path* consists of a sequence of transitions: It is a path from the crawler's current state to a new event to be executed.
    * The URL is not NULL and the *path* consists of a sequence of transitions: A reset path from the initial state leading to an event to be executed.

The P2P RIA Crawl Protocol. Initially, each crawler receives a *Start* message from the coordinator it is associated with, which contains the seed URL. Upon receiving the message, the crawler loads the URL and reaches the initial state. The crawler then sends a *StateInfo* message using the ID of its current state as a key, requesting the receiving coordinator to find a new event to be executed from this state. The coordinator returns in response an *ExecuteEvent* message with an event to be executed or without any event. If the *ExecuteEvent* message contains a new event to be executed, the crawler executes it and sends

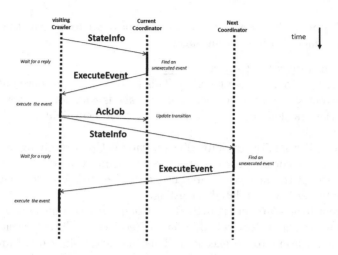

Fig. 2. Exchanged messages during the exploration phase.

an acknowledgment for the executed transition. It has reached a new state and sends a new *StateInfo* message to the coordinator which is associated with the ID of the new current state as a key. In case a crawler receives an *ExecuteEvent* message without an event to execute, it sends a *RequestJob* message to the coordinator it is associated with. This message is forwarded in the ring until a receiving coordinator finds a job or until the system enters a termination phase (Fig. 2).

The following section defines the P2P RIA crawl protocol as executed by the coordinator and the crawler processes.

Coordinator process: UPON RECEIVING STATEINFO
(*stateID, crawlerAddress, currentState*)

1: **if** *stateID* ∉ *myDiscoveredStates* **then**
2:     *add currentState to myDiscoveredStates*
3: **end if**
4: **if** ∃ *t* ∈ *currentState.transitions such thatt.status = unexecuted* **then**
5:     *executionPath ← t*
6:     *t.status ← assigned*
7:     *URL ← ∅*
8: **else if** ∃ *s* ∈ *myDiscoveredStates and t'* ∈ *s.transitions such that t'.status = unexecuted* **then**
9:     *executionPath ← s.path + t'*
10:     *t'.status ← assigned*
11: **end if**
12: *path ←< URL, executionPath >*
13: **send** *ExecuteEvent(crawlerAddress, myAddress, path)*

Coordinator process: UPON RECEIVING ACKJOB
($coordinatorAddress, crawlerAddress, executedTransition$)

1: *Get t from myDiscoveredStates.transitions such that $t.eventID = executedTransition.eventID$*
2: $t.status \leftarrow executed$

Coordinator process: UPON RECEIVING REQUESTJOB
($coordinatorAddress, crawlerAddress, currentState$)

1: **if** $\exists\ s \in myDiscoveredStates$ and $t \in s.transitions$ such that $t.status = unexecuted$ **then**
2:     $executionPath \leftarrow s.path + t$
3:     $t.status \leftarrow assigned$
4:     $path \leftarrow< URL, executionPath >$
5:     **send** $ExecuteEvent(crawlerAddress, myAddress, path)$
6: **else**
7:     **forward** $RequestJob$ to $nextCoordinator$
8: **end if**

Crawler process: UPON RECEIVING START
(URL)

1: $currentState \leftarrow load(URL)$
2: $currentState.path \leftarrow \emptyset$
3: **for all** $e\ \in currentState.transitions$ **do**
4:     $e.status \leftarrow unexecuted$
5: **end for**
6: **send** $StateInfo(stateID, myAddress, currentState)$

Crawler process: UPON RECEIVING EXECUTEEVENT
($crawlerAddress, coordinatorAddress, executionPath$)

1: **if** $executionPath \neq \emptyset$ **then**
2:     **if** $URL \neq \emptyset$ **then**
3:         $currentState \leftarrow load(URL)$
4:         $currentState.path \leftarrow \emptyset$
5:     **end if**
6:     **while** executionPath.hasNext **do**
7:         $currentState \leftarrow process(executionPath.next)$
8:     **end while**
9:     **send** $AckJob(coordinatorAddress, myAddress, executionPath.last)$
10:    $currentState.path \leftarrow executionPath$
11:    **for all** $e\ \in currentState.transitions$ **do**
12:        $e.status \leftarrow unexecuted$
13:    **end for**
14:    **send** $StateInfo(stateID, myAddress, currentState)$
15: **else**
16:    **send** $RequestJob(nextCoordinator, myAddress, currentState)$
17: **end if**

4   Choosing the Next Event to Explore from a Different State

If no event can be executed from the current state of a given crawler, the coordinator that is maintaining this state may look for another state with some unexecuted events, depending on its available knowledge about the executed transitions. In a non-distributed environment, the crawler may have access to all the executed transitions, which allows for the use of a shortest path algorithm to find the closest state with unexecuted events, starting from the current state. However, in the distributed environment, sharing the knowledge about executed transitions may introduce a message overhead and increase the load on the coordinators. Therefore, there is a trade-off between the shared knowledge which improves the choice of the next event to execute, and the message overhead in the system. We introduce different approaches with the aim to reduce the overall time required to crawl RIAs.

Global-Knowledge. This is a theoretical model used for comparison purpose in which we assume that all coordinators have instant access to a globally shared information about the state of knowledge at each coordinator.

Reset-Only. A crawler can only move from a state to another by performing a Reset. In this case, the coordinator returns an execution path, starting from the initial state, allowing the visiting crawler to load the seed URL and to traverse a reset path before reaching a target state with an unexecuted event. Note that Reset-Only approach is a simple way for concurrently crawling RIAs.

Shortest path based on local knowledge. In this case, a visited coordinator may use its local transitions knowledge to find the shortest path from the crawler's current state leading to the closest state with an unexecuted event the coordinator is responsible for. Unlike the Reset-Only approach where only one path from a URL to the target state is stored, coordinators store all executed transitions with their destination states and obtain then a partial knowledge of the application graph. This local knowledge is used to find the shortest path from the current state of the crawler to a state with an unexecuted event. Since the knowledge is partial, this may often lead to a reset path even though according to global knowledge, there exists a shorter direct path to the same state.

Shortest path based on shared knowledge. In this case, the transitions of the *StateInfo* message are locally stored by intermediate coordinators when the message is forwarded through the DHT. Therefore, all forwarding coordinators in the chordal ring, i.e. intermediate coordinators receiving a message that is not designated to them, may also update their transitions knowledge before forwarding it to the next coordinator. This way, the transitions knowledge is significantly increased among coordinators with no message overhead.

Forward exploration. One drawback of the shortest path approach is the distribution of states among coordinators, i.e. each state is associated with a single coordinator in the network. Consequently, shortest paths can be only computed to states the visited coordinator is responsible for. An alternative consists of globally finding the optimal choice based on the breadth-first search.

The forward exploration search is initiated by the coordinator and begins by inspecting all neighboring states from the current state of the crawler if there are no available events on its current state. For each of the neighbor states in turn, it inspects their neighbor states which were unvisited by communicating with their corresponding coordinators, and so on. The coordinator maintains two sets of states for each forward exploration query: The first, referred to as *statesToVisit* is used to tell a receiving coordinator what are the states to visit next, while the second set, referred to as *visitedStates* is used to prevent loops, i.e. states that have been already explored by the forward exploration. Additionally, each state to visit has a history path of ordered transitions from the root state to itself, called *intermediatePath*. This path is used to tell a visiting crawler how to reach a particular state with an unexecuted event from its current state.

Initially, when a visited coordinator receives a *StateInfo* message from a crawler, it will pick an unexecuted event from the crawler's current state. If no unexecuted event is found, the coordinator picks all destination states of the transitions on that state and adds them to the set *statesToVisit*. The *intermediatePath* from the crawler's current state to each of these state is updated by adding the corresponding transition to this path. This coordinator then picks the first state in the list. It first adds it to the set *visitedStates* to avoid loops, and then sends a forward exploration message containing both *statesToVisit*, and *visitedStates* to its appropriate coordinator. When a coordinator receives the forward exploration message, it checks if there is an unexecuted event from the current state. If not, it adds the destination states of the transitions on that state at the beginning of the list *statesToVisit* after verifying that these destination states are not in the set *visitedStates* and that all transitions have been acknowledged on this state. It will then pick the last state in the list *statesToVisit* and send again a forward exploration message which will be received by the coordinator that is responsible for that state.

In order to prevent different coordinators from visiting states that have already been visited and has no unexecuted events, coordinators may share during the forward exploration their knowledge about all executed transitions on these states, with other coordinators in the network. This allows for preventing the states with no unexecuted event that have been already explored, from getting visited again. The knowledge sharing of executed transitions is made by means of the *messageknowledge* parameter included in each of the breadth-first search queries. The *messageknowledge* is updated with the variable *transitions Knowledge* that is maintained by each coordinator upon receiving a *Forward Exploration* message. Notice that all executed transitions must be acknowledged on each visited state before they are added to the *transitionsKnowledge* variable, i.e. for each reached state, a coordinator can only jump over a visited state if and only if all transitions have been executed on that state and are known to a given coordinator.

The following figure describes the forward Exploration protocol, as executed by the coordinator process upon receiving a *ForwardExploration* message. The line 4 to line 13 of *UponReceivingStateInfomessage* are replaced by *UponReceivingForwardExplorationmessage*, allowing for initiating the Forward Exploration.

Coordinator process: UPON RECEIVING FORWARDEXPLORATION (*coordinatorAddress*, *crawlerAddress*, *currentState*, *statesToVisit*, *visitedStates*, *messageKnowledge*)

```
 1:  transitionsKnowledge ← messageKnowledge + transitionsKnowledge
 2:  if ∃ t ∈ currentState.transitions such that t.status = unexecuted then
 3:      executionPath ← currentState.intermediatePath + t
 4:      t.status ← assigned
 5:      URL ← ∅
 6:      path ←< URL, executionPath >
 7:      send ExecuteEvent(crawlerAddress, myAddress, path)
 8:  else
 9:      if ∄ t ∈ currentState.transitions such that t.status = assigned then
10:          for all t ∈ currentState.transitions do
11:              transitionsKnowledge ← t + transitionsKnowledge
12:          end for
13:      end if
14:      for all t ∈ currentState.transitions such that t.status = executed do
15:          if t.destinationState ∉ visitedStates then
16:              t.destinationState.intermediatePath ← currentState.intermediatePath + t
17:              statesToVisit ← t.destinationState + statesToVisit
18:          end if
19:      end for
20:      noJumping ← false
21:      while statesToVisit ≠ ∅ or noJumping = false do
22:          nextState ← statesToVisit.last
23:          remove statesToVisit.last
24:          push nextState to visitedStates
25:          if nextState.transitionsKnowledge ≠ ∅ then
26:              for all t ∈ nextState.transitionsKnowledge do
27:                  if t.destinationState ∉ visitedStates then
28:                      t.destinationState.intermediatePath ← nextState.intermediatePath + t
29:                      statesToVisit ← t.destinationState + statesToVisit
30:                  end if
31:              end for
32:          else
33:              noJumping ← True
34:              send ForwardExploration(nextState.coordinatorAddress, crawlerAddress,
                   nextState, statesToVisit, visitedStates, transitionsKnowledge)
35:          end if
36:      end while
37:      if statesToVisit = ∅ and noJumping = false then
38:          send ExecuteEvent(crawlerAddress, myAddress, ∅)
39:      end if
40:  end if
```

---

5 Evaluation

5.1 Simulation

The simulation software that we developed is written in the Java programming language using the Kepler Service Release 1 of the Eclipse software development environment. For the purpose of simulation, we used the Java SSIM simulation package [15].

5.2   Test-Applications

The first real large-scale application we consider is the JQuery-based AJAX file browser[1] RIA, which is an AJAX-based file explorer. It has 4622 states and 429654 transitions with a reset cost of 12. The second and largest tested real large-scale application is the Bebop[2] RIA. It consists of 5082 states and 468971 transitions with a reset cost of 3. Notice that in an effort to minimize any influence that may be caused by considering events in a specific order, the events at each state are randomly ordered for each crawl.

5.3   Results and Discussion

This section presents the simulation results of crawling the test-applications using our simulation software. Based on our preliminary analysis of experimental results, a coordinator can support up to 20 crawlers without becoming overloaded. For each of the test-applications, we plot the simulated time (in seconds) for an increasing number of coordinators from 1 to 20, with steps of 5, while the number of crawlers is constant and set to 20 crawlers. In this simulation, we plot the cost in time required for crawling each of the test-applications and we compare the efficiency of the proposed schemes to the Global Knowledge scheme where all coordinators have instant access to a globally shared information about the state of knowledge at all coordinators. Notice that the Global Knowledge scheme is unrealistic in our setting and is used only for comparison.

The worst performance is obtained with the Reset-Only strategy, followed by the Shortest Path with Local Knowledge strategy. This is due to the high number of resets performed as well as the partial knowledge compared to all other strategies. Our simulation results also show that the Shortest Path with Local Knowledge strategy converges towards the Reset-Only strategy as the number of coordinators increases, which is due to the low partial knowledge available on each coordinator when the number of coordinators is high.

The Shortest Path based on shared Knowledge strategy comes in the second position and significantly outperforms both the Reset-Only and the Shortest Path based on Local Knowledge strategies as coordinators have more knowledge about the application graph. However, it is worst than the Forward Exploration strategy due to its partial knowledge.

For all applications, the best performance is obtained with the Forward Exploration strategy. This strategy has performed significantly better than the Reset-Only and the Shortest Path based on Local Knowledge strategies and it slightly outperformed the Shortest Path based on shared Knowledge strategy. This is due to the fact that shortest paths can be only computed toward states the visited coordinator is responsible for, while the Forward Exploration

---

[1] http://www.abeautifulsite.net/blog/2008/03/jquery-file-tree/ (Local version: http://ssrg.eecs.uottawa.ca/seyed/filebrowser/).

[2] http://www.alari.ch/people/derino/apps/bebop/index.php/ (Local version: http:// ssrg.eecs.uottawa.ca/bebop/).

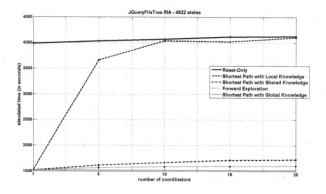

Fig. 3. Comparing different sharing schemes for crawling the JQuery file tree RIA.

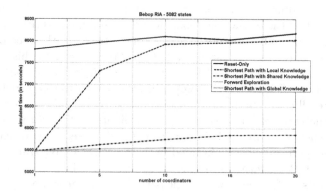

Fig. 4. Comparing different sharing schemes for crawling the Bebop RIA.

strategy consists of finding globally the optimal choice based on the distributed breadth-first search.

We conclude that the Reset-Only, the Shortest Path based on Local Knowledge and the Shortest Path based on shared Knowledge strategies are bad strategies, while the Forward Exploration is the best choice for RIA crawling in a decentralized P2P environment.

Our simulation results show that the simulated time for all schemes increases as the number of coordinators increases, which explains the difficulty of decentralizing the crawling system (Figs. 3 and 4).

5.4 Scalability of Our Approach

The following section illustrates the expected performance when we have 20 crawlers per coordinator, assuming that a coordinator can support up to 20 crawlers without becoming a bottleneck. The behavior of the crawling system is similar across our test-applications. Therefore, we demonstrate the system scalability using the largest test-application we have, which is the Bebop RIA.

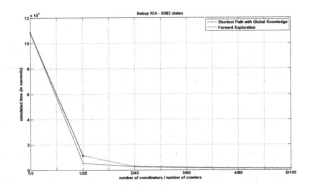

Fig. 5. System scalability for crawling the Bebop RIA.

We consider the strategy with the best performance, which is the Forward Exploration strategy and we plot the simulated time (in seconds) for an increasing number of coordinators from 1 to 5, with 20 crawlers for each coordinator. Our simulation results show that the crawling time decreases near optimally as we increase the number of crawlers, which is consistent with our expectations. We conclude that our system scales with the number of crawlers when the coordinators are not overloaded (Fig. 5).

6   Conclusion

We have presented a new distributed decentralized scheme for crawling large-scale RIAs by partitioning the search space among several controllers that share the information about the explored RIA. This allows for fault tolerance and scalability. Simulation results show that the Forward Exploration strategy is near optimal and outperforms the Reset-Only, the Shortest Path based on Local Knowledge and the Shortest Path based on Shared Knowledge strategies. This is due to its ability to globally find a shortest path, compared to all other strategies that are based on partial knowledge. This makes Forward Exploration a good choice for general purpose crawling in a decentralized P2P environment. However, there is still some room for improvement: We plan to study the system behavior when controllers become bottlenecks. We also plan to apply other crawling strategies besides the greedy strategy.

Acknowledgments. This work is supported in part by IBM and the Natural Science and Engineering Research Council of Canada.

References

1. Mirtaheri, S.M., von Bochmann, G., Jourdan, G.V., Onut, I.V.: GDist-RIA Crawler: a greedy distributed crawler for Rich Internet Applications. In: Noubir, G., Raynal, M. (eds.) NETYS 2014, LNCS 8593, pp. 200–214. Springer, Heidelberg (2014)
2. Zhang, X., Wang, H.: AJAX crawling scheme based on Document Object Model. In: 4th International Conference on Computational and Information Sciences (ICCIS), China, Chongqing, pp. 1198–1201 (2012)
3. Choudhary, S., Dincturk, M.E., Mirtaheri, S.M., Moosavi, A., von Bochmann, G., Jourdan, G.V., Onut, I.V.: Crawling rich Internet applications: the state of the art. In: Conference of the Center for Advanced Studies on Collaborative Research, Toronto, Markham, pp. 146–160 (2012)
4. Benjamin, K., von Bochmann, G., Dincturk, M.E., Jourdan, G.V., Onut, V.: Some modeling challenges when testing rich internet applications for security. In: 1st International Workshop on Modeling and Detection of Vulnerabilities, France, Paris (2010)
5. Xiao, X., Zhang, W.Z., Zhang, H.L., Fang, B.X.: A forwarding-based task scheduling algorithm for distributed web crawling over DHTs. In: Proceedings of the 15th International Conference on Parallel and Distributed Systems (ICPADS), China, Shenzhen, pp. 854–859 (2009)
6. Paulson, L.D.: Building rich web applications with Ajax. Computer **38**, 14–17 (2005). (IEEE Computer Society)
7. Cho, J., Garcia-Molina, H.: Parallel crawlers. In: Proceedings of the 11th International Conference on World Wide Web, WWW, Hawaii, Honolulu, vol. 2 (2002)
8. Schollmeier, R.: A definition of peer-to-peer networking for the classification of peer-to-peer architectures and applications. In: Proceedings of the IEEE 2001 International Conference on Peer-to-Peer Computing (P2P2001), Sweden, Linkping (2001)
9. Stoica, I., Morris, R., Karger, D., Frans Kaashoek, M., Balakrishnan, H.: Chord: a scalable peer-to-peer lookup service for Internet applications. In: Proceedings of ACM SIGCOMM 2001, California, San Deigo (2001)
10. Brin, S., Page, L.: The anatomy of a large-scale hypertextual Web search engine. In: Proceedings of the 7th International Conference on World Wide Web, WWW, Australia, Brisbane, vol. 7 (1998)
11. Misra, J.: Detecting termination of distributed computations using markers. In: PODC'83, Proceedings of the 2nd Annual ACM Symposium on Principles of Distributed Computing, vol. 22, pp. 290–294. ACM, New York (1983)
12. Marini, J.: Document Object Model: Processing Structured Documents. McGraw-Hill/Osborne, New York (2002)
13. Dijkstra, E.W.: A note on two problems in connexion with graphs. Numer. Math. **1**, 269–271 (1959)
14. Loo, B.T., Owen, L., Krishnamurthy, C.S.: Distributed web crawling over DHTs. Technical report (2004)
15. Carzanig, A., Rutheford, M.: SSim: a simple Discrete-event Simulation Library, University of Colorado (2003). http://www.inf.usi.ch/carzaniga/ssim/index.html

GDist-RIA Crawler: A Greedy Distributed Crawler for Rich Internet Applications

Seyed M. Mirtaheri[1](✉), Gregor von Bochmann[1], Guy-Vincent Jourdan[1], and Iosif Viorel Onut[2]

[1] School of Electrical Engineering and Computer Science,
University of Ottawa, Ottawa, Ontario, Canada
staheri@uottawa.ca, {gvj,bochmann}@eecs.uottawa.ca
[2] Security AppScan® Enterprise, IBM, 770 Palladium Dr, Ottawa, Ontario, Canada
vioonut@ca.ibm.com

Abstract. Crawling web applications is important for indexing, accessibility and security assessment. Crawling traditional web applications is an old problem, for which good and efficient solution are known. Crawling Rich Internet Applications (RIA) quickly and efficiently, however, is an open problem. Technologies such as AJAX and partial Document Object Model (DOM) updates only make the problem of crawling RIA more time consuming to the web crawler. One way to reduce the time to crawl a RIA is to crawl a RIA in parallel with multiple computers. Previously published *Dist-RIA Crawler* presents a distributed breath-first search algorithm to crawl RIAs. This paper expands Dist-RIA Crawler in two ways. First, it introduces an adaptive load-balancing algorithm that enables the crawler to learn about the speed of the nodes and adapt to changes, thus better utilize the resources. Second, it present a distributed greedy algorithm to crawl a RIA in parallel, called *GDist-RIA Crawler*. The GDist-RIA Crawler uses a server-client architecture where the server dispatched crawling jobs to the crawling clients. This paper illustrates a prototype implementation of the GDist-RIA Crawler, explains some of the techniques used to implement the prototype and inspects empirical performance measurements.

Keywords: Web crawling · Rich internet application · Greedy algorithm · Load-balancing

1 Introduction

Crawling is the process of exploring and discovering states of a web application automatically. This problem has a long and interesting history. Throughout the history of web-crawling, the chief focus of web-crawlers has been on crawling traditional web applications. In these applications there is a one to one correspondence between the state of the web application and its URL. The new generation of web applications, called *Rich Internet Applications* (RIAs), take

© Springer International Publishing Switzerland 2014
G. Noubir and M. Raynal (Eds.): NETYS 2014, LNCS 8593, pp. 200–214, 2014.
DOI: 10.1007/978-3-319-09581-3_14

advantage of availability of powerful client-side web-browsers and shift some part of application logic to the client. This shift often breaks the assumption of one-to-one correspondance between the URL and the state of the application. Thus, unlike a traditional web application, in crawling a RIA it is not sufficient to discover all application URLs, and it involves discovering all application states.

In a RIA, a client-side page, associated with a single URL, often contains executable code that may change the state of the page as seen by the user. This state is stored within the browser, and is called the *Document Object Model* (DOM). Its structure is encoded in HTML and includes the program fragments executed in response to user input. Code execution is normally triggered by events invoked by the user, such as *mouse over* or *clicking* events. To ensure that a crawler finds all application content it must execute every events from every reachable application states. Thus, under the assumption that a RIA is deterministic, the problem of crawling is reduced to the problem of executing all events in the application across all reachable DOMs.

One can reduce the time it takes to crawl a RIA by executing the crawl in parallel on multiple computational units. By considering each state of the application on the client side (henceforth simply referred to as *state*) as a vertex and each JavaScript event as an edge, the problem of the parallel crawling a RIA is mapped to the problem of parallel exploration of a directed graph.

Dist-RIA Crawler [27] introduced a distributed crawler for RIAs that achieves parallelism by having all the crawlers go to each application state, however, each crawler only explores a specific subset of the events in that vertex. The union of all these events covers all of the events in the state. In Dist-RIA Crawler, each crawler node implements a breath-first search algorithm in its own scope.

Dist-RIA Crawler assigns equal number of events to each node. The underlying assumption is that all nodes have equal processing power, and thus equal workload is to be assigned to the nodes. To enhance Dist-RIA Crawler to take advantage of heterogeneous set of nodes available, this paper introduces a mechanism to adapt to the perceived speed and processing power of the nodes. This algorithm is explained in Sect. 3.

In the context of RIA crawling, crawling strategy refers to the strategy the crawler follows to decide the next event to execute. Dincturk et al. [5,12,14] studied several crawling strategies to optimize the crawl in two dimensions: reducing the total time of the crawl, and finding new application states as soon as possible in the crawl. Among the strategies studied, the greedy algorithm [28] scores well in the majority of cases, and it is much better than breath-first and depth-first search strategies. This algorithm always chooses the closest application state with an un-executed event, goes to the state and execute the event. This paper studies distribution of the greedy algorithm.

In Dist-RIA Crawler, the nodes only broadcast the knowledge of application states, and no single node had the entire knowledge of the transitions between the states. This restriction does not allow a Dist-RIA Crawler to run the greedy algorithm: knowledge of application transitions is a prerequisite for the greedy algorithm. At the same time, broadcasting all transitions to the entire group of workers can make the network a bottleneck.

This paper introduces GDist-RIA Crawler, a client-server architecture to integrate the greedy algorithm into the architecture of the Dist-RIA Crawler. The GDist-RIA Crawler runs the greedy algorithm on the server and runs the crawling jobs to the client nodes. The server node is henceforth referred to as the *coordinator* and the client nodes responsible to crawl the website are henceforth referred to as the *nodes*. Nodes ask the coordinator for tasks to do, the coordinator runs the greedy algorithm on the application graph and responds them with a set of events to execute. Nodes execute the assigned tasks and inform the coordinator about the transition they discovered. The coordinator is the only computer that keeps the knowledge of application graph.

The greedy nature of the algorithm makes the GDist-RIA Crawler superior to the Dist-RIA Crawler (which runs breath-first search) by reducing the total number of events executed to crawl an application. The GDist-RIA Crawler is also superior to the centralized greedy algorithm in that it harnesses the power of multiple nodes to reduce the time it takes to crawl the target application. Further, it does not require the load-balancing algorithm introduced in Sect. 3 that is required by the breath-first search strategy, since only idle nodes ask for work from the coordinator, and thus no node becomes a bottleneck.

This paper contributes to the body of crawling literature by enhancing the previously presented Dist-RIA Crawler in two ways. First by introducing an adaptive load-balancing strategy to harness availability of heterogenous nodes. Second by introducing a client-server architecture to concurrently crawl RIAs. We share our empirical experience with the introduced model and some of the challenges we faced in capturing client-side events.

The rest of this paper is organized as follows: In Sect. 3 we introduce a new adaptive load-balancing algorithm. In Sect. 4 we give an overview of the GDist-RIA Crawler. In Sect. 5 we describe some of the technical aspects of implementing the GDist-RIA crawler. In Sect. 6 we evaluate various performance aspects of the GDist-RIA Crawler. In Sect. 2 we give an overview of the related works. Finally, in Sect. 7 we conclude this paper.

2   Related Works

This work is not the first of its kind in addressing the issue of RIA model construction and model checking. Duda et al. [15,18,23] uses Breadth-First search crawling strategy to crawl RIAs. Crawljax [24,25] leans toward Depth-First search strategy. Other works aim at constructing the FSM model of the application [1–3,22].

Model-based crawling is another area of research that gained momentum in recent years. Benjamin et al. [5,13] present they hypercube model that assumes the target application is a hypercube. Choudhary et al. [9,10] introduce Menu model that assumes events reach the same target state, irrelevant of the source state. Greedy strategy was explored by Peng et al. [28]; and Milani Fard and

Mesbah [26] in a tool called FeedEx. An empirical comparison of different crawling strategies is done by Dincturk et al. [12,13].

Parallel crawling of traditional web applications has been explored extensively in the literature [6–8,16,17,19,20,29,30]. Parallel crawling of RIAs however is a new field and the only work we know of is Dist-RIA Crawler [27]. Dist-RIA Crawler performs a breath-first search over multiple independent nodes. This paper adds a load-balancing algorithm to the breath-first search. It also works on the superior and more efficient greedy algorithm.

A close topic to Model-based crawling is DOM equivalency. Duda et al. [15, 18,23] used equality of DOMs to measure their equivalency. Crawljax [24,25] uses edit distance to do so. Amalfitano et al. [2] compares the two DOMs based on the elements in them. *Imagen* [21] takes into account JavaScript functions closure, event listeners and HTML5 elements as well in identifying the state of the application. In this paper an DOM equality, the most strict form of DOM equivalency, is used.

3   Load-Balancing

The following notations are used in this section and the rest of the paper:

- s: Refers to an application state.
- e: Refers to an event.
- S: The total number of application states.
- E_s: The number of events in the application state s.
- E: Sum of the number of events in all application states.
- N: Number of crawler nodes.
- i: A unique identification number of a node, where $1 \leq i \leq N$.

As described earlier, in each state, Dist-RIA Crawler assigns equal shares of work to the nodes. The load-balancing algorithm presented in this section, refered to as *adaptive* approach, adjusts the portion of events assigned to each node as the crawling proceeds. The manipulation of the portion assigned to the nodes is used as a tool to reduce the workload of the overloaded nodes, and increase the workload of the idle nodes. One of the nodes, called *coordinator*, calculates the portion of the events to be assigned to each node at the time of state discovery. Tasks are not assigned equally, but assigned based on the perceived computational speed of the node and its current workload.

The purpose of the assignment is to drive all nodes to finish together. The portion of events in state s that belong to node i is represented by $P_{s,i}$ where $P_{s,i} \in [0,1]$. The coordinator uses the assignment of tasks to different nodes as a means to increase the chance of all nodes to finish together, and no node becomes a bottleneck. To achieve this goal, for every node i, the coordinator uses the number of events executed so far by the node (called ET_i) to calculate the execution speed of the node. This execution speed is used to forecast the execution rate of the node in the future. Based on the calculated speed for all nodes, and the given remaining workload of each node, the coordinator decides the portion of the tasks that are assigned to each node.

3.1 Adaptive Load-Balancing Algorithm

Assume that a new state s is discovered at time t. The coordinator calculates v_i, the speed of node i, as:

$$v_i = ET_i/t \tag{1}$$

where ET_i is the number of events executed by node i so far. The remaining workload of node i can be calculated as the difference between the number of assigned events (called AT_i) and the number of executed events ET_i. Based on the calculated speed v_i, the coordinator calculates the time it takes for node i to finish execution of remaining events assigned to it. This time to completion is represented by TC_i and is calculated as follow:

$$TC_i = \frac{AT_i - ET_i}{v_i} \tag{2}$$

After the coordinator distributes the new events of a newly discovered state s among the nodes, the time to complete all events will change. Assuming node i will continue executing events at rate v_i, the new estimation for the time to finish, called TC_i', is:

$$TC_i' = TC_i + \frac{P_{s,i} \times E_s}{v_i} \tag{3}$$

To drive all nodes to finish together, the coordinator seeks to make TC' equal for all nodes. That is, it seeks to make the following equation valid:

$$TC_1' = TC_2' = \cdots = TC_N' \tag{4}$$

Equation 4 can be re-written using Eq. 3:

$$TC_1 + \frac{P_{s,1} \times E_s}{v_1} = TC_2 + \frac{P_{s,2} \times E_s}{v_2} = \cdots = TC_N + \frac{P_{s,N} \times E_s}{v_N} \tag{5}$$

Let us take the first two expressions and re-write then:

$$TC_1 + \frac{P_{s,1} \times E_s}{v_1} = TC_2 + \frac{P_{s,2} \times E_s}{v_2} \tag{6a}$$

$$\Rightarrow \frac{(TC_1 + \frac{P_{s,1} \times E_s}{v_1} - TC_2) \times v_2}{E_s} = P_{s,2} \tag{6b}$$

Similarly $P_{s,2}$, $P_{s,3}$, ... and $P_{s,N}$ can all be expressed as follow:

$$\forall i : 2 \leq i \leq N : P_{s,i} = \frac{(TC_1 + \frac{(P_{s,1} \times E_s)}{v_1} - TC_i) \times v_i}{E_s} \tag{7}$$

The coordinator intends to assign all of the events in the newly discovered states to the nodes. Thus the sum of all Ps for state s is 1. Therefore:

$$1 = \sum_{i=1}^{N} P_{s,i} \tag{8}$$

By expanding $P_{s,2}$, $P_{s,3}$, ... and $P_{s,N}$ in Eq. 8, using Eq. 7, we get:

$$1 = P_{s,1} + \sum_{i=2}^{N} \frac{(TC_1 + \frac{(P_{s,1} \times E_s)}{v_1} - TC_i) \times v_i}{E_s} \tag{9a}$$

$$\Rightarrow P_{s,1} = \frac{1 - \sum_{i=2}^{N} \frac{(TC_1 - TC_i) \times v_i}{E_s}}{1 + \frac{E_s}{v_1 \times E_s} \times \sum_{i=2}^{N} v_i} \tag{9b}$$

Given the value of $P_{s,1}$ using Eq. 9, the value of $P_{s,2}$, $P_{s,3}$, ... and $P_{s,N}$ can easily be calculated using Eq. 7.

The adaptive approach does not guarantee that all nodes finish together. The assignment eliminates bottlenecks only if there are enough events in a newly discovered state s to rescue every bottlenecked node. In the other words, if there are not enough events in s, and the workload gap between the nodes is large, the adaptive approach fails to assign enough jobs to all idle nodes and make them busy so that all nodes finish together.

4   Overview of the GDist-RIA Crawler

This section describes the crawling algorithm that the GDist-RIA crawler uses.

4.1   Design Assumptions

The GDist-RIA Crawler makes the following assumptions:

- **Reliability**: Reliability of nodes and communication channels is assumed. It is also assumed that each node has a reachable IP address.
- **Network Bandwidth**: It is assumed that the crawling nodes and the coordinator can communicate at a high speed. This makes the network delay intangible. Note that there is no assumption made about the network delay between the server or servers hosting the target application and the crawling nodes.
- **Target RIA**: The GDist-RIA Crawler only targets deterministic finite RIAs. More formally, the GDist-RIA Crawler assumes that visiting a URL always leads to the same STATE; and from a given STATE, execution of a specific JavaScript event always leads to the same target STATE.

4.2   Algorithm

The GDist-RIA Crawler consists of multiple nodes. The nodes do not share memory and work independently of each other. Nodes communicate with the coordinator using a client-server architecture. Nodes start by contacting the coordinator for the seed URL. After loading the seed URL (i.e. the URL to reach the starting state of the RIA), and after executing any path of events, a node sends the hash of the serialized DOM (henceforth referred to as the ID of s), as well as E_s to the coordinator.

In response, the coordinator who has the knowledge of the application graph calculates the closest application state to s with an unexecuted event and sends a chain of events that lead to that state back to the probing node. This path may start with a reset order by visiting the seed URL. In addition, the coordinator sends the index of the un-executed event in the target state to the probing node.

The probing node executes the assigned event and sends the transition to the coordinator. The coordinator again runs the greedy search algorithm and responds to the client with a new chain of events. This process continues until all the events in all the application states are executed. If at any point the coordinator realizes that there is no path from the state of the probing node to a state with unexecuted events, it orders the node to reset. In effect, by resetting the node jumps back to the seed URL. Since all application states are reachable from the seed URL, the node will find events to execute after the reset.

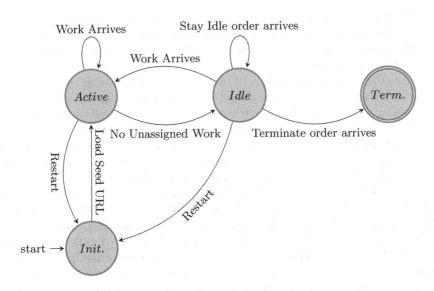

Fig. 1. The node status state diagram.

Figure 1 shows the node state diagram of a crawler node. The crawler starts in the *Initial* state. In this state, the crawler starts up a headless browser process. It then loads the seed URL in the headless browser and goes into the *Active* state. Crawling work happens in the Active state. After finishing the assigned task, the node goes to the *Idle* state. The node stays in the Idle state until either more work becomes available or a termination order from the coordinator marks the end of the crawl. During Active and Idle states, the coordinator may order the node to restart so it can reach states that are unreachable from the current state of the node.

4.3   Termination

When the following two conditions are met the coordinator initiates the termination protocol by sending all nodes a *Terminate* order:

- All nodes are all in Idle state.
- There is no Unassigned work in the coordinator i.e. all events in the discovered states are assigned to the nodes.

5   Implementation

To ensure that the proposed algorithm is practical a prototype of the system was implemented. This section explains some of the technical challenges in implementing the prototype of the GDist-RIA crawler.

5.1   Running a Virtual Headless Browser

The GDist-RIA Crawler uses an engine, called *JS-Engine*, to handle web client events[1]. The primary task of JS-Engine is to execute JavaScript events and it uses *PhantomJS*[2], an open source headless WebKit, to emulate a browser with the capability to do so.

Due to the asynchronous nature of the JavaScript, the crawler can not simply trigger an event and consider the execution finished when the call returns. Executing an event in JavaScript may trigger an asynchronous call to the server, or schedule an event to happen in the future. When these events happen the state of the application may change. More formally, two main types of the events that may have dormant ramifications include: *Asynchronous calls* and *Clock events*.

Upon triggering an event on the target application, the JS-Engine waits until the event and all its ramifications are over. For this to happen successfully, the JS-Engine requires a mechanism to keep track of all asynchronous calls in progress and wait for their completion before continuing. Unfortunately, JavaScript does not offer a method to keep track of AJAX calls in progress. Thus the JS-Engine redefines *send* and *onreadystatechange* methods of *XMLHttpRequest* object, the native JavaScript object responsible for performing asynchronous requests, such that the target web application notifies the crawler application automatically upon start and finish of every asynchronous call (Listing 1.1)[3,4].

---

[1] This paper only focuses on JavaScript events and leaves other client side events such as Flash events to the future studies.

[2] http://phantomjs.org/

[3] *XMLHttpRequest* is the module responsible for asynchronous calls in many popular browsers such as Firefox and Chrome. Microsoft Internet Explorer however does not use module, and instead it uses *ActiveXObject*.

[4] Due to space limitation rest of code snippets in this section are omitted.

Listing 1.1. Hijacking Asynchronous Calls

```
XMLHttpRequest.prototype.sendOriginal = XMLHttpRequest.prototype.send;
XMLHttpRequest.prototype.send = function (x){
        cvar onreadystatechangeOriginal = this.onreadystatechange;
        this.onreadystatechange = function(){
        onreadystatechangeOriginal(this);
        parent.ajaxFinishNotification();
        }
        parent.ajaxStartNotification();
        this.sendOrig(x);
};
```

The second source of asynchronous behaviour of a RIA with respect to the time comes from executing clock functions, such as *setTimeout*. This methods is used to trigger an event in the future. In many cases, such events can help animating the website, and adding fade-in fade-out effects. Knowledge of the existence of such dormant functions may be necessary to the JS-Engine. Similar to the asynchronous events, JavaScript does not offer a method to keep track of the time events. Thus JS-Engine re-defines *setTimeout* to hijack time events.

JS-Engine needs to identify the user interface events (i.e. the events that can be triggered by the user interacting with the interface) in the page. Events that leave a footprint in the DOM are easy to detect: Traversing the DOM and inspecting each element can find these events. Attached events using *addEventListener*, however, do not reflect themselves on the DOM. The final challenge faced by JS-Engine is to detect these client-side events attached through event listeners.

These events are added through a call made to *addEventListener* and are removed through a call made to *removeEventListener*. To handle event listeners, JS-Engine redefines *addEventListener* and *removeEventListener* methods such that whenever a call is made to *addEventListener* an entry is added to a global object, and when a call is made to *removeEventListener* the corresponding element is removed. Hence at any given point, JS-Engine can simply check the contents of this object to get elements with attached events.

6   Evaluation

The coordinator prototype is implemented in PHP 5.3.10 and MySQL 14.14. The coordinator contacts the node using SSH channel. The nodes are implemented using PhantomJS 1.9.2, and they contact the coordinator through HTTP. The coordinator as well as the nodes are hosted on a Linux® Kernel 3.8.0 operating system with an Intel® Intel® Core(TM)2 Duo CPU E8400 @ 3.00 GHz and 3 GB of RAM. The communication happens over a 10 Gbps network.

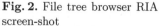

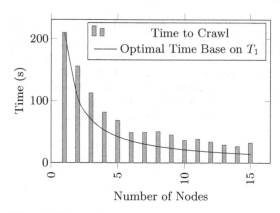

Fig. 2. File tree browser RIA screen-shot

Fig. 3. The total time to crawl the target RIA with multiple nodes.

6.1 Testbed

To measure the performance of the crawler in practice a jQuery based RIA called *jQuery file tree*[5] was chosen. This open source library creates a web interface that allows the user to brows a set of files and directories through a browser. Similar to most file browsers, directories can be expanded and collapsed, leading to the new client side states. Expanding a directory triggers an asynchronous call to the server to retrieve the contents of that directory. Figure 2 shows a picture of a jQuery file tree application.

6.2 Results

To capture the performance of the algorithm as the number of nodes increases, we crawled the target RIA with different number of nodes, from 1 node to 15 nodes.

Figure 3 shows the total time it takes to crawl the RIA as the number of nodes increase (the bar chart) and compares it with the theoretical optimal time to crawl the RIA with multiple nodes (the line chart). The theoretical optimal time it calculated by taking the time it takes to crawl the RIA with one node (T_1), and divide the number by the number of nodes used by the crawler. This theoretical number serves as a base line to measure the efficiency of the crawler. A the figure shows, a good speedup is achieved as the number of nodes increases. The best performance is achieved with 14 nodes.

The performance of the crawler in Fig. 3 is better described by breaking down the time into most time consuming operations. Box plots in Figs. 4, 5, 6 and 7 show this break down:

– Figure 4: This plot shows the time it takes to load the seed URL into JS-Engine. This plot is interesting in that, this operation is the only operation

---

[5] http://www.abeautifulsite.net/blog/2008/03/jquery-file-tree/

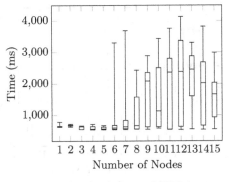

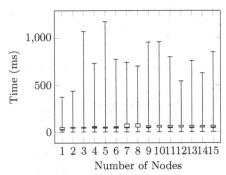

Fig. 4. Time to load the seed URL into JS-Engine.

Fig. 5. Time to update application graph.

that gets more expensive as the number of crawlers increase. Compared to normal asynchronous calls, the seed URL contains large files and libraries. As the number of crawling nodes increase, the host server disk operation becomes a bottleneck and a jump is observed around node 6.

- Figure 5: This plot shows the time it takes for the coordinator to maintain and update the application graph. This includes adding new states and transitions to the application graph stored in the MySQL database. As expected, this operation is impacted by the number of crawlers.
- Figure 6: This plot shows the time it takes for the coordinator to calculate the closest state from the state of the probing node with un-executed events in it. The time to do this calculation does not vary much and it is often close to 50 ms. The calculation itself is rather fast, and the majority of the 50 ms is spent on retrieving the application graph from the database and constructing the auxiliary structures in the memory. As expected, the figure shows that the measured values are independent of the number of crawlers and are not impacted by it.
- Figure 7: Finally this plot shows the time it takes to execute a single JavaScript event. Based on our calculations, executing JavaScript events is fairly fast when there is no asynchronous call to the server. Asynchronous calls make event execution time substantially longer, and often increase the execution time by two orders of magnitude. At the scale we ran the experiments, the application server is not bottlenecked by executing JavaScript events. Eventually as the number of nodes increases, the application server will become a bottleneck and the time it takes to execute asynchronous requests rises.

6.3   Discussion

From the presented break down, it is obvious that the most time consuming operation is loading the seed URL into the JS-Engine. The second most time consuming operation that happens frequently is executing JavaScript events.

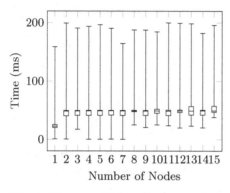
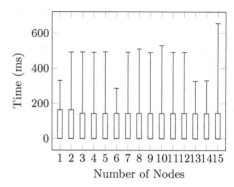
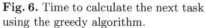

Fig. 6. Time to calculate the next task using the greedy algorithm.

Fig. 7. Time to execute JavaScript events.

Executing a JavaScript event can be particularly time consuming if it involves an asynchronous call to the server.

The design decision of performing the greedy algorithm in a centralized location is inspired by the large discrepancy in the time it takes to find the path greedily and the time it takes to execute the path. As the experiments presented suggests, executing a single asynchronous event can take an order of magnitude longer than calculating the entire shortest path.

At the scale presented in this paper, the coordinator is far from being a bottleneck. As the number of crawling nodes increases, however, the coordinator is bound to become one. In Dist-RIA Crawler [27] nodes uses a deterministic algorithm to autonomously partition the search space and execute JavaScript events in the application. As a future improvement, similar techniques can be used to improve the GDist-RIA crawler by allowing the crawling nodes to autonomously decide (at least partly) the events to execute.

7 Conclusion and Future Improvements

This paper studies distributed crawling of RIAs using a greedy algorithm. A new client-server architecture to dispatch crawling jobs among the crawling nodes, called GDist-RIA Crawler, is introduced. Upon finishing a task, nodes ask the coordinator for the next tasks to do. The coordinator runs the greedy algorithm to assign new task to the probing node, and responds the node with the task. A prototype of the algorithm is implemented and experimental results are provided.

The GDist-RIA Crawler achieves a satisfactory speed up while running the system with up to 15 crawling nodes. This speedup is a result of the low cost of running the greedy search in the application graph at the coordinator, compared to executing the found path by a crawler node. The GDist-RIA Crawler can be improved in many directions, including: Multiple Coordinators to scale better, a peer-to-peer architecture is to shift the greedy algorithm from the coordinator to the crawling nodes, parallelizing other Model-based Crawling strategies (such as probabilistic model or menu model) [4,5,11,14], and Cloud Computing to be more elastic with respect to the resources available and disappearing resources.

Acknowledgments. This work is largely supported by the IBM® Center for Advanced Studies, the IBM Ottawa Lab and the Natural Sciences and Engineering Research Council of Canada (NSERC). A special thank to Sara Baghbanzadeh.

Trademarks

IBM, the IBM logo, ibm.com and AppScan are trademarks or registered trademarks of International Business Machines Corp., registered in many jurisdictions worldwide. Other product and service names might be trademarks of IBM or other companies. A current list of IBM trademarks is available on the Web at "Copyright and trademark information" at www.ibm.com/legal/copytrade.shtml. Intel, and Intel Xeon are trademarks or registered trademarks of Intel Corporation or its subsidiaries in the United States and other countries. Linux is a registered trademark of Linus Torvalds in the United States, other countries, or both. Java and all Java-based trademarks and logos are trademarks or registered trademarks of Oracle and/or its affiliates.

References

1. Amalfitano, D., Fasolino, A.R., Tramontana, P.: Reverse engineering finite state machines from rich internet applications. In: Proceedings of the 2008 15th Working Conference on Reverse Engineering, WCRE '08, pp. 69–73. IEEE Computer Society, Washington, DC (2008)
2. Amalfitano, D., Fasolino, A.R., Tramontana, P.: Experimenting a reverse engineering technique for modelling the behaviour of rich internet applications. In: IEEE International Conference on Software Maintenance, ICSM 2009, pp. 571–574, September 2009
3. Amalftano, D., Fasolino, A.R., Tramontana, P.: Rich internet application testing using execution trace data. In: Proceedings of the 2010 Third International Conference on Software Testing, Verifcation, and Validation Workshops, ICSTW '10, pp. 274–283. IEEE Computer Society, Washington, DC (2010)
4. Benjamin, K., von Bochmann, G., Jourdan, G.-V., Onut, I.-V.: Some modeling challenges when testing rich internet applications for security. In: Proceedings of the 2010 Third International Conference on Software Testing, Verification, and Validation Workshops, ICSTW '10, pp. 403–409. IEEE Computer Society, Washington, DC (2010)
5. Benjamin, K., von Bochmann, G., Dincturk, M.E., Jourdan, G.-V., Onut, I.V.: A strategy for efficient crawling of rich internet applications. In: Auer, S., Díaz, O., Papadopoulos, G.A. (eds.) ICWE 2011. LNCS, vol. 6757, pp. 74–89. Springer, Heidelberg (2011)
6. Boldi, P., Codenotti, B., Santini, M., Vigna, S.: Ubicrawler: a scalable fully distributed web crawler. Proc. Aust. World Wide Web Conf. **34**(8), 711–26 (2002)

7. Boldi, P., Marino, A., Santini, M., Vigna, S.: BUbiNG: massive crawling for the masses. In: WWW (Companion Volume), pp. 227–228 (2014). http://doi.acm.org/10.1145/2567948.2577304

8. Brin, S., Page, L.: The anatomy of a large-scale hypertextual web search engine. In: Proceedings of the Seventh International Conference on World Wide Web 7, WWW7, pp. 107–117. Elsevier Science Publishers B.V., Amsterdam (1998)

9. Choudhary, S.: M-crawler: crawling rich internet applications using menu meta-model. Master's thesis, EECS - University of Ottawa (2012). http://ssrg.site.uottawa.ca/docs/Surya-Thesis.pdf

10. Choudhary, S., Dincturk, M.E., Mirtaheri, S.M., Jourdan, G.-V., Bochmann, G., Onut, I.V.: Building rich internet applications models: example of a better strategy. In: Daniel, F., Dolog, P., Li, Q. (eds.) ICWE 2013. LNCS, vol. 7977, pp. 291–305. Springer, Heidelberg (2013)

11. Choudhary, S., Dincturk, M.E., von Bochmann, G., Jourdan, G.-V., Onut, I.-V., Ionescu, P.: Solving some modeling challenges when testing rich internet applications for security. In: ICST, pp. 850–857 (2012)

12. Choudhary, S., Dincturk, M.E., Mirtaheri, S.M., von Bochmann, G., Jourdan, G.-V., Onut, I.-V.: Crawling rich internet applications: the state of the art. In: Proceedings of the 2012 Conference of the Center for Advanced Studies on Collaborative Research, CASCON '12, IBM Corpm, Riverton (2012)

13. Dincturk, M.E.: Model-based crawling - an approach to design efficient crawling strategies for rich internet applications. Master's thesis, EECS - University of Ottawa (2013). http://ssrg.eecs.uottawa.ca/docs/Dincturk_MustafaEmre_2013_thesis.pdf

14. Dincturk, M.E., Choudhary, S., von Bochmann, G., Jourdan, G.-V., Onut, I.V.: A statistical approach for efficient crawling of rich internet applications. In: Brambilla, M., Tokuda, T., Tolksdorf, R. (eds.) ICWE 2012. LNCS, vol. 7387, pp. 362–9. Springer, Heidelberg (2012)

15. Duda, C., Frey, G., Kossmann, D., Matter, R., Zhou, C.: Ajax crawl: making ajax applications searchable. In: Proceedings of the 2009 IEEE International Conference on Data Engineering, ICDE '09, pp. 78–89. IEEE Computer Society, Washington, DC (2009)

16. Edwards, J., McCurley, K., Tomlin, J.: An adaptive model for optimizing performance of an incremental web crawler (2001)

17. Exposto, J., Macedo, J., Pina, A., Alves, A., Rufino, J.: Geographical partition for distributed web crawling. In: Proceedings of the 2005 workshop on Geographic information retrieval, GIR '05, pp. 55–60. ACM, New York (2005)

18. Frey, G.: Indexing ajax web applications. Master's thesis, ETH Zurich (2007). http://e-collection.library.ethz.ch/eserv/eth:30111/eth-30111-01.pdf

19. Heydon, A., Najork, M.: Mercator: a scalable, extensible web crawler. World Wide Web 2, 219–9 (1999)

20. Li, J., Loo, B., Hellerstein, J., Kaashoek, M., Karger, D., Morris, R.: On the feasibility of peer-to-peer web indexing and search. In: Kaashoek, M.F., Stoica, I. (eds.) IPTPS 2003. LNCS, vol. 2735, pp. 207–15. Springer, Heidelberg (2003)

21. Lo, J., Wohlstadter, E., Mesbah, A.: Imagen: runtime migration of browser sessions for javascript web applications. In: Proceedings of the International World Wide Web Conference (WWW), pp. 815–825. ACM (2013)

22. Marchetto, A., Tonella, P., Ricca, F.: State-based testing of ajax web applications. In: Proceedings of the 2008 International Conference on Software Testing, Verifcation, and Validation, ICST '08, pp. 121–130. IEEE Computer Society, Washington, DC (2008)

23. Matter, R.: Ajax crawl: making ajax applications searchable. Master's thesis, ETH Zurich (2008). http://e-collection.library.ethz.ch/eserv/eth:30709/eth-30709-01.pdf

24. Mesbah, A., Bozdag, E., van Deursen, A.: Crawling ajax by inferring user interface state changes. In: Proceedings of the 2008 Eighth International Conference on Web Engineering, ICWE '08, pages 122–134. IEEE Computer Society, Washington, DC (2008)

25. Mesbah, A., van Deursen, A., Lenselink, S.: Crawling ajax-based web applications through dynamic analysis of user interface state changes. TWEB **6**(1), 3 (2012)

26. Fard, A.M., Mesbah, A.: Feedback-directed exploration of web applications to derive test models. In: Proceedings of the 24th IEEE International Symposium on Software Reliability Engineering (ISSRE), p. 10. IEEE Computer Society (2013)

27. Mirtaheri, S.M., Zou, D., Bochmann, G.V., Jourdan, G.-V., Onut, I.V.: Dist-ria crawler: a distributed crawler for rich internet applications. In: Proceedings of the 8th International Conference on P2P, Parallel, Grid, Cloud and Internet Computing (2013)

28. Peng, Z., He, N., Jiang, C., Li, Z., Xu, L., Li, Y., Ren, Y.: Graph-based ajax crawl: Mining data from rich internet applications. In: 2012 International Conference on Computer Science and Electronics Engineering (ICCSEE), vol. 3, pp. 590–594 (2012)

29. Shkapenyuk, V., Suel, T.: Design and implementation of a high-performance distributed web crawler. In: Proceedings of the International Conference on Data, Engineering, pp. 357–368 (2002)

30. tsang Lee, H., Leonard, D., Wang, X., Loguinov, D.: Irlbot: Scaling to 6 billion pages and beyond (2008)

A New Preference Based Model for Relevant Dimension Identification in Contextual Mobile Search

Sondess Missaoui[1](✉) and Rim Faiz[2]

[1] LARODEC, ISG, University of Tunis, Le Bardo, Tunisia
`sondes.missaoui@yahoo.fr`
[2] IHEC, University of Carthage, Carthage Presidency, Tunis, Tunisia
`Rim.Faiz@ihec.rnu.tn`

Abstract. Mobile search is a significant task in information retrieval and when coupled with context awareness technologies they can become key tools for mobile users for Web search applications. Context awareness techniques can increase the usability of mobile search providing personalized and more focussed content. However, Contextualized Mobile Information Retrieval still remains a challenging problem. This problem is to identify contextual dimensions that improve search effectiveness and should therefore be in the user's focus. We propose a context filtering process based on a new Preference Language Model, and a new relevance measurement. The experiments have been performed with over than 6000 contextual dimensions. The results show the potential of our Preference model in limiting the negative effects of contextual information overload by using the relevance measurement.

Keywords: Mobile information retrieval · Context awareness · User's preferences

1 Introduction

Web search personalization is the process of customizing search results to the needs of specific users, taking advantage of the knowledge acquired from the analysis of the users navigational behavior and many other informations such as user profile data and users physical context. For mobile applications, Web Search personalization becomes a necessity for many reasons. First, mobile users use mobile devices as one of the most important communication tools for daily life. Thus, they expect that when they need information about something, they will get it right away and quickly. Second, mobile phones have gone from being a simple voice-service to become a multipurpose service platform that makes the collect of data about user's behavior, preferences, physical context and social relations easier and faster. This emergence in the use of Mobiles has established new challenges. In fact, mobile queries are often short and ambiguous that traditional search engines cannot guess the user's information demands accurately.

© Springer International Publishing Switzerland 2014
G. Noubir and M. Raynal (Eds.): NETYS 2014, LNCS 8593, pp. 215–229, 2014.
DOI: 10.1007/978-3-319-09581-3_15

In addition, a user's information need may undergo a change through search situations (context of the mobile user). For example, the same request "Broadway" may used to mean restaurant at one particular situation and may used to mean an American street in Manhattan city in other situations. Therefore, without the knowledge of specific search situation, it would be difficult to recognize the correct sense behind a query. The major deficiency of the existing search engines is that they generally lack context modeling. To this end, an optimal Mobile Search engine must incorporate context information to provide an important basis for identifying and understanding users information needs. For such reason, an interesting aspect emerging in Mobile Information Retrieval (Mobile IR) appeared recently, that is related to the several contextual dimensions that can be considered as new features to enhance the user's request and solve "the mismatch query problem" [14]. Hence, in the mobile information environment, the context is a strong trigger for information needs. So the question is "What contextual dimensions reflect better the information need and lead to the appropriate search results?" Owing by this question, the challenge is about selecting the best contextual information that may help to personalize web search and meeting the users demands.

In this paper, we focus our research efforts on an area that has received less attention which is the context filtering. We have brought a new approach that has addressed two main problems: how to identify the user's context dependency of mobile queries? And how to filter this user's context and select the most relevant contextual dimensions? This article is organized as follows. In Sect. 2, we give an overview of Context awareness for Mobile Search. In Sect. 3, we describe our context model. Then in Sect. 4, we present our Filtering approach. Then, in Sect. 5, we discuss experiments and obtained results. Finally, by Sect. 6, we conclude this paper and outline future work.

2   Related Works on Contextual Mobile Search

Mobile context presents challenges of changing location and social context, restricted time for information access, and the need to adapt resources with concurrent physical characteristics of mobile devices. Understanding mobile information needs and associated interaction challenges, is fundamental to improve search browsers. Therefore, Mobile IR systems have evolved to take into account both the user's physical environment and situation. Thence, it was so crucial to integrate context-aware techniques to the aim of modeling contextualized mobile search browsers. The work on context-aware approaches focuses on the adaptation of Mobile IR systems to users needs and tasks. These approaches modelize the user's current context, and exploit it in the retrieval process. Various studies such as [30] and [12] are conducted in order to understand the nature of the information needs of mobile users and their research practices. Indeed, in the context of mobile search, users have less time and screen space for browsing long lists of results. According to [30], users describe their needs in shorter query and using less number of queries by session. Also, they usually consult only the first page of results. Taking this into account, some recent papers have investigated several techniques of context awareness in Mobile IR to recognize user's intention behind the query such as Bouidghaghen et al. [2], and especially to personalize web search such as Tsai et al. [9], Pitkow et al. [28] and Ahn et al. [27]. Personalized web search aims at enhancing the user's query with the his context to better meet the individual needs. To this aim, many research efforts such as [1,4,6,24,29] are performed to modelize context, allowing to identify information that can be usefully exploited to improve search results. The context can include a wide range of dimensions necessary to that characterize the situation of the user. Also, the situation and information demand have more dynamic change in a mobile environment. Owing to the above characteristics, a big challenge appeared which is about selecting the best contextual information that may help to personalize web search and meeting the users demands.

The Related work in the domain can be summarized in terms of three categories. Firstly, approaches which are characterized as "one dimension fits all" using one same contextual dimension to personalize all search queries. Secondly, approaches such as [20] that exploit a set of predefined dimensions for all queries even though these latter are submitted by different users in different contexts. And finally, approaches that are performed to the aim of filtering the user's context and exploit only the relevant information to personalize the mobile search: in this category, our work has proceeded in terms of filtering the mobile context and identifying relevant dimensions to be latter using in contextual ranking approach. The one dimension fits all approaches consider user's mobile context as one dimension at a time sessions. In this category, several research efforts are proposed in the literature to modelize the current user's situation, where location is probably the most commonly used variable in context recognition. Some of these approches such as Bouidghaghen et al. [2], Welch and Cho [21], Chirita et al. [4], Vadrevu et al. [23] and Gravano et al. [18] have build models able to categorize queries according to their geographic intent. Based on localization as the most relevant factor, they define query as "Global" or "local implicit". Indeed, they identify the query sensitivity to location in order to determine whether the user's need is related to his geographic location (local implicit) or not (Global). For local search queries, those approaches personalize the search results using current location. In the same category, Welch and Cho [21], Vadrevu et al. [23] and Gravano et al. [18] use the classification techniques to achieve this goal. Bouidghaghen et al. [2] propose a location query profile in order to automatically classify location sensitive queries on "Local implicit, Local explicit and Global". Location can be considered as an important context dimension but in this field it is not the only one, others can be taken into account. Some queries have no intent for localization (e.g. Microsoft office version, Horoscope) but they are "Time" sensitive. With the aim of recognizing user's intention behind the search, using a unique predefining context's dimension is not accurate. For example, when a mobile user is a passenger at the airport and he is late for check-in, the relevant information often depends in more than time or localization. It is a complex searching task. So, it needs some additional context dimensions such as activities and dates (e.g., flight number inferred from the user's personal calendar or numeric agenda). As another example let us consider a group of users are preparing for an outing with friends for the weekend. If the query "musical event" is formulated by one of them, the query evaluation should produce a different contextual dimensions such as location, time and preferences. The second category of approaches propose to use a set of contextual dimensions for all queries and do not offer any context adaptation models to the specific goals of the users. Several works in this category use 'Here' and 'now', both as the main important concepts for mobile search. Thus, projects as MoBe project of Coppola et al. [5] and Castelli et al. [3] operate including Time and Location as main dimensions besides others in which Bayesian networks are used to automatically infer the user's current context. Most of these approaches use generally classification techniques, and few studies have tried to use semantics and ontological modeling techniques for context such as Gross and Klemke [19], Jarke et al. [10] and Aréchiga et al. [1]. In Mymose system, Aréchiga et al. [1] propose a multidimensional context model, which includes four main dimensions (Spatial, Temporal, Task and Personal model). Those dimensions are supported by ontologies and thesaurus to represent the knowledge required for the system. While all aspects of the operational mobile environment have the potential to influence the outcome search results, only a subset is actually relevant. For such reason, the last category of approaches such as [11,17] are proposed to identify the appropriate contextual information in order to tailor the search engine results to the specific user's context. Kessler [11] approach is built to automatically identifying relevant context parameters. He proposes a cognitively plausible dissimilarity measure "DIR". The approach is based on the comparison of result rankings stemming from the same query posed in different contexts. This measure aims to calculate the effects of context changes on the IR results. Another research effort, Stefanidis et al. [17], specify context as a set of multidimensional attributes. They identify user's preferences in terms of their ability to tailor with the context state of a query. In order to improve understanding the user's needs and to satisfy them by providing relevant responses, we propose a novel model inspired by the last category of approaches. It allows to define the most relevant and influential user's context dimensions for each search situation. Comparing to the previously discussed approaches, our main contribution is to filter the mobile user's context in order to tailor search results with the intention behind his query. We formulate the context filtering problem as the problem of identifying those contextual dimensions whic are eligible to encompass the user's preferences. We provide a new score that allows to compute the relevance degree of each dimension. The idea is: "the more relevant the context dimension is, the more effective the personalized answer can be".

3   Our User's Context Model

Within Mobile IR research, context information provides an important basis for identifying and understanding users information needs [7]. In fact, mobile devices

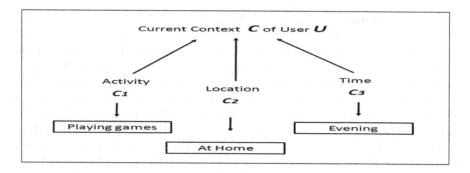

Fig. 1. An instance of a modeled context.

provide more context information than personal computers, such as location information, Time, SMS Clicks, Friends Contacts, Tags, Profiles, Traffic, and certain social networks. All those can be considered as context dimensions and then be used as additional features to create an efficient representation of the user's situation. In our work, the context is modeled through a finite set of special purpose attributes, called context dimensions c_i, where $c_i \in C$ and C is a set of n dimensions $\{c_1, c_2..., c_n\}$ For instance we adopt a context model that represents the user's context by only three dimensions Location, Time, Activity. The Fig. 1 shows the concept of user's context C with an instance of a finite set of contextual dimensions Location, Time, Activity. The user's current context is the user's physical, environmental and organizational situations in the moment of search. It can be considred as the current state at the time of the query submission. For example, when a query such as "Restaurant" is formulated by a parent, his current situation can be definite as Location: Sousse - Tunisia; Time: Evening-12/09/2012; Activity: Outing with family. We present in the next section our filtering model including the main features that allow to filter the user's current context and specify the most relevant contextual dimensions to narrow the search.

4   Context Filtering Process Based on Preference Language Model

A user's context is multidimensional and contains lots of information. Those dimensions are changing from one situation to another and may have an important effect for a query and haven't the same importance for another. Hence, including all context's dimensions for each search can decrease the reliability and robustness of search engine in terms of response time and efficiency. Thus, we propose to filter the context in order to retain only relevant dimensions. In order to identify relevant contextual dimension we measure the effect of each dimension on mobile queries performance according to two language models:

- Query Language Model proposed by Cronen et al. [22]
- and our Preference Language Model, which we proposed and described in this section.

4.1   Query Language Model

Query Language Model is used in many research such as [8] and [2] to the aim of analyzing the user's query and its sensibility to the context. However the best way to analyze a context dimension is to look at its effect on the query. Thence, its effect on the type of documents the query retrieves. In our work we use the Query language model approach as described in [22] which allow to examine the performance of the query. To this aim, we follow those steps:

- **Step 1:** We begin by selecting the top N (cf. Sect. 5) search results of intial user's query (Q_{in}).
- **Step 2:** In the second step, we refine the query by adding the contextual dimension c_i. We obtaine a refined query (Q_{c_i}) for which we select also the top N search results.
- **Step 3:** We measure the effect of the dimension c_i on the query outcomes by comparing the search results of both intial query (Q_{in}) and refining query (Q_{c_i}) using the language model as described in [22]. The assumption is that the more the dimension enhance this model the more it is relevant.

In a language modeling approach [13,16], we rank the documents in a collection according to their likelihood of having generated the query. Given a query Q and a document D,this likelihood is presented by the following equation:

$$P(Q \mid D) = \prod_{w \in Q} P(w \mid D)^{q_w} \qquad (1)$$

We denote, q_w as the number of times the word w occurs in query Q which was restricted to 0 or 1. Thus, in [25] the document language models $P(w \mid D)$, are estimated using the words in the document. This ranking allows to build a query language model, $P(w \mid Q)$, out of the top N documents:

$$P(w \mid Q) = \sum_{D \in R} P(w \mid D) \frac{P(Q \mid D)}{\sum_{D \in R} P(Q \mid D')} \qquad (2)$$

Where R is the set of top N documents. At this point, we use Kullback-Leibler divergence to calculate the gap between the query language models (unigram distributions) of (Q_{in}) and (Q_{c_i}). (Q_{in}) is the initial query submitted by the user. (Q_{c_i}) is the refined query by adding the contextual dimension c_i to (Q_{in}). Thus, This gap between the both models, can be considered as the effect of the contextual dimension c_i (cf. Sect. 5.1) on the mobile query performance.

$$D_{kl}(P(w \mid Q_{c_i}), P(w \mid Q_{in})) = \sum_{w \in Q} P(w \mid Q_{c_i}) \log \frac{P(w \mid Q_{c_i})}{P(w \mid Q_{in})} \qquad (3)$$

Where $P(w \mid Q_{in})$, is the language model of the initial query, used as a background distribution. $P(w \mid Q_{c_i})$ is the language model of the refined query.

4.2   Preference Language Model

In the following, we propose a preference language model to incorporate user's preferences information into the language model so that we induce the effictivness of a query to return results related to user's preferences. Which mean, its ability to describe well the user's information need. Thus we wish to examine some preferences profile of a query Q. E.g., Searching for some "events", the mobile search system must take into account the user's preference "Art". Hence relevant retrieved results must contain cultural or musical events. By analogy to the "Query Language Model", we create a "Preferences Language Model" described as the maximum likelihood estimates.

$$\hat{P}(Pre \mid Q) = \sum_{D \in R} \hat{P}(Pre \mid D) \frac{P(Q \mid D)}{\sum_{D \in R} P(Q \mid D)} \tag{4}$$

Where "Pre" is a term that describes a user preferences category from a data base containing all user's preferences (his profile). For example if a user is interested by "Music" a set of terms such as (Classical songs, Opera, Piano, Saxophone) are defined as "Pre". The maximum likelihood estimate of the probability "Pre" under the term distribution for document D is:

$$\hat{P}(Pre \mid D) = \begin{cases} 1 & if \; Pre \in Pre_D \\ 0 & Otherwise \end{cases} \tag{5}$$

Where Pre_D is the set of categories names of interests contained in document D (e.g. Art, Music, News, Cinema, Horoscope ...). The profile, that describes the user's interests and preferences could be explicitly set by the user or gathered implicitly from the user search history. In our experiments, a profile is collected explicitly before starting the search session. Similar to a regular query language model, the preference model also needs to be smoothed to solve the zero probability problem and to penalize common terms. To this aim, We consider a popular smoothing method Jelinek-Mercer [26]. We use the distribution of the initial query Q_{in}(reference-model) over preferences as a background model. This background model is defined by:

$$\hat{P}(Pre \backslash Q_{in}) = \frac{1}{|N|} \sum_D \hat{P}(Pre \mid D) \tag{6}$$

Thus, the smoothing method is given by:

$$P'(Pre \mid Q) = \lambda \hat{P}(Pre \mid Q) + (1 - \lambda) \hat{P}(Pre \mid Q_{in}) \tag{7}$$

Given λ as a smoothing parameter.

Figure 2 shows an example for the effect of different dimensions on the Preference Language Model (preferences profile) of the query "Olympic sports". For our experiments, we choose as dimensions three contextual informations which are Time, Location and Activity. In this example the initial query presents a flat preferences profile, while Time, location and Activity dimensions have profiles

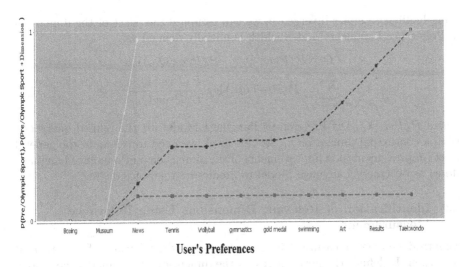

Fig. 2. Comparison between the preferences profiles of the query "Olympic sports", an enhanced queries using three contextual dimensions.

with distinctive peaks spread over many user's preferences. Looking in depth on this graph of Fig. 2, we can see the difference between calculated preferences profile for the initial query $P(Pre \mid Q_{in})$ and preference profile for the query enhanced by a contextual dimension c_i is "Time" $P(Pre \mid Q_{Time})$. Indeed, Time dimension makes a clear improvement for some preferences (Results, Taekwando) over the others profiles. But for some others user's preferences $P(Pre \mid Q_{Time})$ is less or equal to $P(Pre \mid Q_{in})$. The assumption of this analysis is that irrelevant dimension's Preference Language Model show no variance comparing to the initial query Preference Language Model. Given that, this contextual dimension is not important for a query and shouldn't be selected. In contrast, a relevant dimension provides query Preference Language Model with at least one peak. At this point, we need to analyze a context dimension's effect on the Preference Language Model. Thence, we follow those steps:

- **Step 1:** We begin by selecting the top N (cf. Sect. 5) search results of intial user's query (Q_{in}). Then we calculate the Preference language model of Q_{in}.
- **Step 2:** In the second step, we refine the query by adding the contextual dimension c_i. We obtain a refined query (Q_{c_i}) for which we select also the top N search results. Also, Then we calculate the Preference language model of Q_{c_i}.
- **Step 3:** We measure the effect of the dimension c_i on the Preference language model using Kullback-Leibler divergence.

Using Kullback-Leibler divergence, we can estimate the effect of the dimension on Preference Language Model, which is initially defined as:

$$D_{kl}\left(P\left(Pre \mid Q_{c_i}\right), P\left(Pre \mid Q_{in}\right)\right) =$$

$$\sum_{Pre \in Pre_D} P\left(Pre \mid Q_{c_i}\right) \log \frac{P\left(Pre \mid Q_{c_i}\right)}{P\left(Pre \mid Q_{in}\right)} \tag{8}$$

Where $P\left(Pre \mid Q_{c_i}\right)$ is Preferences Language Model for the refined query Q_{c_i} using a contextual dimension c_i. At this level, we need to calculate the general effect (improvement/non improvement) of the dimension on Preference Language Model as on Query Language Model to predict its relevance degree.

4.3 Identification of Relevant Dimensions Using Relevance Measurement

We introduce a new measure that allows to specify the relevance of a contextual dimension. It defines the performance of the dimension at enhancing the mobile query. Our measure named "Relevance score" combines linearly the effect of such dimension on Query Language Model and Preference Language Model using the following formula:

$$Relevance\left(c_i, Q\right) =$$

$$\left[D_{kl}\left(P\left(Pre \mid Q_{c_i}\right), P\left(Pre \mid Q_{in}\right)\right) + D_{kl}\left(P\left(w \mid Q_{c_i}\right), P\left(w \mid Q_{in}\right)\right)\right] \tag{9}$$

with $Relevance(c_i, Q)$ on $[0, 1]$. where c_i and C represent respectively, contextual dimension and user's current context. Once this Relevance score is calculated, we define experimentally a threshold value γ. A relevant dimension c_i must have a relevance degree that goes beyond γ, otherwise it is considered irrelevant and will be not including in the personalization as an element of the accurate user's current context C. The proposed context-based measurement model can be expressed in a formal manner with the use of basic elements toward mathematic interpretation that build representative values from 0 to 1, corresponding to the intensity of dimension's relevance. Being null values indicative of non importance for that dimension (it should not be integrated in personalization of mobile information retrieval process). In the experiment, we will try to define the threshold that a dimension should obtain to be classified as relevant or irrelevant information. In the next section, we will also evaluate the effectiveness of our metric measure "Relevance score" to classify the contextual dimensions.

5   Experimental Evaluation

Our goal is to evaluate the "Relevance score" measure. In this section, we present our training and test collection, our evaluation protocol, which has been greatly improved compared to [15], then we describe and discuss the obtained results. We have improved our system performance which is achieved, through the size augmentation of our database (from 300 to 2200 queries), and the creation of a new user's context model with over than 6000 dimensions. which enhances the stability and reliability of our system.

5.1   Dataset

For the experiments reported in this work, we used a real-world dataset which is a fragment submitted to the America Online search engine. We had access to a portion of the 2006 query log of AOL[1]. We had relied on some experts in the field of Information Retrieval to pick manually 2200 initial set of queries based on the signification of their terms. Also experts have select queries which may be related to the user's environmental and physical context. After a filtering step to eliminate duplicate queries, we obtained a set of 2000 queries. Where three contextual dimensions (Time, Location and Activity) are assigned to each query to indicate the user current situation. To obtain the top N Web pages that match each query, we use a Web search engine namely Google via the Google Custom Search API[2]. We considered only the first 10 retrieved results, which is reasonable for a mobile browser, because mobile users aren't likely to scroll through long lists of retrieved results. Then, for each query in the test set we classified manually their related contextual dimensions. Each dimension is associated to a label to indicate whether it is irrelevant or relevant. The criterion to assess whether a given dimension is relevant, is based on whether the mobile user expects to see search results related to this contextual information ordered high on the results list of a search engine. E.g., for a query such as "weather" the user can express his intention to see search results related higher to location and time information. Since, these dimensions are judged relevant. These steps left us, in our sample test queries, with 34 % irrelevant dimensions and 65.6 % relevant.

5.2   Evaluation Protocol: Assessment of the Classification Performance of Relevance Score

Our experimental design allows us to evaluate the effectiveness of our technique to identify user's relevant contextual dimensions. For this purpose, we propose an evaluation methodology of obtained results using manually labeled contextual dimensions. In fact, a contextual dimension's class is correct only if it matches the labeled results. Using the Relevance score as a classification feature, we build a context intent classifier. In order to compute the performance of the classifiers in predicting the parameter types, we use standard precision, recall and F-measure measures. We use also classifiers implemented as part of the Weka[3] software. We test the effectiveness of several supervised individual classifiers (Decision trees, Naive Bayes, SVM,and a Rule-Based Classifier) in classifying contextual parameters using Relevance score as classification feature.

---

[1] http://www.gregsadetsky.com/aol-data/

[2] https://developers.google.com/custom-search/

[3] http://www.cs.waikato.ac.nz/ml/weka/

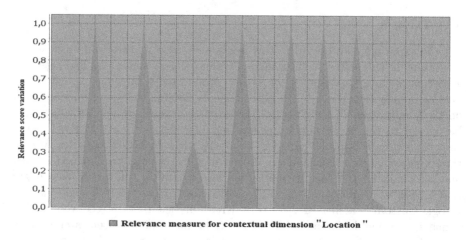

Relevance score variation

■ **Relevance measure for contextual dimension "Location"**

Fig. 3. Distribution of Relevance measure for geographic dimension (Location).

5.3   Results and Discussion

Analysis of Relevance Score Measure. At this level we analyze the "Relevance score" distribution for each category of contextual parameters. Figure 3 shows distribution of Relevance score measure over different values of Location parameters for different queries. In this figure we notice that there is a remarkable drops and peaks in the value of 'Relevance score' for the Location parameters. Moreover, the distribution of this measure for temporal parameters, presented in Fig. 4, has a clear variation with multiple values which clearly support our assumption here. Indeed, the relevance of a contextual parameter is independent on his type or value but it depends on the query and the intention of mobile user behind such query. Hence, Relevance score measure hasn't a uniform distribution for those contextual parameters. It is still depending on the user's query. We can conclude that the measure based on language model approach succeeds to measure the sensitivity of user's query to each contextual dimension.

Table 1 presents the two lowest and two highest values for each parameter class, obtained from our sample test queries and their user's context. Those values allow to confirm a possible correlation between parameter intent class and 'Relevance score' feature. Hence, we define a threshold value for each parameter class. And in the following, we will evaluate the effectiveness of thus thresholds to classify those dimensions.

Effectiveness of Contextual Parameter Classification. Our goal in this evaluation is to assess the effectiveness of our classification attribute 'Relevance score' to identify the type of contextual dimension from classes: relevant and irrelevant. As discussed above, we tested different types of classifiers and Table 2 presents the values of the evaluation metrics obtained by each classifier. In fact, all the classifiers were able to distinguish between the both contextual parameter

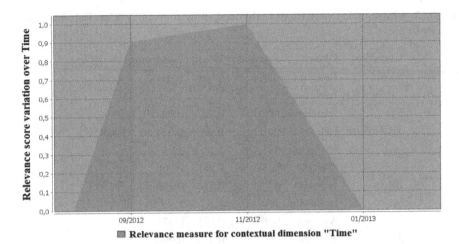

Fig. 4. Distribution of Relevance measure for temporal dimension (Time).

Table 1. The fourth lowest and highest values for each dimension class.

Query	Parameters	Relevance score	Class
"house for sale"	Activity: At home	0.432	Relevant
"check in airport"	Time: 12/09/2012	0.550	
"house for sale"	Location: Tunisia	0.985	
"check in airport"	Activity: Walking	0.999	
"outdoor tiki hut bars"	Time: 30/08/2012	0.147	Irrelevant
"eye chart"	Activity: Working	0.169	
"weather"	Activity: Walking	0.199	
"new bus federation"	Activity: Study	0.279	

classes. Fmeasures, Precision and Recall ranging from 96 % to 99 %. But "SVM" classifier achieves the highest accuracy with 99 % for the F-measure. This first experiment implies the effectiveness of our approach to accurately distinguish the both types of user's current contextual information. It especially allows to correctly identify irrelevant contextual information with an evaluation measure over 1. When relevant achieving over 97 % classification accuracy.

In a second experiment, we evaluated the classification effectiveness of our approach comparatively to DIR approach developed by Kessler [11]. The DIR measure enables distinguishing between irrelevant and intended context. Whence, we compared the two approaches only on this basis. We implemented the DIR approach using the SVM classifier which achieves one of the best classification performance using one simple rule: analyzing the individual results in two rankings for the same query expanded by different contextual parameters. Intended or relevant contextual information must have an impact that goes beyond a threshold value.

Table 2. Classification performance obtained using a classifier with Relevance score as a feature.

Classifier	Class	Precision	Recall	F-measure	Accuracy
SVM	Relevant	0.978	0.989	0.981	99 %
	Irrelevant	1	1	1	
	Average	0.991	0.99	0.99	
JRIP rules	Relevant	0.911	0.953	0.924	96.3 %
	Irrelevant	1	1	1	
	Average	0.965	0.962	0.962	
Bayes	Relevant	1	0.933	0.966	97 %
	Irrelevant	1	1	1	
	Average	0.973	0.971	0.971	
J48	relevant	1	0.933	0.966	97 %
	irrelevant	1	1	1	
	average	0.973	0.971	0.971	

Table 3. Classification performance on Relevant and Irrelevant dimensions: comparison between our approach and DIR measure approach.

Approach	DIR approach			Our approach: Relevance score					
Class	Relevant	Irrelevant	Average	Relevant	Impro	Irrelevant	Impro	Avrege	Impro
Precision	1	0.968	**0.982**	1	0 %	0.984	1.7 %	**0.991**	1 %
Recall	0.956	1	**0.981**	0.978	2.3 %	1	0 %	0.99	1 %
F-measure	0.977	0.984	**0.981**	0.989	1.3 %	0.992	0.9 %	0.99	1 %
Accuracy	**98 %**			**99.5 %**					1.5 %

Hence, we should obtain a high value of DIR measure to classify a context as relevant. Table 3 presents the precision, recall, F-measure and accuracy achieved by the SVM classifier according to the both approaches. The result of comparison show that, our approach gives higher classification performance than DIR approach with an improvement of 1 % at accuracy. This improvement is mainly over Relevant context parameters with 1.3 % at Recall.

6   Conclusion

We proposed in this paper a filtering model for mobile user's context that evaluates the quality of contextual dimensions using different features and selects the most appropriate among them. Those dimensions will improve the retrieval process to produce reliable and in context results. This approach is based on the language models approach. We have built a new metric measure namely Relevance score that allows to effectively classify the contextual dimensions on Relevant and irrelevant according to their ability to enhance the search results.

Our experimental evaluation on a part of the AOL corpus shows that some contextual dimensions are more relevant and influential then others. Whence, we evaluated the classification performance of our metric measure comparatively to a cognitively plausible dissimilarity measure namely DIR. For future work, we plan to extend filtering model using others contextual dimensions and to exploit our proposed automatic method to personalize mobile Web search. We will customize the search results for queries by considering the determined user's contextual dimensions classified as relevant.

References

1. Aréchiga, D., Vegas, J., De la Fuente Redondo, P.: Ontology supported personalized search for mobile devices. In: Proceedings of the ONTOSE (2009) (Mymose)
2. Bouidghaghen, O.: Accés contextuel à l'information dans un environnement mobile: approche basée sur l'utilisation d'un profil situationnel de l'utilisateur et d'un profil de localisation des requêtes. Thesis of Paul Sabatier University (2011)
3. Castelli, G., Mamei, M., Rosi, A.: The whereabouts diary. In: Hightower, J., Schiele, B., Strang, T. (eds.) LoCA 2007. LNCS, vol. 4718, pp. 175–192. Springer, Heidelberg (2007)
4. Chirita, P., Firan, C., Nejdl, W.: Summarizing local context to personalize global Web search. In: Proceedings of the Annual International Conference on Information and Knowledge Management, pp. 287–296 (2006)
5. Coppola, P., Della Mea, V., Di Gaspero, L., Menegon, D., Mischis, D., Mizzaro, S., Scagnetto, I., Vassena, L.: CAB: the context-aware browser. IEEE Intell. Syst. **25**(1), 38–47 (2010)
6. De Virgilio, R., Torlone, R.: Modeling heterogeneous context information in adaptive web based applications. In: Proceedings of ICWE 2006, 6th International Conference on Web Engineering, pp. 56–63. IEEE Computer Society (2006)
7. Abowd, G.D., Dey, A.K.: Towards a better understanding of context and context-awareness. In: Gellersen, H.-W. (ed.) HUC 1999. LNCS, vol. 1707, pp. 304–307. Springer, Heidelberg (1999)
8. Diaz, F., Jones, R.: Using temporal profiles of queries for precision prediction. In SIGIR, vol. 4, pp. 18–24, July 2004
9. Tsai, F.S., Xie, X., Lee, W.C., Yang, Q.: Intro for mobile IR mobile information retrieval: a survey. J. Eur. J. Sci. Res. **55**, 394–400 (2010)
10. Jarke, M., Klemke, R., Nicki, A.: Broker's lounge-an environment for multi-dimensional user-adaptive knowledge management. In: Proceedings of the 34th Annual Hawaii International Conference on System Sciences, 3–6 Jan 2001, pp. 1–10 (2001). doi:10.1109/HICSS.2001.926339
11. Kessler, C.: What is the difference? a cognitive dissimilarity measure for information retrieval result sets. J. Knowl. Inf. Syst. **30**(2), 319–340 (2012)
12. Kamvar, M., Baluja, S.: A large scale study of wireless search behavior: google mobile search. In: Proceedings of the SIGCHI Conference on Human Factors in Computing Systems, ACM Journal, pp. 701–709 (2006)
13. Lavrenko, V., Croft, W.B.: Relevance-based language models. In: Proceedings of the 24th International ACM SIGIR Conference on Research and Development in Information Retrieval, vol. 24, pp. 120–127 (2001)
14. Mario, A., Cantera, J.M., Fuente, P., Llamas, C., Vegas, J.: Knowledge-Based Thesaurus Recommender System in Mobile Web Search (2010)

15. Missaoui, S., Faiz, R.: Context filtering process for mobile web search. In: Proceedings of the 10th ACS/IEEE International Conference on Computer System and Application (AICCSA 2013)
16. Ponte, J.M., Croft, W.B.: A language modeling approach to Information retrieval. In: Proceedings of the 21st International ACM SIGIR Conference on Research and Development in Information Retrieval, pp. 275–281 (1998)
17. Stefanidis, K., Pitoura, E., Vassiliadis, P.: Adding context to preferences. In: Proceedings of the 23rd International Conference on Data Engineering (ICDE), vol. 23 (2007)
18. Gravano, L., Hatzivassiloglou, V., Lichtenstein, R.: Categorizing web queries according to geographical locality. In: Proceedings of the Twelfth International Conference on Information and Knowledge Management, pp. 325–333 (2003)
19. Gross, T., Klemke, R.: Context modelling for information retrieval: requirements and approaches. J. WWW/Internet 1, 29–42 (2003)
20. Yau, S., Liu, H., Huang, D., Yao, Y.: Situation-aware personalized Information retrieval for mobile internet. In: Proceedings of the Annual International Computer Software and Applications Conference, vol. 27 (2003)
21. Welch, M., Cho, J.: Automatically identifying localizable queries. In: Proceedings of the 31st Annual International ACM SIGIR Conference on Research and Development in Information Retrieval, vol. 31, pp. 1185–1186 (2008)
22. Cronen-Townsend, S., Zhou, Y., Croft, W.B.: Predicting query performance. In: Proceedings of the 25th Annual International ACM SIGIR Conference on Research and Development in Information Retrieval, pp. 299–306. ACM Press, (2002). Commun. ACM J. 50–55 (2002)
23. Vadrevu, S., Zhang, Y., Tseng, B., Sun, G., Li, X.: Identifying regional sensitive queries in web search. In: Proceedings of the 17th International Conference on World Wide Web WWW '08, vol. 8, pp. 507–514 (2008)
24. Poslad, S., Laamanen, H., Malaka, R., Nick, A., Buckle, P., Zipf, A.: Crumpet, creation of user-friendly mobile services personalised for tourism. In: J. 3G Mobile Communication Technologies, pp. 28–32 (2001)
25. Croft, W.B., Lafferty, J.: Language Modeling for Information Retrieval. Kluwer Academic Publishers, Dordrecht (2003)
26. Jelinek, F., Mercer, R.L.: Interpolated estimation of markov source parameters from sparse data. In: Proceedings of the Workshop on Pattern Recognition in Practice (1980)
27. Ahn, J., Brusilovsky, J.P., He, D., Grady, J., Li, Q.: Personalized web exploration with task modles. In: Proceedings of the International Conference on World Wide Web, vol. 17, pp. 1–10 (2008)
28. Pitkow, J., Schutze, H., Cass, T., Cooley, R., Turnbull, D., Edmonds, A., Adar, E., Breuel, T.: Personalized search. Commun. ACM J. 45(9), 50–55 (2002)
29. Ingwersen, P., Jarvelin, K.: The Turn: Integration of Information Seeking and Retrieval in Context. Springer, Dordrecht (2005)
30. Hollan, J.D., Sohn, T., Li, K.A., Griswold, W.G.: A Diary Study of Mobile Information Needs. In: Proceedings of the Data Collection, Florence, Italy (2008)

Intelligent Multipath Optimized Link State Routing Protocol for QoS and QoE Enhancement of Video Transmission in MANETs

Abdelali Boushaba[1(✉)], Adil Benabbou[1], Rachid Benabbou[2], Azeddine Zahi[2], and Mohammed Oumsis[1,3,4]

[1] LIM laboratory, Faculty of Sciences Dhar El Mahraz,
Sidi Mohamed Ben Abdellah University, Fez, Morocco
{abdelali.boushaba, adil.benabbou}@usmba.ac.ma
[2] LSIA laboratory, Faculty of Sciences and Technology,
Sidi Mohamed Ben Abdellah University, Fez, Morocco
benabbou@yahoo.com, dinzahi@yahoo.fr
[3] LRIT laboratory Associate Unit to CNRST (URAC 29),
Mohammed V-Agdal University, Rabat, Morocco
[4] High School of Technology-Salé, Mohammed V-Agdal University,
Rabat, Morocco
oumsis@yahoo.com

Abstract. Video transmission over Mobile Ad hoc Networks (MANETs) is a challenging task due to instability and limited resources in such networks. Transmission of video streams through multipath routing protocols in MANETs can enhance the quality of video transmission. To this end, we propose an extension of MP-OLSR (Multipath Optimized Link State Routing Protocol), named FQ-MP-OLSR (Fuzzy based Quality of service MP-OLSR), which integrates two fuzzy systems. The first receives as inputs three links Quality of Service (QoS) metrics: delay, throughput and Signal to Interference plus Noise Ratio (SINR) and return as output multi-constrained QoS metric used to find the best paths. The second fuzzy system is applied to adapt cost functions used to penalize paths previously computed by Dijkstra's algorithm. To schedule multimedia traffic among heterogeneous multiple paths, FQ-MP-OLSR integrates also the Weighted Round-Robin (WRR) scheduling algorithm, where the path weights, needed for scheduling, are computed using the multi-constrained QoS metric provided by the first fuzzy system. These mechanisms allow FQ-MP-OLSR to improve video QoS and QoE (Quality of Experiment), against the MP-OLSR that uses classical mechanisms such as hop count as single metric, cost functions without adaptation and Round-Robin (RR) as scheduling algorithm. Implementation and simulation experiments with Network Simulator NS2 are presented in order to validate our proposed approach. The results show that FQ-MP-OLSR achieves a significant improvement of the video streaming quality in term of QoS and QoE.

Keywords: MANETs · Multi-paths · Multi-constrained metric · MP-OLSR · FQ-MP-OLSR · WRR · Video streaming · QoS · QoE

© Springer International Publishing Switzerland 2014
G. Noubir and M. Raynal (Eds.): NETYS 2014, LNCS 8593, pp. 230–245, 2014.
DOI: 10.1007/978-3-319-09581-3_16

1 Introduction

Mobile Ad hoc Networks (MANETs) are characterized by a dynamic topology and non-centralized administration. The instability and limited resources have large impacts on the performances of video transmission over MANETs. The video transmission demands high throughput, low data loss and low delay. Consequently, for a good quality video transmission, it is important to enhance video transmission taking account multiple Quality of Service (QoS) parameters. Using multipath routing protocols in MANETs allows to improve load distribution, reliability, fault tolerance, security, energy preservation and QoS [1]. To this end, we propose, in this paper an extension of MP-OLSR (Multipath Optimized Link State Routing Protocol) [2], named FQ-MP-OLSR (Fuzzy based Quality of service MP-OLSR). Like original MP-OLSR, FQ-MP-OLSR uses the multipath Dijkstra's algorithm without eliminating nodes or links which compose the previous computed paths, the aim is to obtain (in case when it is not possible to find node or link-disjoint paths) the inter-twisted multiple paths that may share one or more links. The multipath Dijkstra's algorithm obtains considerable flexibility and scalability by using the cost functions, route recovery and loop detection mechanisms in order to improve QoS of MANETs. Rather than using hop count as a single metric in MP-OLSR, FQ-MP-OLSR uses a new routing metric based on multiple link quality metrics to find the best path in term of QoS. This metric is computed by the first proposed Fuzzy Logic Controller (FLC). As well, FQ-MP-OLSR adapts the cost functions as function of network conditions by using second proposed FLC. Finally, FQ-MP-OLSR integrates Weighted Round-Robin (WRR) scheduling algorithm for supporting heterogeneous multiple paths with different QoS. Implementation and simulation experiments with Network Simulator NS2 are presented in order to validate our proposed goals. The results show that our enhancement achieves a significant improvement of the quality of video streaming in term of QoS and QoE metrics.

This paper is organized as follows: Sect. 2 summarizes some related works. Section 3 describes the MP-OLSR functionality. Section 4 presents our improvement made to MP-OLSR. Section 5 describes simulation parameters and results. Finally, Sect. 6 concludes the paper.

2 Related Works

Several multipath routing protocols based OLSR have already been proposed. Xuekang et al. [3] proposed an OLSR multipath version, which compute two nodes-disjoint best paths from source to a destination. The first path is used to send data and the second is alternate and is used only if the first breaks, to select paths that improve QoS, authors introduces a new cross-layer parameter which is define as the ratio between SNR (Signal to Noise Ratio) and delay metrics.

Hung et al. proposed in [4, 5] respectively, two new multiple paths variant of OLSR called LIA-MPOLSR (Link-disjoint Interference-Aware Multipath OLSR) and HIA-MPOLSR (Hybrid Interference-Aware Multipath OLSR) which are based interference metric calculated by considering the geographic distance between nodes. The performance evaluation shows that LIA-MPOLSR and HIA-MPOLSR enhances the performances in terms of packet delivery ratio, routing overhead and normalized routing load. However, the metric based interference used to select paths is not always available, GPS (Global Position System) is needed to know position of neighbors for computing this metric.

Adoni et al. [6] proposed a multipath OLSR variant based energy metric, the aim is to get energy optimization of all nodes in the network, and make energy expenditure of all nodes uniform. Another multipath OLSR variant based energy and moving mode metrics is proposed by Huang et al. [7], the aim is to increase living time of nodes and links and reliability of selected paths. However, moving mode metric require neighbors nodes position, so this information is not always available.

All cited multipath variants of OLSR use a removing strategy of nodes or links to find disjoint paths. However, under particular cases, this strategy could not find disjoint paths. Thus, this strategy sometimes leads to find paths with a high number of hops, which increases packets transmission delay and causes a high rate of broken links and then a high rate of packet loss.

In our knowledge, the only multipath variant of OLSR trying to increase the chance of constructing disjoint paths is MP-OLSR proposed by Yi et al. [2, 8]. Thereafter, we propose to improve this variant while keeping its advantages. Before presenting our improvements made to MP-OLSR, we describe the basic functionality of MP-OLSR in the next section.

3   Multipath Optimized Link State Routing Protocol (MP-OLSR)

MP-OLSR [2] is a multipath enhanced variant of the standard OLSR [9]. MP-OLSR improves quality of data transmission by enhancing packet delivery ratio and load balancing. MP-OLSR inherits some characteristics of OLSR, each node in the Ad hoc network maintains network topology using a periodic exchange of protocol messages such as HELLO and Topology Control (TC) messages. To reduce TC messages, like in OLSR, MP-OLSR uses a Multipoint Relays (MPR) selection algorithm. Differently to OLSR, MP-OLSR does not maintain routing tables to all reached nodes in the network. The multipath computation procedure is made in a source node by following an on-demand computation, so the source node triggers multipath computation when there are data packets need to be sent to a destination node.

Based on the network topology database, MP-OLSR computes the multiple paths using multipath Dijkstra's Algorithm (see Algorithm 1) without eliminating nodes or links that compose the computed paths. The aim is to construct multiple paths in case where the ad hoc network does not contain strictly node-disjoint or link-disjoint paths.

As presented in Algorithm 1, the *MultipathDijsktra* function computes and returns a set of t paths P = $(P_1, P_2, ..., P_t)$, connecting a source node s and a destination node d, from a graph G = (V,E,c), where V is the set of vertices (i.e. nodes), E $\subset$ V $\times$ V is the set of edges (i.e. links) and c : V $\times$ V $\rightarrow$ $\mathcal{R}^{*+}$ is the cost function which define the set of weights associated at each edge belonging to E, so for each edge e_q = (v_q, v_{q+1}) $\in$ E, there exists a weight $c(e_q)$ associated with it. $c(e_q)$ represents the cost or metric associate to edge e_q, by default MP-OLSR use hop count as metric to select multiple paths, so in this case $c(e_q)$ is equal 1 for each edge $e_q \in E$.

Algorithm 1. Multipath Dijkstra's algorithm

```
1   Function MultiPathDijkstra(s, d, G, t)
2       c₁ ← c;
3       G₁ ← G;
4       for (i ← 1 to t) do
5           SourceTreeᵢ ← Dijkstra(Gᵢ, d);
6           Pᵢ ← GetPath(SourceTreeᵢ, d);
7           foreach (arc eq ∈ E) do
8               if (eq is in Pᵢ or Reverse(eq) is in Pᵢ) then
9                   cᵢ₊₁(eq) ← fₚ(cᵢ(eq));
10              else if (the vertex Head(eq) ∩ Pᵢ ≠ Ø) then
11                  cᵢ₊₁(eq) ← fₑ(cᵢ(eq));
12              else
13                  cᵢ₊₁(eq) ← cᵢ(eq);
14              end if
15          end for
16          Gᵢ₊₁ ← (V, E, cᵢ₊₁);
17      end for
18  return (P₁, P₂, ..., Pₜ);
```

The function $Dijkstra(G, s)$ used in $MultipathDijsktra$ function is the standard Dijkstra's algorithm [10] that returns a source tree of the shortest path from node s in graph G. Initially, the cost of all the links is set to one. The function $GetPath$ $(SourceTree, d)$ extracts the path P_i from node s to node d and the function $Reverse(e_q)$ returns the opposite edge (v_{q+1}, v_q) of e_q so that $e_q = (v_q, v_{q+1})$. The function $Head$ (e_q) returns the vertex from edge which e_q points, i.e., v_{q+1}. The paths in P are not necessarily disjoint, when a path P_i is computed, the cost function f_p called also incremental function is used to increase the cost of the arc e_q or $Reverse(e_q)$ that belongs to the path P_i. This will make future paths tend to be link-disjoint. The cost function f_e is used to increase the cost of the arcs if $Head(e_q)$ belongs to P_i, then this will make the arcs tend to be node-disjoint. The paths constructed by function Mul-$tipathDijsktra$ do not need to be strictly disjoint. The cost functions $f_p(c) = 3c$ and $f_e(c) = 2c$ are used by MP-OLSR [2], i.e. a penalty is applied to the used links and nodes. The computation procedure is repeated t times until t paths P are obtained from source node s to destination node d.

4   The Improvements Made to MP-OLSR

4.1   Link Cost Based Multiple Link Quality Metrics Computation

MP-OLSR uses a hop count as single routing metric. By using this metric, MP-OLSR do not find the best path in term of QoS. Generally, using single metric may satisfy only one criterion metric. So, efficient routing in MANETs requires selecting routes that considers multiple QoS. However, Selecting route which satisfies multiple QoS routing metrics is an NP-complete problem [11]. There is no accurate mathematical model to describe it. To this end, we propose a new metric based on multiple link quality metrics by using fuzzy logic. This technology provides an efficient tool to solve multi-constraint problem, it is able to calculate results fast and precisely. Fuzzy logic has proven efficiency in many applications such as decision support and intelligent control, especially where a system is difficult to be characterized. Since MANETs need simple and fast methods to make decision, fuzzy logic is qualified as suitable method to make decision in such networks. The input parameters considered by the proposed fuzzy logic system are delay, throughput, and SINR (Signal to Interference plus Noise Ratio). Thus, each node can build a weighted graph where link weights (link costs) are computed by the fuzzy logic system. Based on this graph, multipath Dijkstra's algorithm is used to find paths with minimum cost (where the cost of a path is equal to the sum of link costs in the path). Due to lack of space, the strategies used for computing the three input link quality metrics (delay, throughput and SINR) of the proposed fuzzy-logic system are not described in this paper. For more information about these three metrics, the reader can refer to [12–14]. To compute the links cost based multiple QoS metrics (delay, throughput and SINR) we developed a first Fuzzy Logic Controller (FLC). The following paragraphs describe the Fuzzy concepts and the components needed to construct the first FLC for computing link costs.

Fuzzy Logic and Fuzzy Set Theory. Fuzzy logic theory [15] is based on fuzzy set theory [16], which are proposed by Lotfi Zadeh to solve problems that are difficult to solve for classical set theory and logic. Fuzzy logic theory has been widely employed for supporting intelligent systems. Fuzzy set theory, allows an element x in universal set X to partially belong to a fuzzy set A. Then, a fuzzy set can be described by a membership function μ_A defined as follow: $\mu_A: X \rightarrow [0, 1]$. For all $x \in X$, The membership value $\mu_A(x)$ is the degree of truth of x in fuzzy set A, it indicates the certainty (or uncertainty) that x belongs to fuzzy set A. The fuzzy set A is completely determined by the set of tuple $A = \{(x, \mu_A(x)) \mid x \in X, \mu_A(x) \in [0, 1]\}$.

FLC for Link Cost Computation. The proposed FLC is shown in Fig. 1, it receives as input the normalized delay, throughput and SINR of a link, and returns as output the cost of this link. The fundamental components of the proposed FLC are described as follows:

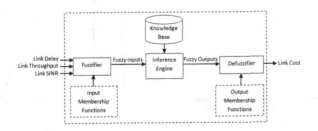

Fig. 1. FLC for link cost computation

Fuzzifier. It is based on the input membership functions (MFs), the fuzzifier converts a numerical input variable (real number or crisp variable) into fuzzy input sets needed for the Inference Engine. Triangular and rectangular MFs are used here as the reference because they have a lower processing cost compared to other MFs. Figure 2(a), (b) and (c), show respectively, the normalized link delay MFs, link throughput MFs and link SINR MFs of the proposed FLC. They have three linguistic variables *Low (L)*, *Medium (M)* and *High (H)*.

Knowledge Base. Called also rule base, it contains a collection of fuzzy IF-THEN rules that are expressed as fuzzy conditional statements. The rule base represents the knowledge and experience of a human expert of the system. In our proposed FLC and based on the fuzzy values of link delay, throughput, and SINR, the mobile node uses the IF-THEN rules (as defined in Table 1) to calculate the link cost metric.

Inference Engine. It derives conclusions from the fuzzy IF-THEN rules, it maps fuzzy inputs sets received from the Fuzzifier onto fuzzy outputs sets which will be converted into crisp value by the Defuzzifier.

Defuzzifier. It performs defuzzification process to return a numeric (crisp) value based on a predefined output MFs. Figure 2(d) shows the defined output MFs for link cost. It has three linguistic variables Low (L), Medium (M) and High (H). Defuzzifier aggregates the fuzzy set into a single value. One of the most popular defuzzification methods is the Mamdani's Center of Gravity (COG) method [17]. It is used here to defuzzify the fuzzy outputs sets received from Inference Engine component. The center of gravity is calculated as follows:

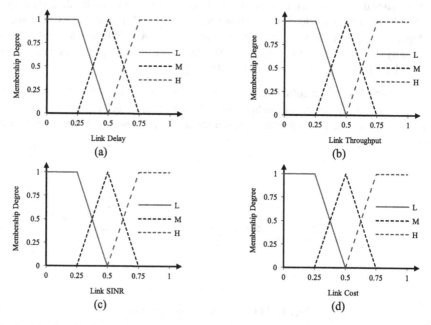

Fig. 2. Membership functions for (a) link delay, (b) link SINR (c) link throughput and (d) link cost

Table 1. Rule base for link cost computation

Link Delay	Link Throughput	Link SINR	Link Cost	Link Delay	Link Throughput	Link SINR	Link Cost	Link Delay	Link Throughput	Link SINR	Link Cost
Low	Low	Low	High	Medium	Low	Low	High	High	Low	Low	High
Low	Low	Medium	High	Medium	Low	Medium	High	High	Low	Medium	High
Low	Low	High	Medium	Medium	Low	High	Medium	High	Low	High	Medium
Low	Medium	Low	High	Medium	Medium	Low	High	High	Medium	Low	High
Low	Medium	Medium	Medium	Medium	Medium	Medium	Medium	High	Medium	Medium	High
Low	Medium	High	Low	Medium	Medium	High	Medium	High	Medium	High	Medium
Low	High	Low	Medium	Medium	High	Low	High	High	High	Low	High
Low	High	Medium	Low	Medium	High	Medium	Medium	High	High	Medium	Medium
Low	High	High	Low	Medium	High	High	Low	High	High	High	Medium

$$COG = \frac{\int_a^b \mu(x)x\,dx}{\int_a^b \mu(x)\,dx} \tag{1}$$

Where $\mu(x)$ denotes the membership degree of element x, $[a, b]$ is the interval of the result aggregated MF, and COG is the returned numeric value from Defuzzifier. In the implementation and experimental design, COG presents the link cost returned by the function *FuzzyLinkCost* that presents the proposed FLC. The *FuzzyLinkCost* function will be called by the function *LinksCostAssignement* presented by the Algorithm 1. *LinksCostAssignement* function is used to assign links cost of MANET's graph G and is called by modified multipath Dijkstra's algorithm (line 2 in Algorithm 2).

Algorithm 2. Links cost assignment algorithm

1   **Function** LinksCostAssignement(*G*)
2   *maxLD* ← *MaxLinkDelay(G);*
3   *maxLT* ← *MaxLinkThroughput(G);*
4   *maxLSINR* ← *MaxLinkSINR(G);*
5   **foreach** (arc e_q ∈ E) **do**
6   *NLD* ← *linkDelay(e_q)/maxLD;*
7   *NLT* ← *linkThroughput(e_q)/maxLT;*
8   *NLSINR* ← *linkSINR(e_q)/maxLSINR;*
9   *linkCost(e_q)* ← *FuzzyLinkCost(NLD, NLT, NLSINR);*
10   **end for**

In the links cost assignment algorithm (Algorithm 2), the functions *MaxLinkDelay*, *MaxLinkThroughput* and *MaxLinkSINR* compute, respectively, the maximum values of link delay, link throughput and link SINR in the graph G. These values are used to compute, for each link e_q in the graph G, the normalized QoS metrics *NLD*, *NLT* and *NLSINR*, respectively, of link delay, link throughput and link SINR. The three normalized link QoS metrics *NLD*, *NLT* and *NLSINR* are used as input parameters of the function *FuzzyLinkCost* to assign link cost to the link e_q.

4.2   Cost Functions Adaptation

We propose to adapt cost functions as function of MANET conditions; in our scheme, the link cost and the hop count metrics are used. Our idea is to penalize links (belonging to current computed path by Dijkstra's algorithm) with high values if they have high costs and belonging to long path, inversely, penalize links with low values if they have low costs and belonging to short path. The aim is to favor the sharing links that have low costs and belonging to short paths and, inversely, disfavor the sharing links that have high costs and belonging to long paths. So, long path having high sharing links increase packets delay transmission and loss. To adapt cost functions we developed a second FLC which is independent to the first FLC used to compute links cost. The second proposed FLC receives two inputs the cost of link and the hop count of the current path computed by Dijkstra's algorithm and contain this link. This new FLC returns as output the penalization parameter c_0 used to increment the cost of this link.

Figure 3(a) shows the link cost MFs, it has three linguistic variables *Low* (*L*), *Medium* (*M*) and *High* (*H*). The hop count MFs and the penalization parameter c_0 MFs are show, respectively, in Fig. 3(b) and (c). They have five linguistic variables *Very Low* (*VL*), *Low* (*L*), *Medium* (*M*), *High* (*H*) and *Very High* (*VH*). In our new proposed FLC and based on the fuzzy values of link cost and hop count metrics, mobile node uses the IF-THEN rules, as defined in Table 2, and Mamdani's Center of Gravity (COG) method [17] for computing the penalization parameter c_0. In the implementation and experimental design, the proposed FLC for cost function adaptation is presented by the function *FuzzyCostFunctionAdaptation*. This function is used by the modified

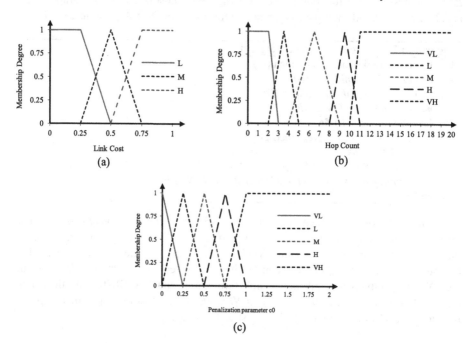

Fig. 3. Membership functions for (a) link cost, (b) path hop count and (c) penalization parameter

Table 2. Rule base for link penalization computation

Link cost	Hop count	Link penalization	Link cost	Hop count	Link penalization	Link cost	Hop count	Link penalization
Low	Very low	Very low	Medium	Very low	Low	High	Very low	High
Low	Low	Low	Medium	Low	Low	High	Low	Medium
Low	Medium	Low	Medium	Medium	Medium	High	Medium	High
Low	High	Medium	Medium	High	High	High	High	High
Low	Very high	High	Medium	Very high	High	High	Very high	Very high

multipath Dijkstra's algorithm to increase the cost of the link. It receives as input the current link cost and the hop count of the path containing this link (see Algorithm 3).

4.3   Load Balancing

The important role of load distribution is to select path to carry packets from source to destination. In MP-OLSR protocol, packets are distributed into different paths by using Round-Robin (RR) algorithm [18]. RR is simple and no additional network information is required for path selection. However, RR is incapable to balance load among heterogeneous multiple paths. So, if the cost of each path is different, RR can cause problems such as over-utilization of a path with high cost and under-utilization of a path with low cost. To this end, we propose to integrate Weighted Round-Robin (WRR) scheduling mechanism [19] to MP-OLSR for supporting heterogeneous multiple paths.

Each path was assigned a weight, an integer value that indicates the capacity of path. In our proposed scheme we compute the weight ω_i of path P_i as function of path cost (pc) by the following formulate:

$$\omega_i = Int\left[\left(\frac{\frac{1}{pc_i}}{\sum_{i=1}^{t}\left(\frac{1}{pc_i}\right)}\right) \times 100\right] \tag{2}$$

Where pc_i is the path cost of the path P_i which equals the sum of the cost of links belonging to this path and Int is rounding function from float value to lowest integer value.

To compute the weight ω_i for each path P_i we have added the lines 5, 9 and 23 to 27 in multipath Dijkstra's algorithm (see Algorithm 3). The algorithm returns multiple paths with its assigned weights. In this case, paths with higher weights (low costs) could carry a higher number of packets than those with less weights. In other words, the numbers of packets assigned to paths are limited by weights of the paths. Traffic load distribution based WRR algorithm is performed by node source s to distribute packets into the t paths to destination node d based on weights parameters.

Algorithm 3. The modified multipath Dijkstra's algorithm
1   **Function** ModifiedMultiPathDijkstra(s, d, G, t)
2    $LinksCostAssignement(G)$;
3    $c_1 \leftarrow c$;
4    $G_1 \leftarrow G$;
5    $SumInvPathCost \leftarrow 0$;
6   **for** ($i \leftarrow 1$ to t) **do**
7        $SourceTree_i \leftarrow Dijkstra(G_i, d)$;
8        $P_i \leftarrow GetPath(SourceTree_i, d)$;
9        $pc_i \leftarrow PathCost(Pi)$;
10       $h_i \leftarrow HopCount(P_i)$;
11   **foreach** (arc $e_q \in E$) **do**
12   **if** (e_q is in P_i or $Reverse(e_q)$ is in P_i) **then**
13               $c_0 \leftarrow FuzzyCostFunctionAdaptation(linkCost(e_q), h_i)$;
14               $c_{i+1}(e_q) \leftarrow (1+ c_0) \times c_i(e_q)$;
15   **else if** (the vertex $Head(e_q) \cap P_i \neq \emptyset$) **then**
16               $c_0 \leftarrow FuzzyCostFunctionAdaptation(linkCost(e_q), h_i)$;
17               $c_{i+1}(e_q) \leftarrow (1+ c_0) \times c_i(e_q)$;
18   **else**
19               $c_{i+1}(e_q) \leftarrow c_i(e_q)$;
20   **end if**
21   **end for**
22       $G_{i+1} \leftarrow (V, E, c_{i+1})$;
23       $SumInvPathCost \leftarrow SumInvPathCost + \frac{1}{pc_i}$;
24   **end for**
25   **for** ($i \leftarrow 1$ to t) **do**
26       $\omega_i \leftarrow Int\left[\left(\frac{\frac{1}{pc_i}}{SumInvPathCost}\right) \times 100\right]$;
27   **end for**
28   **return** $((P_1, \omega_1), ..., (P_t, \omega_t))$;

5   Simulation Model

5.1   Simulation Parameters

To evaluate our enhancement, we conducted simulation experiments for the original MP-OLSR and the enhanced variant of MP-OLSR denoted FQ-MP-OLSR. The traffic considered in the evaluation focuses on video stream transmission over MANET. The obtained results are also compared. The simulations were performed with the Network Simulator NS2 [20] according to the MP-OLSR implementation [8] based on UM-OLSR [21] which is corrected and validated in our previous works [22]. The proposed correction is made, particularly, to the Multipoint Relays (MPR) selection algorithm [9] responsible for optimizing the broadcasting topology control (TC) packets. For more credible simulation we use the wireless IEEE 802.11 implementation from [23]. This implementation includes IEEE 802.11 bug fixes, realistic channel propagation, multiple data transmission rates and adaptive auto rate fallback (AARF).

In all simulations, we use a network consisting of 50 mobile nodes. These nodes are randomly moved in square area of size 1000 m × 1000 m according to the Random Waypoint Mobility Model [24]. Video transmissions have been carried out by using the video quality evaluation tool Evalvid [25, 26], integrated in NS2. Evalvid generates the input source file from the information of video frames. The video source used in the simulation is *akiyo_cif.yuv* [26] that have 300 frames in YUV CIF (352 × 288) format. This video sequence is compressed by MPEG-4 codec and sent from a source to destination at 10th second with a rate 30 frames/s. Each frame was fragmented into packets before transmission, and the maximum transmission packet size over the simulated network is 1000 bytes. The sources background traffic used in simulations is CBR (Constant Bit Rate) associated with the UDP. CBR connections are randomly generated by using a traffic generator and are started at times uniformly distributed between 5 and 100 s.

Like in [2], the number t of paths is set to 3, for both, original and enhanced MP-OLSR variants. The main simulation parameters are summarized in Table 3.

5.2 Evaluation Criteria

The objective of the experiments with the network simulator NS2 is to validate our proposed enhancement, by analyzing the impact of the MP-OLSR and FQ-MP-OLSR on the quality of real video sequences. To this end we analyze three QoS metrics:

Table 3. Simulation parameters

Parameters used for traffic model	
Simulation time	100 s
Type of multimedia traffic	MPEG-4
Multimedia sequence name	Akiyo
Type of background traffic	CBR/UDP
Number of background traffic connections	15 connections
Background traffic packets size	512 bytes
Background traffic packets rate	10 packets/s
Parameters used for mobility model	
Ad hoc network area	1000 m × 1000 m
Number of nodes	50
Pause time	5 s
Maximum speed of nodes	0, 1.5, 5, 10, 15, 20, 25 and 30 m/s
Mobility model	Random Waypoint
Parameters used for physical and link layers	
MAC protocol	IEEE 802.11
Propagation model	Two-ray ground
Transmission range	250 m
Bandwidth	11 Mbps
Maximum queue size	50 packets

- **Packet loss ratio**: is the ratio between the number of dropped data packets and those sent by the sources;
- **Delay**: is the time elapsing from the sending of a packet by the source until it is received by the destination;
- **Jitter**: is the average of the difference in transmission delays of two successively received packets belonging to the same data stream.

To assess how video streams are perceived by users, we analyze also three QoE (Quality of Experiment) metrics [27]:

- **PSNR** (Peak Signal to Noise Ratio): compares frame by frame the quality of the video received by the user with the original one. PSNR computes the Mean Square Error (MSE) of each pixel between the original and received frames. PSNR is represented in dB. Frames with more similarity will result in higher PSNR values;
- **SSIM** (Structural Similarity): measures the video structural distortion trying to get a better correlation with the user's subjective impression. SSIM combines luminance, contrast, and structural similarity of the frames to compare the correlation between the original frame and the received one. The values of SSIM vary between 0 and 1. The closer the metric gets to 1, the better the video quality;
- **VQM** (Video Quality Metric): measures the perception damage the video experienced based on human visual system characteristics including in a single metric factors such as blurring, noise, color distortion, and distortion blocks. The closer the metric gets to 0, the better the video quality.

5.3   Simulation Results and Discussions

Figure 4(a) illustrates the packet loss ratio of the video traffic in different mobility scenarios. It shows that, in all mobility scenarios, the packet loss ratio of FQ-MP-OLSR is lower compared to MP-OLSR. As shown in Table 4, FQ-MP-OLSR can decrease packet loss ratio up to 77.4 % compared to MP-OLSR. The high packet loss ratio achieved by MP-OLSR can be explained by the fact that it uses the hop count as single metric for routing decision. This metric cannot avoid instable paths that produce high packet loss. The scheduling mechanism is another factor that may influence packet loss ratio. So, the RR algorithm that is used by MP-OLSR, the not take into account heterogeneous paths, it may cause problems such as over-utilization of instable paths

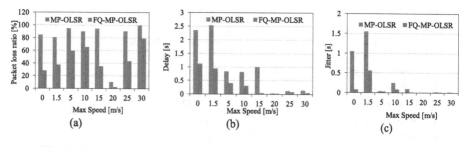

Fig. 4. QoS metrics (a) Packets loss ratio, (b) delay and (c) jitter for video traffic

with a low throughput and SINR and under-utilization of stable paths with a high throughput and SINR. All these factors may increase packet loss ratio by MP-OLSR. However, FQ-MP-OLSR adopts an intelligent routing decision process allowing the selection of best and the most stable paths using multi-constrained QoS metric based delay, throughput and SINR. Especially, taking into account throughput and SINR in routing decision reduce packet loss ratio. FQ-MP-OLSR, uses also WRR scheduling algorithm for balancing packets transmission among heterogeneous paths. The weights of paths, used by WRR algorithm, are computed as function of the multi-constrained QoS metric previously computed by fuzzy system. As well, FQ-MP-OLSR adapts links penalization to avoid paths with higher cost (lower multi-constrained QoS metric) and higher hop count when computing multiple paths by Dijkstra's algorithm. So, if the hop counts of paths are high, then they are vulnerable to broken links and more packet losses are generated.

Our enhancements also reduce packets transmission delay. Figure 4(b) illustrates the average end to end delay of the video traffic in different mobility scenarios. It shows that, in all mobility scenarios, the end to end delay is significantly less for FQ-MP-OLSR compared to original MP-OLSR. The decrease of the end to end delay by FQ-MP-OLSR is mainly introduced by multi-constrained QoS metric which the delay is one of it component. This metric is used for routing decision and also by WRR scheduling mechanism to balances traffic between heterogeneous paths having different delay and adapts links penalization to avoid paths with higher cost and higher hop count when computing multiple paths by Dijkstra's algorithm.

As shown in Table 4, FQ-MP-OLSR can decrease delay up to 96.3 % compared to MP-OLSR. The average jitter is also decreased by FQ-MP-OLSR. Figure 4(c) illustrates the average jitter in different mobility scenario. It shows that, whatever the speed of mobile nodes, the average jitter of the FQ-MP-OLSR version is lower compared to original MP-OLSR. Thus, as shown in Table 4, FQ-MP-OLSR decrease jitter up to 88.5 % compared to MP-OLSR. Hence, FQ-MP-OLSR increases the quality level of multimedia transmissions, where delay and jitter are the keys metrics that influence multimedia quality transmission.

Table 4. Performance metrics improvement by FQ-MP-OLSR for video traffic

Max speed	Packet loss ratio	Delay	Jitter	PSNR	SSIM	VQM
0 m/s	↓66.93 %	↓52.32 %	↓92.45 %	↑77.17 %	↑54.92 %	↓80.68 %
1.5 m/s	↓53.30 %	↓63.01 %	↓64.07 %	↑76.35 %	↑51.32 %	↓79.65 %
5 m/s	↓37.33 %	↓52.61 %	↓20.90 %	↑73.12 %	↑49.65 %	↓72.58 %
10 m/s	↓27.03 %	↓62.46 %	↓66.87 %	↑11.72 %	↑17.53 %	↓24.70 %
15 m/s	↓62.55 %	↓96.27 %	↓88.52 %	↑49.51 %	↑48.51 %	↓71.64 %
20 m/s	↓77.44 %	↓24.01 %	↓7.40 %	↑1.84 %	↑0.31 %	↓3.22 %
25 m/s	↓52.03 %	↓31.51 %	↓14.15 %	↑60.78 %	↑51.78 %	↓80.62 %
30 m/s	↓20.74 %	↓62.25 %	↓52.75 %	↑37.77 %	↑42.09 %	↓63.13 %

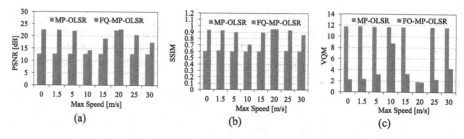

Fig. 5. QoE metrics (a) PSNR, (b) SSIM and (c) VQM for video traffic

Figure 5 compares the video quality in term of QoE metrics considering MP-OLSR and FQ-MP-OLSR. It can be seen that FQ-MP-OLSR has the best values compared to original MP-OLSR. Thus, as summarized in Table 4, FQ-MP-OLSR increases PSNR and SSIM, respectively, up to 77.2 % and 54.9 %. It shows also, that VQM is reduced up to 80.7 %.

6 Conclusion and Future Work

We proposed and implemented an improved variant of MP-OLSR protocol called FQ-MP-OLSR. The aim is to reach acceptable QoS and QoE for video transmission in MANETs. To this end, we developed two fuzzy systems for FQ-MP-OLSR. The first is used to compute multi-constrained QoS metric based three QoS metrics. The second is applied to adapt cost functions used to penalize paths previously computed to find next paths by Dijkstra's algorithm. We integrated also the WRR scheduling algorithm to FQ-MP-OLSR for scheduling multimedia traffic among heterogeneous multiple paths, the weights of paths, needed for scheduling, are computed based multi-constrained QoS metric computed by the first fuzzy system. These mechanisms allow FQ-MP-OLSR to improve video QoS and QoE, against the MP-OLSR that uses classical mechanisms such as hop count as single metric, cost functions without adaptation and Round-Robin (RR) as classical scheduling algorithm.

Simulation experiments with Network Simulator NS2 show that FQ-MP-OLSR achieves a significant improvement of the quality of video streaming in term of QoS and QoE. Thus, FQ-MP-OLSR can decrease packet loss ratio, end-to-end delay and average jitter, respectively, up to 77.4 %, 96.3 % and 88.52 %. It increases PSNR and SSIM, respectively, up to 77.2 % and 54.9 %. Finally, it reduces VQM up to 80.7 % compared to original MP-OLSR.

The FQ-MP-OLSR protocol can be further improved by reducing topology control traffic. Thus, in the future work, we would like to study and integrate optimal MPR selection heuristics [28] to FQ-MP-OLSR and confirm our improvements by setup test-bed environment to show the efficiency of the proposed enhancements in real scenarios.

References

1. Mueller, S., Tsang, R.P., Ghosal, D.: Multipath routing in mobile ad hoc networks: issues and challenges. In: Calzarossa, M.C., Gelenbe, E. (eds.) MASCOTS 2003. LNCS, vol. 2965, pp. 209–234. Springer, Heidelberg (2004)
2. Yi, J., Adnane, A., David, S., Parrein, B.: Multipath optimized link state routing for mobile ad hoc networks. Ad Hoc Netw. 9(1), 28–47 (2011)
3. Xuekang, S., Wanyi, G., Xingquan, X., Baocheng X., Zhigang, G.: Node discovery algorithm based multipath OLSR routing protocol. In: WASE International Conference on Information Engineering, ICIE '09, vol. 2, pp. 139–142 (2009)
4. Le, P.H., Pujolle, G.: A link-disjoint interference-aware multi-path routing protocol for mobile ad hoc network. In: Cherifi, H., Zain, J.M., El-Qawasmeh, E. (eds.) DICTAP 2011, Part I. CCIS, vol. 166, pp. 649–661. Springer, Heidelberg (2011)
5. Le, P.H., Pujolle, G.: A hybrid interference-aware multi-path routing protocol for mobile ad hoc network. In: Gelenbe, E., Lent, R., Sakellari, G. (eds.) Computer and Information Sciences II, pp. 179–183. Springer, London (2012)
6. Adoni, K.A., Joshi, R.D.: Multipath OLSR with energy optimization in Mobile Adhoc NETwork (MANET). In: Meghanathan, N., Chaki, N., Nagamalai, D. (eds.) CCSIT 2012, Part III. LNICST, vol. 86, pp. 552–561. Springer, Heidelberg (2012)
7. Huang, M., Liang, Q., Xi, J.: A parallel disjointed multi-path routing algorithm based on OLSR and energy in ad hoc networks. J. Netw. 7(4), 613–620 (2012)
8. Yi, J., Cizeron, E., Hamma, S., Parrein, B., Lesage, P.: Implementation of multipath and multiple description coding in OLSR. In: 4th OLSR Interop/Work Shop, Ottawa (2008)
9. Clausen, T., Jacquet, P.: Optimized Link State Routing Protocol (OLSR). In: Internet Request for Comments RFC 3626, Internet Engineering Task Force (2003)
10. Dijkstra, E.W.: A Short Introduction to the Art of Programming. Technische Hogeschool Eindhoven, Eindhoven (1971)
11. Wang, Z., Crowcroft, J.: Quality-of-service routing for supporting multimedia applications. IEEE J. Sel. Areas Commun. 14(7), 1228–1234 (1996)
12. Frikha, M.: Quality of service in MANETs. In: Ad Hoc Networks, pp. 89–114. Wiley, Hoboken (2013)
13. Kazantzidis, M., Gerla, M.: End-to-end versus explicit feedback measurement in 802.11 networks. In: Seventh International Symposium on Computers and Communications, ISCC 2002, pp. 429–434 (2002)
14. Moh, S., Kang, M., Chung, I.: Link quality aware robust routing for mobile multihop ad hoc networks. In: Wang, X. (ed.) Mobile Ad Hoc Networks: Protocol Design. InTech, Shanghai (2011)
15. Zadeh, L.A.: Fuzzy logic. Computer 21(4), 83–93 (1988)
16. Zadeh, L.A.: Fuzzy sets. Inf. Control 8(3), 338–353 (1965)
17. Mamdani, E.H.: Application of fuzzy algorithms for control of simple dynamic plant. Proc. IEEE 121(12), 1585–1588 (1974)
18. DNS Server Round-Robin Functionality for Cisco AS5800. Cisco. http://www.cisco.com/en/US/docs/ios/12_1t/12_1t3/feature/guide/dt_dnsrr.html
19. Prabhavat, S., Nishiyama, H., Ansari, N., Kato, N.: On load distribution over multipath networks. IEEE Commun. Surv. Tutor. 14(3), 662–680 (2012)
20. The Network Simulator: NS-2. http://www.isi.edu/nsnam/ns/
21. Francisco, J.R.: UM-OLSR: OLSR implementation for NS-2, University of Murcia (Spain). http://masimum.inf.um.es/fjrm/?page_id=116

22. Boushaba, A., Benabbou, A., Benabbou, R., Zahi, A., Oumsis, M., Ouatik, S.E.: Credibility of wireless ad hoc networks simulations: case studies. Int. Rev. Comput. Softw. (IRECOS) **7** (6), 3195–3205 (2012)
23. Fiore, M.: NS-2.29 Wireless Update Patch. http://perso.citi.insa-lyon.fr/mfiore/
24. Camp, T., Boleng, J., Davies, V.: A survey of mobility models for ad hoc network research. Wirel. Commun. Mob. Comput. **2**(5), 483–502 (2002)
25. Klaue, J., Rathke, B., Wolisz, A.: EvalVid – a framework for video transmission and quality evaluation. In: Kemper, P., Sanders, W.H. (eds.) TOOLS 2003. LNCS, vol. 2794, pp. 255–272. Springer, Heidelberg (2003)
26. EvalVid - A Video Quality Evaluation Tool-set. http://www.tkn.tu-berlin.de/menue/research/evalvid/
27. Serral-Gracià, R., Cerqueira, E., Curado, M., Yannuzzi, M., Monteiro, E., Masip-Bruin, X.: An Overview of Quality of Experience Measurement Challenges for Video Applications in IP Networks. In: Osipov, E., Kassler, A., Bohnert, T.M., Masip-Bruin, X. (eds.) WWIC 2010. LNCS, vol. 6074, pp. 252–263. Springer, Heidelberg (2010)
28. Boushaba, A., Benabbou, A., Benabbou, R., Zahi, A., Oumsis, M.: Optimization on OLSR protocol for reducing topology control packets. In: International Conference on Multimedia Computing and Systems, ICMCS'12, pp. 539–544 (2012)

Improved Ant Colony Optimization Routing Protocol for Wireless Sensor Networks

Asmae El Ghazi[✉], Belaïd Ahiod, and Aziz Ouaarab

LRIT, Associated Unit to CNRST (URAC 29) Faculty of Sciences,
Mohammed V-Agdal University, Rabat, Morocco
{as.elghazi,aziz.ouaarab}@gmail.com, ahiod@fsr.ac.ma

Abstract. Wireless Sensor Networks (WSNs) consist of autonomous
nodes, deployed to monitor various environments (even under hostility).
Major challenges arise from its limited energy, communication failures
and computational weakness. Many issues in WSNs are formulated as
NP-hard optimization problems, and approached through metaheuristics. This paper outlines an Ant Colony Optimization (ACO) used to
solve routing problems in WSNs. We have studied an approach based
on ACO. So, we designed an improved one that reduces energy consumption and prolongs WSN lifetime. Through simulation results, our
proposal efficiency is validated.

Keywords: Wireless Sensor Network · Metaheuristic · Routing ·
Ant Colony Optimization

1 Introduction

Wireless Sensor Network (WSN) is a new kind of network composed of a large
number of sensors working in uncontrolled areas [1]. Many physical parameters like temperature, humidity, acoustic vibration, pressure, and electromag-
netism can be detected by different kinds of sensor nodes [2]. For those various
nodes and their communication abilities, WSN can be used for many applications
such as disaster relief, environmental control, precision agriculture, medicine and
health care [3]. This new technology is receiving increased interest, due to its
advantages. Its easy deployment reduces installation cost. It can be distributed
over a wide region and has capacity of self-organization. Nonetheless there are
some intrinsic limitations for sensors like low processing capacity, low power,
and limited lifetime [4]. Hence, new theoretical problems and challenges appear
in operations research and optimization field. Some basic optimization problems
are related to coverage, topology control, scheduling, mobility and routing [5,6]
But, many researches have tended to focus on routing problems rather than all
the previously mentioned problems.

Routing in WSN is very challenging, as it has more different characteristics
than that in traditional communication networks [7]. It's qualified as an NP-hard
optimization problem [5]. That means we need robust and efficient techniques

© Springer International Publishing Switzerland 2014
G. Noubir and M. Raynal (Eds.): NETYS 2014, LNCS 8593, pp. 246–256, 2014.
DOI: 10.1007/978-3-319-09581-3_17

to solve this kind of problems, such as metaheuristics [8]. Metaheuristics use search strategies to explore the solution space. These methods begin with a set of initial solutions or an initial population, and then they examine step by step a sequence of solutions to reach or hope to approach the optimal solution of the problem of the interest.

Many metaheuristics, such as Genetic Algorithms (GA) [9], Artificial Bee Colony (ABC) [10], Particle Swarm Optimization (PSO) [11] and Ant Colony Optimization (ACO) [12] are used to solve routing problems [13]. The ACO metaheuristic has been successfully applied to solve routing problem in WSN [12,14, 15]. Its optimization procedure can be easily adapted to implement an ant based routing algorithm for WSNs. To date, various methods have been developed to solve WSN routing problem, such as Sensor-driven Cost-aware Ant Routing (SC), the Flooded Forward Ant Routing (FF) algorithm, and the Flooded Piggy-backed Ant Routing (FP) algorithm [14], Adaptive ant-based Dynamic Routing (ADR) [16], Adaptive Routing (AR) and Improved Adaptive Routing (IAR) algorithm [17], and E&D ANTS [18].

We studied an approach based on ACO for WSN routing problem, proposed by S. Okdem and D. Karaboga [15]. In addition to its safety and efficacy, this approach can be enhanced. So, we proposed an improved one by adding a new kind of ants' communication, to supply prior information to the other ants.

The remaining of this paper is organized as follows: Sect. 2 gives the WSN routing problem statement. Section 3 introduces Ant Colony Optimization (ACO). Section 4 presents our ACO-based algorithm for the routing problem. Section 5 shows the performance evaluation of our results. Finally, Sect. 6 concludes our work.

2   Routing Problem in Wireless Sensor Networks

Routing is forwarding data from source to destination. The route between both extremities is determined by many techniques relatively to the application field. Routing in wireless sensor networks differs from routing in classical networks. In the case of WSNs we can talk about unreliable links, energy requirements and no infrastructure. Many routing algorithms developed for wireless sensor networks depend on mobility of sensors or sinks, application field and network topology. Overall, the routing techniques are classified according to network structure or protocol operation (routing criteria) [7].

Figure 1 shows that in WSN routing protocols, based on network structure, are classified into three categories based on: flat, hierarchical networks, and location based routing. Moreover, these protocols can be classified into multipath, query, negotiation, QoS, and coherent, by considering protocol operation [7]. The studied protocol ranked among flat networks. Routing problem consists on stable sensors and sink. The purpose is to find the best paths that minimize energy consumption, guarantee links reliability (by using acknowledgement signals) and manage bandwidth [15]. All these requirements are considered in the conception of the ACO routing protocol, which described in the following sections.

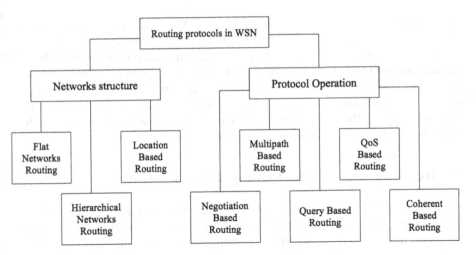

Fig. 1. Routing protocols in WSN: taxonomy [7]

3 Ant Colony Optimization

Ant colony is considered among the colonies of insects that have a very high capacity to explore and exploit their environment despite their displacement way which is very limited (walking) compared to other species (flying). This moving inconvenience is offset by skills in manipulating and using environment. They use their environment as a medium of storage, processing and sharing information between all the ants in the colony. Inspired from this behavior, M. Dorigo and G. Di Caro have developed in 1999 ant colony optimization algorithms [19]. ACO basic steps are summarized in the Algorithm 1 [20].

Algorithm 1. ACO

Objective function $f(x_{ij}), (i,j) \in \{1, 2, ..., n\}$
Initialize the pheromone evaporation rate ρ
while (criterion) **do**
    for *Loop over n nodes* **do**
        Generate the new solutions (using Eq. 1)
        Evaluate new solutions
        Mark the best routes with the pheromone $\delta\tau_{ij}$
        Update Pheromone : $\tau_{ij} \leftarrow (1 - \rho)\tau_{ij} + \delta\tau_{ij}$
    end for
    Daemon actions
end while
Output the best results and pheromone distribution.

This algorithm discusses two interesting points: The first one is related to the probability of choosing routes, which is used basically in ACO (Eq. 1) to let node s make a choice by calculating the probability of any node in its coverage area, and then choosing the node r with the highest probability value. The second one depends on pheromone. At the start ants take routes randomly and left an amount of pheromone τ in these routes. This quantity of pheromone is not stable. On one hand it can be decreased by environmental factors (wind, sun, ...), where those factors are presented by the pheromone evaporation rate parameter ρ. On the other hand it increases because all the other ants, when they choose the route, they leave an amount of pheromone $\delta\tau$.

4   Routing-Based Ant Colony Optimization

S. Okdem and D. Karaboga [15], present a new kind of routing protocol based on ACO where they try to maximize WSN lifetime and minimize energy consumption of sensors. After detecting an event, source node splits data to N parts, every part is transmitted to the next destination by an ant. Ants choose next hop by using two heuristic functions. The first one is related to the quantity of the pheromone, and the second depends on energy. These values appear, where ant k moving from node s to node r, in the following probabilistic decision rule (Eq. 1):

$$P_k(r,s) = \begin{cases} \frac{[\tau(r,s)]^\alpha \cdot [\eta(r,s)]^\beta}{\sum_{r \in R_s}[\tau(r,s)]^\alpha \cdot [\eta(r,s)]^\beta} & \text{if } k \notin tabu^r \\ \\ 0 \quad \text{otherwise} \end{cases} \tag{1}$$

Where $\tau(r,s)$ is a function that returns the pheromone value between node s and r, η is the first heuristic value related to nodes' energy level, R_s are receiver nodes, α and β are two parameters that control the relative influence of the pheromone trail and the heuristic information, and $tabu^r$ is the list of packet identities already received by node r [15]. Pheromone trails are connected to each $arc(r,s)$ which has a trail value $\tau \in [0,1]$. The heuristic value τ of the node r is expressed by Eq. 2:

$$\tau(r,s) = \frac{(I - e_s)^{-1}}{\sum_{r \in R_s}(I - e_r)^{-1}} \tag{2}$$

Where I is the initial energy, and e_r is the current energy level of receiver node r. According to this rule, node having information chooses a node destination to forward this information, and so on until sink. This approach gives good results, relatively to routing protocol EEABR proposed by T. Camilo et al. [21]. But these results can be improved, by adding more accuracy to make a choice especially when probabilities are equal. In its decision a node chooses randomly the following node, so it may make wrong choice and loses data in uncovered area, or packets travel a long path to the sink. Therefore many nodes lose power (just because choice was bad), delay of delivery and lifetime decreases. To reduce the number of wrong choices, we improved this approach [15]. we kept the same ACO solution modeling as in [15] but we made decision rule more precise by adding a new heuristic value δ. So, the new probabilistic decision rule is as follows (Eq. 3):

$$P_k(r,s) = \begin{cases} \dfrac{[\tau(r,s)]^\alpha \cdot [\eta(r,s)]^\beta \cdot [\delta(r,s)]^\gamma}{\sum_{r \in R_s} [\tau(r,s)]^\alpha \cdot [\eta(r,s)]^\beta \cdot [\delta(r,s)]^\gamma} & \text{if } k \notin tabu^r \\ \\ 0 \quad \text{otherwise} \end{cases} \tag{3}$$

The heuristic value δ (Eq. 4) is used to distinguish the best neighbor, avoiding the use of the wrong nodes, so do not exhausting it. δ is related to sensors field R_c. According to Dorigo experimentation [19], the control parameters values are: $\alpha = 1$, $\beta = 5$. After many tests, we conclude that the best value of γ is 1. By using this heuristic value δ, sensors transmit information about sink.

$$\delta(r,s) = \begin{cases} \dfrac{E_s}{\sum_{r \in R_s} E_r} & \text{if Sink} \in R_c \\ \\ v \quad \text{otherwise} \end{cases} \tag{4}$$

Where E_r is the residual energy of node r (residual energy is the energy of node at the end of simulation) and v is a constant that depends on the simulation environment. Node r having sink in its collection field, must inform neighboring nodes about this detail, to have more chances to be chosen, because packets will attain sink definitely. When sink is not in the r field, only energy and pheromone are considered in the probabilistic rule. This information allows to take the right choice, and then get a new approach which gives a good result, mainly in energy consumption, WSN lifetime, reliability and packet delivery ratio (PDR) .

5   Simulation and Results

In order to show the performance of our proposal, we simulate the both approaches, improved and original one, in same conditions, using basically MATLAB for implementation. We used a model of sensors based on "First Order Radio Model" of Heinzelman et al. [22] (see Fig. 2). To send and receive a message, power requirements are formulated as follows:

- To send k bits to a remote receiver by d meters, transmitter consumes:
  $E_{Tx}(k,d) = (E_{elec} \times k) + (\epsilon_{amp} \times k \times d^2)$
- To receive k bits, receiver consumes:
  $E_{Rx}(k) = E_{elec} \times k$

Where $E_{elec} = 50\,\text{nJ/bit}$ and $\epsilon_{amp} = 100\,\text{nJ/bit/m}^2$ are respectively energy of electronic transmission and amplification.

Aiming to test several situations, we apply routing protocol on several WSNs with different densities. We deploy randomly a number of sensors varied according to coverage area. We distribute 10 nodes over $200 \times 200\,\text{m}^2$, 20 nodes over $300 \times 300\,\text{m}^2$, 30 nodes over $400 \times 400\,\text{m}^2$, 40 nodes over $500 \times 500\,\text{m}^2$ and finally for $600 \times 600\,\text{m}^2$ we deploy different WSNs, composed by 50, 60, 70, 80 and 100

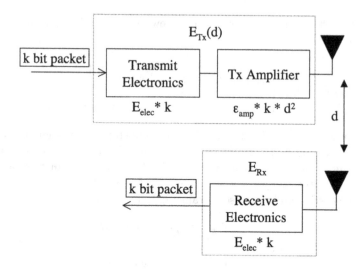

Fig. 2. First Order Radio Model [22]

sensor nodes. The main task of this deployment is to monitor a static phenomenon, and transmit all collected data to the sink, which has an unknown location. In the same setting, related to the original protocol, and using the same metrics (average residual energy) we perform simulation of improved protocol for the purpose of comparing results and confirming their efficiency.

By performing many simulations we prove that the improved protocol is better than the original one. Figure 3 shows that our improved approach is higher than original approach by considering the average residual energy of 15 runs. Thus, the power consumption is minimized, and the WSN lifetime is maximized especially when densities are high. In order to confirm the efficiency of our proposal, we simulated the transmission of 256 packets in different coverage areas where it deployed randomly a number of nodes (from 10 to 100 nodes). The shown results in Fig. 4 represent the average residual energy of 15 runs.

Figure 4 presents residual energy normalized (all values between 0 and 1) after reception of 256 packets by Sink, for many WSNs with diverse number of nodes. Packet Delivery Ratio (PDR) is the ratio of the correctly received packets at the receiver to the total number of packets sent by the sender. A straightforward method to calculate PDR is to send a number of packets in a period of time. The receiver counts the successful received packets and calculates the PDR [23]. According to this definition, the PDR can be calculated as in Eq. 5.

$$PDR = \frac{\text{Number of received packets}}{\text{Number of transmitted packets}} \tag{5}$$

This metric allows knowing if a protocol is able to ship all sent packages. In order to compare PDR of studied and improved approaches, we simulate sending 256 packets, using various WSNs (changing number of nodes). Our approach

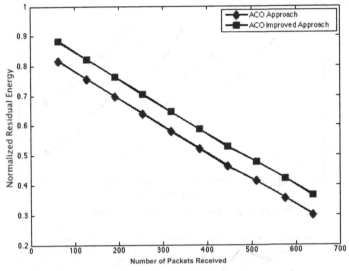

(a) 20 *nodes, density is* $222 \text{x} 10^{-6} nodes/m^2$

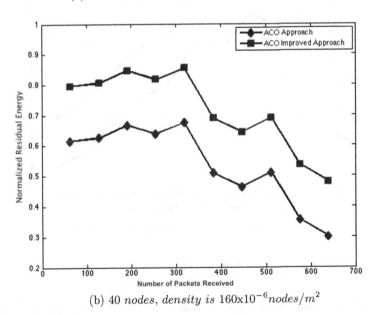

(b) 40 *nodes, density is* $160 \text{x} 10^{-6} nodes/m^2$

Fig. 3. Simulation results for different WSNs

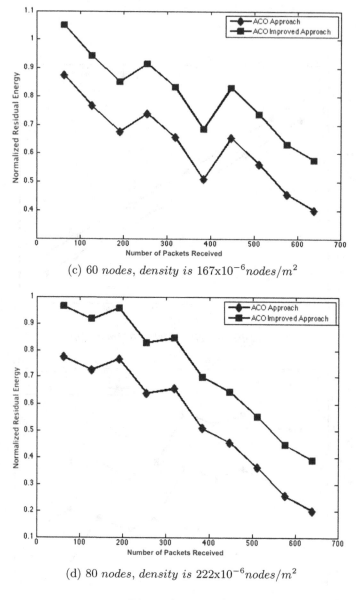

(c) 60 *nodes, density is* $167\text{x}10^{-6} nodes/m^2$

(d) 80 *nodes, density is* $222\text{x}10^{-6} nodes/m^2$

Fig. 3. (*continued*)

reduces energy consumption, since the number of lost packets is minimal (Fig. 5). Packets are lost because of many reasons such as dead of nodes in the path, or the lack of the active neighbour nodes.

Figure 5 presents a PDR (%) after reception of 256 packets by Sink for many WSNs with diverse numbers of nodes.

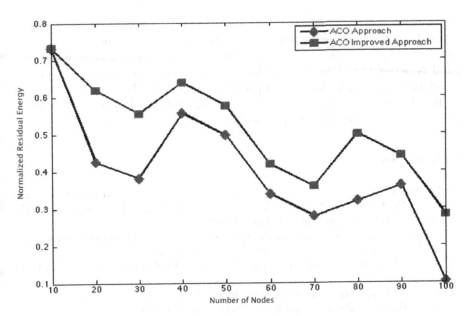

Fig. 4. Residual energy for different WSNs

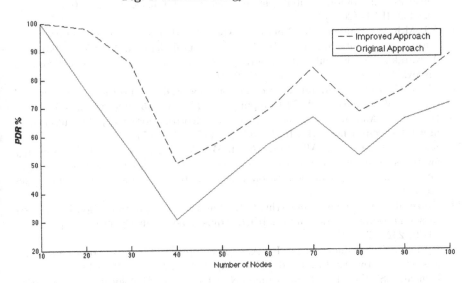

Fig. 5. Packet Delivery Ratio for different WSNs

6   Conclusion

This paper presents an improved protocol for WSN routing. The protocol is achieved by using an enhanced ant colony algorithm to optimize the node power consumption and increase network lifetime as long as possible, while data transmission is attained efficiently. To evaluate the performance of our protocol, we implemented in the same conditions, both approaches original and improved one. From the comparison it is concluded that overall performance of our proposal is better than Okdem and Karaboga approach [15], in terms of energy consumption, network lifetime and packet delivery ratio. The future work could be investigate other methods and compare the ant-based algorithm for other proactive and reactive routing protocols.

References

1. Potdar, V., Sharif, A., Chang, E.: Wireless sensor networks: a survey. In: International Conference on Advanced Information Networking and Applications Workshops, WAINA'09, pp. 636–641. IEEE (2009)
2. Akyildiz, I.F., Su, W., Sankarasubramaniam, Y., Cayirci, E.: Wireless sensor networks: a survey. Comput. Netw. **38**(4), 393–422 (2002)
3. Xu, N.: A survey of sensor network applications. IEEE Commun. Mag. **40**, 102–114 (2002)
4. Masri, W.: QoS requirements mapping in TDMA-based Wireless Sensor Networks. Ph.D. thesis, Toulouse University III-Paul Sabatier (2009)
5. Gogu, A., Nace, D., Dilo, A., Mertnia, N.: Optimization problems in wireless sensor networks. In: Complex, Intelligent and Software Intensive Systems (CISIS), pp. 302–309. IEEE (2011)
6. Ali, M.K.M., Kamoun, F.: Neural networks for shortest path computation and routing in computer networks. IEEE Trans. Neural Netw. **4**, 941–954 (1993)
7. Al-Karaki, J.N., Kamal, A.E.: Routing techniques in wireless sensor networks: a survey. Wirel. Commun. **11**(6), 6–28 (2004)
8. Blum, C., Roli, A.: Metaheuristics in combinatorial optimization: overview and conceptual comparison. ACM Comput. Surv. (CSUR) **35**, 268–308 (2003)
9. Hussain, S., Matin, A.W., Islam, O.: Genetic algorithm for energy efficient clusters in wireless sensor networks. In: ITNG, pp. 147–154 (2007)
10. Saleh, S., Ahmed, M., Ali, B.M., Rasid, M.F.A., Ismail, A.: A survey on energy awareness mechanisms in routing protocols for wireless sensor networks using optimization methods. Transactions on Emerging Telecommunications Technologies (2013)
11. Kulkarni, R.V., Venayagamoorthy, G.K.: Particle swarm optimization in wireless-sensor networks: a brief survey. IEEE Trans. Syst. Man Cybern. C Appl. Rev. **41**(2), 262–267 (2011)
12. Fathima, K., Sindhanaiselvan, K.: Ant colony optimization based routing in wireless sensor networks. Int. J. Adv. Netw. Appl. **4**(4), 1686–1689 (2013)
13. Iyengar, S.S., Wu, H.C., Balakrishnan, N., Chang, S.Y.: Biologically inspired cooperative routing for wireless mobile sensor networks. IEEE Syst. J. **1**(1), 29–37 (2007)
14. Zhang, Y., Kuhn, L.D., Fromherz, M.P.J.: Improvements on ant routing for sensor networks. In: Dorigo, M., Birattari, M., Blum, C., Gambardella, L.M., Mondada, F., Stützle, T. (eds.) ANTS 2004. LNCS, vol. 3172, pp. 154–165. Springer, Heidelberg (2004)
15. Okdem, S., Karaboga, D.: Routing in wireless sensor networks using an ant colony optimization (ACO) router chip. Sensors **9**, 909–921 (2009)

16. Lu, Y., Zhao, G., Su, F.: Adaptive ant-based dynamic routing algorithm. In: Fifth World Congress on Intelligent Control and Automation, WCICA 2004, vol. 3, pp. 2694–2697. IEEE (2004)
17. Ghasem Aghaei, R., Rahman, M.A., Gueaieb, W., El Saddik, A.: Ant colony-based reinforcement learning algorithm for routing in wireless sensor networks. In: Instrumentation and Measurement Technology Conference Proceedings, pp. 1–6. IEEE (2007)
18. Wen, Y.F., Chen, Y.Q., Pan, M.: Adaptive ant-based routing in wireless sensor networks using energy* delay metrics. J. Zhejiang Univ. SCI. A 9(4), 531–538 (2008)
19. Dorigo, M., Di Caro, G.: Ant colony optimization: a new metaheuristic. In: Proceedings of the 1999 Congress on Evolutionary Computation CEC 99, pp. 1–8. IEEE (1999)
20. Yang, X.S.: Engineering Optimization: An Introduction with Metaheuristic Applications. Wiley, New York (2010)
21. Camilo, T., Carreto, C., Silva, J.S., Boavida, F.: An energy-efficient ant-based routing algorithm for wireless sensor networks. In: Dorigo, M., Gambardella, L.M., Birattari, M., Martinoli, A., Poli, R., Stützle, T. (eds.) ANTS 2006. LNCS, vol. 4150, pp. 49–59. Springer, Heidelberg (2006)
22. Heinzelman, W.R., Chandrakasan, A., Balakrishnan, H.: Energy-efficient communication protocol for wireless microsensor networks. In: Proceedings of the 33rd Annual Hawaii International Conference on System Sciences, pp. 1–10. IEEE (2000)
23. Guo, C., Zhou, J., Pawelczak, P., Hekmat, R.: Improving packet delivery ratio estimation for indoor ad hoc and wireless sensor networks. In: Consumer Communications and Networking Conference, pp. 1–5. IEEE (2009)

UMTS Base-Station Location Problem for Uplink Direction Using Genetic Algorithms and Fuzzy Logic

Mohammed Gabli[✉], El Miloud Jaara, and El Bekkaye Mermri

Department of Mathematics and Computer Science, Faculty of Science,
University Mohammed Premier, BV Mohammed VI, Oujda, Morocco
{medgabli,emjaara}@yahoo.fr,
b.mermri@fso.ump.ma

Abstract. In this paper, we address the problem of planning the universal mobile telecommunication system (UMTS) base stations location for uplink direction. The objective is to maximize the total trafic covered and minimize the total installation cost. To define the cost, researchers used the current period market prices. But prices may change over time. Our aim here is to deal with the imprecise and uncertain information of prices. For this we address this problem using fuzzy Logic. We propose an algorithm based on the hybridization of genetic algorithm (GA) with Local Search method (LS). To code the solutions of the problem, we have used an encoding method which combines binary and integer coding. To validate the proposed method some numerical examples are given. The obtained results show the efficiency of our approach.

Keywords: UMTS · Optimization · Fuzzy logic · Genetic algorithm · Local search · Hybridization

1 Introduction

Universal Mobile Telecommunications System (UMTS) is a third generation mobile cellular technology for networks based on the Global System for Mobile Communications standard (GSM). The deployment of UMTS networks involves a colossal investment for the operators. In this context, the optimization of these networks becomes, for an operator, a fundamental task.

The problem of planning second-generation cellular systems adopting a time-division multiple access (TDMA)-based access scheme has usually been simplified by subdividing it into a coverage planning problem and a frequency planning problem which are driven by a coverage and a capacity criterion, respectively [1–3]. Using the wideband code-division multiple access (W-CDMA) air interface of UMTS, the two-phase approach is not appropriate mainly because the bandwidth is shared by all active connections and no actual frequency assignment is strictly required. The access scheme allows for a more flexible use of

© Springer International Publishing Switzerland 2014
G. Noubir and M. Raynal (Eds.): NETYS 2014, LNCS 8593, pp. 257–269, 2014.
DOI: 10.1007/978-3-319-09581-3_18

radio resources and the capacity of each cell (e.g., the number of connections) is not limited a priori by a fixed channel assignment as in TDMA systems, but it depends on the actual interference levels which determine the achievable signal-to-interference ratio (SIR) values. As these values depend on both traffic distribution and base stations (BSs) positions, BS location in UMTS networks cannot only be based on coverage but it must also be capacity driven [1,2]. Furthermore, since interference levels depend both on the connections within a given cell and on those in neighboring cells, the SIR values and the capacity are highly affected by the traffic distribution in the whole area [1,4].

UMTS networks planning problems have been the interest of many researchers (see for instance [5–10]). In this article we focus on the problem of Amaldi et al. [1,4] in which they investigate mathematical programming models for supporting the decisions on where to install new base stations and how to select their configuration so as to find a trade-off between maximizing coverage and minimizing costs.

But the cost estimation differs from one author to another. In [6,7] the total cost of an UMTS access network is composed of two variable factors: the cost of the radio network controller (RNC) stations and the cost of the links. In [1,4,10] authors consider that an installation cost is associated with each candidate site. In [11] the cost estimation is limited to engineering and license costs. In [9] the total cost is composed of Infrastructure cost and license cost. In [12] the combined costs for operators can be broken into 8 categories: license cost, operational cost, network set up, content acquisition, product development, customer acquisition, handset subsidization and fixed marketing costs. For Great Britain [11], the costs are estimated for a single UMTS network over 10 years. The auctioned license will contribute about 25 % of the costs. Cost of operation will be 24 %, network deployment 12 %, customer acquisition 11 %, subsidies for phones 11 %, marketing 8 %, acquisition of content 7 %, and product development 2 % (see [11]). In all of these articles, authors used the current period market prices. But prices may change over time. The question is how to define the cost estimation then? In order to investigate more realistic systems, it is necessary to consider the situation that one makes a decision on the basis of data involving fuzziness (see [13], for instance).

In this paper, we address the UMTS Base-station Location problem for Uplink direction using fuzzy Logic to deal with the imprecise and uncertain information of prices. For this we apply three inputs (license cost, operational cost and content acquisition) to produce one output (the estimated cost). We propose an algorithm based on the hybridization of the genetic algorithm (GA) with the Local Search method (LS).

In Sect. 2, we describe the problem and we present its mathematical modelling, and in Sect. 3 we propose the fuzzy logic model. In Sect. 4, we introduce an approach using metaheuristics and fuzzy Logic. In Sect. 5 we give an application of our approach, then we present the obtained numerical results. Finally, in Sect. 6 we give some concluding remarks.

2 Problem Statement and Model Presentation

Consider a territory to be covered by an *UMTS* service. Let $S = \{1, ..., m\}$ be a set of candidate sites (CS) where a base station (*BS*) can be installed and $I = \{1, ..., n\}$ a set of test points (*TPs*). Each site j has a cost denoted by c_j. We denote by u_i The required number of simultaneously active connections for *TP* index i (TP_i). In this section we will need the following notations:

$P_{\text{reçue}}$	Received power
P_{target}	Target power
P_{max}	Maximum power
SIR	The signal-to-interference ratio
H_b	Height of the base (in meters)
H_m	Height of the mobile station (in meters)
F	Signal frequency (in megahertz)
dB	Decibels
dBm	Power ratio in dB of the measured power referenced to one milliwatt (mW)
CS	Candidate site
TP	Test points
BS	Base station
g_{ij}	Propagation factor of the radio link between TP_i and a candidate site CS_j
d_{ij}	Distance between TP_i and candidate site CS_j
SF	Spreading factor; the ratio between the spread signal rate and the user rate

2.1 Mechanism of Power Control (PC) and Radio Propagation

In UMTS networks, it is important to implement a mechanism that allows to a mobile terminal to adjust its power of emission while guaranteeing a good reception of the base station. This power problem also arises for the power emitted by the base station to limit the intercellular interferences. Two PC mechanisms are commonly considered [4]:

1. *PC mechanism based on the received power:* The transmitted power is adjusted so that the power received on each channel is equal to a given target value P_{target}.
2. *PC mechanism based on the estimated SIR:* The transmitted power is set so that the SIR is equal to a target value SIR_{target}.

The propagation channel in a mobile radio environment is mainly related to the type of environment to be considered, urban, rural, indoor, etc.; and to physical phenomena that the wave undergoes during the propagation namely reflection, diffraction and diffusion. In this paper we consider the Hata's propagation model presented in [14], which gives the attenuation due to the signal propagation. In particular, the attenuation between a BS_j and TP_i for urban areas, measured in decibels (dB) and denoted by L_u, is given by [14]:

$$L_u(d_{ij}) = 69.55 + 26.16\log(F) - 13.82\log(H_b)$$
$$- a(H_m) + [44.9 - 6.55\log(H_b)]\log(d_{ij}), \qquad (1)$$

where the parameter $a(H_m)$ is a correction factor depending on the height of the antenna of the mobile station and on the environment. The value of $a(H_m)$ is given by:

– For a medium sized city:

$$a(H_m) = (1.1\log(F) - 0.7)H_m - (1.56\log(F) - 0.8) \qquad (2)$$

– For a large city:

$$a(H_m) = 3.2(\log(11.75H_m)]^2 - 4.97 \qquad (3)$$

2.2   Model Presentation

Let $S = \{1, ..., m\}$ be a set of candidate sites (CS) where a base station can be installed and $I = \{1, ..., n\}$ a set of test points. Each base station BS_j has a cost denoted by c_j. Let u_i be the required number of simultaneously active connections for a TP_i. Let us define the two following classes of decision variables:

$$y_j = \begin{cases} 1 & \text{if a } BS \text{ is installed in a site } j, \\ 0 & \text{otherwise,} \end{cases} \qquad \text{for } j \in S, \qquad (4)$$

and

$$x_{ij} = \begin{cases} 1 & \text{if a } TP_i \text{ is assigned to a } BS_j, \\ 0 & \text{otherwise.} \end{cases} \qquad \text{for } i \in I \text{ and } j \in S. \qquad (5)$$

We see that the variable x depends on y. An illustrative example is presented in Fig. 1. In this example we have four CSs and six TPs. We see that the BS_2 is not installed and the TP_3 is not covered; TP_1 and TP_2 are assigned to BS_1; TP_4 and TP_5 are assigned to BS_3 and TP_6 is assigned to BS_4. We consider a power-based PC mechanism. Suppose we have directive BSs with three identical $120°$ sectors and with an omnidirectional antenna diagram along the horizontal axis. Let the index set $I_j^\sigma \subseteq I$ denotes the set of all TPs that fall within the sector σ of the BS installed in the candidate site CS_j. Since we wish to maximize the total trafic covered and minimize the total installation cost subjected to some constraints, then the problem can be expressed as (see [1,4]):

$$\begin{cases} \text{Maximize } f(x) = \displaystyle\sum_{i=1}^{n}\sum_{j=1}^{m} u_i x_{ij}, \\ \text{Minimize } g(y) = \displaystyle\sum_{j=1}^{m} c_j y_j, \end{cases} \qquad (6)$$

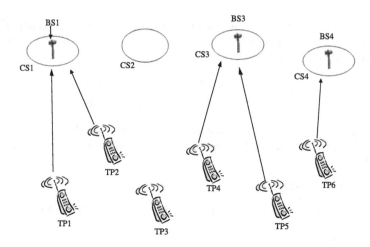

Fig. 1. Illustration of the problem

subject to:

$$\sum_{j=1}^{m} x_{ij} \leq 1 , \quad i \in I, \tag{7}$$

$$x_{ij} \leq \min\{1, g_{ij}P_{max}/P_{target}\}y_j, \quad i \in I , j \in S, \tag{8}$$

$$y_j \sum_{i \in I_j^\sigma} \sum_{t=1}^{m} (\frac{u_i g_{ij}}{g_{it}} x_{it} - 1) \leq SF/SIR_{min}, \quad j \in S, \sigma \in \Sigma, \tag{9}$$

$$x_{ij} , y_j \in \{0,1\}, \quad i \in I, j \in S, \tag{10}$$

where the propagation factor of the radio link between a TP_i and a candidate site CS_j is given by:

$$g_{ij} = (10^{L_u(d_{ij})/10})^{-1}, \tag{11}$$

where the attenuation L_u is calculated by relation (1).

Amaldi et al. [1,4] have transformed the multi-objective problem (6) into a mono-objective one as follows:

$$\text{Maximize} \sum_{i=1}^{n} \sum_{j=1}^{m} u_i x_{ij} - \lambda \sum_{j=1}^{m} c_j y_j, \tag{12}$$

subject to the constraints (7), (8), (9) and (10), where $\lambda > 0$ is a tradeoff parameter between maximizing coverage and minimizing costs.

In this model, the costs c_j, $1 \leq j \leq m$ are taken constants. But prices may change over time. To deal with the imprecise and uncertain information of prices we introduce a fuzzy logic model as follows:

$$\text{Maximize} \sum_{i=1}^{n} \sum_{j=1}^{m} u_i x_{ij} - \lambda \sum_{j=1}^{m} \tilde{c}_j y_j, \tag{13}$$

subject to the constraints (7), (8), (9) and (10), where $\lambda > 0$ is a tradeoff parameter between maximizing coverage and minimizing costs, and $\tilde{c}_j$, $1 \leq j \leq m$ is a fuzzy cost with the membership function presented in Fig. 2.

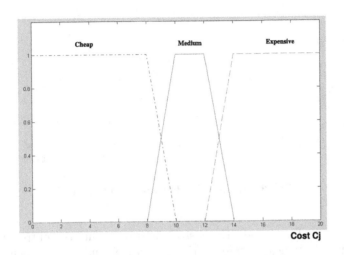

Fig. 2. Membership function of input cost

3   Proposed Fuzzy Logic Model

Certainty and precision are much too often used as an absolute standard in reasoning and decision making. Fuzzy logic is based on the notion of relative graded membership and can deal with information arising from computational perception and cognition that is uncertain, imprecise, vague, partially true, or without sharp boundaries [15]. The concept of fuzzy sets has been published in 1965 by Lotfi Zadeh in his famous paper *Fuzzy sets* [16]. Fuzzy set can be defined as a set with membership degree with values in the interval [0, 1].

A fuzzy inference system (FIS) is composed of four components: fuzzifier, rules, inference engine, and defuzzifier. In general, FIS has multiple inputs and multiple outputs [17]. The fuzzifier converts the crisp input into membership degree value. The inference engine process the inference mechanism from the rulebase information and finally the crisp output is computed by a defuzzifier process. In this paper we use fuzzy logic to deal with the imprecise information of prices. Following the expert advice in the field of telecommunications in Morocco, we apply three inputs: license cost (44 %), operational cost (43 %) and content acquisition (13 %) to produce one output (the estimated cost). The fuzzy logic is described as follows.

– *Membership function.* The three inputs are fed into a fuzzifier, which transforms them into fuzzy sets. We consider that these inputs have the same membership function values of fuzzy input. We define these inputs as follow:

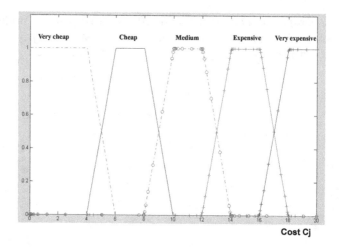

Fig. 3. Membership function of output cost

"Cheap", "Medium" and "Expensive", and we define the output as follow: "Very cheap", "Cheap", "Medium", "Expensive" and "Very expensive". The membership function values of fuzzy input is shown in Fig. 2 and the membership function values of fuzzy output is shown in Fig. 3.

– *Fuzzy rules.* We applied a set of fuzzy IF-THEN rules to obtain fuzzy decision sets. The IF-THEN rules are shown in Table 1.
– *Fuzzy inference system methods.* We use the Zadeh operators and the Mamdani type fuzzy model. This model is widely accepted for capturing expert knowledge and it allows us to describe the expertise in more intuitive, more human-like manner (see [18]). For the defuzzification, we use center of gravity method.

To achieve this model, we propose an algorithm based on the hybridization of genetic algorithm (GA) with local search method (LS) (see the next section). These hybridizations (see e.g. [19,20]) are proven to be more efficient than the evolutionary algorithms (including GAs) themselves. The reason behind this is the combination of global exploration and local exploitation [21].

4 Proposed Approach Using Metaheuristics and Fuzzy Logic

Consider the problem presented in Sect. 2.2 and described by Eq. (13).

4.1 Chromosome Representation

To code the chromosome we use the encoding method introduced by the authors in [22]. This encoding method combines binary coding, for test points (TPs),

Table 1. IF-THEN fuzzy rules

IF			THEN
License cost	Operational cost	Content acquisition	Estimated cost
Cheap	Cheap	Cheap	Very cheap
Cheap	Cheap	Medium	Very cheap
Cheap	Cheap	Expensive	Cheap
Cheap	Medium	Cheap	Cheap
Cheap	Medium	Medium	Cheap
Cheap	Medium	Expensive	Medium
Cheap	Expensive	Cheap	Medium
Cheap	Expensive	Medium	Medium
Cheap	Expensive	Expensive	Medium
Medium	Cheap	Cheap	Medium
Medium	Cheap	Medium	Medium
Medium	Cheap	Expensive	Medium
Medium	Medium	Cheap	Medium
Medium	Medium	Medium	Medium
Medium	Medium	Expensive	Medium
Medium	Expensive	Cheap	Expensive
Medium	Expensive	Medium	Expensive
Medium	Expensive	Expensive	Expensive
Expensive	Cheap	Cheap	Medium
Expensive	Cheap	Medium	Medium
Expensive	Cheap	Expensive	Medium
Expensive	Medium	Cheap	Expensive
Expensive	Medium	Medium	Expensive
Expensive	Medium	Expensive	Expensive
Expensive	Expensive	Cheap	Very expensive
Expensive	Expensive	Medium	Very expensive
Expensive	Expensive	Expensive	Very expensive

and integer coding for base stations (BSs). If we have m base stations and n test points, the chromosome will have $m + n$ genes, where the first m genes are formed by the code of the base stations and the remanning digits are formed by the test points code. Hence each chromosome will indicate if a TP is covered or not, and to which BS is assigned. For example, if we have $m = 7$ and $n = 13$ the chromosome can be encoded as: $4; 3; 1; 0; 1; 7; 4; 7; 2; 3; 2; 5; 6; 0111001$. Finally, we must always take care not to fall in the case where a TP is assigned to a BS that is not installed. To do this we use a small correction which reassigns the TP to another BS (see [22] for more detail).

4.2   Initial Population, Crossover and Mutation

Now, we show how to create an initial population and how to apply crossover and mutation operators of the GA to this type of encoding.

- *Initial population.* Suppose we have n TPs and m BSs. To define each chromosome of the population we generate $n + m$ random genes; the first n genes are integers in the set $\{0, \ldots, m\}$ and the remaining m genes are binary digits. Then, we use the correction procedure defined above.
- *Crossover.* We use the usual crossover followed by the procedure of correction.
- *Mutation.* We used the usual mutation followed by the procedure of correction. If the gene to mutate is a TP, we replace it by an integer chosen randomly from the set $\{1, 2, \ldots, m\}$, otherwise we transform the 0 to 1 and the 1 to 0 in the selected gene.

4.3   Hybridization Approach

For genetic algorithms (GAs), local search (LS) is often used for the improvement of the solutions and the intensification of research [23]. In this paper we exploit this hybridization as follows:

- We seek the best solution by the method of GAs;
- We take this solution as the initial configuration of LS;
- We apply the method of LS on this configuration.

5   Application

5.1   Data Description

To evaluate the performance of the proposed algorithm, we consider uplink instances generated by using Hata's propagation model. For each instance, we consider a rectangular service area, a number of candidate sites in which to locate omnidirectional antennas, and a number of TPs. Using a pseudorandom number generator each candidate site and each TP is assigned a position with uniform distribution in the service area. We considered two families instances of a urban environment. The simulation parameters are:

- Size of the service area (in km): 0.4×0.4 in the first instance and 1×1 in the second instance;
- Number of TPs: 95 in the first instance and 400 in the second instance;
- Number of BSs: 22 in the first instance and 120 in the second instance;
- $u_i = 1$, the required number of simultaneously active connections for a TP_i;
- $F = 2000 \, \mathrm{MHz}$;

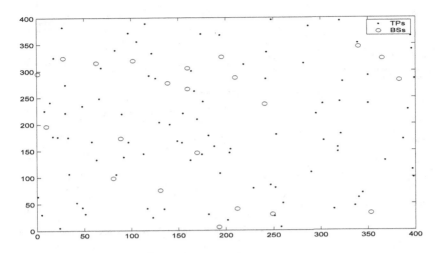

Fig. 4. First instance: location of 95 TPs and 22 BSs in a service area of 0.4 × 0.4 (Km)

- $H_m = 1\,\text{m}$;
- $H_b = 10\,\text{m}$;
- $P_{target} = -100\,\text{dBm}$ (about $10^{-10}\,\text{mW}$);
- $P_{max} = 30\,\text{dBm}$;
- $SF = 128$;
- $SIR_{min} = 0.03125\,\text{dB}$;
- $SIR_{target} = 6\,\text{dB}$;
- Input costs c_i: are taken randomly between 1 and 20 units.

Figures 4 and 5 illustrate the distribution of the TPs and BSs in the area service of the two instances, respectively.

5.2   Computational Results

The algorithms were coded in JAVA programming language and implemented on a machine of *CPU Intel Core2Duo-2GHz* and memory *RAM 2Go*. In the GA approaches we have used three selection methods; roulette, scaling and sharing. The parameters of GA are set as follows: crossover probability $p_c = 0.4$, mutation probability $p_m = 0.01$, population size $ps = 30$, and maximum number of

Table 2. Number of TPs covered and BSs installed for n = 95 and m = 22

Method of selection	Served TPs	BSs not installed	Cost	Total cost	Time in second
Roulette	92	1	278	281	75
Scaling	92	1	274	281	75.6
Sharing	**93**	1	**270**	**281**	76.4

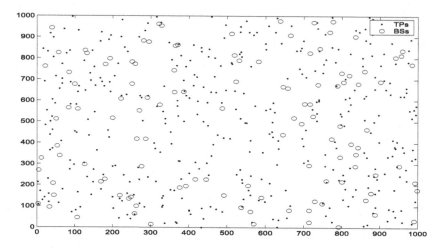

Fig. 5. Second instance: location of 400 TPs and 120 BSs in a service area of 1 × 1 (Km)

Table 3. Number of TPs covered and BSs installed for n = 400 and m = 120

Method of selection	Served TPs	BSs not installed	Cost	Total cost	Time in second
Roulette	397	5	1273	1719	230
Scaling	**398**	8	**1238**	**1719**	231
Sharing	396	5	1280	1719	233

generations 5000. In the sharing selection method, the threshold of dissimilarity between two parents is taken as $\sigma_s = ps/2$, and $\alpha = 1$. Each experiment were conducted on ten times. Tables 2 and 3 show number of TPs covered, number of BSs installed and costs for the two instances problem, respectively. Now, we comment results of each experiment.

First instance problem: 95 TPs and 22 BSs.

The best solution consists of installing 21 BSs instead of 22, which cover 93 TPs among 95, with a cost equal to 270, see last line in Table 2. Then we have a gain of 11, since the cost of installing all BSs is 281. We obtained a gain of approximately 4 % of costs of BSs.

Second instance problem: 400 TPs and 120 BSs.

This time, the best solution consists of installing 112 BSs instead of 120, which cover 398 TPs among 400, with a cost equal to 1238, see line 2 in Table 3. Then we have a gain of 481, since the cost of installing all BSs is 1719. We realized a gain of approximately 28 % of cost of BSs.

6 Conclusion

In this paper we have considered an UMTS base station (BS) location planning problem for uplink direction based on propagation models with power control. The objective is to maximize the total trafic covered and minimize the total installation cost. To deal with the imprecise and uncertain information of prices we address this problem using a fuzzy Logic. For this we apply three inputs to produce one output (the estimated cost). Our goal is to make the resolution of the problem more realistic.

In order to solve the problem we have proposed an algorithm based on the hybridization of genetic algorithm (GA) with Local Search method (LS). To code the solutions of the problem, we have used an encoding method which combines binary and integer coding, then we have described the crossover and mutation operators. We have applied our approach to two instances problem. The obtained results show the performance of our method.

References

1. Amaldi, E., Capone, A., Malucelli, F.: Planning UMTS base station location: optimization models with power control and algorithms. IEEE Trans. Wirel. Commun. **2**, 939–952 (2003)
2. Berruto, E., Gudmundson, M., Menolascino, R., Mohr, W., Pizarroso, M.: Research activities on UMTS radio interface, network architectures, and planning. IEEE Commun. Mag. **36**, 82–95 (1998)
3. Naghshineh, M., Katzela, I.: Channel assignment schemes for cellular mobile telecommunication systems: a comprehensive survey. IEEE Pers. Commun. **3**, 10–31 (1996)
4. Amaldi, E., Capone, A., Malucelli, F., Signori, F.: Radio planning and optimization of W-CDMA systems. In: Conti, M., Giordano, S., Gregori, E., Olariu, S. (eds.) PWC 2003. LNCS, vol. 2775, pp. 437–447. Springer, Heidelberg (2003)
5. St-Hilaire, M., Chamberland, S., Pierre, S.: Uplink UMTS network design-an integrated approach. Comput. Netw. **50**, 2747–2761 (2006)
6. Juttner, A., Orban, A., Fiala, Z.: Two new algorithms for UMTS access network topology design. Eur. J. Oper. Res. **164**, 456–474 (2005)
7. Hashemi, S.M., Moradi, A., Rezapour, M.: An ACO algorithm to design UMTS access network using divided and conquer technique. Eng. Appl. Artif. Intell. **21**, 931–940 (2008)
8. Meunier, H.: Algorithmes évolutionnaires parallèles pour l'optimisation multi objectif de réseaux de télécommunications mobiles. Ph.D. thesis, University of Sciences and Technologies, Lille (2002)
9. Dréo, J., Pétrowski, A., Siarry, P., Taillard, E.: Métaheuristiques pour l'optimisation difficile. Eyrolles, Paris (2003)
10. Amaldi, E., Capone, A., Malucelli, F.: Radio planning and coverage optimization of 3G cellular networks. Wirel. Netw. **14**, 435–447 (2008)
11. Mundt, T.: How much is a byte? A survey of costs for mobile data transmission. In: 2004 Proceedings of the Winter International Symposium on Information and Communication Technologies (WISICT) (2004)

12. Yang, Y.: UMTS investment study. Technical report T-109.551. Helsinki University, Telecommunication Business II (2003)
13. Katagiri, H., Mermri, E.B., Sakawa, M., Kato, K., Nishizaki, I.: A possibilistic and stochastic programming approach to fuzzy random MST problem. IEICE Trans. Inf. Syst. **E88–D**(8), 1912–1919 (2005)
14. Hata, M.: Empirical formula for propagation loss in land mobile radio services. IEEE Trans. Veh. Technol. **VT–29**, 317–325 (1980)
15. Sakawa, M.: Fuzzy Sets and Interactive Multiobjective Optimization. Springer, New York (1993)
16. Zadeh, L.A.: Fuzzy sets. Inf. Control **8**(3), 338–353 (1965)
17. Peng, P.K., Hitam, M.S.: Multiobjective optimization using fuzzy genetic algorithms. Empowering Science, Technology and Innovation Towards a Better Tomorrow, UMTAS (2011)
18. Kaur, A., Kaur, A.: Comparison of mamdani-type and sugeno-type fuzzy inference systems for air conditioning system. Int. J. Soft Comput. Eng. (IJSCE) **2**(2), 2231–2307 (2012)
19. Moscato, P.: On Evolution, search, optimization, genetic algorithms and martial arts: towards memetic algorithms. Caltech Concurrent Computation Program (report 826) (1989)
20. Molina, D., Lozano, M., Garcia-Martinez, C., Herrera, F.: Memetic algorithms for continuous optimisation based on local search chains. Evol. Comput. **18**(1), 27–63 (2010)
21. Mandal, A., Das, A.K., Mukherjee, P., Das, S.: Modified differential evolution with local search algorithm for real world optimization. In: IEEE Congress on Evolutionary Computation (CEC), pp. 1565–1572 (2011)
22. Gabli, M., Jaara, E.M., Mermri, E.B.: Planning UMTS base station location using genetic algorithm with a dynamic trade-off parameter. In: Gramoli, V., Guerraoui, R. (eds.) NETYS 2013. LNCS, vol. 7853, pp. 120–134. Springer, Heidelberg (2013)
23. Bontoux, B.: Techniques hybrides de recherche exacte et approche: application des problèmes de transport. Ph.D. thesis, University of Avignon and the Vaucluse (2008)

FL-EDCA: A QoS-Aware and Energy-Efficient Mechanism for IEEE 802.11e EDCA Standard

Hicham Touil[1(✉)] and Youssef Fakhri[1,2]

[1] Laboratory LaRIT, Team Network and Telecommunication,
University Ibn Tofaïl, Kenitra, Morocco
Touil.hm@gmail.com,
fakhri-youssef@univ-ibntofail.ac.ma
[2] LRIT, Unité Associée au CNRST (URAC 29), Faculty of Sciences,
Mohammed V-Agdal University, Rabat, Morocco

Abstract. The IEEE 802.11e EDCA standard was developed to guarantee the Quality of Service (QoS) requirements of the different traffic types (voice, video, data, etc.) in WLAN. However, several studies have shown that this standard performs poorly under heavy load traffic due to the high collision rate. On the other hand, EDCA was also used in the battery constrained devices. But, very few studies have tried to improve the energy-efficiency of this standard. For these reasons, we propose in this paper a Fuzzy-Logic-based (FL) mechanism to improve both energy-efficiency and traffic performance of the IEEE 802.11e EDCA, and also to favor real-time traffic when traffic load is heavy. The proposed FL-EDCA decreases the collision probability considerably, through a dynamic adaptation of the contention windows, using fuzzy logic controller. Our simulation results show that FL-EDCA outperforms EDCA by improving significantly energy-efficiency and traffic performance.

Keywords: IEEE 802.11e · EDCA · MAC protocol · Energy-efficiency · Traffic performance · WLAN

1 Introduction

The rapid evolution and accessibility of the IEEE 802.11 WLAN [1] technologies have led to their adoption all over the world. This technology has been used in many fields, and become dominant in some fields, seen its flexibility and evolution. The IEEE 802.11 WLAN is deployed at large, e.g., in offices, homes, public hotspots, etc. With the emergence of multimedia applications that require well-defined QoS levels for their good functioning, improving the IEEE 802.11 WLAN standard has become a necessity. This improvement should ensure an appropriate level of QoS to satisfy the applications requirements in terms of delay, jitter, throughput, etc. For this reason, the IEEE 802.11 Working Group has proposed as an improvement the IEEE 802.11e WLAN [2], which has today become a reference for QoS-Wireless Communication Networks. This standard provides service/traffic differentiation at the MAC Layer, using four Access Categories (AC). The IEEE 802.11e standard defines a third coordination function called Hybrid Coordination Function (HCF). HCF defines two modes of channel access:

G. Noubir and M. Raynal (Eds.): NETYS 2014, LNCS 8593, pp. 270–281, 2014.
DOI: 10.1007/978-3-319-09581-3_19

(i) EDCA MAC protocol that is a distributed contention-based channel access mechanism, (ii) and HCF Controlled Channel Access (HCCA) MAC protocol that is a centralized polling-based channel access mechanism. The EDCA and HCCA are improvements of DCF and PCF MAC protocols of the IEEE 802.11 standard.

The EDCA is distributed channel access method and can be used in ad hoc networks. The communication management within an Ad hoc WLAN with multiple priority traffic is a difficult task. For this reason, the IEEE 802.11e EDCA [2] has been deployed at the MAC layer to manage traffics according to their priority, in order to ensure a good traffic performance. However, several studies have shown that EDCA MAC protocol performs poorly under heavy traffic load due to the high collision rate [3]. On the other hand, greening the communication protocols is recognized as a primary design goal. The IEEE 802.11(e) technology is also used in the battery constrained devices (notebook computers, smart phones, eBook readers, etc.). The research works conducted on the EDCA have invested a lot in the field of improving traffic performance (delay, throughput, jitter, etc.). But, little research has invested in the energy-efficiency side of the EDCA. So, a good improvement of EDCA must consider both traffic performance and energy-efficiency, hence our proposal of FL-EDCA protocol in this paper.

The proposed FL-EDCA MAC protocol is an enhanced version of the EDCA. The FL-EDCA integrates a QoS Mechanism which is based on a Fuzzy Logic Controller (FLC) to dynamically adapt the contention windows of EDCA. This QoS Mechanism reduces the probability that a collision occurs, something that significantly improves the traffic performance and energy-efficiency. In addition, FL-EDCA favors real-time traffic when traffic load is heavy. The strength of the FL-EDCA protocol is that, it is based on two types of decision metrics: (i) Preventive metric represented by the remaining energy of the station; and (ii) Healing metric represented by the collision rate seen by the station.

The rest of this paper is structured as follows. Section 2 presents the related work. Section 3 outlines a brief overview of the IEEE 802.11e EDCA standard. In Sect. 4, we present our proposed FL-EDCA MAC protocol. Performance evaluation is presented in Sect. 5. Finally, conclusions and future work are presented in the last section.

2 Related Work

Several research studies have tried to improve the EDCA protocol. All improvements proposed by these studies include just the traffic performance side. But, few of them have addressed the energy-efficiency side of the EDCA. One of the few studies that have tried to improve both traffic performance and energy-efficiency is the EDCA/CA MAC protocol proposed by Chen and Cheng [4]. The EDCA/CA tries to improve traffic performance and energy-efficiency by reducing the number of collisions, by defers the transmissions of some traffic when traffic load is heavy. But, the EDCA/CA slightly increases the video delay when traffic is light. On the other hand, to improve the energy-efficiency of EDCA, the IEEE 802.11 Working Group has developed an energy conservation mechanism called Automatic Power Save Delivery (ASPD) [5]. This mechanism consists in reducing the idle listening state of the communication interface, which represents one of the main sources of energy waste in EDCA. But, there are other sources of energy waste, such as collisions, overhead, etc. [6]. Therefore, the development of a QoS Mechanism that reduces collisions is another solution to further improve the energy-efficiency of the EDCA. In addition, this QoS Mechanism will enable us to improve also the traffic performance.

To the best of our knowledge, there are no studies that have tried to improve both traffic performance and energy-efficiency of EDCA, by adjusting the contention windows CWmin and CWmax. This need has motivated us to propose the FL-EDCA MAC protocol to improve both traffic performance and energy-efficiency of EDCA, and also to favor real-time traffic when traffic load is heavy.

Fuzzy logic is used in many fields because it allows simulate human reasoning. In wireless networks, several studies have used this mathematical theory. We cite as an example, the study made by Nyirenda et al. [7] that has used a Fuzzy Logic Congestion Detection (FLCD) in IEEE 802.11 WLAN environment. Simulation results of this study have showed that the FLCD minimizes UDP traffic delay, and also reduces packet loss rate. As well, fuzzy logic has been used as a basis for a localization solution in Wireless Sensor Networks (WSN) [8]. Other studies have proposed mechanisms based on fuzzy logic at the routing layer of WSN to maximize lifetime [9, 10].

3   The IEEE 802.11e EDCA MAC Protocol

The IEEE 802.11e Enhanced Distributed Channel Access (EDCA) [2] is an enhancement of the IEEE 802.11 DCF MAC protocol [1]. As shown in Fig. 1, the EDCA uses eight Traffic Categories (TC) defined by the IEEE 802.1D Bridges Specification [11]. These eight TC are mapped to four Access Categories (AC), in order to ensure traffic/service differentiation at the MAC Layer.

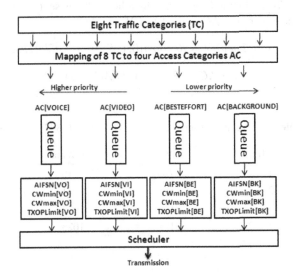

Fig. 1. The EDCA MAC structure

- AC[VOICE] <= TC(6 and 7) : Higher priority traffic,
- AC[VIDEO] <= TC(4 and 5),
- AC[BESTEFFORT] <= TC(0 and 3),
- AC[BACKGROUND] <= TC(1 and 2) : Lower priority traffic.

Each AC is represented by a Drop-Tail MAC-Queue (Dropping a packet that arrives at a full queue) that uses the technique First In First Out (FIFO). The priority of each MAC-Queue is maintained by four MAC parameters that are: Arbitration Inter Frame Space Number (AIFSN), Contention Window minimum (CWmin), Contention Window maximum (CWmax), and Transmission Opportunity Limit (TXOPLimit). The default values of these MAC parameters for each AC (with the IEEE 802.11b at the physical layer) are given in Table 1. Each AC has its own AIFS[AC] and CW[AC] parameters, see (1) and (2). The values of aSlotTime and SIFS parameters are fixed according to the used physical layer. For example, for the IEEE 802.11b PHY: aSlotTime = 20 μs and SIFS = 10 μs.

$$AIFS[AC] = SIFS + AIFSN[AC] \times aSlotTime \tag{1}$$

$$CWmin[AC] \leq CW[AC] \leq CWmax[AC] \tag{2}$$

The two parameters CWmin and CWmax determine the value of CW[AC]. At the beginning, CW[AC] = CWmin[AC]. If the station has a packet to transmit, it waits a AIFS[AC] time. If all throughout the AIFS[AC] the channel was free, the station sends the packet directly. Otherwise, the station must wait until the channel becomes free, wait for another time AIFS[AC], and then wait a random time called Backoff Timer (BT), see (3). If during the decrement of BT[AC] the channel becomes busy, the decrement is suspended. Once the channel becomes free the station waits AIFS [AC], and then continues decrementing the BT[AC]. If the BT[AC] time expires, the station can send the packet. When there is a transmission error of a packet, the CW[AC] value of the concerned AC is doubled, see (4). When the packet is sent successfully, the CW [AC] value of the concerned AC is reset to CWmin[AC].

$$BackoffTime[AC] = Random(0, CW[AC]) \times aSlotTime \tag{3}$$

$$CWnew[AC] = 2 \times (CWold[AC] + 1) - 1 \tag{4}$$

Table 1. MAC parameters values of EDCA (IEEE 802.11b PHY)

AC	AIFSN	CWmin	CWmax	TXOPLimit
AC_VO	2	7	15	3.264 ms
AC_VI	2	15	31	6.016 ms
AC_BE	3	31	1023	0 ms
AC_BK	7	31	1023	0 ms

4　The proposed FL-EDCA MAC Protocol

In this section we describe in detail the FL-EDCA protocol that we propose in this paper. The FL-EDCA is an enhanced version of the EDCA, which incorporates a QoS Mechanism to reduce the probability that a collision occurs. For reducing this probability, the FL-EDCA dynamically adapts (at run time) the contention windows CWmin and CWmax of the four AC, using Fuzzy Logic Controller (FLC), as shown in Fig. 2. When the collision rate increases the FLC increases the size of the Contention Windows (CWs) to reduce the collision probability. To adjust the size of CWs, the FLC uses two decision metrics. The first decision metric is preventive represented by the Remaining Energy (RE) of the station. The FLC increases slightly the CWs according to the remaining energy. In this way, when the remaining energy decreases, we will try to reduce the probability of future collisions. The second decision metric is healing represented by the Collision Rate (CR). The FLC increases the CWs according to the collision rate seen by the station, in order to reduce the probability of future collisions.

The operating mode of the QoS Mechanism (Based on a FLC) incorporated in our proposed FL-EDCA protocol is as follows:

After each time period P, we must make the following steps:

- **STEP 1**: We count the number of packets sent and the number of collisions that have occurred during this period P.
  - P = (5000 × aSlotTime) according to [12].
  - We use the IEEE 802.11b at the physical layer, so aSlotTime = 20 μs.
- **STEP 2**: We calculate the Collision Rate (CRnew) after the expiration of each period P.

$$CRnew = NColl/NPSent \tag{5}$$

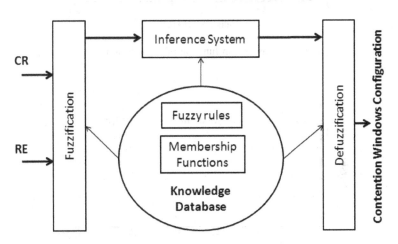

Fig. 2. FLC architecture incorporated in FL-EDCA.

- NColl: Collisions number in P period.
- NPSent: Packets sent number in P period.
- **STEP 3**: We use after step 2 an estimator of Exponentially Weighted Moving Average (EWMA), to smoothen the estimated values of the collision rate.

$$CRavg(new) = (1 - \alpha) * CRnew + \alpha * CRavg(old) \qquad (6)$$

- $\alpha = 0.8$ according to [12].
- **STEP 4**: We apply the new calculated values of the collision rate CRavg(new) and remaining energy (in %) as input to the FLC.
- **STEP 5**: The controller fuzzifies the value of the two inputs using their membership functions (see Figs. 3 and 4). Then look in the inference rules (see Table 2) to determine the correspondent decision. And finally the FLC defuzzifies the decision, and gives as output the proper configuration CWs(out) of the four AC (see Table 3).

The two membership functions (MF) are used to convert the value of CR and RE to a fuzzy set (Low, Medium, or High) according to the degree of truth. The values of S1, S2, S3 and S4 of each MF define the fuzzy sets. There is no standard that allows

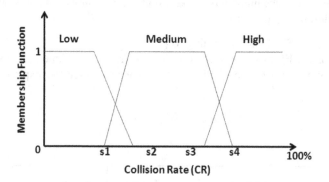

Fig. 3. Membership function of the collision rate

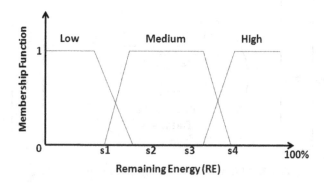

Fig. 4. Membership function of the remaining energy

Table 2. Fuzzy inference rules

Rules	CR	RE	CWs(out)
R1	Low	High	Config A
R2	Low	Medium	Config A
R3	Low	Low	Config A
R4	Medium	High	Config B
R5	Medium	Medium	Config B
R6	Medium	Low	Config C
R7	High	High	Config D
R8	High	Medium	Config D
R9	High	Low	Config E

Table 3. Contention windows configurations

CWs(out)	Configurations				
	A	B	C	D	E
CWmin[VO]	7	7	15	15	31
CWmax[VO]	15	15	31	31	63
CWmin[VI]	15	31	31	63	63
CWmax[VI]	31	63	63	127	127
CWmin[BE]	31	63	63	127	127
CWmax[BE]	1023	1023	1023	1023	1023
CWmin[BK]	31	63	63	127	127
CWmax[BK]	1023	1023	1023	1023	1023

determining the values of the threshold {S1, S2, S3, S4} of CR and RE. We have set the values of {S1, S2, S3, S4} of CR based on the reference [13], which analyzed the impact of CWmin and CWmax values on packet loss. To set the values of {S1, S2, S3, S4} of RE, we have divided the interval [0,100 %] on three equal fuzzy sets.

The used fuzzy inference rules in Table 2 are in the following form:

if CR is X **and** RE is Y **then** CWs(out) is Z

Table 2 shows the different possible combinations (rules) between the fuzzy sets of the two membership functions. For each rule, an output configuration of CWs is chosen. The output configurations are detailed in Table 3, and their values are chosen based on the results of the reference [13] and the recommendations of the IEEE 802.11e [2]. The CWs are attributed to the rules in such a way that, the CWmin and CWmax values increase gradually with the increase of CR and the decrease of RE. The values of CWs(out) configurations were well chosen to support real-time traffic. As shown in Table 3, the values of CWmin[VO] and CWmax[VO] always keep a safe distance with the CWmin and CWmax values of the others ACs. Such a configuration allows keeping priority of the real-time traffic, regardless the traffic load in the network.

How a node can compute the number of collisions? The determination of the cause of packet loss (collision or weak signal) in real time is impossible in wireless networks, because the antenna can't transmit data and listen to the channel at the same time [14]. Such a problematic has prompted the IEEE 802.11 Working Group to propose an intermediate solution. This solution consists in assigning the problem of packet loss to a collision, but after a certain number of unsuccessful retransmission of the packet (set from Short/Long Retry Count parameters), the problem of loss is attributed to a weak signal [14]. In the case of a packet loss due to a collision, the Binary Exponential Backoff (BEB) is invoked to double CW, see (4). In the case of a packet loss due to a weak signal, the data-rate adaptation algorithm is invoked.

5   Performance Evaluation

We have simulated our network using the simulation environment Network Simulator 2 (NS-2). We have implemented the EDCA protocol in NS-2 based on the code that was proposed by Sven et al. [15]. To properly assess the energy-efficiency and traffic performance, we realized several scenarios by varying the density of nodes (2, 4, 6, 8, 10, 12, 14, 16 and 18) and the traffic load in the network. The simulated network contains no hidden or mobile stations. All stations belong to a single Independent Basic Service Set (IBSS). In our study, the energy-efficiency is represented by the average lifetime of nodes, and the traffic performance is represented by the sum of the gains of the delay, throughput and packets delivery rate of FL-EDCA compared to EDCA. Table 4 shows in detail the Constant Bit Rate (CBR) traffics exchanged between nodes. Figure 5 shows the topology used in the different scenarios. The simulation time in the different scenarios is 10000 seconds. The used simulation parameters and the energetic characteristics of the communication interface [16] are detailed in Table 5.

5.1   Results and Discussion

Figure 6 shows the lifetime guaranteed by EDCA and FL-EDCA MAC protocols. Preliminary results show that the FL-EDCA can ensure greater energy-efficiency through the QoS Mechanism that it integrates. This significant improvement in lifetime is due to the ability of FL-EDCA to reduce the collision probability. This decrease in collisions avoids wasted energy during a collision, and also the wasted energy during the retransmission of the packet after collision. In addition, this significant energy-efficiency guaranteed by FL-EDCA is due to the two decision metrics (preventive and healing) on which is based the FLC integrated in our QoS Mechanism. Since, through

Table 4. Exchanged traffics

Traffic	Voice	Video
Packet size (Bytes)	160	625
Packet interval (ms)	20	12.5
Traffic rate (Kbps)	64	400

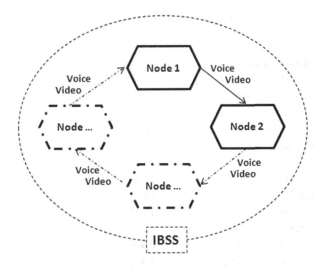

Fig. 5. Simulation topology

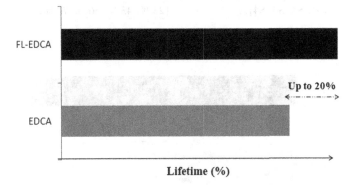

Fig. 6. Guaranteed lifetime by EDCA and FL-EDCA protocols

these metrics the FLC can correctly predict the proper configuration of CWs, in an attempt to avoid as much as all future collisions.

Figure 7 shows the guaranteed traffic performance. The traffic performance represent in this figure the sum of the gains of the delay, throughput and packets delivery rate of FL-EDCA compared to EDCA. Preliminary results show that the FL-EDCA can provide more traffic performance. This is due to the ability of the QoS Mechanism integrated in our FL-EDCA protocol to significantly reduce the number of contentions in the network, something that significantly reduces the number of collisions. Because reducing the number of collisions prevents the time loss due to collisions and re-transmissions, something that improves the delay, throughput and packet delivery rate. In addition, this significant improvement in traffic performance is due to the two decision metrics (preventive and healing) on which is based the FLC integrated in our QoS Mechanism. Since, through these metrics the FLC can correctly predict the proper

Table 5. Simulation parameters

Parameter	Value(s)
Simulation time	10 000 s
Simulation area	100 m x 100 m
Number of nodes	2, 4, 6, 8, 10, 12, 14, 16, 18
Pause time	0 s
Queue size	50
Physical layer	IEEE 802.11b
SIFS	10 μs
SlotTime	20 μs
DIFS	50 μs
Data rate	11 Mbps
IDLE energy	0.740 W
Reception energy	0.900 W
Transmission energy	1.350 W
Sleep energy	0.050 W
$\{S1, S2, S3, S4\}_{CR}$	$\{1\ \%, 2\ \%, 10\ \%, 20\ \%\}$
$\{S1, S2, S3, S4\}_{RE}$	$\{23\ \%, 43\ \%, 56\ \%, 76\ \%\}$

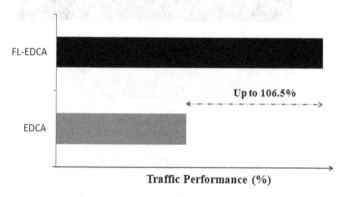

Fig. 7. Guaranteed traffic performance by EDCA and FL-EDCA protocols

configuration of CWs, in an attempt to avoid as much as all future collisions. The FL-EDCA ensures better QoS characteristics compared to EDCA protocol (Delay gain: up to 30.2 %, Throughput gain: up to 44.9 %, Packets delivery rate gain: up to 31.4 %).

6 Conclusion and Future work

In this paper we have proposed an enhanced version of EDCA called FL-EDCA. This proposed MAC protocol incorporates a QoS Mechanism that is based on a fuzzy logic controller to reduce the probability that a collision occurs, through dynamic adaptation (at run time) of the contention windows. Simulation results show that FL-EDCA outperforms EDCA by improving significantly energy-efficiency and traffic performance.

In our future study, we will try to find the optimal values of the intervals of the three states (Low, Medium and High) of the membership functions, to maximize both traffic performance and energy-efficiency guaranteed by our FL-EDCA protocol.

References

1. IEEE-802.11 LAN MAN Standards Committee of the IEEE Computer Society ANSI/IEEE Std 802.11, Part 11: Wireless LAN Medium Access Control (MAC) and Physical Layer (PHY) Specifications (1999)
2. IEEE 802 Committee of the IEEE Computer Society, IEEE 802.11e Amendment to IEEE Std 802.11, Part 11: Wireless LAN Medium Access Control (MAC) and Physical Layer (PHY) Specifications: Medium Access Control (MAC) Quality of Service (QoS) Enhancements (2005)
3. Villalón, J., Cuenca, P., Orozco-Barbosa, L.: B-EDCA: a new IEEE 802.11e-based QoS protocol for multimedia wireless communications. In: Boavida, F., Plagemann, T., Stiller, B., Westphal, C., Monteiro, E. (eds.) NETWORKING 2006. LNCS, vol. 3976, pp. 148–159. Springer, Heidelberg (2006)
4. Jyh, C.C., Kai, W.C.: EDCA/CA: enhancement of IEEE 802.11e EDCA by contention adaption for energy efficiency. IEEE Trans. Wirel. Commun. 7, 2866–2870 (2008)
5. Perez, C.X., Camps, M.D.: IEEE 802.11E QoS and power saving features overview and analysis of combined performance. IEEE Wirel. Commun. 17, 88–96 (2010)
6. Bachir, A., Dohler, M., Watteyne, T., Leung, K.K.: MAC essentials for wireless sensor networks. IEEE Commun. Surv. Tutor. 12, 222–248 (2010)
7. Nyirenda, C.N., Dawoud, D.S.: Fuzzy logic congestion control in IEEE 802.11 wireless local area networks: a performance evaluation. In: AFRICON, 26–29 Sept 2007, pp. 1–7 (2007)
8. Chiang, S.-Y., Wang, J.-L.: Localization in wireless sensor networks by fuzzy logic system. In: Velásquez, J.D., Ríos, S.A., Howlett, R.J., Jain, L.C. (eds.) KES 2009, Part II. LNCS, vol. 5712, pp. 721–728. Springer, Heidelberg (2009)
9. Chiang, S.-Y., Wang, J.-L.: Routing analysis using fuzzy logic systems in wireless sensor networks. In: Lovrek, I., Howlett, R.J., Jain, L.C. (eds.) KES 2008, Part II. LNCS (LNAI), vol. 5178, pp. 966–973. Springer, Heidelberg (2008)
10. Chi, S.H., Cho, T.H.: Fuzzy logic based propagation limiting method for message routing in wireless sensor networks. In: Gavrilova, M.L., Gervasi, O., Kumar, V., Tan, C., Taniar, D., Laganá, A., Mun, Y., Choo, H. (eds.) ICCSA 2006. LNCS, vol. 3983, pp. 58–67. Springer, Heidelberg (2006)
11. IEEE-802.1D: IEEE Standard for Local and Metropolitan Area Networks – Media Access Control (MAC) Bridges (2004)
12. Romdhani, L., Qiang, N., Turletti, T.: Adaptive EDCF: enhanced service differentiation for IEEE 802.11 wireless ad hoc networks. IEEE Wirel. Commun. Netw. 2, 1373–1378 (2003)
13. Touil, H., Fakhri, Y., Benattou, M.: Contention window MAC parameters tyning for wireless multimedia sensor networks. In: 10th ACS/IEEE International Conference on Computer Systems and Applications, pp. 1–4 (2013)

14. Rayanchu, S., Mishra, A., Agrawal, D., Saha, S., Banerjee, S.: Diagnosing wireless packet losses in 802.11: separating collision from weak signal. In: Proceedings of IEEE INFOCOM, pp. 735–743 (2008)
15. Sven, W., Emmelmann, M., Christian, H., Adam, W.: TKN EDCA model for ns-2. Technical report TKN-06-003, Telecommunication Networks Group, Technische Universität Berlin (2006) [online]
16. Cunha, D.O., Costa, L.H.M.K., Duarte, O.C.M.B.: Analyzing the energy consumption of IEEE 802.11 ad hoc networks. In: IFIP/IEEE International Conference on Mobile and Wireless Communications Networks (2004)

Loss Minimization and Delay Differentiation for Optical Burst Switching Over Star Networks

Salek Riadi[(⊠)], Abdelilah Maach, and Driss El Ghanami

Computer Science Department, Mohammadia School of Engineers,
Mohammed V-Agdal University, Rabat, Morocco
salek.riadi@gmail.com, {maach,elghanami}@emi.ac.ma

Abstract. In OBS networks, lost bursts can be recovered proactively using burst cloning, or reactively using burst retransmission. Burst cloning has advantage of low delay but it suffers from low throughput. Burst retransmission has advantage of high throughput but at the cost of high delay. To minimize delay while keeping high throughput in star OBS networks, we propose three schemes: (1) enhanced burst retransmission scheme that controls the retransmissions; (2) hybrid loss recovery scheme that integrates efficiently burst cloning and burst retransmission; (3) differentiated QoS scheme that provides differentiation between two classes in terms of delay using burst cloning and burst retransmission. Both analytical and simulation results show that the proposed schemes achieve high throughput. We find that, compared to basic burst retransmission scheme, first scheme reduces delay only at moderate and high load, however, second and third scheme reduce delay at every load. Third scheme can also give good differentiation.

Keywords: Performance analysis · Optical burst switching · Loss minimization · Delay differentiation

1 Introduction

Optical Burst Switching (OBS) is proposed as a switching paradigm to support tremendous traffic of current and next generation Internet over wavelength division multiplexing networks [1–3]. OBS networks use one-way reservation that leads to burst contention, which is the principal reason of burst loss. Burst loss affects negatively the performance of the higher layers. Contention occurs at both edge and core node. At edge node, contending burst may be electronically queued in finite burst queue and, consequently, a new arriving burst can be lost if the burst queue is full. Whereas at core node, which lacks of optical memory and wavelength conversion capability, contending burst will be lost.

Burst cloning mechanism can proactively recover lost bursts by transmitting two or more duplicates of the same burst in order to enhance the probability that at least one duplicate will reach destination [4]. We have previously proposed two burst cloning schemes for star networks [5]. First scheme, called basic burst cloning scheme, can reduce burst loss at low load, however at high load, it leads to a significant burst loss at

© Springer International Publishing Switzerland 2014
G. Noubir and M. Raynal (Eds.): NETYS 2014, LNCS 8593, pp. 282–297, 2014.
DOI: 10.1007/978-3-319-09581-3_20

edge nodes due to burst queue saturation. The second scheme, called opportunistic burst cloning scheme, aims to overcome this shortcoming by disabling burst cloning mechanism when the burst queue size reaches a preset Threshold (T). Whereas burst cloning mechanism has advantage of low burst delay, it suffers from low bandwidth utilization. Lost bursts can be also recovered reactively by retransmitting contending bursts [6]. For star networks, the authors of [7] proposed a basic burst retransmission scheme. Burst retransmission mechanism has advantage of high bandwidth utilization but at the cost of high burst delay.

In order to minimize burst delay while keeping high bandwidth utilization in star OBS networks, we propose, in this work, three schemes. The first scheme is an enhanced burst retransmission scheme, which aims to control the retransmissions through a simple technique to enable/disable burst retransmission mechanism. The second scheme is a new hybrid loss recovery scheme, which aims to integrate efficiently burst cloning and burst retransmission mechanism. The third scheme is a differentiated QoS scheme that provides differentiation between two classes in terms of burst delay by using burst cloning and burst retransmission. We propose analytical models for basic burst retransmission scheme, enhanced burst retransmission scheme, hybrid loss recovery scheme and differentiated QoS scheme. The accuracy of our analytical model is verified through simulation. Both analytical and simulation results show that the proposed schemes achieve high bandwidth utilization. We find that, compared to basic burst retransmission scheme, the first scheme reduces burst delay only at moderate and high load, however, the second and third scheme reduce delay at every load. The third scheme can offer also a good differentiation in terms of burst delay.

The outline of this paper is: in Sect. 2, we present and analyze the basic burst retransmission scheme; in Sect. 3, we propose and analyze the enhanced burst retransmission scheme; in Sect. 4, we propose and analyze the hybrid loss recovery scheme; in Sect. 5, we propose and analyze the differentiated QoS scheme; in Sect. 6, we show the analytical and simulation results. Finally, we conclude this paper in Sect. 7.

2   Basic Burst Retransmission Scheme

In Basic Burst Retransmission Scheme (BBRS) [7, 8], both new arriving and retransmitting burst are scheduled through EPMV-VF algorithm [9]. We consider that burst queue is finite and, consequently, both new arriving and retransmitting burst will be lost when the burst queue is saturated. Each new arriving burst should be kept in retransmission buffer and assigned a unique id. The life duration of burst copy in retransmission buffer is controlled by setting a timer to the value of Round Trip Time (RTT) between edge and core node. A control packet is sent before data burst to reserve a data wavelength at the core node and if this reservation is failing, a Negative Acknowledgment (NACK) packet with burst id is sent from the core node to the edge node, which is the source of the control packet. When the NACK packet reaches the edge node, which has an unsaturated burst queue, the timer is set to RTT and the new control packet is sent again, and so on. The burst copy is still in the retransmission buffer until it either reaches its destination or is lost due to burst queue saturation.

2.1 Modeling of Edge Node

The burst queue of the edge node in conventional OBS is modeled with $M/M/W/K$ queue; where the number of servers W represents the number of data wavelengths per single fiber, and the number of system places K represents the sum of the number of data wavelengths and the number of burst queue places; the burst arrival from burst assembler to the burst queue is assumed Poisson process with rate λ bursts per second and the distribution of burst time is exponential with a mean of $1/\mu$ seconds [5]. In BBRS, the total burst arrival to the burst queue Λ includes the new burst arrival from burst assembler λ and the arrival of retransmitted bursts δ:

$$\Lambda = \lambda + \delta. \tag{1}$$

We model the burst queue in BBRS with the same $M/M/W/K$ queue as conventional OBS except that the burst arrival is Λ. The equilibrium probability (p_n) is expressed in terms of p_0 as follows:

$$p_n = \frac{1}{n!} \left(\frac{\Lambda}{\mu} \right)^n p_0, \text{ for } n = 1, \ldots, W, \tag{2}$$

$$p_n = \frac{W^W}{W!} \left(\frac{\Lambda}{W\mu} \right)^n p_0, \text{ for } n = W+1, \ldots, K. \tag{3}$$

The normalization condition of the total probability is expressed as follows:

$$\sum_{n=0}^{K} p_n = 1. \tag{4}$$

Consequently, p_0 is given by:

$$p_0 = \left(\sum_{n=0}^{W} \frac{1}{n!} \left(\frac{\Lambda}{\mu} \right)^n + \frac{W^W}{W!} \sum_{n=W+1}^{K} \left(\frac{\Lambda}{W\mu} \right)^n \right)^{-1}. \tag{5}$$

The burst queue is saturated with the probability (f):

$$f = p_K. \tag{6}$$

The utilization of each outgoing data wavelength (ρ) is given by:

$$\rho = \frac{\Lambda(1 - p_K)}{W\mu}. \tag{7}$$

The Queuing Delay (QD) is given based on Little's law [10]:

$$QD = \frac{\sum_{n=1}^{K} n p_n}{\Lambda(1 - p_K)}. \tag{8}$$

2.2 Modeling of Core Node

Let g be the probability of a data-wavelength reservation failure in core node. g is given by the following formula, which is given and proved in [5]:

$$g = \frac{\alpha(N-1)}{\mu N + 2\alpha(N-1)}. \tag{9}$$

Where N is the number of edge nodes and α is given by:

$$\alpha = \frac{\mu\rho}{1-\rho}. \tag{10}$$

The arrival of retransmitted bursts δ is:

$$\delta = \sum_{i=1}^{\infty} ((1-f)g)^i \lambda, \tag{11}$$

that is,

$$\delta = \frac{(1-f)g}{1-(1-f)g} \lambda. \tag{12}$$

To get δ we need the 2-tuple (f, g) and to obtain the 2-tuple (f, g) we need δ, which leads to the following iterative algorithm. In the initialization step, we assume that δ is zero. In the iterative step, we calculate the 2-tuple (f, g); and then we calculate δ. We repeat the iterative step until δ converges.

2.3 Performances of Network

Since the burst is lost only in edge nodes due to burst queue saturation, the Burst Loss Probability (BLP) is given by:

$$BLP = \sum_{i=0}^{\infty} f((1-f)g)^i. \tag{13}$$

Thus,

$$BLP = \frac{f}{1-(1-f)g}. \tag{14}$$

The Normalized Throughput (NT) is the ratio of bandwidth utilization. NT is given by:

$$NT = \frac{\lambda(1-BLP)}{W\mu}. \tag{15}$$

The BD depends on QD, Offset Time (OT), Propagation Delay (PD), Processing Time (PT) of each of control packet and NACK packet, and average number of retransmissions (r). BD is given by:

$$BD = QD + OT + r \overbrace{(2PD + 2PT)}^{RTT} + 2PD, \tag{16}$$

such as r is given by:

$$r = \sum_{i=1}^{\infty} i((1-f)g)^i (1-(1-f)g), \tag{17}$$

that is,

$$r = \frac{(1-f)g}{1-(1-f)g}. \tag{18}$$

3 Enhanced Burst Retransmission Scheme

At low load, the BBRS can minimize significantly the burst loss probability with reasonable burst delay. At high load, the BBRS can also minimize the burst loss probability but not as significantly with unreasonable high burst delay. To overcome this shortcoming, we propose Enhanced Burst Retransmission Scheme (EBRS), which aims to control the retransmissions through a simple technique to enable/disable burst retransmission mechanism. In EBRS, retransmission mechanism is enabled or disabled in accordance with the current state of the burst queue. When the NACK packet reaches the edge node, if the burst queue size is less than a preset threshold, the timer is set to *RTT* and the new control packet is sent to the core node; else, the burst copy is deleted from retransmission buffer and, consequently, the burst is finally lost.

3.1 Modeling of Edge Node

We model the burst queue of edge node with the Markov chain shown in Fig. 1, where Λ is given by (1) and T denotes the threshold. Based on the global balance equation for the cut between states $(n-1)$ and n, we can express p_n in terms of p_0 as follows:

$$p_n = \frac{1}{n!}\left(\frac{\Lambda}{\mu}\right)^n p_0, \text{ for } n = 1,\ldots,W, \tag{19}$$

$$p_n = \frac{W^W}{W!}\left(\frac{\Lambda}{W\mu}\right)^n p_0, \text{ for } n = W+1,\ldots,T, \tag{20}$$

$$p_n = \frac{W^W}{W!}\left(\frac{\Lambda}{\lambda}\right)^T\left(\frac{\lambda}{W\mu}\right)^n p_0, \text{ for } n = T+1,\ldots,K. \tag{21}$$

Consequently, p_0 is given by:

$$p_0 = \left(\sum_{n=0}^{W}\frac{1}{n!}\left(\frac{\Lambda}{\mu}\right)^n + \frac{W^W}{W!}\left(\sum_{n=W+1}^{T}\left(\frac{\Lambda}{W\mu}\right)^n + \left(\frac{\Lambda}{\lambda}\right)^T\sum_{n=T+1}^{K}\left(\frac{\lambda}{W\mu}\right)^n\right)\right)^{-1}. \tag{22}$$

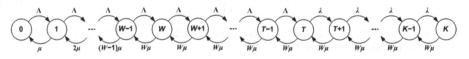

Fig. 1. State transition diagram for burst queue of an edge node in EBRS

The new burst arrival from burst assembler will be dropped with probability (f_1):

$$f_1 = p_K. \tag{23}$$

The arrival of the retransmitting bursts will be dropped with probability (f_2):

$$f_2 = \sum_{n=T}^{K} p_n. \tag{24}$$

ρ are given as follows:

$$\rho = \frac{\sum_{n=1}^{K} \min(W, n) p_n}{W}, \tag{25}$$

QD is given based on Little's law as follows:

$$QD = \frac{\sum_{n=1}^{K} n p_n}{W \mu \rho}. \tag{26}$$

3.2 Modeling of Code Node

g is calculated as in BBRS except that the arrival of retransmitted bursts δ is given by:

$$\delta = (1 - f_1)g \sum_{i=1}^{\infty} ((1 - f_2)g)^{i-1} \lambda, \tag{27}$$

that is:

$$\delta = \frac{(1 - f_1)g}{1 - (1 - f_2)g} \lambda. \tag{28}$$

3.3 Performances of Network

The new burst is lost due to burst queue saturation whereas the retransmitted burst is lost if the burst queue size is greater than the threshold. The *BLP* is given by:

$$BLP = f_1 + (1 - f_1)f_2 g \sum_{i=1}^{\infty} ((1 - f_2)g)^{i-1}, \tag{29}$$

that is,

$$BLP = \frac{f_1 + (f_2 - f_1)g}{1 - (1 - f_2)g}. \tag{30}$$

The *NT* is given based on (15). The *BD* is calculated using (16) such as average number of retransmissions (r) is given by:

$$r = \sum_{i=1}^{\infty} i((1-f_2)g)^i(1-(1-f_2)g), \tag{31}$$

that is,

$$r = \frac{(1-f_2)g}{1-(1-f_2)g}. \tag{32}$$

4 Hybrid Loss Recovery Scheme

In this section, we propose a Hybrid Loss Recovery Scheme (HLRS), which aims also to improve bandwidth utilization while keeping burst delay as low as possible in star OBS networks. HLRS integrates burst retransmission mechanism, which has advantage of high bandwidth utilization but it suffers from high burst delay, with burst cloning mechanism, which has advantage of low burst delay but it suffers from low bandwidth utilization. In HLRS, we divide the burst queue into three parts with two thresholds. When the burst queue size is less than the first threshold, the both mechanisms are enabled. When the burst queue size is between the first threshold and the second threshold, only burst retransmission mechanism is enabled. When the burst queue size is more than the second threshold, the both mechanisms are disabled. When a new arriving burst is ready, if the burst queue is saturated, then, the new arriving burst is lost, else, it is kept in retransmission buffer, the timer is set to *RTT*, and if the burst queue size is less than the first threshold, then, two copies of the new arriving burst are sent to the core node, else, only one copy of the new arriving burst is sent to the core node. When the NACK packet reaches the edge node, if the burst queue size is more than the second threshold, the burst copy is deleted from retransmission buffer and the burst is finally lost, else, the timer is set to *RTT* and if the burst queue size is less than the first threshold, then, two copies of retransmitting burst are sent to the core node, else, only one copy of retransmitting burst is sent to the core node.

4.1 Modeling of Edge Node

We model the burst queue of edge node queue in HLRS with the Markov chain shown in Fig. 2, where T_1 denotes the first threshold and T_2 denotes the second threshold. Λ is given by (1). We can express p_n based on the global balance equation for the cut between states $(n-1)$ and n:

$$p_1 = \frac{\Lambda}{\mu} p_0, \text{ for } n = 1, \tag{33}$$

$$p_n = \frac{\Lambda}{\min(W,n)\mu}(p_{n-1} + p_{n-2}), \text{ for } n = 2, \ldots, T_1, \tag{34}$$

$$p_n = \frac{\Lambda}{\min(W,n)\mu} p_{n-1}, \text{ for } n = T_1 + 1, \ldots, T_2, \tag{35}$$

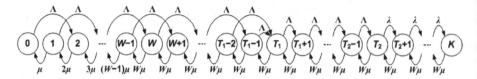

Fig. 2. State transition diagram for burst queue of an edge node in HLRS

$$p_n = \frac{\lambda}{\min(W, n)\mu} p_{n-1}, \text{ for } n = T_2 + 1, \ldots, K. \tag{36}$$

Based on (33), (34), (35), (36) and the normalization condition of the total probability, we can calculate any state probability p_n. The following way computes all state probabilities of the system: let u_n be the un-normalized probability of the state n, we initialize u_0 to one; for $n \geq 1$, we calculate u_n as in (33), (34), (35) and (36); finally, we calculate p_n as follows:

$$p_n = \frac{u_n}{\sum_{i=0}^{K} u_i}, \text{ for } n = 0, \ldots, K. \tag{37}$$

The probability that a new burst will be dropped is:

$$f_1 = p_K. \tag{38}$$

The probability that a retransmitted burst will be dropped is:

$$f_2 = \sum_{n=T_2}^{K} p_n. \tag{39}$$

ρ and QD are given by (25) and (26) respectively. If a burst is not lost, then it will be cloned with the probability c:

$$c = \frac{W\mu\rho}{\Lambda \sum_{n=0}^{T_2-1} p_n + \lambda \sum_{n=T_2}^{K-1} p_n} - 1. \tag{40}$$

4.2   Modeling of Core Node

The load may be considered in core node is:

$$l = \frac{(1 + cg)\rho}{1 + c}. \tag{41}$$

Where g is given by (9), such as α is given by:

$$\alpha = \frac{\mu l}{1 - l}. \tag{42}$$

If the burst is cloned, then it is retransmitted only when the both data wavelength reservations are failed. However, if the burst is not cloned, then the burst is retransmitted when one data wavelength reservation is failed. Therefore, the arrival of retransmitted bursts δ is given by:

$$\delta = (1 - f_1)((1 - c)g + cg^2) \sum_{i=1}^{\infty} \left((1 - f_2)((1 - c)g + cg^2)\right)^{i-1} \lambda, \qquad (43)$$

that is:

$$\delta = \frac{(1 - f_1)((1 - c)g + cg^2)}{1 - (1 - f_2)((1 - c)g + cg^2)} \lambda. \qquad (44)$$

To get δ we need the 4-tuple (f_1, f_2, c, g) and to obtain the 4-tuple (f_1, f_2, c, g) we need δ, which leads to an iterative algorithm. We propose the following iterative algorithm. In the initialization step, we assume that δ is zero and g is zero. In the iterative step, we calculate the 4-tuple (f_1, f_2, c, g); and then we calculate δ. We repeat the iterative step until δ converges.

4.3   Performances of Network

The new burst is lost due to burst queue saturation however the retransmitted burst is lost if the burst queue size is greater than the second threshold T_2. Therefore, BLP is:

$$BLP = f_1 + (1 - f_1)f_2((1 - c)g + cg^2) \sum_{i=1}^{\infty} \left((1 - f_2)((1 - c)g + cg^2)\right)^{i-1}, \qquad (45)$$

that is,

$$BLP = \frac{f_1 + (f_2 - f_1)((1 - c)g + cg^2)}{1 - (1 - f_2)((1 - c)g + cg^2)}. \qquad (46)$$

The NT is given based on (15). We calculate the BD by (16) such as r is given by:

$$r = \sum_{i=1}^{\infty} i\left((1 - f_2)((1 - c)g + cg^2)\right)^i \left(1 - (1 - f_2)((1 - c)g + cg^2)\right), \qquad (47)$$

thus,

$$r = \frac{(1 - f_2)((1 - c)g + cg^2)}{1 - (1 - f_2)((1 - c)g + cg^2)}. \qquad (48)$$

5   Differentiated Quality of Service Scheme

Here, we propose a Differentiated Quality of Service Scheme (DQSS), which aims to provide a differentiation between two classes in terms of burst delay while keeping the burst loss as low as possible for both classes and high bandwidth utilization in star OBS networks. The bursts of the First Class of Service (CoS_1) contain non-real-time traffic (e.g. best-effort services), however, the bursts of the Second Class of Service (CoS_2)

contain real-time traffic (e.g. voice and video conferencing) which demands lowest delay. In DQSS, bursts of CoS_1 are processed as in EBRS, however, bursts of CoS_2 are processed as in HLRS. When the burst queue size is less than the first threshold, burst retransmission mechanism is enabled for bursts of CoS_1 and CoS_2, however, burst cloning mechanism is enabled only for bursts of CoS_2. When the burst queue size is between the first threshold and the second threshold, only burst retransmission mechanism is enabled for bursts of CoS_1 and CoS_2. When the burst queue size is more than the second threshold, the both mechanisms are disabled.

5.1 Modeling of Edge Node

The burst arrival from burst assembler to the burst queue includes the arrival of CoS_1 (λ_1) and the arrival of CoS_2 (λ_2):

$$\lambda = \lambda_1 + \lambda_2. \tag{49}$$

The total burst arrival of a CoS_i to the burst queue includes the new burst arrival of the CoS_i (λ_i) and the arrival of retransmitted bursts of the same CoS_i (δ_i):

$$\Lambda_i = \lambda_i + \delta_i. \tag{50}$$

We model the burst queue of edge node queue in DQSS with the Markov chain shown in Fig. 3, where Λ is given by:

$$\Lambda = \Lambda_1 + \Lambda_2. \tag{51}$$

We can express p_n based on the global balance equation for the cut between states $(n-1)$ and n:

$$p_1 = \frac{\Lambda}{\mu}p_0, \quad \text{for } n = 1, \tag{52}$$

$$p_n = \frac{\Lambda p_{n-1} + \Lambda_2 p_{n-2}}{\min(W, n)\mu}, \quad \text{for } n = 2, \ldots, T_1, \tag{53}$$

$$p_n = \frac{\Lambda}{\min(W, n)\mu}p_{n-1}, \quad \text{for } n = T_1 + 1, \ldots, T_2, \tag{54}$$

$$p_n = \frac{\lambda}{\min(W, n)\mu}p_{n-1}, \quad \text{for } n = T_2 + 1, \ldots, K. \tag{55}$$

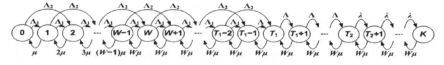

Fig. 3. State transition diagram for burst queue of an edge node in DQSS

We calculate p_n as follows: we initialize the un-normalized probability of the state 0 (u_0) to one; for $n \geq 1$, we calculate u_n as in (52), (53), (54) and (55); finally, we calculate p_n using (37). f_1, f_2, p, QD and c are given by (38), (39), (25), (26) and (42) respectively. If a burst of CoS_2 is not lost, then it will be cloned with the probability q:

$$q = \frac{c\Lambda}{\Lambda_2}. \tag{56}$$

5.2 Modeling of Core Node

l is given by (41). The arrival of retransmitted bursts of CoS_1 is given by:

$$\delta_1 = (1 - f_1)g \sum_{i=1}^{\infty} ((1 - f_2)g)^{i-1} \lambda_1, \tag{57}$$

that is:

$$\delta_1 = \frac{(1 - f_1)g}{1 - (1 - f_2)g} \lambda_1. \tag{58}$$

The arrival of retransmitted bursts of CoS_2 is given by:

$$\delta_2 = (1 - f_1)((1 - q)g + qg^2) \sum_{i=1}^{\infty} ((1 - f_2)((1 - q)g + qg^2))^{i-1} \lambda_2, \tag{59}$$

that is:

$$\delta_2 = \frac{(1 - f_1)((1 - q)g + qg^2)}{1 - (1 - f_2)((1 - q)g + qg^2)} \lambda_2. \tag{60}$$

To get the 2-tuple (δ_1, δ_2) we need the 4-tuple (f_1, f_2, q, g) and to obtain the 4-tuple (f_1, f_2, q, g) we need the 2-tuple (δ_1, δ_2). We propose the following iterative algorithm. In the initialization step, we assume that δ_1 is zero, δ_2 is zero and g is zero. In the iterative step, we calculate the 4-tuple (f_1, f_2, q, g); and then we calculate the 2-tuple (δ_1, δ_2). We repeat the iterative step until g converges.

5.3 Performances of Network

The Burst Loss Probability of CoS_1 (BLP_1) is given as in (30). The Burst Loss Probability of CoS_2 (BLP_2) is given by:

$$BLP_2 = f_1 + (1 - f_1)f_2((1 - q)g + qg^2) \sum_{i=1}^{\infty} ((1 - f_2)((1 - q)g + qg^2))^{i-1} \tag{61}$$

that is,

$$BLP_2 = \frac{f_1 + (f_2 - f_1)((1 - q)g + qg^2)}{1 - (1 - f_2)((1 - q)g + qg^2)}. \tag{62}$$

Consequently, the *BLP* is given by:

$$BLP = \frac{(\lambda_1 BLP_1 + \lambda_2 BLP_2)}{\lambda}. \tag{63}$$

The *NT* is given based on (15). The Burst Delay of CoS_1 (BD_1) is given by (16) such as r is given by (32). The Burst Delay of CoS_2 (BD_2) is given by (16) such as r is given by:

$$r = \sum_{i=1}^{\infty} i\left((1-f_2)((1-q)g + qg^2)\right)^i \left(1 - (1-f_2)((1-q)g + qg^2)\right), \tag{64}$$

thus,

$$r = \frac{(1-f_2)((1-q)g + qg^2)}{1 - (1-f_2)((1-q)g + qg^2)}. \tag{65}$$

Consequently, the *BD* is given by:

$$BD = \frac{(\lambda_1(1 - BLP_1)BD_1 + \lambda_2(1 - BLP_2)BD_2)}{\lambda(1 - BLP)}. \tag{66}$$

6 Numerical Results

We implemented Conventional OBS (COBS), Basic Burst Cloning Scheme (BBCS), Opportunistic Burst Cloning Scheme (OBCS), BBRS, EBRS, HLRS and DQSS in ns-2 simulator [11] using OBS-ns extension [12]. In the considered star network, the core node is connected to 15 edge nodes (i.e. $N = 15$) through 15 different bi-directional dual-fibers. We assume that there are no control packet losses and no NACK packet losses, $W = 8$, $K = 24$, $PD = 10^{-3}$ s, $PT = 10^{-6}$ s. $OT = 10^{-5}$ s, wavelength capacity is 10 Gbps and $\mu^{-1} = 0.0008$ s. The generated load (*L*) by each burst assembler can be set

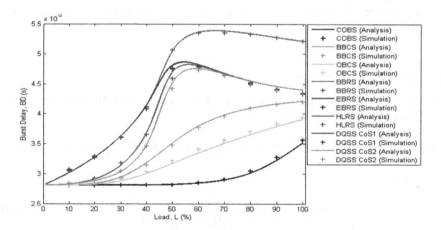

Fig. 4. Burst delay, *BD*

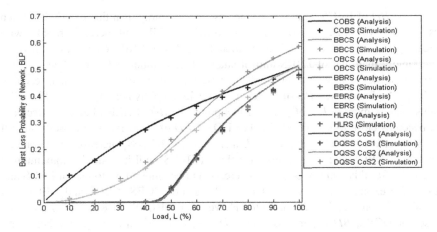

Fig. 5. Burst loss probability, *BLP*

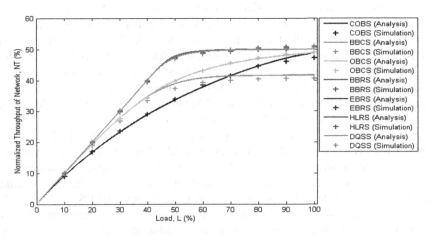

Fig. 6. Normalized Throughput of network, *NT*

by adjusting the rate λ such as $L = \lambda(W\mu)^{-1}$. In Figs. 4, 5 and 6, we plot respectively analytical and simulation results of *BD*, *BLP* and *NT*, as function of L for: COBS; BBCS with $R = 2$; OBCS with $T = 16$; BBRS; EBRS with $T = 20$; HLRS with $T_1 = 8$, $T_2 = 20$; DQSS with $T_1 = 8$, $T_2 = 20$, $\lambda_1/\lambda = 0.9$, $\lambda_2/\lambda = 0.1$. Note that the analytical model of COBS, BBCS and OBCS are given in [5].

The results shown in Figs. 4, 5, and 6 demonstrate that, our analytical models achieve a good approximation in comparison with the simulation results.

In Fig. 4, we observe that, *BD* of COBS remains less than that of BBCS, OBCS, BBRS, EBRS, HLRS and both classes of DQSS for every load. The *BD* of COBS remains constant and near to end-to-end propagation delay until the load reaches 50 %; after this point, it begins to increase slowly with increasing L. When L is below 30 %, *BD* of OBCS is close to that of BBCS and increases slowly; however, when L is more than 30 %, *BD* of BBCS continues to increase more rapidly than that of OBCS. When *L* is less than 40 %, *BD* of EBRS is close to *BD* of BBRS and increases rapidly with increasing *L*; however, when *L* is more than 40 %, *BD* of BBRS continues to increase more rapidly than that of EBRS until it attains its maximum at *L* = 66 % and then it decreases slowly with increasing *L*. *BD* of EBRS becomes to decrease when reaching *L* = 54 %. As *L* increases, *BD* of HLRS increases less rapidly than that of EBRS until it attains its maximum at *L* = 56 %; after this point, the *BD* of HLRS begins to decrease and becomes close to that of EBRS. For DQSS, *BD* of CoS_1 remains close to that of EBRS under every load; however, as *L* increases, *BD* of CoS_2 increases more rapidly than that of BBCS and less rapidly than that of HLRS until it attains its maximum at *L* = 60 %; after this point, it begins to decrease and becomes close to that of EBRS and HLRS. We explain the above results as follows. For COBS, BBCS and OBCS, *BD* depends only on *OT*, *PD*, *PT* and *QD*. However, for BBRS, EBRS, HLRS and both classes of DQSS, *BD* depends on *OT*, *PD*, *PT*, *QD* and on average number of re-transmissions (*r*) as shown in (16). Since *OT* and *PD* remain constant, the variation of *BD* for COBS, BBCS and OBCS is due to *QD* and the variation of *BD* for BBRS, EBRS, HLRS and both classes of DQSS is due to *QD* and *r*. COBS has zero extra load, which leads to smaller *QD*, and, consequently, lower *BD*. For BBCS, the extra load of burst cloning increases as the load increases, however, OBCS reduces ratio of extra load as the load increases. Thus, OBCS can also reduce *QD* and, consequently, *BD* more than BBCS. At low load, the extra load of burst retransmission of EBRS is very similar to that of BBRS, thus EBRS and BBRS achieve the same *QD* and *r*. Consequently, EBRS and BBRS achieve the same *BD* at low load. However, at moderate and high load, as we increase load EBRS reduces the ratio of the extra load more than BBRS that means that EBRS minimizes *QD* and reduces *r* more than BBRS. Consequently, EBRS can achieve a *BD* that is less than *BD* of BBRS at moderate and high load. At low and moderate load, HLRS allows each transmitted burst more opportunity to avoid retransmission by transmitting two duplicates of the burst using burst cloning mechanism that leads to reduce significantly *r*. Consequently, HLRS achieves a *BD* that is less than *BD* of EBRS at low and moderate load. In DQSS, only the bursts of CoS_2 that benefits by burst cloning mechanism, therefore the bursts of CoS_2 have an opportunity to avoid retransmission more than that of bursts of HLRS at low and moderate load. Consequently, CoS_2 of DQSS achieves a *BD* that is less than *BD* of HLRS at low and moderate load. At high load, HLRS and DQSS disable burst cloning mechanism and reduces the ratio of the extra load, due to burst retransmission mechanism, as EBRS. Consequently, HLRS, CoS_1 of DQSS and EBRS achieve the same *BD* at high load. By compared to arrival of CoS_1, the arrival of CoS_2, which is processed as in EBRS, is very high, consequently, CoS_1 of DQSS achieves a *BD* that is near to that of EBRS at every load.

In Fig. 5, we show that, *BLP* of OBCS remains less than that of both BBCS and COBS for every load. When *L* is less than 40 %, *BLP* of OBCS is very close to that of BBCS and increases slowly. When *L* is more than 40 %, *BLP* of BBCS increases more rapidly than that of OBCS and when *L* is above 70 %, it becomes above that of COBS. The *BLP* of BBRS is close to that of EBRS, HLRS and both classes of DQSS, it remains less than that of OBCS under every load. The *BLP* of BBRS, EBRS, HLRS and both classes of DQSS remains close to zero until the load reaches 40 %; after this point, it increases with increasing L. In Fig. 6, we observe that OBCS offers better NT compared with both COBS and BBCS. When L is less than 40 %, NT of OBCS is close to that of BBCS and it increases with increasing L. When L is more than 40 %, NT of BBCS increases slowly and when L is more than 70 %, it will be less than NT of COBS. However, when L is more than 40 %, NT of OBCS becomes greater than that of BBCS and continues to increase with increasing L. BBRS, EBRS, HLRS and DQSS achieve the same NT under every load. At low load, the NT of BBRS, EBRS, HLRS and DQSS increases more rapidly than that of COBS, BBCS and OBCS. At high load, the NT of BBRS, EBRS, HLRS and DQSS remains almost constant and above than that of COBS, BBCS and OBCS. We interpret the above results as follows. In COBS, BBCS and OBCS, burst loss occurs at edge node and core node. COBS has no extra load because it uses no loss recovery mechanisms. Thus, COBS has better burst loss probability at edge node (LPE) and worse burst loss probability at core node (LPC). BBCS aims to reduce LPC by cloning all new arriving bursts that leads to saturation of burst queue. Consequently, BBCS suffers from high LPE. In OBCS, the edge node prevents saturation of burst queue by disabling the burst cloning mechanism when the load is high. OBCS achieves an optimal combination of LPE and LPC than COBS and BBCS. Consequently, OBCS has better BLP and NT than COBS and BBCS. In BBRS, EBRS, HLRS and DQSS, burst loss occurs only in edge node. The extra load of retransmission increases as the load increases until the burst queue is near to saturation state; after this point, if no action is taken such as in BBRS, the burst queue is saturated, which leads to a loss of both new arriving and retransmitting bursts. EBRS prevents saturation of burst queue at high load by disabling burst retransmission mechanism. This technique keeps more opportunity for new arriving bursts at high load when burst retransmission becomes inefficient to reduce burst lost. In order to allow each transmitted burst more opportunity to avoid retransmission, HLRS efficiently uses the unused bandwidth of EBRS at low load through burst cloning mechanism. DQSS uses also this unused bandwidth but only for burst of CoS_2. Thus, BBRS, EBRS, HLRS and both classes of DQSS achieve the same BLP. Consequently, BBRS, EBRS, HLRS and DQSS achieve the same NT.

7 Conclusion

In this paper, three schemes are proposed for star OBS networks to improve bandwidth utilization while keeping burst delay as low as possible. The first scheme is an enhanced burst retransmission scheme, which aims to control the retransmissions through a simple technique to enable/disable burst retransmission mechanism. The second scheme is a hybrid loss recovery mechanism, which aims to integrate efficiently burst cloning and burst retransmission mechanisms. The third scheme is a differentiated QoS scheme that provides differentiation between two classes in terms of burst delay by using burst cloning and burst retransmission. We analytically modeled basic burst retransmission scheme, enhanced burst retransmission scheme, hybrid loss recovery scheme and differentiated QoS scheme over star networks. The results obtained from simulation present a good agreement with analytical results. We found that the proposed schemes achieve high bandwidth utilization; compared to basic burst retransmission scheme, the first scheme reduces burst delay only at moderate and high load, however, the second and third scheme reduce delay at every load; the third scheme can offer also a good differentiation in terms of burst delay.

References

1. Qiao, C., Yoo, M.: Optical burst switching (OBS) — a new paradigm for an Optical Internet. J. High Speed Netw. **8**(1), 69–84 (1999)
2. Yao, S., Mukherjee, B., Dixit, S.: Advances in photonic packet switching: an overview. IEEE Commun. Mag. **38**(2), 84–94 (2000)
3. Baldine, I., Rouskas, G.N., Perros, H.G., Stevenson, D.: JumpStart: a just-in-time signaling architecture for WDM burst-switched networks. IEEE Commun. Mag. **40**(2), 82–89 (2002)
4. Huang, X., Vokkarane, V.M., Jue, J.P.: Burst cloning: a proactive scheme to reduce data loss in optical burst-switched networks. In: Proceedings of IEEE International Conference on Communications (ICC), Seoul, South Korea, May 2005
5. Riadi, S., Maach, A., El Ghanami, D.: An opportunistic burst cloning scheme for optical burst switching over star networks. J. Microw. Optoelectron. Electromagnet. Appl. **12**(SI-2), 167–180 (2013)
6. Zhang, Q., Vokkarane, V.M., Wang, Y., Jue, J.P.: Evaluation of burst retransmission in optical burst-switched networks. In: Proceedings of IEEE BROADNETS, pp. 276–282, October 2005
7. Maach, A., Bochmann, G., Mouftah, H.T.: Robust optical burst switching. In: Proceedings of Networks 2004, Vienna, Austria, pp. 447–452, June 2004
8. Agustí-Torra, A., Bochmann, G., Cervelló-Pastor, C.: Retransmission schemes for optical burst switching over star networks. In: Proceedings of the 2nd IFIP International Conference on Wireless and Optical Communications Networks, WOCN 2005, Dubai, UAE, March 2005
9. Li, H., Thng, I.L.-J.: Edge node buffer usage in optical burst switching networks. Photon Netw. Commun. **13**(1), 31–51 (2007)
10. Little, J.D.: A proof for the queueing formula $L = \lambda W$. Oper. Res. **9**, 383–387 (1961)
11. ns-2 Network Simulator (2009). http://www.isi.edu/nsnam/ns
12. OIRC OBS-ns Simulator (2009). http://wine.icu.ac.kr/~obsns/index.php

A Formal Driving Behavior Model for Intelligent Transportation Systems

Afaf Bouhoute$^{(\boxtimes)}$, Ismail Berrada, and Mohamed El Kamili

LIM, Faculty of Science, USMBA, Fez, Morocco
{afaf.bouhoute,ismail.berrada,mohamed.elkamili}@usmba.ac.ma

Abstract. Vehicular Ad hoc Networks are considered recently as a fertile field of research. Their applications are showing a growing importance as they are expected to improve road safety and traffic efficiency, through the development of vehicle safety applications whose main goal is to provide the driver with assistance in dangerous situations. Thanks to vehicular communications, drivers can permanently receive information about road conditions which help them to make more reliable decisions. The idea behind this paper is to enable an adaptive assistance to drivers in different situations, based on their past driving experience. As a first step, we focus on the modeling and learning of individual driving behavior at a picoscopic level. This paper proposes a formal description of a driver-centric model, using the formalisms of hybrid IO automata and rectangular automata. Then, an online passive learning based approach for the construction of the described model is proposed. Having a model that describe the behavior of drivers can enable us to predict and recognize a driver preferences in different driving context, enabling thus an adaptive assistance.

Keywords: VANET · Driver behavior modeling · Hybrid I/O automata · Rectangular automata · Behavior learning

1 Introduction

With the fast development in wireless and sensor technologies, Vehicular ad-hoc networks (VANETs) have emerged as a core component of intelligent transportation systems (ITS). The main goal of VANETs is to enhance traffic safety and efficiency by enabling the exchange of information among connected cars. The amount of information that can be disseminated through vehicular communication provides a great opportunity for the development of driver assistance systems. Equipped with a sophisticated on-board unit (OBU), vehicles are able to collect information about road conditions, driving situations and other vehicle's information. This information can be used to make driving more convenient by providing a reliable assistance to the driver and warn him in-time about potential danger and hazardous situations. Thus, the driver will have a better chance to avoid and react properly to dangerous situations. Despite the important role of

© Springer International Publishing Switzerland 2014
G. Noubir and M. Raynal (Eds.): NETYS 2014, LNCS 8593, pp. 298–312, 2014.
DOI: 10.1007/978-3-319-09581-3_21

the dissemination of information in road safety, the behavior of drivers towards this information remains a dominant factor for safety enhancement. The motivation of this work is to enable an adaptive driving assistance to individual drivers, based on their observed behavior in the previous encountered driving situations. Therefore, we focus primarily on the modeling of driving behavior. Driving behavior models were considered by researchers as a promising tool to develop advanced assistance systems, allowing the emergence of driver's adapted vehicles. We assume that the analysis and study of these models are important to predict the behavior of drivers, thus ensuring safer roads.

In this paper, we investigate the description and construction of a driver-adapted behavior model in the context of VANET, taking into account the different real time information and warnings a driver receives while driving. A new formal framework for capturing and modeling driving behavior is then proposed. This behavior can be captured using mixed discrete and continuous parameters. This is why we chose the hybrid automata formalism as a basis of our approach. To describe the proposed framework, we define the formalism of Rectangular Hybrid I/O Automata (RHIOA) with urgent transitions. Then to gather and encode driving behavior within the proposed framework, an online-passive learning based approach using the theory of Learning Automata (LA) is proposed. The constructed model will represent the behavior of the individual driver according to which it was built, and can be used to provide him with a personalized assistance. The rest of the paper is structured as follows. Section 2 presents related works. A formal description of the framework of our model is given in Sect. 3. In Sect. 4, we describe driving behavior within the proposed framework. The approach used for the construction of the model is presented in Sect. 5. Then in Sect. 6, we clarify our approach using an example of application of our model. Section 7 concludes and draws perspectives.

2   Related Work

Driving behavior has been recently investigated by many studies, leading to the appearance of a huge variety of behavioral models. Driving behavior models have different purposes, and differ in terms of strategies and approaches used to capture the driving behavior. A schematic grouping of these approaches is presented in [2]. In this section, we give examples of some of these models presented in the literature.

The work proposed in [3] aims to model the driving behavior to detect if the driver is distracted due to a secondary task. Steering wheel angle, brake status, acceleration status and vehicle speed were used as parameters to model the behavior. The models were then evaluated to classify driving actions (long term behavior/constant or neutral driving), detect the driver distraction and identify the driver by his driving behavior characteristics. The paper [12] focuses on the impact of contextual information on the driver's performance, and tries to model and recognize driver maneuvers. After a training stage, seven driver maneuvers were modeled. The proposed behavior model was able to recognize and classify the maneuver 1 second before any significant change in the car signals. In [16], two different and complementary approaches were proposed. The goal of these approaches was to obtain generic model (driver independent model of the maneuvers and the route) that can be used for driver identification and distraction detection. The authors of [8] propose an analysis of car-pedal use and car-following habits to build driver models that were evaluated in driver identification.

Other researchers have focused on the modeling of driving behavior in specific scenarios. In [11], the lane change scenario was modeled based on the steering behavior. The model recognizes three different maneuvers: lane keeping, normal lane change and emergency lane change. The paper [7] proposes a situation aware predictive braking system that implements predicted behavioral information, vehicle information and surrounded information in the braking system. Therefore, the system will be able to identify the need for braking action and detect if a braking action is planned by the driver. An application of the learning of driver behavior in an adaptive cruise control system was presented in [14]. The goal of [14] is to optimize the interactions between drivers and the system by automatically adjusting the gap setting based on driver type and the context of the drive. According to the driving style, three types of drivers were defined: hunter, glider and follower. In [15], a series of experiments was conducted to learn and model the usual behavior of drivers at the stop sign before an intersection. The model was used to detect deviations from the usual behavior and to decide if assistance is necessary. In [13], a Partially Autonomous Driving Assistance System is proposed. The system provides the driver with a longitudinal support to avoid collisions in a car following situation. The considered scenario is divided into three stages: the pre-collision, the collision warning and the automatic emergency braking. For the first two stages, the driver is in complete control of the vehicle while the system takes the full control in the case of the emergency braking. A reinforcement learning scheme is used to find an optimal warning and intervention strategy for the assistance system. A probabilistic approach for driving behavior prediction was considered in [5]. It considers an intersection situation and focuses on the prediction of the stop probability during a driver's side turn.

A recent approach of modeling presented in [17] uses concepts from behavioral psychology. The authors consider driving behavior as a result of an optimization process. They formalize their idea within a formal framework of hybrid automata, and introduce a theoretical variable to represent the consequences of possible behavior. A scenario of a driver entering the freeway was used as a Testbed to evaluate their model. Although the authors use hybrid automata to model and predict qualitatively distinct driving maneuvers, they do not consider a decision process. The goal of their model is to find an optimal driving trajectory for a given situation.

Most of the researches presented in the literature rely on modeling approaches to create prototypes models that allow them to classify the observed driving behavior. They focus mainly on the driver behavior without taking into account the information about the driving environment. In this paper, we intend to fill

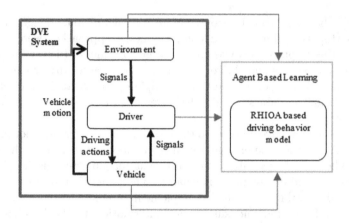

Fig. 1. The framework of the proposed model

the lack of approaches that address the human driving behavior in the context of VANET. In contrast to the researches presented above, we propose an approach that tries to construct a model for an individual driver based on his observed behavior, taking into consideration the reaction of the driver to different traffic information received either from VANET or from on-board sensors.

3   Presentation of the Modeling Framework

The design of a framework for modeling human driving behavior is a challenging task that might be faced with several limiting factors, such as:

- The diversity of parameters intervening in driving, that have to be included within the framework.
- The interactions of the model with the external environment.
- The approach used to gather and encode knowledge within the model.

Even though the driver is the main actor in the driving activity, the environment in which the driver is moving and the driven vehicle play an important role in the determination of driving behavior. Driver, Vehicle, Environment and their interactions are referred to as DVE system [10]. In this paper we describe a new framework for a driver-centered modeling of driving behavior. The overall framework of our approach is represented in Fig. 1. The goal of our approach is to model the observed driving behavior of an individual driver. The model captures:

- Signals received from the external environment (e.g. traffic signs, collision warnings, traffic information...)
- Signals received from the vehicle (e.g. played music, phone call...)
- Driving actions performed by the driver.

The description of our framework relies on a mix of notions from the theories of hybrid input/output and rectangular automata. Hybrid IO Automaton (HIOA) is a well known formal model, which can be used to describe discrete and continuous behavior of a system. It is a kind of finite state machine with a set of continuous variables. HIOA has been widely used to describe and analyze different examples of hybrid transportation systems, such as automotive control systems, automated transportation systems and intelligent vehicle highway systems. Rectangular automata are an important subclass of hybrid automata that was proposed to deal with decidability questions about hybrid automata. Their advantage consists of providing a better analysis of hybrid systems.

Our formal model consists of an adaptation of hybrid IO automata [6] and rectangular automata [4] with urgent transitions [1]. Hybrid I/O automata allows us to differentiate input and output actions, while rectangular hybrid automata allows us to define rectangular inequalities over variables. And, we express urgency using the concept of urgent transitions. Urgent transitions are transitions that occur as soon as their guard becomes true, without any delay. Formally, we define Rectangular Hybrid I/O Automaton with urgent transitions (RHIOA) as a tuple $(H,U,Y,Q,\Theta,inv,E,I,O,urgent,D)$, where:

- H is a set of internal variables, U is a set of input variables and Y is a set of output variables. H,U and Y are disjoint from each other and we write $X \triangleq H \cup U \cup Y$.
- $Q \subseteq val(H)$ is a set of states, where $val(H)$ is the set of valuations of H.
- Θ is a set of initial states.
- $inv : Q \rightarrow Rect(H)$ is an invariant function, where $Rect(H)$ is the set of all rectangular predicates over H. A rectangular predicate ϕ over H is a conjunction of rectangular inequalities; it defines the set of vectors $[\![\phi]\!] = \{z \in \mathbb{R}^n \mid \phi\,[H := z]\,is\,true\}$. A rectangular inequality over H is a formula $h_i \sim c$, where $h_i \in H$, c is an integer constant and $\sim$ is one of $<, \leq, >, \geq$. The function inv maps each state to its invariant condition.
- E,I and O are sets of internal, input and output actions, respectively. An internal action of E will be denoted later by "?".
- D is a set of discrete transitions. A discrete transition is labeled with an action, and is defined as a triple (q, o, g, q') where q is a source state, o is an action, $g \in Rect(H)$ is a guard on the transition, and q' is a target state. To simplify, if the guard is true we will only refer to a transition as a triple (q, o, q').
- $urgent$ is a set of urgent transitions.

4   Description of Driving Behavior Model Using RIOHA

The idea of our modeling approach is to capture and analyze the driving behavior in a continuous basis. The goal is to be able to characterize the driving behavior in a specific state within specific environmental conditions. We distinguish three categories of driving behavior:

- Convenient behavior: is a driving behavior that is in compliance with the environmental conditions. Environmental conditions are determined as the traffic rules, hazardous events... An example of convenient driving behavior is when the driver respects the speed limitation on a road.
- Tolerable behavior: is every behavior deviated with a predefined value from the convenient behavior. The deviation has a predetermined value. For example, exceeding the speed limited by a traffic sign with 10 % can be tolerable.
- Risky behavior: is a behavior of driver who does not respect the environment conditions. For example, an overtake maneuver on road where overtaking is prohibited is characterized as risky.

By continuously observing the driver, the system characterizes his behavior in real time as one of the categories cited above. While driving, the driver may also transit between them. In this section, we will firstly present a description of a convenient driving behavior model. Then, we extend it by integrating a description of the risky driving behavior.

4.1   Convenient Driving Behavior

The proposed model is a description of the behavior of a driver in interaction with the vehicle and the driving environment. The driver receives information about roads from the environment, and makes control decisions. Vehicles receive the control decisions from the driver and move in the environment accordingly. Following the driver, the automaton describing the driving behavior is supposed to be in a state. A state is defined by a set of internal variables. We restrict ourselves to the parameters presented in Table 1 (the variables *clock* and *isSafe* are related to risky behavior, their semantic is explained later). This set might be extended later with additional variables, such as GPS position, physical state of the driver, weather... For the availability of these parameters, we assume that the vehicle is equipped with a set of sensors capable of measuring the value of the vehicle's parameters.

The automaton resides in a state q as long as the variables stay inside the invariant interval $[\![inv(q)]\!]$. $inv(q)$ is conjunction of rectangular inequalities presented in Fig. 2. The Domains D_V, D_{lane}, D_d, D_θ contain the values used as boundaries to construct the inequalities. As a domain of velocity, we can use the values of speed panels provided by the traffic code. This will allow us to have a set of speed intervals which will be useful to characterize the behavior of the driver related to an encountered speed panel. The same goes for the other domains; they can be constructed based on the panels defined by the traffic code. The information transmitted to the driver (received from the environment) is modeled as input actions of the automaton while the driving actions performed by the driver are represented as output actions. The set of input actions consists of signals and events received from the vehicle or the environment, either using the different on-board sensors and/or a vehicular communication. Table 2 resumes some of the possible input and output actions used by our model. Transitions are defined as triples (q, l, q'), where q is a source state, l is a label associated

Table 1. List of internal variables

Parameter		Description
V		Velocity
lane		Lane used by the vehicle
d		Following distance
θ		Steering angle $(-30 < \theta < 30)$
Vehicle characteristics	l	Length of the vehicle
	w	Width of the vehicle
	h	Height of the vehicle
	m	Weight of the vehicle
clock		System clock used to control the period of time the vehicle can be in the current state
isSafe		Locally controlled variable to determine if a state is safe

$V \sim c$	$/c \in D_v$	$l \sim c$	$/c \in D_l$
$lane \sim c$	$/c \in D_{lane}$	$w \sim c$	$/c \in D_w$
$d \sim c$	$/c \in D_d$	$h \sim c$	$/c \in D_h$
$\theta \sim c$	$/c \in D_\theta$	$m \sim c$	$/c \in D_m$

Fig. 2. Rectangular inequalities over H

to the transition and is expressed as a couple (I/O) [where I is an input action received in state q and O is an output action performed according to I], and $q\prime$ is a target state.

4.2   Risky Driving Behavior

The driving environment plays a crucial role to determine the category of driving behavior. In our model, we characterize driving according to the contextual situation determined by a received input. Therefore, we extend the model described in the previous paragraph by defining:

- The set of input variables presented in Table 3. Input variables are determined by the received input actions; they provide the allowed values corresponding to the internal variables of Table 1. For example, if an input action limiting the speed to 90 km h is received, the system receives also the input variable $speed_{max} = 90$. These variables are used later to construct predicate on urgent transitions.
- The new state internal variable $isSafe$ used as etiquette to evaluate the safety of the current state.

Table 2. Example of eventual input and output actions

Input actions		Output actions
Traffic signs based	VANET warnings	
- Max/min speed limit	- Collision warning	- Accelerate
- Stop	- Accident warning	- Turn right
- Min safety distance	- Traffic congestion warning	- Change lane
- No turn left/right	- Emergency vehicle warning	- Maintain speed
- No U-turn	- Parking space allocation	- Give way
- No overtaking		- Decelerate
- One way		- Turn left
- Closed road		- Overtake
- Length/Width limit		- Stop
- Height limit		- Go straight
- weight limit		- Make U turn

Table 3. The Set of input variables

Input variables		
Minimum allowed values	Maximum allowed values	Description
$speed\_min$	$speed\_max$	Allowed speed
$lane\_min$	$lane\_max$	Allowed lane
$min\_headway$	$max\_headway$	Allowed headway distance
θ_min	θ_max	Allowed steering angle
$lentgh\_min$	$lentgh\_max$	Allowed length of the vehicle
$width\_min$	$width\_max$	Allowed width of the vehicle
$height\_min$	$height\_max$	Allowed height of the vehicle
$weight\_min$	$weight\_max$	Allowed weight of the vehicle

- The internal variable *clock* used to represent the time. The automaton can be tolerated to be in a temporary safe state for a predetermined period of time. This period is controllable by a timer, the system moves automatically to an unsafe state once this timer expires.

5   Construction of the Driving Behavior Model

The previous paragraph describes the characteristics of our model. However, it does not determine how the adapted model will be constructed. The construction of the model consists mainly of the filling of the set D of transitions. This set is initially empty and will be learned based on the observed behavior of the driver. Thus, we ensure the construction of personalized models that depend on driving characteristics of individual drivers. We propose the use of the theory of learning automata [9] as a base of our approach. Through an online passive learning process, the learning agent will construct the driving behavior model by observing the interactions between the driver, vehicle and environment. The set of states in learning automata has to be finite.

5.1   Convenient Driving Behavior

The construction of the behavior model includes the definition of states, transitions between states and transition probabilities. The states consist of disjoint valuations of the internal variables, and we associate to each state an invariant condition. The sets D_i (where $i = V, lane, d, \theta, l, w, h, m$) are supposed to be finite. Therefore, the set of states is also finite. Transitions are enabled when a change of state, with or without reception of input actions, is observed. We suppose that the system is capable of recognizing driver actions, and transitions are stochastic. Without any prior information about the driver behavior, the set of transitions is empty. The role of the Learning Agent (LA) is to learn the possible transitions according to the observed driving behavior and their probabilities. The initial state of the system is the state that assigns 0 to variables $(V, lane, d, \theta)$. The scheme of the process of construction is as follows.

- The LA is initially in state $q_{initial}$.
- The LA observes the driver and his interactions with the vehicle and the environment.
- If the driver receives an input I_j and performs an output action O_i that changes the current state of the system to $q\prime$, a new transition $tr = (q, (I_j/O_i), q\prime)$ is added to the set of transitions.
- If the driver receives an input I_j, performs an output action O_i without a change in the current state, the transition $tr = (q, (I_j/O_i), q)$ is added to the set of transitions.
- If the driver receives an input I_j and does not perform any output action, the transition $tr = (q, (I_j/?), q)$ is added to the set of transitions.
- If the driver performs an output action O_i without a reception of an input action, a new transition $tr = (q, (?/O_i), q\prime)$ [or $tr = (q, (?/O_i), q)$ if we stay at the same state] is added to the set of transitions.
- The LA updates the probabilities of transition based on the following reinforcement scheme; the probability is distributed over the outgoing transitions from q. A transition with high probability is a transition that was frequently traversed by the automaton.

$$P(q, tr) = P(q, tr) + \frac{1}{r}(1 - P(q, tr))$$

$$P(q, tr\prime) = P(q, tr\prime) + \frac{1}{r}(P(q, tr\prime)), for \ tr \neq tr\prime$$

(1)

Where $P(q, tr)$ is the probability of transition tr in q, r is the number of enabled transitions outgoing from q and $tr\prime$ is a transition outgoing from q.

The constructed automaton will refer to all the possible states and weighted transitions (I/O), (?/O) and (I/?) that have been explored by the driver.

5.2 Risky Driving Behavior

The determination of risky driving behavior consists of an evaluation of the safety of a state. This evaluation is possible by verifying if the variables of the current state respect the values determined by input variables. Let $Vect = \{(h_1, h_2, ..., h_n)|h_i \in H\}$ a vector of the current values in a state q. Input variables are divided into two vectors U_{min} and U_{max} for minimum and maximum allowed values. We define the following rectangular inequalities (RI).

- $RI_1 : Vect \leq U_{max}$ if for all $i, Vect_i \leq U_{max_i}$
- $RI_2 : Vect \geq U_{min}$ if for all $i, Vect_i \geq U_{min_i}$
- $RI_3 : Vect \leq U_{min}$ if for all $i, Vect_i \leq U_{min_i}$
- $RI_4 : Vect \geq U_{max}$ if for all $i, Vect_i \geq U_{max_i}$
- $RI_5 : Vect \geq U_{min} - \epsilon$ if for all $i, Vect_i \geq U_{min_i} - \epsilon$
- $RI_6 : Vect \leq U_{max} + \epsilon$ if for all $i, Vect_i \leq U_{max_i} + \epsilon$
  With ϵ a vector of tolerable deviation values over H.

A rectangular predicate ϕ is defined as a conjunction of rectangular inequalities: $\phi = \bigwedge_i RI_i$. We define three predicates:

- $\phi_1 = RI_1 \wedge RI_2$ defines the rectangular constraint $Vect \in [U_{min}, U_{max}]$.
- $\phi_2 = RI_3 \wedge RI_4$ defines the rectangular constraint $Vect \notin [U_{min}, U_{max}]$.
- $\phi_3 = RI_5 \wedge RI_6$ defines the rectangular constraint $Vect \in [U_{min} - \epsilon, U_{max} + \epsilon] \backslash [U_{min}, U_{max}]$.

Based on the classification of driving behavior provided previously, we define 3 levels of safety of a state q:

- Safe state: refers to a convenient behavior. We say that a state is safe, if the current values $Vect$ satisfy the predicate ϕ_1.
- Temporarily safe state: refers to a tolerable behavior. We say that a state is temporarily safe, if the current values $Vect$ satisfy the predicate ϕ_3 (the predicate ϕ_1 with a tolerable deviation of ϵ).
- Unsafe state: refers to a risky behavior. We say that a state is unsafe, if the current values $Vect$ satisfy predicates ϕ_2.

Based on these safety levels, we can define 3 possible values of $isSafe$:

$$q.safe = \begin{cases} -1 & \text{if } Vect \in [\![\phi_2]\!] \\ 0 & \text{if } Vect \in [\![\phi_3]\!] \\ 1 & \text{if } Vect \in [\![\phi_1]\!] \end{cases}$$

The definition of $isSafe$ and its semantic is considered as important for evaluating driving behavior and identifying risky behaviors due to infringements of the traffic code. It is useful for example to capture and model the behavior of

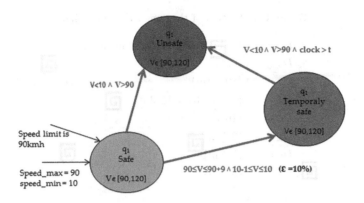

Fig. 3. Example of risky behavior

a driver who exceeds the speed limit, and take relative actions, such as warning the driver, controlling the vehicle or sending alerts to the Police. The modeling of this risky behavior is an extension of the convenient behavior model, by adding to every state q (safe state) two other associated states q_{unsafe}, q_{T_safe} referring to the unsafe and temporary safe versions of the state q. The values of internal variables of the new states remain the same; expect the value of the variable $isSafe$. The transitions between $safe$, $temporarily\_safe$ and $unsafe$ states are modeled as internal guarded urgent transitions:

- $q_{safe} \overset{\phi_2}{\rightarrow} q_{unsafe}$
- $q_{safe} \overset{\phi_3}{\rightarrow} q_{T\_safe}$
- $q_{T\_safe} \overset{\phi_2 \wedge clock > t}{\longrightarrow} q_{unsafe}$

Figure 3 shows an example of the modeling of a risky behavior in a state where the speed is limited to 90. To simplify, the example shows only the invariant of the velocity and the input variable $speed_{max}$. The system in state q compares the current value of speed with the input value $speed_{max} = 90$. If a little deviation is detected and this latter is tolerable, the system moves internally to a temporary safe state. Otherwise if the value of V is far away from the tolerable speed, the system moves to an unsafe state. The system can authorize to stay in a temporary safe state until the expiration of a timer t. The timer has a predetermined value that varies according to situations. Once this latter is expired, the system moves to an unsafe state. Depending on the applications, an action can be taken in temporary safe and unsafe states such as warning the driver or sending alerts to authorities through a vehicular communication.

6   Example of Driving Behavior Modeling

In this section, we present an example of human driving behavior modeling based on the model described in the previous section. To determine the invariants of

Table 4. Definition of the constraints domains

$D_V =$	$\{0, 30, 50, 70, 90, 110, 240\,\mathrm{km\,h}\}$
$D_{lane} =$	$\{0, 1\}$
$D_d =$	$\{50, 70\,\mathrm{m}\}$
$D_\theta =$	$\{-30, -15, 0, 15, 30°\}$
$D_l =$	$\{10\,\mathrm{m}\}$
$D_w =$	$\{2, 5\,\mathrm{m}\}$
$D_h =$	$\{3, 5\,\mathrm{m}\}$
$D_m =$	$\{5, 5\,\mathrm{m}\}$

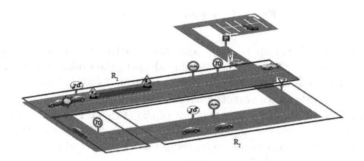

Fig. 4. Scenario of the example

states, we restrict ourselves to some of the existing traffic signs. The set of states is constructed by forming disjoint combinations of intervals of variables defined based on the sets in Table 4. Based on these sets, 2304 states are constructed.

Let use as an example the scenario shown in Fig. 4. The driver of the blue car is driving from and to the parking through a non-motorway main route. The road consists of two-lanes and one way, and we want to model the behavior of the driver during one trip. As already explained, inputs are received from the encountered traffic panels and vehicles. To explain our approach for model construction, we suppose that the driver behaves as shown in Table 5. This latter contains for every input received the output actions performed by the driver, this latter can also perform some driving actions without the reception of inputs. For a better comprehension, we represent only the states explored by the model following the example of the supposed behavior; the description of the states is given in Table 6. To illustrate the evolution of the construction of the automaton, we decompose the route traveled by the driver into 2 parts (R1, R2). The driver is initially in the state q_1, the evolution of the model is shown in Figs. 5 and 6. The red and orange states refer to temporary and unsafe states.

The constructed automaton corresponds to the supposed behavior of the driver in one trip, exploration of other states and the updates of transitions probabilities are possible in next trips. The goal of the proposed example is

Table 5. Description of inputs and outputs

Received input		Driver's output
Action	Variable	
-	-	O_2: Accelerate
I_2: give right of way	$speed_{min} = 0$ $speed_{max} = 20$	O_5: Give way
-	-	O_2: Accelerate
I_1: allowed speed 70 km h	$speed_{max} = 70$	O_1: Decelerate
I_3: No overtaking	$lane_{min} = 0$ $lane_{max} = 0$	O_3: Keep lane
I_4: Road construction	$lane_{min} = 1$ $lane_{max} = 1$	O_4: Change lane
I_5: End of road construction	$lane_{min} = 0$ $lane_{max} = 0$	O_4: Change lane
I_6: End of allowed speed	$speed_{min} = 0$ $speed_{max} = 120$	O_2: Accelerate
I_7: Accident warning	$lane_{min} = 0$ $lane_{max} = 0$ $\theta_{min} = 5$	O_4: Change lane
-	-	O_4: Change lane
I_1: allowed speed 70kmh	$speed_{max} = 70$	O_1: Decelerate
-	-	O_4: Change lane
I_3: No overtaking	$lane_{min} = 0$ $lane_{max} = 0$	O_3: Keep lane
I_2: give right of way	$speed_{min} = 0$ $speed_{max} = 20$	O_5: Give way
-	-	O_2: Accelerate
I_8: Parking	$speed_{min} = 0$ $speed_{max} = 20$	O_1: Decelerate

Table 6. Description of states

State ID	Description			
	V	lane	θ	d
q_1	[0,30]	0	[0,15]	$> V/2$
q_2	[30,50]	0	[0,15]	$> V/2$
q_3	[50,70]	0	[0,15]	$> V/2$
q_4	[50,70]	1	[0,15]	$> V/2$
q_5	[70,90]	0	[0,15]	$> V/2$
q_6	[70,90]	1	[0,15]	$> V/2$

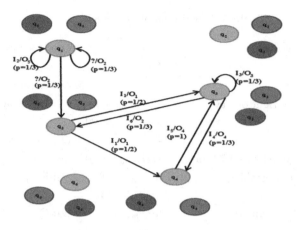

Fig. 5. First step of construction (part R_1)

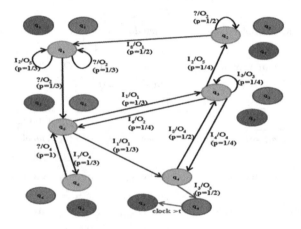

Fig. 6. The completed driving behavior model of the scenario

to illustrate the idea of our modeling approach and how it can be applied. We mention that our model and the learning scheme used to construct it are not completely implemented yet.

7 Conclusion

The analysis and prediction of driving behavior through human driving models is considered as an important step in the development of adaptive assistance systems. In this paper, we proposed a driver-centric approach to model the driving behavior in vehicular ad-hoc networks. A formal description of our model was given using the framework of hybrid I/O automata. The theory of stochastic learning automata was then used to define transitions and construct the automaton. The idea of our work is to construct the automaton following the observed behavior of individual drivers. To explain the idea of our modeling approach, an example of driving behavior in road scenario was presented. This paper is considered as an introduction of our work, the implementation of the model and the learning process used to construct it a considered as further work.

References

1. Barbuti, R., Tesei, L.: Timed automata with urgent transitions. Acta Informatica **40**(5), 317–347 (2004)
2. Boyraz, P., Sathyanarayana, A., Hansen, J.L., Jonsson, E.: Driver behavior modeling using hybrid dynamic systems for driver-aware active vehicle safety. In: Proceedings of the Enhanced Safety of Vehicles, pp. 1–8 (2009)
3. Choi, S., Kim, J., Kwak, D., Angkititrakul, P., Hansen, J.H.L.: Analysis and classification of driver behavior using in-vehicle can-bus information. In: Biennial Workshop on DSP for In-Vehicle and Mobile Systems, pp. 17–19 (2007)
4. Henzinger, T.A., Kopke, P.W.: Discrete-time control for rectangular hybrid automata. Theor. Comput. Sci. **221**(1), 369–392 (1999)
5. Kumagai, T., Sakaguchi, Y., Okuwa, M., Akamatsu, M.: Prediction of driving behavior through probabilistic inference. In: Proceedings of the 8th International Conference Engineering Applications of Neural Networks, pp. 117–123 (2003)
6. Lynch, N., Segala, R., Vaandrager, F.: Hybrid i/o automata. Inf. Comput. **185**(1), 105–157 (2003)
7. McCall, J.C., Trivedi, M.M.: Driver behavior and situation aware brake assistance for intelligent vehicles. Proc. IEEE **95**(2), 374–387 (2007)
8. Miyajima, C., Nishiwaki, Y., Ozawa, K., Wakita, T., Itou, K., Takeda, K., Itakura, F.: Driver modeling based on driving behavior and its evaluation in driver identification. Proc. IEEE **95**(2), 427–437 (2007)
9. Narendra, K.S., Thathachar, A.L.M.: Learning Automata: An Introduction. Courier Dover Publications, New York (2012)
10. Ni, D.: Picoscopic Modeling. Lecture Notes in Traffic Flow Theory (2013)
11. Nobuyuki, K., Tomohiro, Y., Osamu, S., Andrew, L.: A driver behavior recognition method based on a driver model framework. SAE Trans. **109**(6), 469–476 (2000)
12. Oliver, N., Pentland, A.P.: Driver behavior recognition and prediction in a smartcar. In: AeroSense 2000, pp. 280–290. International Society for Optics and Photonics (2000)
13. Pietquin, O., Tango, F., et al.: A reinforcement learning approach to optimize the longitudinal behavior of a partial autonomous driving assistance system. In: ECAI, pp. 987–992 (2012)
14. Rosenfeld, A., Zevi, B., Goldman, C.V., Kraus, S., LeBlanc, D.J., Tsimhoni, O.: Learning driver's behavior to improve the acceptance of adaptive cruise control. In: IAAI (2012)
15. Sakaguchi, Y., Okuwa, M., Takiguchi, K., Akamatsu, M.: Measuring and modeling of driver for detecting unusual behavior for driving assistance. In: Proceedings of 18th International Technical Conference on the Enhanced Safety of Vehicles (2003)
16. Sathyanarayana, A., Boyraz, P., Hansen, J.H.L.: Driver behavior analysis and route recognition by hidden markov models. In: IEEE International Conference on Vehicular Electronics and Safety, ICVES 2008, pp. 276–281. IEEE (2008)
17. Schwarze, A., Buntins, M., Schicke-Uffmann, J., Goltz, U., Eggert, F.: Modelling driving behaviour using hybrid automata. IET Intell. Transport Syst. **7**(2), 251–256 (2013)

Short: Blind Separation of the Multiarray Multisensor Systems Using the CP Decomposition

Awatif Rouijel[1]([✉]), Khalid Minaoui[1], Pierre Comon[2],
and Driss Aboutajdine[1]

[1] University Mohamed V-Agdal, LRIT Associated Unit to the CNRST-URAC N29,
Avenue des Nations Unies, Agdal, BP.554, Rabat-Chellah, Morocco
awatifrouijel@gmail.com
[2] GIPSA-Lab, CNRS UMR5216, Grenoble Campus, BP.46,
38402 St Martin d'Heres Cedex, France

Abstract. Sensor arrays are used in many applications, where their ability to localize signal sources is essential. One of the sensor applications is the signal processing of multi antennas with multi sensors. In this paper, we present an application of the proposed Canonical Polyadic decomposition (CP decomposition), with isolation of scaling matrix to multiarray multisensor systems. A simple blind receiver based on the enhanced alternating least squares (E-ALS) algorithm is presented. For illustrating this application, computer simulations are provided and demonstrate the good behavior of these algorithm compared to the old ALS algorithm.

Keywords: CP decomposition · Multiarray · Multisensor · Blind separation · Optimization · ALS

1 Introduction

For many years, systems with multiple sensors have been used to receive or send signals through a wireless channel [1]. Sensor array systems have several advantages over single sensor systems. First, they can increase the signal-to-noise ratio (SNR). Second, sensor arrays can steer the transmitting or receiving beams, then multiple signals can be separated. This is very useful in applications such as multi-user wireless communications which require the processing of as many signals as possible without mutual interference, and passive radar which need to localize signal source locations.

Recently, the use of multi-linear algebra methods has attracted attention in several areas such as data mining, signal processing and particularly in wireless communication systems. Wireless communication data can sometimes be viewed as components of a high order tensor (order larger than 3). Solving the problem of source separation returns then to find a decomposition of this tensor and

© Springer International Publishing Switzerland 2014
G. Noubir and M. Raynal (Eds.): NETYS 2014, LNCS 8593, pp. 313–318, 2014.
DOI: 10.1007/978-3-319-09581-3_22

determining its parameters. One of the most popular tensor decompositions is the CP decomposition, which decomposes the tensor into a sum of rank-one components [2]. The interest of the CP decomposition lies in its uniqueness under certain conditions, and it has been exploited and generalized in several works, for solving different signal processing problems [3] such as multi-array multi-sensor signal processing [4]. The typical algorithm for finding the CP components is alternating least squares (ALS) optimization. As proposed in [5, 6], this algorithm neglect the scaling matrix in the optimization process. Herein, we propose an improvement of ALS optimization algorithms taking into account the scaling matrix in the CP decomposition. An application of the proposed Algorithm to multiarray multisensor system is presented. The proposed multiarray multisensor system is a tensor of three dimensions: the first one represents the number of sensors, the second one is equal to the number of arrays and the third one defines the length of transmitted signal.

2   Notation

Let us first introduce some essential notation. Vectors are denoted by boldface lowercase letters, e.g., $\mathbf{a}$; matrices are denoted by boldface capital letters, e.g., $\mathbf{A}$. Higher-order tensors are denoted by boldface Euler script letters, e.g., $\mathcal{T}$. The pth column of a matrix $\mathbf{A}$ is denoted $\mathbf{a}_p$, the (i, j) entry of a matrix $\mathbf{A}$ is denoted by A_{ij}, and element (i, j, k) of a third-order tensor $\mathcal{T}$ is denoted by T_{ijk}. The outer (tensor) product is represented by the symbol $\circ$, the Kronecker product by $\otimes$ and The Frobenius norm by $\|\mathcal{T}\|_F$.

Any tensor $\mathcal{T}$ admits a decomposition into a sum of rank-1 tensors, called CP decomposition. In the case of a 3rd order tensor, this decomposition takes the form below:

$$\mathcal{T} = \sum_{r=1}^{R} \lambda_r \mathbf{a}_r \circ \mathbf{b}_r \circ \mathbf{c}_r \tag{1}$$

Denote by $()^T$ matrix transposition, λ_r real positive scaling factors, and R the tensor rank. Vectors $\mathbf{a}_r$ (resp. $\mathbf{b}_r$ and $\mathbf{c}_r$) live in a linear space of dimension I (resp. dimension J and K).

As given in (1), the explicit writing of decomposable tensors is subject to scale indeterminacies. In the tensor literature, optimization of the CP decomposition (1) has been done without taking into account scaling factor $\mathbf{\Lambda}$. In [7], we propose to pull real positive factors λ_r outside the product, which permits to monitor the conditioning of the problem. Scaling indeterminacies are then clearly reduced to unit modulus but are not completely fixed.

3   Existence and Uniqueness

In the literature, the existing results in [8] showed that under certain conditions, a third-order tensor of rank R can be uniquely represented as sum of

R rank-1 tensors. In practice, it is preferred to adapt to a lower multi-linear model of a fixed rank $R < rank\{T\}$, so that we have to deal with a problem of approximation. The best rank-R approximate is defined by the minimum of the objective function:

$$\Upsilon(\mathbf{A}, \mathbf{B}, \mathbf{C}, \mathbf{\Lambda}) = \|T - \sum_{r=1}^{R} \lambda_r A_{ir} B_{jr} C_{kr}\|_F^2 \tag{2}$$

By expanding the Frobenius norm in (2), and canceling the gradient with respect to $\boldsymbol{\lambda}$, we will calculate the optimal value of $\mathbf{\Lambda}$, which satisfy the following linear system:

$$\mathbf{G}\boldsymbol{\lambda} = \mathbf{f} \tag{3}$$

where $\mathbf{f}$ is R-dimensional vector and $\mathbf{G}$ represents the $R \times R$ Gram matrix defined by: $G_{pq} = (\mathbf{a}_p \otimes \mathbf{b}_p \otimes \mathbf{c}_p)^H (\mathbf{a}_q \otimes \mathbf{b}_q \otimes \mathbf{c}_q)$. In view of matrix $\mathbf{G}$, we can see that the coherence plays a role in the conditioning of the problem, and has deeper implications, particularly in existence and uniqueness of the solution to Problem (2). See [7] for further details.

4   Algorithm for CP Decomposition

The Alternating Least Squares (ALS) algorithm is the classical solution to minimize the objective function (2) [9]. In this paper we propose a new version of the ALS algorithm, that we call E-ALS (Enhanced Alternating Least Squares). E-ALS consists to estimate one of the three loading matrices at each step by minimizing the function error (2) and taking into account the scaling matrix $\mathbf{\Lambda}$.

The E-ALS algorithm can be described by the pseudo-code below:

1. Initialize $(\mathbf{A}(0), \mathbf{B}(0), \mathbf{C}(0))$ to full-rank matrices with unit-norm columns.
2. Compute $\mathbf{G}(0)$ and $\mathbf{f}(0)$, and solve $\mathbf{G}(0)\,\boldsymbol{\lambda} = \mathbf{f}(0)$ for $\boldsymbol{\lambda}$, as defined in Sect. 3 by (3). Set $\mathbf{\Lambda}(0) = \text{Diag}\{\boldsymbol{\lambda}\}$.
3. For $k \geq 1$ and subject to a stopping criterion, do
    (a) Estimate $\mathbf{A}(k)$: $\widehat{\mathbf{A}} = \mathbf{T}^{I,KJ}(\mathbf{\Lambda}(k-1)(\mathbf{C}(k-1) \odot \mathbf{B}(k-1))^\dagger)^T$
    (b) Update $\mathbf{A}(k) = \widehat{\mathbf{A}}$
    (c) Estimate $\mathbf{B}(k)$: $\widehat{\mathbf{B}} = \mathbf{T}^{J,KI}(\mathbf{\Lambda}(k-1)(\mathbf{C}(k-1) \odot \mathbf{A}(k))^\dagger)^T$
    (d) Update $\mathbf{B}(k) = \widehat{\mathbf{B}}$
    (e) Estimate $\mathbf{C}(k)$: $\widehat{\mathbf{C}} = \mathbf{T}^{K,JI}(\mathbf{\Lambda}(k-1)(\mathbf{B}(k) \odot \mathbf{A}(k))^\dagger)^T$
    (f) Update $\mathbf{C}(k) = \widehat{\mathbf{C}}$
    (g) Normalize the columns of $\mathbf{A}(k)$, $\mathbf{B}(k)$ and $\mathbf{C}(k)$
    (h) Compute $\mathbf{G}(k)$, $\mathbf{f}(k)$ and solve Eq. (3) for $\boldsymbol{\lambda}$. Set $\mathbf{\Lambda}(k) = \text{Diag}\{\boldsymbol{\lambda}\}$,

where $(\ )^\dagger$ denotes the Moore-Penrose pseudo inverse. The convergence at the kth iteration is declared when the error between tensor T and its reconstructed from the estimated loading matrices, does not significantly change between iterations k and $k+1$ (a change smaller than a predefined threshold).

5   Application to Multi Array Multi Sensor System

Sensor arrays consist of multiple sensors which are located at different points in space. In other words, the array signal is a propagating signal sampled both spatially and temporally by the sensor array. We assume that there are J arrays having the same number I of sensors, where two different arrays may share one or more sensors. The sensors are located in space by a vector $\mathbf{m}_i \in \mathbb{R}^2$, $i = 1, \cdots, I$, and the $J - 1$ subarray are deduced from the reference array, by translation in space defined by $\Delta_j \in \mathbb{R}^2$, $j = 1, \cdots, J$. Lets P signals impinge on an array from P different directions. The signal received by the sensor i in the jth array at discrete time k, can be written as:

$$S_{i,j}(k) = \sum_{p=1}^{P} \sigma_p(k) \exp(\jmath \frac{\omega}{C}(\mathbf{m}_i^T \mathbf{d}_p + \Delta_j^T \mathbf{d}_p)) \tag{4}$$

where $\sigma_p(k)$ denotes the complex envelope of the pth source, ω is the central pulsation, C the wave celerity, $\jmath^2 = -1$ and $\mathbf{d}_p$ is direction of arrival of the pth path. Now, rewriting $T_{ijk} = S_{i,j}(k)$, $A_{ip} = \exp(\jmath \frac{\omega}{C} \mathbf{m}_i^T \mathbf{d}_p)$, $B_{jp} = \exp(\jmath \frac{\omega}{C} \Delta_j^T \mathbf{d}_p)$ and $C_{kp} = \sigma_p(k)$, gives us the relation resembling the CP decomposition:

$$T_{ijk} = \sum_{p=1}^{P} \lambda_p A_{ip} B_{jp} C_{kp} \tag{5}$$

Hence, estimating the signal waveforms $\sigma_p(k)$ and the directions of arrival $\mathbf{d}_p$ is then equivalent to decompose the tensor $\mathcal{T}$ into a sum of P contributions.

5.1   Computer Simulations

In this section, we present some simulation results for illustrating the performances of the proposed blind receiver of Multiarray Multisensor system. In this experiment, we consider a multiarray multisensor system with, $J = 3$ arrays, $I = 4$ sensors and $P = 6$ sources of size $K = 10$. As presented in Fig. 1, the arrays are composed of 4 sensors located by the matrix $\mathbf{M}$. The sensors are linearly placed and the arrays 2 and 3 are obtained by a translation Δ. The angles-of-arrival are $(-90, -60, -30, 0, 30, 60)$. Figure 2 illustrates the performance of our blind receiver E-ALS and those of the ALS receiver. These results indicate that the proposed receiver E-ALS gives a better estimation of signal waveforms matrix $\mathbf{C}$ than the ALS one. By computing the CP decomposition of tensor $\mathcal{T}$ of Eq. (5), it is possible to estimate the directions of arrival d_p of each propagation path if $\mathbf{m}_i$ or Δ_j are known. Figure 3 illustrates the directions of arrival (DOAs) estimations as a function of SNR. From this figure, we can see an exact estimation of the angles of arrival for the SNR higher than zero.

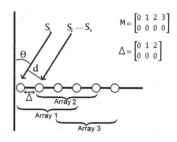

$$M = \begin{bmatrix} 0 & 1 & 2 & 3 \\ 0 & 0 & 0 & 0 \end{bmatrix}$$

$$\Delta = \begin{bmatrix} 0 & 1 & 2 \\ 0 & 0 & 0 \end{bmatrix}$$

Fig. 1. Sensor array example with linear arrays.

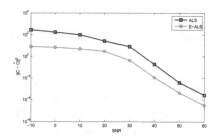

Fig. 2. Matrix Estimation error (MEE) versus SNR results for scenario: $I = 4$, $J = 3$, $K = 10$, $P = 6$ and $(\theta_1, \theta_2, \theta_3, \theta_4, \theta_5, \theta_6) = (-90, -60, -30, 0, 30, 60)$.

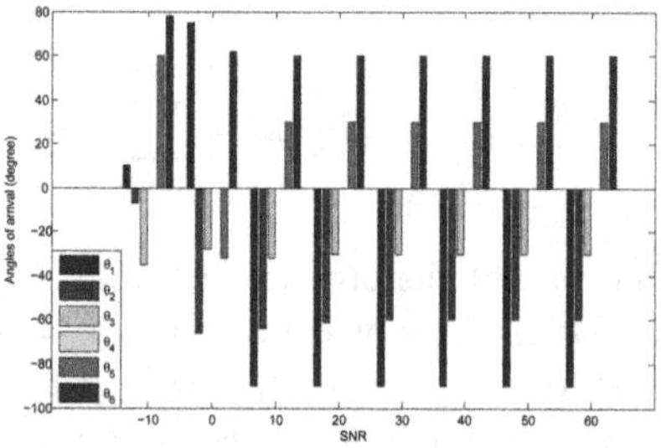

Fig. 3. Angles of arrival Estimation versus SNR results for scenario: $I = 4$, $J = 3$, $K = 10$, $P = 6$ and $(\theta_1, \theta_2, \theta_3, \theta_4, \theta_5, \theta_6) = (-90, -60, -30, 0, 30, 60)$.

6   Conclusion

This paper presents an enhanced version of ALS algorithm, which take into account the scaling matrix. The conditioning of the optimal scaling matrix Λ computation depends on coherences via a Gram matrix. An application of the CP decomposition to Multiarray Multisensor system has been presented. Finally, the computer simulations demonstrate the good behavior of our algorithm, compared to the classical ALS one used in the literature, and its usefulness in Multiarray Multisensor applications.

References

1. Johnson, D., Dudgeon, D.: Array Signal Processing: Concepts and Techniques. Prentice Hall, Englewood Cliffs (1993)
2. Harshman, R.A.: Foundations of the PARAFAC procedure: models and conditions for an "explanatory" multi-modal factor analysis. UCLA working papers in phonetics, pp. 1–84 (1970)
3. Comon, P.: Tensor decompositions, state of the art and applications. In: IMA Conference on Mathematics in Signal Processing, Warwick, UK (2000)

4. Lim, L.-H., Comon, P.: Multiarray signal processing: tensor decomposition meets compressed sensing. Compte-Rendus Mcanique de l'Academie des Sciences **338**(6), 311–320 (2010)
5. Comon, P., Luciani, X., De Almeida, A.L.F.: Tensor decompositions, alternating least squares and other tales. J. Chemometrics **23**, 393–405 (2009)
6. Acar, E., Dunlavy, D.M., Kolda, T.G.: A scalable optimization approach for fitting canonical tensor decompositions. J. Chemometrics **25**, 67–86 (2011)
7. Comon, P., Minaoui, K., Rouijel, A., Aboutajdine, D.: Performance index for tensor polyadic decompositions. In: 21th EUSIPCO, Marrakech, Morocco (2013)
8. Kruskal, J.B.: Three-way arrays: rank and uniqueness of trilinear decompositions. Linear Algebra Appl. **18**, 95–138 (1977)
9. Smilde, A.K., Bro, R., Geladi, P.: Multi-way analysis. Applications in the Chemical Sciences. Wiley, Chichester (2004)

Short: A Lightweight and Secure Session Management Protocol

Yassine Sadqi$^{(\boxtimes)}$, Ahmed Asimi, and Younes Asimi

Information Systems and Vision Laboratory,
Department of Mathematics and Computer Sciences, Faculty of Sciences,
Ibn Zohr University, Agadir, Morocco
{yassine.sadqi,asimiahmed2008,asimi.younes}@gmail.com

Abstract. Secure session management is a challenging problem for Web applications. In fact, three of the ten most critical security risks included in the OWASP top ten 2013 can lead to session hijacking attacks. Best practices advocate the transmission of the session identifiers over HTTPS. However, this approach does not solve the session problems, and can't be deployed on a wide range of HTTP-only applications. This paper presents a lightweight session management design deployed over HTTP, which allows much of the existing infrastructure of the web to remain unchanged, while at the same time strengthening authentication. Our work leverages the following key insights. (1) Users already have shared secrets with their web applications (e.g. password). (2) HTTPS is primarily used to protect the authentication information. (3) A secure session management should be built on a secure initial mutual authentication. Our proposed protocol guaranties the authenticity, confidentiality, integrity, and anti-reply of authentication credentials.

Keywords: Session management · Authentication · HTTP/HTTPS · Web application

1 Introduction

The Hypertext Transfer Protocol (HTTP) is a stateless protocol, which means that an HTTP server cannot determine if two different requests come from the same user. Unfortunately, almost all modern Web applications need a mechanism to keep track of user's personal settings and authentication information. This task is known as session management. In particular, because session management plays a key role in today Web authentication, it is a prime target of malicious attacks. Instead of stealing the user's original credentials, a wide range of attacks focus on session management weaknesses. Beside that they are two motivations for the research presented in this paper. The first is the enormous demand for secure Web session management. For instance, between the OWASP Top ten security risks of 2010 and 2013, "broken authentication and session management" has raised from the third to the second position [1]. The second is the absence of a lightweight and secure approach that protect the confidentiality and integrity of user authentication security parameters (e.g. password, session identifier). Best practices advocate the transmission of session identifiers over HTTPS. However,

© Springer International Publishing Switzerland 2014
G. Noubir and M. Raynal (Eds.): NETYS 2014, LNCS 8593, pp. 319–323, 2014.
DOI: 10.1007/978-3-319-09581-3_23

this approach does not solve session problems, and cannot be deployed on a wide range of HTTP-only applications [2, 3]. In this paper we show the most common vulnerabilities of session management, the current solutions to overcome these vulnerabilities and their limitations. Finally, a high level overview a lightweight novel approach for secure session management is presented.

2   Current State of Web Authentication

2.1   Authentication Phases

At first, personal websites employed the built-in HTTP authentication specification. The RFC 2617 defines the digest scheme as an extension for HTTP/1.1. It is a security enhancement alternative that avoids most serious flaws of basic HTTP authentication. However, it is known that both basic and digest authentication contain multiple security risks.

Currently with the wide adoption of dynamic web programming, HTTP authentication is used rarely in real-world web application. In fact the dominant scenario for user authentication includes two related phases [4]:

1. Login: In this phase, the web application provides a mechanism for initial user authentication to verify the user identity using a special authenticator.
2. Session management: After successful login phase, the web application associates a unique session identifier (SID) with this specific client. Next, the web application sends the SID to that client as part of an HTTP server response. The web application then identifies the client using an association between a specific user and its SID. Without this phase, a user would have to reenter the authentication credentials in each HTTP request.

2.2   Session Management Vulnerabilities

Until the writing of this paper, there is no standard mechanism for session management. This means that each web application built its unique session management system. As a result, session management vulnerabilities will generally belong to either: (1) Defects in the generation of session identifiers (SIDs), or (2) defects in the handling of SIDs throughout their lifecycle: while they are at rest (e.g., on hard disk), and while they are in transit (e.g., during login). Although most today web applications rely on mature platforms mechanism to generate session identifiers [3], none of them offer a complete secure session management.

Furthermore, our analysis to current session management practices concluded that one of the root causes of sessions attacks is the bearer token concept [5]. For instance, any party in possession of a valid session ID can use it to access the associated user protected resources no matter what channel over which the session identifier is transmitted or whoever presents it. Specifically, the static nature of the session IDs on a specific period of time (i.e. cookie life time) provides attackers with a hijacking window [6], which gives the attacker a change to impersonate a legitimate user, during the life time of this session identifier. Therefore, even with the submission of authentication parameters over HTTPS, an attacker profits from the hijacking window, to execute one of the well-known session attacks to retrieve the token.

2.3   Current Solutions

Several protocols have been proposed to improve the security of session management. X. Liu et al. [4] demonstrated the shortcomings of multiple cookie security enhancement propositions [7–9] and present a secure cookie scheme based on a hashed-based message authentication code (HMAC) and HTTPS.

Dietz et al. [5] proposed a new TLS extension. It is based on the origin bound certificate concept (OBC). Unlike typical certificates, and their use in SSL/TLS client authentication, an OBC is generated by the browser without the user's interaction, as needed and contains no user-identification information. It is primarily used to establish an authenticated channel between the browser and the web application that can be later reestablished. To strengthen cookie-based authentication and withstand network active attacks, the scholars presented channel bound cookie in that the generated session identifier is associated with the client's origin bound certificate (OBC).

Dacosta et al. [2] presented One Time Cookie (OTC), a solution that guarantees session integrity of HTTP request and resist session hijacking attacks. OTC relies on HTTPS in its set up phase to share a secret key, which is used to generate dynamic single-user authentication token for each request. Additionally, an OTC token is tied to the requested resources.

While these solutions are helpful to build strong Web session schemes, we primary identified two key limitations: (1) The security of all these protocols either require a full HTTPS deployment, or rely on HTTPS in its set up phase, especially to exchange secrets parameters [2, 10]. (2) Multiple schemes built secure session management on a weak initial user authentication [2, 4, 7, 10]. It is known that a system is only as strong as its weakest point. Therefore, we cannot build a secure session management on a weak initial authentication. Otherwise, some of the most secure and robust methods can be easily compromise the login phase (e.g. phishing, Cross-Site Request Forgery).

3   High-Level Overview of Our Solution

Our work leverages the following key insights: (1) HTTP-only applications lack a secure session management mechanism (which represent in some large Web study 41 % of all tested applications [11]). (2) A secure session management should be built on a secure initial mutual authentication. (3) Users already have shared secrets with their web applications (e.g. password).

As a solution, our proposed protocol should assure the authenticity, confidentiality, integrity and anti-reply of user's initial login and URL requests authentication credentials (i.e. password and the shared master session key). Therefore, we plan to construct LSSM from the following basic building blocks:

- *Server side authentication using public key certificate*: Our protocol does not require HTTPS deployment, but does not abundant server authentication based on a public key certificate. After receiving the server certificate and a digital signature using the associated server private key, the browser validates the server identity based on the same mechanism used in HTTPS. If succeed, the browser decrypts the digital signature via the public key of the certificate. Otherwise, halt the communication and shows a message error indicating a certificate or signature validation problem. In addition, *LSSM* security will not depend solely on the browser certificate validation, but add a second factor (i.e. the hash and salted password).
- *Asymmetric cryptography for secure session key establishing*: The browser generates a pre-master session key and encrypts it with the already validated server public key. We assume a valid certificate, thus only the server that possess the associated private key is able to decrypt the pre-master session key. After that, both the web application and the browser compute the master session key that will be used in the next step.
- *Trusted path for password entry and submission*: Transmitting passwords using HTML form attribute present several security threats [12]. Thus, in our work we will instead use a new private built-in browser window that enables users to enter their passwords. Furthermore, the password is never transmitted over the network. The browser uses only its hash and salted version to compute a unique signature based on hashed-based message authentication code (HMAC).
- *Request signature*: After a successful first login and secure key establishment, the browser generates a signature based on the already exchanged master session key and other parameters. This signature guaranties the requests authenticity and integrity.
- *Mutual authentication*: After each exchange, both the browser and the server verify the origin of each message base on the following parameters: (i) the pre-master and master session keys, (ii) the shared secret in the registration phase (e.g. the hash of the salted password), (iii) the secure random numbers generated by both the client and the server in each exchange.

4 Conclusion and Future Work

As we discussed secure session management is a challenging problem for Web applications. Best practices advocate the transmission of the session identifiers over HTTPS. However, this approach does not solve the session problems, and cannot be deployed on a wide range of HTTP-only applications. In this paper we presented a lightweight secure session management protocol (LSSM) deployed over HTTP, which allows much of the existing infrastructure of the web to remain unchanged, while at the same time strengthening authentication. We first overviewed the current state of user's authentication on the Web, and present the shortcomings of the most relevant proposed solutions. After that, we introduced a high-level overview of our work-in-progress. Future scope in this work is to develop a complete prototype implementation of the proposed solution. We also plan to give a security analysis to verify the security properties of user's authentication credentials. While LSSM needs to be lightweight, then we will provide extensive performance analysis on multiple platforms.

References

1. Open Web Application Security Project: TOP 10 2013. https://www.owasp.org/, https://www.owasp.org/index.php/Top_10_2013

2. Dacosta, I., Chakradeo, S., Ahamad, M., Traynor, P.: One-time cookies: preventing session hijacking attacks with stateless authentication tokens. ACM Trans. Internet Technol. TOIT **12**, 1 (2012)

3. Stuttard, D., Pinto, M.: The Web Application Hacker's Handbook Finding and Exploiting Security Flaws. Wiley, Indianapolis (2011)

4. Liu, A.X., Kovacs, J.M., Gouda, M.G.: A secure cookie scheme. Comput. Netw. **56**, 1723–1730 (2012)

5. Dietz, M., Czeskis, A., Balfanz, D., Wallach, D.S.: Origin-bound certificates: a fresh approach to strong client authentication for the web. In: Proceedings of 21st USENIX Security Symposium, 2012 (2012)

6. Wedman, S., Tetmeyer, A., Saiedian, H.: An analytical study of web application session management mechanisms and HTTP session hijacking attacks. Inf. Secur. J. Glob. Perspect. **22**, 55–67 (2013)

7. Fu, K., Sit, E., Smith, K., Feamster, N.: Dos and Don'ts of client authentication on the web. In: Proceedings of the 10th USENIX Security Symposium, pp. 251–268 (2001)

8. Park, J.S., Sandhu, R.: Secure cookies on the Web. Internet Comput. IEEE. **4**, 36–44 (2000)

9. Xu, D., Lu, C., Dos Santos, A.: Protecting web usage of credit cards using one-time pad cookie encryption. In: Proceedings of the 18th Annual Computer Security Applications Conference, 2002 , pp. 51–58 (2002)

10. Adida, B.: Sessionlock: securing web sessions against eavesdropping. In: Proceedings of the 17th International Conference on World Wide Web, pp. 517–524 (2008)

11. Bonneau, J., Preibusch, S.: The password thicket: technical and market failures in human authentication on the web. In: Proceedings of the 9th Workshop on the Economics of Information Security (2010)

12. Sandler, D., Wallach, D.S.: <input type="password"> must die. In: Presented at the Web 2.0 Security & Privacy (2008)

Short: Intrusion Detection Quality Analysis for Homogeneous Wireless Sensor Networks

Noureddine Assad[1][✉], Brahim Elbhiri[2], Sanaa El Fkihi[3],
My Ahmed Faqihi[3], Mohamed Ouadou[1], and Driss Aboutajdine[1]

[1] LRIT, Associated Unit to CNRST (URAC 29),
Med V-Agdal University, Rabat, Morocco
assad.noureddine@gmail.com
[2] EMSI Rabat, Rabat, Morocco
[3] RIITM, ENSIAS, Mohammed-V University Souissi, Rabat, Morocco

Abstract. In this paper we analyze the intrusion detection in a homogeneous Wireless Sensor Network that is defined as a mechanism to monitor and detect unauthorized intrusions or anomalous moving attackers in area of interest. The quality of deterministic deployment can be determined sufficiently by analysis, before the deployment. However, when random deployment is required, determining the deployment quality becomes challenging and depends directly on node density. The major question is centered on the network coverage problem, how can we guarantee that each point of the region is covered by the required number of sensors? To deal with this, probabilistic intrusion detection models are adopted, called single and multi sensing probability detection and the deployment quality issue is surveyed and analyzed in terms of coverage. We evaluate our probabilistic model in homogeneous wireless sensor network, in term of sensing range, node density, and intrusion distance.

Keywords: Intrusion detection probability · Problem coverage network · Sensing range and sensing detection

1 Introduction

Advances in technology have made possible to develop small low-cost devices, called sensors, which may be deployed in large numbers to form a wireless sensor network (WSN) that can be used in many applications. Each sensor senses a field of interest and communicates the collected data to the sink, where the end-user can access them [1]. This article focuses on WSN surveillance applications like detecting unauthorized/unusual moving intruders. Intrusion detection model introduces as parameters sensing range and node density. Each field of interest point must be within the sensing range of at least one sensor and a WSN must be able to adapt to changing network because an intruder may be detected by single or multi sensors, that is modeled by single or multi sensing detection.

Some works are targeted at particular applications, but the main idea is still centered on a coverage issue that is addressed by several authors. References [2,3]

© Springer International Publishing Switzerland 2014
G. Noubir and M. Raynal (Eds.): NETYS 2014, LNCS 8593, pp. 324–329, 2014.
DOI: 10.1007/978-3-319-09581-3_24

showed how well an area is monitored by sensors, while [4,5] derived analytical expressions to enhance the deployment quality because the network coverage concept is a measure of the quality of service. These issues are motivated by random network topology, which implies the efficient deployment of the required coverage. Specifically, given a monitoring region, how can we guarantee that each region point is covered by the required sensor number? Thus, we need to recognize which areas are covered by enough sensors, to enhance the intrusion detection probability and to limit an intruder to exceed a threshold distance.

This paper major contributions are developing a probabilistic approach by deriving analytical expressions to characterize topological properties of network coverage, designing and analyzing the intrusion detection probability in a homogeneous WSN in single and multi sensing detection. In Sect. 2, we analytically evaluate the intrusion detection model in a homogeneous WSN. Section 3 presents the simulation results while conclusions are drown in Sect. 4.

2 Intrusion Detection Model in a Homogeneous WSN

Intrusion detection in a WSN is defined as a mechanism to detect unauthorized intrusions or anomalous moving attackers, for deterministic node deployment. The deterministic deployment quality can be determined by analysis before deployment, however, when random deployment is required, it becomes challenging [6]. To assess a sensor deployment quality, it is fundamental to characterize WSN parameters like node density and sensing range, for high detection probability.

2.1 Collaborating Sensors

Consider two nodes N_i and N_j located at ξ_i and ξ_j respectively. N_k ($k = 1, 2$) covers the surface area S_{N_k}. Let us note d_{ij} the distance between N_i and N_j. The collaborating set of N_i and N_j is defined as the union between S_{N_i} and S_{N_j}. Besides, N_i and N_j are said to be collaborating if and only if $d_{ij} = |\xi_i - \xi j| \leq 2R_{SENS}$ (R_{SENS}: sensing range). In general, the collaborating sensor set N_i is:

$$S_{col}(N_i) = \cup_{\{N_j : |\xi_i - \xi_j| \leq 2R_{SENS}\}} S_{N_j} \qquad (1)$$

2.2 Sensing Model Probability

We consider a random network topology where all nodes are randomly deployed; we note λ its node density. We adopt a sensing model probability where sensor can detect any events located in its sensing area. All sensors are assumed to be homogeneous and have the same sensing coverage R_{SENS}. An intruder starts from a random WSN point and moves in a random fashion as illustrated in Fig. 1. The sensing model, where exactly k sensors detect the intruder, follows a poisson distribution:

$$P(k) = \frac{(S\lambda)^k}{k!} e^{(-S\lambda)} \qquad (2)$$

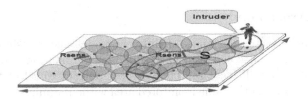

Fig. 1. An intruder starts from a random point in the WSN and moves in a random fashion, and sweeps the surface area S following a trajectory L.

where S is the area swept by the intruder following a trajectory L. It is given by

$$S = 2R_{SENS}L + \pi R_{SENS}^2 \tag{3}$$

2.3 Single-Sensing Detection

The probability that no sensor in an area of interest can detect an event is $\overline{P} = e^{-\lambda S}$. The complement of $\overline{P}$ is the probability that there is at least one sensor which detects an event. This sensing model probability is determined by:

$$P = 1 - \overline{P} = 1 - e^{-\lambda S} \tag{4}$$

According to the intrusion scenario given in Sect. 2.2, the probability that an intruder does not exceed the threshold distance L_{THR} is:

$$P(0 \leq L < L_{THR}) = 1 - e^{-(2R_{SENS}L_{THR} + \pi R_{SENS}^2)\lambda} \tag{5}$$

2.4 Multi-sensing Detection

In a WSN, the number of required sensors depends on the coverage quality. An area may require that multiple nodes monitor each of its points [7]. This constraint is known as k-coverage; where k is the number of nodes that watch each point. To achieve a coverage degree k, we derive the probability P that an intruder can be detected within threshold intrusion distance L_{THR} in k-sensing. The multi-sensing detection model is (S is given in Eq. (3)):

$$P(0 \leq L < L_{THR}) = 1 - \sum_{i=1}^{k} \frac{(S\lambda)^i}{i!} e^{-S\lambda} \tag{6}$$

While increasing the sensing coverage and the number of nodes per unit, the intrusion detection probability in single/multi sensing increases; all events that happen in the network, are covered. Optimal values of sensing coverage and node density to cover an area, can be determined in advance by the above formulas.

2.5   Node Availability

In a dense network, sensing areas of different nodes may be similar to their neighbor nodes, so nodes will transmit redundant information and WSN total energy consumption will increase. Thus, it is important to select the effective sensor number covering the same monitored area without diminishing the overall field coverage. It is appropriate to take into account the node availability rate p in our analysis. Each sensor can decide whether to become active with probability p or to move to the sleep mode with probability $1 - p$. So, the sensing model probability that exactly k sensors detect an intruder is:

$$P(n = k) = \frac{(Sp\lambda)^k}{k!} e^{(-Sp\lambda)} \tag{7}$$

The probabilities that an intruder can be detected without exceeding a threshold distance L_{THR} in an homogeneous WSN, with node density λ, sensing range R_{SENS} and node availability p, in the single and the multi sensing are:

$$P(0 \leq L < L_{THR}) = 1 - e^{-Sp\lambda} \tag{8}$$

$$P(0 \leq L < L_{THR}) = 1 - \sum_{i=1}^{k} \frac{(S)^i}{i!} e^{-Sp\lambda} \tag{9}$$

3   Discussions Results

In this section, we evaluate our intrusion detection model by using MATLAB software. We consider a random homogeneous WSN composed of static sensors which are independent and distributed uniformly in a square area 10×100.

The results illustrated in Fig. 2(a) show that the intrusion detection probability P is determined by the node density λ and the sensing range R_{SENS}. Intrusion detection may need a large sensing range or a high node density, thus increasing the WSN deployment cost.

We can note that if we increase the node density λ or the sensing range R_{SENS}, the probability to cover an intrusion happens in the network increases too. This is because the increase of sensing range/node density significantly enhances the network coverage. However, increasing more λ or R_{SENS} the probability attend 1 and remains constant, will not affect the robustness of detection. Consequently, for a given value of sensing range R_{SENS}, we can find the optimal node number which can be deployed to cover efficiently the controlled region and reciprocally. This node number and sensing range will be the optimal values, which must be used to totally cover an area of interest.

The Fig. 2(b) shows intrusion detection probability curves as a function of the intrusion distance for different values of node availability rate p. It is obvious that if the intrusion distance L increases, the detection probability P increases too. In the normal cycle, the node availability p is usually less than 1.0, it is considered

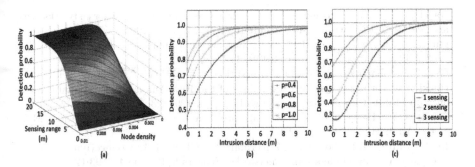

Fig. 2. (a) Intrusion detection probability as a function of node density and sensing range. (b) Intrusion detection probability withe different values of node availability. (c) Single-sensing detection probability versus multi-sensing detection probability.

to be satisfied to monitored an area as much as possible without diminishing the overall field coverage. If an intruder is detected by a node, an alarming message is broadcasting over the entire network, to improve the detection efficiency by assuring the network connectivity, it is illustrated by node availability rate $p = 1$.

We plot in Fig. 2(c), the detection probability in multi-sensing detection as a function of intrusion distance. The detection probability increases with the increase of the intrusion distance. At the same time, the single-sensing detection probability ($k = 1$) is higher than that of multi-sensing detection ($k = 2$ and $k = 3$). This is because the multi-sensing detection imposes a more strict requirement on detecting an intruder in the network, at least $k = 2$ ($k = 3$) sensors are required.

4   Conclusion

In this paper, we developed a probabilistic approach by deriving analytical expressions to characterize the topological properties of network coverage, designing and analysing the intrusion detection probability in a homogeneous WSN with taking into account various parameters such as sensing range, node density or availability, and intrusion distance. We investigate our model for intrusion detection in WSN to single-sensing and multi-sensing detection. Our results enable us to design and analyse the homogeneous WSN and help us to select the critical parameters of network in order to meet the WSN application requirements.

References

1. Akyildiz, I.F., Su, W., Sankarasubramaniam, Y., Cayirci, E.: Wireless sensor networks: a survey. Comput. Netw. **38**(4), 393–422 (2002)
2. Mulligan, R., Ammari, H.M.: Coverage in wireless sensor networks: a survey. Netw. Protoc. Algorithms **2**(2), 27–53 (2010)

3. Ravelomanana, V.: Extremal properties of three-dimensional sensor networks with applications. IEEE Trans. Mob. Comput. **3**(3), 246–257 (2004)
4. Onur, E., Ersoy, C., Deliç, H.: How many sensors for an acceptable breach detection probability? Comput. Commun. **29**(2), 173–182 (2006)
5. Gui, C., Mohapatra, P.: Power conservation and quality of surveillance in target tracking sensor networks. In: Proceedings of the 10th Annual International Conference on Mobile Computing and Networking, pp. 129–143. ACM (2004)
6. Huang, C.F., Tseng, Y.C.: The coverage problem in a wireless sensor network. Mob. Netw. Appl. **10**(4), 519–528 (2005)
7. Li, J., Andrew, L.L., Foh, C.H., Zukerman, M., Chen, H.H.: Connectivity, coverage and placement in wireless sensor networks. Sensors **9**(10), 7664–7693 (2009)

Short: A Case Study of the Performance of an OpenFlow Controller

Fouad Benamrane$^{(\boxtimes)}$, Mouad Ben Mamoun, and Redouane Benaini

LRI, Faculty of Sciences at Rabat, Mohammed V-Agdal University, Rabat, Morocco
benamranefouade@gmail.com,
{ben_mamoun,benaini}@fsr.ac.ma

Abstract. Over the last four years there has been significant growth in the interest that researchers and IT industry have shown in a new network architecture approach called Software-Defined Networking (SDN). This new approach is based on the separation between the control plane (routing decisions) and the data plane (packet forwarding). Communication between these two planes is mainly established today by the OpenFlow protocol. The interest of SDN is that it allows network programmability through applications acting on the control plane and hence it facilitates the development of new network protocols and services. However, there are some problems of performance and scalability when a single centralized controller is deployed in an SDN architecture. In this paper, we briefly introduce SDN, OpenFlow and review performance studies. After, we study through some experiments the performance issues of the Ruy OpenFlow controller especially in a large-scale network case.

Keywords: Software-defined networking · OpenFlow · Performances · Scalability

1 Introduction

The Internet has become a universal digital infrastructure essential for billions of people. Nevertheless, its architecture has some weaknesses in security, quality of service and performance and must cope with new needs due to the continuous increase in traffic and changing uses. However, because of the enormous installation of equipments and difficulty of testing new protocols in operational networks, this infrastructure has remained static and no significant progress has been made on its fundamental architecture in nearly three decades. The initial objective of the "Software Defined Networks (SDN)" approach that has recently emerged is to solve this problem and open network infrastructure for innovation. The idea is to allow researchers to run experimental code on programmable switches and routers that could handle packets from the experimental traffic without disrupting the operation of the production network [1]. After the emergence of SDN, several recent work has shown that this approach is suitable for

© Springer International Publishing Switzerland 2014
G. Noubir and M. Raynal (Eds.): NETYS 2014, LNCS 8593, pp. 330–334, 2014.
DOI: 10.1007/978-3-319-09581-3_25

applications in various environments such as distributed data centers, wireless networks and enterprise networks [2,3].

In SDN architecture, the control plane is supported by centralized software application called a controller and the switches becomes simple packet forwarding devices. This architecture raises the problem of controller performance and its capacity to handle all the network devices, especially for large and highly distributed networks.

In this paper, we try to contribute to the efforts of analyzing performances of SDN controllers by studying the performances of Ryu OpenFlow controller [4] through some experiments. The paper is organized as follows: Sect. 2 is devoted to some works on performances of OpenFlow controllers. Section 3 presents the used tools and scenarios of the experiments. Simulation results are given in Sect. 4. Finally, we give some conclusions in Sect. 5.

2 Related Works

The OpenFlow protocol is an open source protocol normalized by the Open Networking Foundation (ONF) [5], it specifies how a software controller and a switch should communicate in an SDN architecture. Openflow allows users to implement rules into switches flow tables. The communication between the flow table and the remote controller will be established through Secure Shell (SSH), using the OpenFlow protocol agent to exchange messages and configuration management with the switch. Currently, there are several available OpenFlow controllers, for example, Floodlight [6], NOX [7] and Ryu [4]. The differences between these controllers relies on programming language, performances and application domain.

As SDN is a new technology, the performance issue is not yet sufficiently studied. We mention here some works that are interested in this problem. In [8], the authors present a study of SDN controller performance using some publicly-available OpenFlow controllers. They show that the problem of performances is not an intrinsic limitation of the SDN control plane, but of the available controllers which are not optimized for performance. To prove this, they propose a multi-threaded controller called NOX-MT (a new release of the NOX controller) that improves the performance of NOX by more than 30 times.

In [9], the authors consider the FloodLight OpenFlow controller and show how the latency between an OpenFlow switch and its controller affect the performances of the whole network. The SDN fundamental concept is to centralize the control plane through a single controller, but thereafter researchers suggest to deploy multiple controllers to manage different components of the network.

In [10], the authors studied the impact of the number of controllers to deploy and their placement on performances. They conclude that there are no placement rules that applies to every network and that the controllers number depends on the network topology and the metric choice. The mentioned works and also other studies show that there are many facets to analyze the performances of a network based on SDN approach.

In the next two sections, we consider the Ryu OpenFlow controller and perform some experiments to evaluate its scalability.

3   Study Description

In this section, we give a description of our testbed, we specify the hardware configuration and the different tools used in our experiments.

To emulate an SDN platform, we must have an SDN controller, an SDN software switch and an SDN emulation tool. In our testbed, we use the Ryu OpenFlow controller [4], which is based on python language and provides software components with well defined API. We also use a programmable switch called Open Vswich (OVS) [11], and the Mininet emulation environment [12], developed by Stanford University. We note that all the results shown in the next section depend on the lab device[1] used to conduct the experiment.

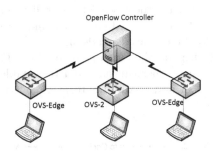

Fig. 1. Linear OVS topology

The goal of this study is to analyze the scalability issue. For this, we consider a basic network topology as shown in (Fig. 1), we vary the number of nodes and measure the network delay. We consider two scenarios with and without (w/o) centralized controller to clearly see the impact of the controller. In the first case, every packet sent to an unknown address will be delivered to the controller to decide what to do with it. The other case (w/o) corresponds to a proactive technique where we pre-populates the flow table in each switch before receiving the first packets from the data plane. In fact, the second scenario can be viewed as the limit case (for the first scenario) when the controller is never solicited. Hence, the delay difference between the two scenarios gives an idea about the delay caused by the solicitation of the controller.

In both cases, we generate an ICMP messages (Ping) and measure the time delay between the two edges. In the case without controller, this time is the sum of the traditional packet-network latency to which will be added flow setup time, the necessary time to insert the appropriate rules in each OVS flow table. In the other case, the flow setup time is added each time the controller receives a packet, hence the measured time is already the sum of all delays. In the next section, we give results of both scenarios.

---

[1] All senarios run in Ubuntu 12.04.3 LTS 3.2.0-57-generic-pae i686, gcc 4.8, Boost 1.46.1, Sun Java 1.6.0.27,Core(TM)2 Duo CPU, 2.00GHz. Ryu (v.3.2), Mininet (v.2.0) and Open vSwitch 2.0.90.

4   Simulation Results

There are various performance metrics to quantify for an SDN controller. We focus here on the latency metric (delay to respond to data path requests), which have an impact on the network time delay. Figure 2 gives this delay according to the OVS nodes number. We can observe that until 60 nodes, the delay difference between the two scenarios (with and w/o) is very low and becomes more important as the number of nodes increases. In fact, when the network size increases, the controller becomes much solicited and could not handle all the requests within a reasonable time. For example, in the case of 100 nodes, the time delay is equal to 4 s, while it's less than 2 s in the scenario without controller. We can also observe that up to 60 nodes, the delay is less than or nearly equal to a second, even in the case with controller. So, we can benefit from simplicity management of a centralized controller and a reasonable time delay. Obviously, the threshold of 60 nodes depends on this case study and may change according to the lab device and the considered topology. From this experiment, we can deduce that one controller can handle a reasonable number of switches such as a network of small and medium enterprise, but it could not handle a large-scale network.

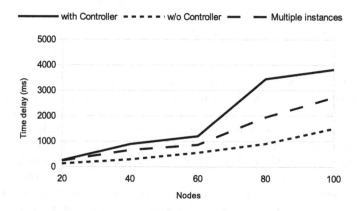

Fig. 2. Time delay variation according to the OVS nodes number of different scenarios

To investigate more the performances of one centralized controller, we propose to apply the multiple instances technique that is widely used in today's complex systems with virtualization technologies. In the previous experiment, the network is managed by only one instance of the controller. The exchanged messages (Packet_In, Packet_Out et Flow_mod) are on only one port (by default 6633), which can cause an overload on the controller in larger networks. In the multiple instances scenario, each instance manages a small part of the network and communicates with the nodes on a unique port. In Fig. 2, we consider the case of 4 instances. We can observe that the time delay decreases in comparison of the single instance case. Therefore, this technique alleviates the problem of scalability. However, we think that it is not sufficient to solve the problem.

5   Conclusion

SDN is undoubtedly one of the important trends in networking area. A large networking community in industry and academia is interested and works on different aspects of this topic. In this paper, we investigated the performance issue and focused especially on scalability. The results of our experiments confirm that effectively scalability may be an issue and a single centralized controller could not handle a large size network. The multiple instances technique may help to reduce the effect of the scalability limitation. However, we think that the real solution is to have several controllers and to design new protocols to communicate between controllers. We note that this idea has been already proposed in some works, but there is no protocol that was developed and tested yet in the best of our knowledge.

References

1. Casado, M., Freedman, M.J., Pettit, J., Luo, J., McKeown, N., Shenker, S.: Ethane: taking control of the enterprise. ACM SIGCOMM Comput. Commun. Rev. **37**, 1–12 (2007)
2. Wang, R., Butnariu, D., Rexford, J.: OpenFlow-based server load balancing gone wild. In: Proceedings of the 11th USENIX Conference on Hot Topics in Management of Internet, Cloud, and Enterprise Networks and Services, p. 12. USENIX Association (2011)
3. Bansal, M., Mehlman, J., Katti, S., Levis, P.: Openradio: a programmable wireless dataplane. In: Proceedings of the First Workshop on Hot Topics in Software Defined Networks, pp. 109–114. ACM (2012)
4. Ryu SDN framework. http://osrg.github.io/ryu
5. Open networking foundation. https://www.opennetworking.org/
6. Floodlight OpenFlow controller. http://floodlight.openflowhub.org/
7. Nox open controller. http://www.noxrepo.org/
8. Tootoonchian, A., Gorbunov, S., Ganjali, Y., Casado, M., Sherwood, R.: On controller performance in software-defined networks. In: USENIX Workshop on Hot Topics in Management of Internet, Cloud, and Enterprise Networks and Services (HotICE) (2012)
9. Phemius, K., Thales, M.B.: OpenFlow: why latency does matter. In: 2013 IFIP/IEEE International Symposium on Integrated Network Management (IM 2013), pp. 680–683 (2013)
10. Heller, B., Sherwood, R., McKeown, N.: The controller placement problem. In: Proceedings of the First Workshop on Hot Topics in Software Defined Networks, pp. 7–12 (2012)
11. Open vswitch. http://openvswitch.org/
12. Lantz, B., Heller, B., McKeown, N.: A network in a laptop: rapid prototyping for software-defined networks. In: Proceedings of the 9th ACM SIGCOMM Workshop on Hot Topics in Networks, p. 19 (2010)

Short: Gossip-Based Sampling in Social Overlays

Mansour Khelghatdoust$^{(\boxtimes)}$ and Sarunas Girdzijauskas

Royal Institute of Technology (KTH), Stockholm, Sweden
{mansourk,sarunasg}@kth.se

Abstract. Performance of many P2P systems depends on the ability to construct a random overlay network among the nodes. Current state-of-the-art techniques for constructing random overlays have an implicit requirement that any two nodes in the system should always be able to communicate and establish a link between them. However, this is not the case in some of the environments where distributed systems are required to be deployed, e.g., Decentralized Online Social Networks, Wireless networks, or networks with limited connectivity because of NATs/firewalls, etc. In this paper we propose a gossip based peer sampling service capable of running on top of such restricted networks and producing an on-the-fly random overlay. The service provides every participating node with a set of uniform random nodes from the network, as well as efficient routing paths for reaching those nodes via the restricted network.

Keywords: Peer sampling · Social overlay · Gossip · Random overlay

1 Introduction

At the heart of many gossip protocols, lies a *Peer Sampling Service*, which provides each node with a continuously changing random samples to ensure correctness of the protocols. The assumption of the existing gossip based sampling services, such as [3,6], is that a node can directly contact any other node from its sampled set. However, some applications do not allow such communication freedom between nodes. E.g., nodes behind firewalls, NATs or strictly friend-to-friend online social networks, where communications are limited to immediate friends only, mainly for privacy reasons. In this paper, we provide a solution for executing gossip based sampling service on restricted networks. We ensure that every node is provided not only with the set of random nodes but, crucially, with the routing directions towards these random nodes. I.e., each node maintains routing paths using only the available paths of the underlying restricted network. The main contribution of the paper is a novel on-the fly path pruning technique which exploits the local knowledge of the restricted network at the nodes that forward the gossip messages. The main target of this protocol is particularly for push based gossip applications where nodes update their state only if they have been selected as sample by any participating node to receive information.

© Springer International Publishing Switzerland 2014
G. Noubir and M. Raynal (Eds.): NETYS 2014, LNCS 8593, pp. 335–340, 2014.
DOI: 10.1007/978-3-319-09581-3_26

2 Solution

We model the underlying restricted overlay as an undirected graph with unweighted edges. We assume every node has knowledge (IP address) of its immediate neighbors and neighbors-of-neighbors. We also assume non-malicious behavior of the nodes, i.e., the nodes are willing to act as relay for message forwarding. Apart from knowledge of restricted overlay, nodes keep a fixed-sized and continuously changing cache of C entries of paths towards samples. Similar to [3], in order to acquire truly random samples at each node, nodes periodically exchange with each other the subsets of their caches, called *Swapping Cache*. In particular, in each round every node selects a copy of the longest waiting entry e from the cache, contacts it through routing path and sends to e a copy of swapping cache. Also, it receives a random subset of e's cache entries. Each node then updates its cache with the exchanged set. More precisely, each node updates its cache by replacing entries that are selected as swapping cache more (propagated more) in its cache with the received entries. In our experiments we show that such shuffling strategy converges very fast to random samples at each node and accordingly, a random overlay is continuously being constructed on the fly.

However, since cache entries to the sampled nodes indicate paths which always start at the source node, after swapping, cache paths do not indicate a path from recipient node to the sampled node. A naive way to solve this issue is to merge reversed path from source node to destination node with the path towards the sampled node in the swapped cache. The problem of this approach is that such paths grow prohibitively large and do not scale. We propose an algorithm to prune swapping cache paths upon forwarding gossip messages at each node by exploiting the local knowledge of nodes and discovering shortcuts locally. In this algorithm, source node, destination node and relay nodes (nodes within path) that are involved in a gossiping round execute this algorithm once they have received swapping cache. Every node parses the current path, and prunes it if it can construct a shorter path by using knowledge of its own routing tables or the tables of its neighbors. The message is continued to be relayed through the updated path. The details of the algorithm is given in (Algorithm 1).

Since the underlying restricted overlay can be arbitrary, the resulting routing paths will inevitably exhibit all range of lengths, and can be as short as one hop. Such variation in routing path lengths imply that the communication times between nodes will vary greatly during the exchange process. This in turn will create a bias in selection of random nodes. To this end, we introduce a delay mechanism and define two system parameters called α (maximum threshold of path length) and β (maximum delay). Recipient nodes reject paths with larger length than α to ensure having short length paths. Furthermore, length of gossiping rounds are equalized using β that is preferably equivalent to α. In other words, a gossiping round is postponed to a time that is obtained from the difference between β and the length of the selected path.

From practical perspective, each entry other than path consists of two variables. *WaitingTime*, represents time that entry is waiting to be selected for

---

Algorithm 1. PATH CONSTRUCTION

1: **function** RECONSTRUCT PATH(path)
2:      resultPath = *emptyList*
3:      **if** self.Id is sourceNode **then**   ▷ Current node is gossip round initiator
4:          resultPath.addFirst(self.Id)
5:          **return** resultPath
6:      **end if**
7:      **for all** *id* ∈ *path.reverse*() **do**
8:          **if** self.isNeighbor(id) **then**   ▷ id is immediate neighbor of current node
9:              resultPath.addFirst(id)
10:             **break**
11:         **else if** self.isTwoHopNeighbor(id) **then**   ▷ id is two-hop neighbor
12:             resultPath.addFirst(id)
13:             resultPath.addFirst(self.getNeighbor(id))
14:             **break**
15:         **else**
16:             resultPath.addFirst(id)
17:         **end if**
18:     **end for**
19:     **if** self.Id is relayNode **then**   ▷ Current node is within path acting as relay
20:         resultPath.addFirst(self.Id)
21:     **end if**
22:     **return** resultPath
23: **end function**

---

gossiping. *Swapped*, denotes the number of times that the entry was selected as one of the swapping cache entries in current node. The protocol is performed by letting the initiating peer P execute the following 9 steps:

1. Increase by one *waitingTime* of all entries.
2. Select copy of entry Q with the highest *waitingTime* from the cache, and copy of S − 1 other random entries as swapping cache.
3. Increase by one the *swapped* field of all selected S − 1 entries within cache.
4. Set *waitingTime* entry Q within cache to zero.
5. Execute path construction algorithm for all entries of the swapping cache.
6. Wait w.r.t delay, send updated cache to next node of the path towards Q.
7. Receive from one of its social neighbors of reverse path a subset of no more than S of Q's entries and execute path construction algorithm for them.
8. Discard the entries with a path longer than α (Maximum path length).
9. Update P's cache, by *firstly* replacing the same entries already existed with longer path, (if any), and *secondly* replacing entries with the highest *swapped*.

On reception of a swapping cache request, node Q randomly selects a copy of subset of its own entries, of size S, execute step 3 for S entries, executes step 5 and sends it to one of its social neighbors in the constructed reverse path, execute step 7, insert sender entry to the received swapping cache and executes steps 8, 9.

Table 1. DATASET

Data set	$|V|$	$|E|$	Type	Diameter
Wiki-Vote	7066	103663	Social	7
AstroPh	17903	197031	Collaboration	14
Facebook	63391	817090	Social	16

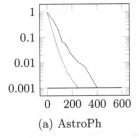
(a) AstroPh

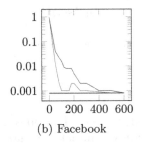
(b) Facebook

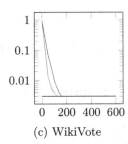
(c) WikiVote

Fig. 1. The figure shows clustering coefficient (CC). X and Y axis-es show cycle and average CC respectively. In blue and gray diagrams both α and β are set 2d and d respectively. Black line represents CC of random graph (Color figure online).

Any relay node involved in gossiping, execute path construction algorithm and cooperate in building reverse path.

3   Experiments

We implemented the algorithm on PEERSIM [5]. The properties of the graphs are given in Table 1. The clustering coefficient (CC) of a node is formulated by division of C over $N - 1$ that C is cache size and N is network size ($\frac{C}{N-1}$). We calculate it to ensure that CC of resulting overlay is equivalent to random overlay. Neighbors in random overlay are target nodes of paths within caches. Two scenarios are executed ($\alpha = d$, $\beta = d$; $\alpha = 2d$, $\beta = 2d$) where d is diameter of the network. (C = 20, S = 5). As Fig. 1 exhibits, CC of the graphs converge to random graph ensuring global randomness. Larger value for α increases the speed of convergence but gives better local randomness. In another experiment we evaluate In-degree distribution of nodes to see whether the sampling bias is removed in random graph. We calculate degree distribution of target nodes of paths over random graph. The ideal case is to have a degree distribution with low standard deviation. It ensures an unbiased sampling independent of node degrees in social graph. In Fig. 2, the results show a normal distribution in which 70 % of nodes have in degree 20 ± 20 %, a value between 16, 24 (C = 20). In the extended version of our work [4] we perform experiments with churn and show that our algorithm is robust to churn and correlated failures.

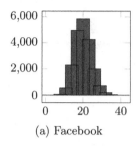

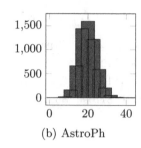

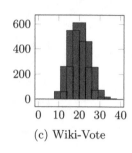

(a) Facebook   (b) AstroPh   (c) Wiki-Vote

Fig. 2. In-degree distribution. X-axis shows degree. Y-axis shows nodes count.

4   Related Work

In [1], a random walk based approach is proposed for sampling on restricted networks. Every node periodically initiates a Maximum Degree random walk, passing its own id and the random walk's mixing time as parameters and using reverse random walk as routing to construct view for keeping samples. This protocol assumes network size and maximum degree are known. So, it needs extra protocols to obtain them. It requires large mixing time and produced average path length is large. It is suitable for small size networks but might not scale in large networks. The idea of constructing a virtual overlay network on top of static networks has already been used in VRR [2]. It is a network routing protocol inspired by overlay routing algorithms in Distributed Hash Tables (DHTs) but it does not rely on an underlying network routing protocol. VRR routes using only fixed location independent identifiers that determine the positions of nodes in a virtual ring. Each node maintains a small number of paths to its virtual neighbors that can be used to forward messages between any pair of nodes. VRR has different usage from our algorithm. It solves routing problem on link layer networks while our algorithm addresses random sampling problem on such networks.

References

1. Bar-Yossef, Z., Friedman, R., Kliot, G.: RaWMS - random walk based lightweight membership service for wireless ad hoc networks. ACM Trans. Comput. Syst. (TOCS) **26**(2), 5 (2008)
2. Caesar, M., Castro, M., Nightingale, E.B., O'Shea, G., Rowstron, A.: Virtual ring routing: network routing inspired by DHTs. ACM SIGCOMM Comput. Commun. Rev. **36**, 351–362 (2006)
3. Jelasity, M., Voulgaris, S., Guerraoui, R., Kermarrec, A.-M., Van Steen, M.: Gossip-based peer sampling. ACM Trans. Comput. Syst. (TOCS) **25**(3), 8 (2007)
4. Khelghatdoust, M.: Gossip based peer sampling in social overlays. Master's thesis, The Royal Institute of Technology (KTH), Stockholm, Sweden (2014)

5. Montresor, A., Jelasity, M.: PeerSim: a scalable P2P simulator. In: Proceedings of the 9th International Conference on Peer-to-Peer (P2P'09), Seattle, WA, pp. 99–100, September 2009
6. Voulgaris, S., Gavidia, D., Van Steen, M.: Cyclon: inexpensive membership management for unstructured p2p overlays. J. Netw. Syst. Manag. **13**(2), 197–217 (2005)

Short: Graphical Specification and Automatic Verification of Business Process

Outman El Hichami[1]([✉]), Mohammed Al Achhab[2], Ismail Berrada[3],
and Badr Eddine El Mohajir[1]

[1] Faculty of Sciences, UAE, Tetouan, Morocco
el.hichami.outman@taalim.ma, b.elmohajir@ieee.ma
[2] National School of Applied Sciences, UAE, Tetouan, Morocco
alachhab@ieee.ma
[3] Faculty of Sciences and Technology, USMBA, Fez, Morocco
iberrada@univ-lr.fr

Abstract. This paper deals with the integration of the formal verification techniques of business process (*BP*) in the design phase. In order to achieve this purpose, we use the graphical notation of Business Process Modeling Notation (*BPMN*) for modeling *BP* and specifying constraint properties to be verified. A formal semantics for some response properties are given.

Keywords: Business process · BPMN · Dynamic behaviors · Formal verification

1 Introduction

Nowadays company has become more dependent on software systems, not only in safety-critical areas, but also in areas such as finance and administration. Emerging methods for enterprise systems analysis rely on the representation of work practices in the form of business processes modeling [1]. The Business Process Modeling Notation (*BPMN*) [2] is a standard notation used for business process modeling in order to define, analyze and deploy Business Processes (*BP*). It provides symbols to a simple graphical specification for defining the control flow of the business process in the early phases of process development.

In this paper, we propose the integration of the formal verification techniques of *BPMN* models in the design phase. Most specification formalisms in this domain are a bit tricky to use. To make them easier to use, our patterns come with descriptions that illustrate how to map well-understood, conceptions of *BP* behavior into precise statements in common formal specification languages like linear temporal logic (*LTL*) [3] and computation tree logic (*CTL*) [4]. We are particularly interested in responses properties.

Unlike our work presented in this paper, existing works [5–8] in this area are largely concentrated on a translation of *BPMN* models to a formal language, and the specification of the properties was written with a temporal logic

G. Noubir and M. Raynal (Eds.): NETYS 2014, LNCS 8593, pp. 341–346, 2014.
DOI: 10.1007/978-3-319-09581-3_27

[3,4], and do not consider a visual language for specifying these properties to be verified. Dijkman et al. [9] uses Petri Nets [10] to formalize and analyze *BPMN* and it considers to verify only the safety properties. In [11], the authors have developed a tool called *ProM*[1] to verify *BPMN* models. The temporal property specification logic supported by *ProM* is restricted to (*LTL*).

To the best of our knowledge, the above works show that the verification phase comes after the design phase, and the knowledge of the logic used for the specification of properties is needed. Our approach has the objective of integrating the verification process at the design stage.

This paper is organized as follows: In Sect. 2 we provide definitions and notations of *BPMN*, while Sect. 3 describes a visual language for specifying properties to be verified. Finally, some conclusions are drawn in Sect. 4.

2 Business Process Modeling Notation (BPMN)

In this section, we give the basic notations of *BPMN* (see Fig. 1) used in this paper. *BPMN* models are composed of:

1. Events:
    (a) Start Event: it indicates where a particular process will start;
    (b) End Event: it indicates where a process will end.
2. Task: is a generic type of work to be done during the course of a *BP*.
3. Sequence flow: it links two objects in a process diagram.
4. Gateways:
    (a) And-split Gateway: is where a single branch is divided into two or more parallel branches which are executed concurrently;
    (b) And-join Gateway: is where two or more different branches of the process merge into one single branch;
    (c) Or-split Gateway: it routes the sequence flow to exactly one of the outgoing branches based on conditions;
    (d) Or-join Gateway: it awaits one incoming branch to complete before triggering the outgoing flow.

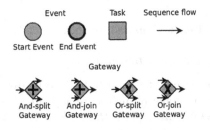

Fig. 1. The basic elements of *BPMN*

---

[1] http://www.promtools.org/prom6/

3 Visual Language for Specifying Response Properties

In this section, we show how the designer specifies the properties to be verified by using a graphical interface. At this stage, the framework uses this specification as a guide to implement the transformation to LTL or CTL temporal logic. These logics use the following quantifiers: (i) A: all paths, (ii) E: at least there exists one path, (iii) $\Diamond$: eventually in the future, and (iv) $\Box$: now and forever in the future. For more details see [3,4].

In this paper, we focus on the definition of five of the most frequently used response properties by providing a graphical representation and corresponding temporal logic semantics:

1. ($\Phi1$): task t_i will always be followed by task t_j;
2. ($\Phi2$): task t_i will always be followed by tasks t_j and t_k, while t_j and t_k will be executed in parallel.
3. ($\Phi3$): task t_i will always be followed by tasks t_j or t_k.
4. ($\Phi4$): task t_k will be executed after the end of task t_i and task t_j, while t_i and t_j are already executed in parallel.
5. ($\Phi5$): task t_k will be executed after the end of task t_i or task t_j.

The designer can use a graphical interface to specify the source and the target extremities of property to be verified. Then, the framework proposes the collection of the gateways and arrow types in order to choose the desirable semantic (Figs. 2, 3, 4, 5, and 6):

Specification language and semantics of $\Phi1$

$$\Phi1 \Leftrightarrow \begin{cases} \text{-1- There exists one potential path that connects } t_i \text{ to } t_j : \\ (t_i \Rightarrow E\Diamond t_j), \text{ (CTL formula).} \\ \text{-2- All paths from } t_i \text{ to } t_j : \\ (t_i \Rightarrow A\Diamond t_j), \text{ (CTL formula).} \\ \text{-3- Every time } t_i \text{ is executed, } t_j \text{ has to be executed afterwards:} \\ \Box(t_i \Rightarrow \Diamond t_j), \text{(LTL formula).} \end{cases}$$

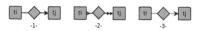

Fig. 2. Graphical specification of $\Phi1$

Specification language and semantics of $\Phi2$

$$\Phi2 \Leftrightarrow \begin{cases} \text{-1- When } t_i \text{ is executed, } t_j \text{ and } t_k \text{ have to be executed afterwards,} \\ \text{while the two outgoing branches are activated in parallel, each} \\ \text{branch on one potential path: } (t_i \Rightarrow (E\Diamond t_j \wedge E\Diamond t_k)), \text{ (CTL formula).} \\ \text{-2- When } t_i \text{ is executed, } t_j \text{ and } t_k \text{ have to be executed afterwards,} \\ \text{while the two outgoing branches are activated in parallel, each} \\ \text{branch on all potential paths: } (t_i \Rightarrow (A\Diamond t_j \wedge A\Diamond t_k)), \text{ (CTL formula).} \\ \text{-3- Every time } t_i \text{ is executed, } t_j \text{ and } t_k \text{ have to be executed in} \\ \text{parallel afterwards: } \Box(t_i \Rightarrow (\Diamond t_j \wedge \Diamond t_k)), \text{ (LTL formula).} \end{cases}$$

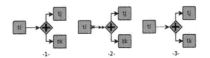

Fig. 3. Graphical specification of $\Phi 2$

Specification language and semantics of $\Phi 3$

$$\Phi 3 \Leftrightarrow \begin{cases} \text{-1- One of the tasks } t_j \text{ or } t_k \text{ eventually is executed after the task } t_i \\ \text{on one potential path: } (t_i \Rightarrow (E\Diamond t_j \vee E\Diamond t_k)), \text{ (CTL formula).} \\ \text{-2- One of the tasks } t_j \text{ or } t_k \text{ eventually is executed after the task } t_i \\ \text{on each potential path: } (t_i \Rightarrow (A\Diamond t_j \vee A\Diamond t_k)), \text{ (CTL formula).} \\ \text{-3- Every time } t_i \text{ is executed, one of the tasks } t_i \text{ or } t_k \\ \text{has to be executed afterwards: } \Box(t_i \Rightarrow (\Diamond t_j \vee \Diamond t_k)), \text{ (LTL formula).} \end{cases}$$

Fig. 4. Graphical specification of $\Phi 3$

Specification language and semantics of $\Phi 4$

$$\Phi 4 \Leftrightarrow \begin{cases} \text{-1- When merging parallel branches, outgoing branch on one} \\ \text{potential path: } ((t_i \wedge t_j) \Rightarrow E\Diamond t_k), \text{ (CTL formula).} \\ \text{-2- When merging parallel branches, outgoing branch on all} \\ \text{potential paths: } ((t_i \wedge t_j) \Rightarrow A\Diamond t_k), \text{ (CTL formula).} \\ \text{-3- Every time tasks } t_i \text{ and } t_j \text{ are simultaneously executed, } t_k \text{ has} \\ \text{to be executed afterwards: } \Box((t_i \wedge t_j) \Rightarrow \Diamond t_k), \text{ (LTL formula).} \end{cases}$$

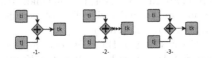

Fig. 5. Graphical specification of $\Phi 4$

Specification language and semantics of $\Phi 5$

$$\Phi 5 \Leftrightarrow \begin{cases} \text{-1- One of the tasks } t_i \text{ or } t_j \text{ is eventually followed by the task } t_k \\ \text{on one potential path: } ((t_i \vee t_j) \Rightarrow E\Diamond t_k), \text{ (CTL formula).} \\ \text{-2- One of the tasks } t_i \text{ or } t_j \text{ will be eventually followed by the} \\ \text{task } t_k \text{ on each potential path: } ((t_i \vee t_j) \Rightarrow A\Diamond t_k), \text{ (CTL formula).} \\ \text{-3- Every time one of the tasks } t_i \text{ or } t_j \text{ is executed, it is followed} \\ \text{by the task } t_k: \Box((t_i \vee t_j) \Rightarrow \Diamond t_k), \text{ (LTL formula).} \end{cases}$$

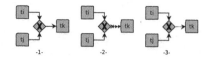

Fig. 6. Graphical specification of $\Phi 5$

4 Conclusion

In this paper, we presented a new approach to integrate the formal verification techniques of *BP* in the design phase. We proposed the use of *BPMN* to modelize *BP*. A visual graphical language is given to specify the properties that will be verified and corresponding temporal logic semantics. In this way, the designer can automatically and intuitively validate constraint specifications on the designed processes at this early stage, while the knowledge of the temporal logic used for the specification of properties is not needed.

References

1. Lodhi, A., Koppen, V., Saake, G.: Business process modeling: active research areas and challenges. Technical report 1, Faculty of Computer Science, University of Magdeburg, p. 38 (2011)
2. OMG. Business Process Modeling Notation (BPMN) Version 2.0. OMG Final Adopted Specification. Object Management Group (2011)
3. Manna, Z., Pnueli, A.: The Temporal Logic of Reactive and Concurrent Systems. Springer, New York (1992)
4. Heljanko, K.: Model checking the branching time temporal logic CTL. Research report A45, Digital Systems Laboratory, Helsinki University of Technology, Espoo, Finland (1997)
5. Takemura, T.: Formal semantics and verification of BPMN transaction and compensation. In: Proceedings of APSCC 2008, pp. 284–290. IEEE (2008)
6. EI Hichami, O., AI Achhab, M., Berrada, I., Oucheikh, R., El Mohajir, B.E.: An approach of optimisation and formal verification of workflow Petri nets. J. Theor. Appl. Inf. Technol. **61**(3), 486–495 (2014)
7. van der Aalst, W.M.P., van Dongen, B.F.: Discovering Petri nets from event logs. In: Jensen, K., van der Aalst, W.M.P., Balbo, G., Koutny, M., Wolf, K. (eds.) Transactions on Petri Nets and Other Models of Concurrency VII. LNCS, vol. 7480, pp. 372–422. Springer, Heidelberg (2013)
8. Fahland, D., Favre, C., Koehler, J., Lohmann, N., Volzer, H., Wolf, K.: Analysis on demand: instantaneous soundness checking of industrial business process models. Data Knowl. Eng. **70**(5), 448–466 (2011)
9. Dijkman, R.M., Dumas, M., Ouyang, C.: Formal semantics and analysis of BPMN process models using Petri nets. Technical report 7115, Queensland University of Technology, Brisbane (2007)

10. Murata, T., Koh, J.Y.: Petri nets: properties, analysis and applications. an invited survey paper. Proc. IEEE **77**(4), 541–580 (1989)

11. van der Aalst, W.M.P., van Dongen, B.F., Günther, C.W., Mans, R.S., de Medeiros, A.K.A., Rozinat, A., Rubin, V., Song, M., Verbeek, H.M.W.E., Weijters, A.J.M.M.T.: ProM 4.0: comprehensive support for *real* process analysis. In: Kleijn, J., Yakovlev, A. (eds.) ICATPN 2007. LNCS, vol. 4546, pp. 484–494. Springer, Heidelberg (2007)

Author Index

Printed in the United States
By Bookmasters